Anonymous

Report of Evidence

Taken before the Royal Commission appointed to Inquire into the Value of the

Central Prison Labour

Anonymous

Report of Evidence
Taken before the Royal Commission appointed to Inquire into the Value of the Central Prison Labour

ISBN/EAN: 9783337170813

Printed in Europe, USA, Canada, Australia, Japan

Cover: Foto ©ninafisch / pixelio.de

More available books at **www.hansebooks.com**

REPORT OF EVIDENCE

TAKEN BEFORE THE

ROYAL COMMISSION

APPOINTED TO INQUIRE INTO

THE VALUE OF

THE CENTRAL PRISON LABOUR.

REPORTED BY RICHARDSON, BRADLEY & LUMSDEN.

Toronto:
PRINTED BY HUNTER, ROSE & CO., 25 WELLINGTON STREET.
1877.

CENTRAL PRISON LABOUR COMMISSION.

COMMISSIONERS :—HON. W. PEARCE HOWLAND, Chairman;
Z. R. BROCKWAY;
JAMES NOXON.

COUNSEL :—Hon. A. S. Hardy, for the Government; Messrs. Morrison, Wells & Gordon, for the Canada Car and Manufacturing Company.

SECRETARIES AND SHORT-HAND WRITERS :—Messrs. Richardson, Bradley & Lumsden.

CENTRAL PRISON
LABOUR COMMISSION.

The Commissioners appointed to consider questions in dispute between the Canada Car Company and the Government of the Province of Ontario, respecting the value of prison labour furnished to the Company by the Government, met at Ten o'clock, a. m., on Wednesday, June 20th, in the Parliamentary Buildings, Toronto. The Commissioners were—the Hon. W. P. Howland, Z. R. Brockway, Esq., and James Noxon, Esq.

Hon. W. P. Howland, was, on motion, unanimously chosen Chairman of the Commission.

Messrs. Richardson, Bradley and Lumsden were appointed Secretaries and Short-hand writers.

Hon. Mr. Hardy appeared on behalf of the Government. Hon. Mr. Wells represented the Company. Mr. Langmuir, Inspector of Prisons, was in attendance.

The Commission, authorizing the enquiry, was read, as follows :—

[L. S.]   D. A. MACDONALD.

PROVINCE OF ONTARIO.

VICTORIA, by the Grace of GOD, of the United Kingdom of Great Britain and Ireland, Queen, Defender of the Faith, &c., &c., &c.

To the Honourable WILLIAM PEARCE HOWLAND, of the City of Toronto, Z. R. BROCKWAY, Superintendent of the Adult Reformatory, Elmira, State of New York, and JAMES NOXON, of the Town of Ingersoll, Ontario, Esquire, our Commissioners in this behalf.

GREETING :

WHEREAS, in and by a Statute of the Province passed in the thirty-first year of our reign, entitled, "An Act to repeal Chapter B. of the Consolidated Statutes of Canada, so far as the same relates to Ontario, to authorize the publication, in the *Ontario Gazette*, and to make provision for inquiries concerning public matters and official notices," it is enacted, that whenever the Lieutenant-Governor in Council deems it expedient to cause inquiry to be made into and concerning any matter connected with the good government of this Province, or the conduct of any part of the public business thereof, or the administration of Justice therein, and such enquiry is not regulated by any special law, the Lieutenant-Governor may, by the Commission in the case, confer upon the Commissioners or persons by whom such enquiry is to be conducted, the power of summoning before them any party or witness, and of requiring them to give evidence on oath, orally or in writing (or on solemn affirmation if they be parties entitled to affirm in civil matters), and to produce such documents and things as such Commissioners deem requisite to the full investigation of the matters into which they are appointed to examine, and that the Commissioner or Commissioners shall then have the same power to enforce the attendance of such witnesses and to compel them to give evidence, as is vested in any Court of Law in civil cases.

And whereas, acting under the authority of the Government of Ontario, the Inspector of Prisons for Ontario, did heretofore enter into an agreement with the Canada Car and

Manufacturing Company (limited), they carrying on business under the name and style of the Canada Car Company (limited), dated 17th day of March, A. D., 1873, with reference to the hiring of the said Company of the labour of a number of prisoners, of the Central Prison of Ontario, and for providing certain works, machinery and plant, for the use of the said company.

And whereas, by a certain other agreement, dated the twenty-seventh day of January, A.D 1876, between the said Inspector of Prisons, acting as aforesaid, of the first part, the Commissioner of the Public Works of the Province also acting as aforesaid, of the second part, and the said Canada Car and Manufacturing Company (limited), of the third part, the terms of the said first mentioned agreement were varied in the manner and to the extent in the said agreement of twenty-seventh January, set forth.

And whereas, at the time at which the said last mentioned agreement was executed the said company alleged and still allege, that the price agreed to be paid in the said original contract for the said prison labour, was and is in excess of its real value, and whereas, without admitting any right of claim on the part of the said Company to a reduction in the said price, but for the purpose of satisfying the said Government and the said Company, as to what is under all the circumstances of the case, and having regard to the value of the works, machinery and plant, provided by the said Government, a fair price to be paid therefor by the said Company, the said Commissioner of Public Works acting as aforesaid, in the said agreement last mentioned, agreed to name either one or more Commissioners, not being officers of the Government, to enquire into the whole subject and to report to the Government the result of such inquiry, and the price thereinafter to be paid for such labour should be considered by the Government, and that subject to ratification by resolution of the Legislative Assembly of Ontario, regulated or readjusted according to what the Government should consider fair and just.

And whereas our said Commissioner of Public Works has, in pursuance of the said agreement, nominated and recommended that you, the Hon. William Pearce Howland, Z. R. Brockway, and James Noxon, should be named as Commissioners for the purpose aforesaid.

And whereas, the Lieutenant Governor of our Province in Council deems it expedient that inquiry should be made into and concerning the said matters.

Now know ye that we, having and reposing full trust and confidence in you, the said William Pearce Howland, Z. R. Brockway and James Noxon, do hereby, by and with the advice of the Executive Council of our said Province, appoint you, the said William Pearce Howland, Z. R. Brockway and James Noxon, our Commissioners in this behalf, to examine into and report to us, your opinion as to the value of the prison labour agreed to be furnished by the Government of the said Province to the said Canada Car and Manufacturing Company (Limited), having regard to the value of the works, machinery and plant provided by the Government of Ontario as aforesaid, under the said first mentioned agreement, or otherwise howsoever. And we hereby give you, our said Commissioners, full power and authority to summon before you any witness or witnesses, and to require him or them to give evidence on oath orally or in writing (or on solemn affirmation if such witness or witnesses is, or are parties entitled to affirm in civil matters), and to produce before you, our said Commissioners, such documents and things as you may deem requisite to the full investigation of the premises, together with all and every other power and authority in the said Act mentioned and authorized to be by us conferred on any Commissioners appointed by authority or in pursuance thereof. And we do require you, our said Commissioners, forthwith after the conclusion of such inquiry, to make a full report to us, touching the said investigation, together with a return of all or any evidence taken by you concerning the same, and to report not later than the 1st day of August next.

In testimony whereof we have caused these our letters to be made patent, and the great seal of our said Province of Ontario to be hereunto affixed. Witness the Honourable Donald Alexander Macdonald, Lieutenant-Governor of our Province of Ontario, at our Government House, in our City of Toronto, in our said Province, this first day of June, in the year of our Lord one thousand eight hundred and seventy-seven, and in the fortieth year of our reign.

By Command,

I. R. ECKART,
Assistant Secretary.

The agreement made between the Government and the Company was read, as follows:—
This Agreement, made the seventeenth day of March, A.D. 1873, between the Inspector of Prisons for Ontario for and on behalf of Her Most Gracious Majesty, of the first part, and
The Canada Car Company (limited), of the City of Toronto and Province of Ontario, of the second part;
Whereas the said Inspector, acting for and on behalf of Her Majesty, and with the authority of the Government of Ontario, has entered into a contract with the said Canada Car Company for the hire to them of the labour of certain of the prisoners who may hereafter be imprisoned in the Central Prison for the Province of Ontario, now being erected at Toronto, and to allow the said Company to use the workshops, coal-sheds, and grounds in connection with such prison, in the manner hereinafter set forth, and has also agreed that such workshops shall be completed and fitted up to the extent hereinafter particularly described:

Now, it is hereby witnessed as follows: The said Inspector, for and on behalf of Her Majesty, as aforesaid, agrees with the said Company, to hire and let to the said company, the labour of as many prisoners as may be received into the Central Prison aforesaid, between the first day of January, 1874, and the first day of July, 1874, except such as may be required for the domestic work of the prison, and to hire and let to the said Company, from the first day of July, 1874, until the thirtieth day of June, 1881, the labour of two hundred and fifteen such prisoners at least, to be employed as is hereinafter specified.

The Inspector further agrees that the Company may, during the said periods, use the prison workshops, coal-sheds, drying kilns, four cupolas, two travelling cranes, two steam-engines of fifty-horse power (nominal), with boilers for the said engines, suitable and complete, connected therewith, as now being built and erected on the prison grounds, and shown upon the drawings produced; that the Government of Ontario shall sufficiently light and heat the said workshops, and shall sufficiently supply the same with water, and shall also provide and put in working order the roads, railway tracks, switches and turn tables, and provide suitable foundations for machines, and fit up two suitable offices and a wash-room, the same to be completed and put in working order, in accordance with the drawings produced at the time of the execution of these presents.

The Inspector further agrees that the Government of Ontario shall provide, in case the same can be had and put in for the sum of seven thousand dollars, but not otherwise, two fans with blast pipes and troughs for foundry and forging shops, three hoists, six furnaces, and two nail ovens, and shall also expend to the extent of one thousand dollars, if necessary, in making the small building at the end of the south shop suitable for a brass foundry, with small furnaces and blow pipes, if desired by the Company.

The Inspector further agrees that the Government shall furnish main and intermediate shafting, also to furnish and connect with the engines all pulleys, belting, and fixtures necessary to run the said main and intermediate shafting, also fixtures and bolts to receive the Company's counter-shafting in each workshop, to the extent shown in plan now produced, the Company to connect and attach to the machines.

The Inspector further agrees that the Company will be allowed the yard room space coloured red on drawings produced, for piling lumber and other material, as well as the use of the tracks and other things agreed to be provided and put in working order as aforesaid, but if such yard space is found to be insufficient, then the Company shall apply to the Inspector for a further allotment of the enclosed space.

The Inspector further agrees that the workshops, tracks, roads, plant and machinery, which the company is to be entitled to use under these presents (except those as to which the limitations of seven thousand dollars and one thousand dollars are herein before made), shall be substantially completed on the first day of October, 1873, and that from and after the first day of July, 1873, the said company shall be entitled to use the same, in order to fit the same up for the purposes contemplated by these presents.

The Inspector further agrees that the dietaries of the prison shall be liberal, and in all respects sufficient for the requirements of working men.

And the said company agree with the said Inspector, that they will accept and pay for the labour of as many prisoners as may be furnished or tendered to them up to the number of two hundred and sixty, between the said first day of January, 1874, and thirtieth day of June, 1881, inclusive, at the rate of fifty cents per prisoner, per day, for the first two years and a half of the subsistence of this contract, commencing on the first day of January, 1874; fifty-five cents per prisoner per day, for the second period of two years and a half, and sixty cents per prisoner per day, during the third period of two years and a half. And it is further agreed that the book-keeper of the prison (or other officer appointed in that behalf), may as often as he receives prisoners into said prison, between the first day of January, 1874, and the first day of July, 1874, notify in writing the manager of the said " Canada Car Company " or the foreman of their said works, of the number of prisoners ready to be placed at work, and shall furnish with such notice a list of the names of such prisoners, and also state the occupation the prisoners were engaged in before confinement, if any. Payment for each of such prisoners shall commence one week after such notice shall have been given, unless the said company employ such prisoners or any of them before the expiration of such week, in which case payment shall commence from the time of such employment.

It is further agreed that one roll of the prisoners shall be kept by an officer of the said company at the said works, and another by the book-keeper of the said prison, and such rolls shall be checked and compared every day, and the amount owing in respect of such labour shall be made up at the close of each week and a certificate thereof, signed by the said officer of said company, delivered by him to the Inspector on the Monday thereafter, and on the first day of each month the said company shall pay the amount owing up to the Saturday then next preceding in respect of the said prisoners, by depositing the same at Toronto to the credit of the Treasurer of the Province of Ontario, in such of the banks of this Province as may be from time to time directed by such Treasurer, and shall deliver to the said Treasurer a deposit receipt therefor.

And the said company further agrees to employ said prisoners in the preparing of wood-work of any description for railway cars and equipments, and in construction of steam and sailing vessels, and building purposes generally, and in the manufacture of articles from steel, iron, brass and other metals for the said construction of railway cars, and for the other purposes above described. But should the company desire to manufacture articles from other materials than those above named, then, in that case, the same must be submitted to the Inspector and approved by him in writing.

The company further agrees to provide a sufficient number of instructors in the various branches of industry prosecuted, and in the several shops, who shall instruct the prisoners and supervise the labour of the prison, the company to have the right of introducing and employing in the prison workshops ordinary skilled artizans, and skilled labourers, but shall not employ such persons in the proportion of more than one such person for every six prisoners, and the persons so introduced, shall not at any one time exceed forty-three.

The company further agree that the officers, supervisors, instructors, skilled artizans, and labourers, and other persons, employees of the said company, who are hereby permitted, or may be permitted under the regulations, to enter the said prison workshops or grounds, shall conform to all the rules and regulations which are, or may be provided for the good government and general administration of the prison, and shall not allow conversation between the prisoners, or between prisoners and visitors, or between prisoners and such skilled artizans, or between prisoners and such instructors and supervisors, unless actually necessary in giving instructions or orders in connexion with the work in which they are engaged, and that no such person shall take or receive letters or other communications from any prisoner to his friends, or from any person to any prisoner, and that no such person shall be in any way the means of communication between any prisoner and any person outside of such prison, and that no such person shall barter with any prisoner or sell any article to any prisoner, or give any liquor or tobacco to any prisoner, and that all cases of insubordination or refusal to work on the part of any prisoner, on the order of a supervisor, shall be forthwith reported to the warden of the prison for such action as may be considered proper, and that in case any of the employees of the said company breaks any of the regulations in this clause of this agreement contained, and the same comes to the knowledge of the foreman of the said company, he will report the same forthwith from time to time to the warden, and in case the Inspector of Prisons shall so direct, such person shall be thereafter excluded from such Central Prison premises by the said company.

The company further agree to take all reasonable and proper care of the buildings and the plant, tracks, engines, boilers, furnaces and machinery therein or upon the premises ; and that they will make good any damage done to the buildings, or such plant, tracks, engines, boilers, furnaces or machinery, ordinary wear and tear, damage by fire and the action of the elements excepted; and that in case any trade (such as that of a grinder,) is so hard on prison clothing as to require prisoners engaged therein to be supplied with clothing at a rate greater than two suits per annum, the company shall pay such an amount as the Inspector may adjudge sufficient to cover the additional cost.

The company agree that they will not use or permit to be used any space in the yard or grounds of said prison for piling lumber or other material not allotted to them, and will not permit any material or manufactured article to remain in such yard or grounds without the consent of the Inspector; and that the company shall once in every week, and oftener if required, remove from the said shops and prison premises all filth, dirt, cinders, ashes, refuse, lumber and waste matter that may accumulate therein from the industries aforesaid.

It is further agreed that the prisoners whose labour is to be furnished under this agreement, shall be persons who shall be sentenced to imprisonment in the Central Prison for periods not less than two months, or such persons as may be removed from other prisons to such Central Prison, and who, at the time of such removal, have not less than two months of their sentences then unexpired, the company to have a right to reject any prisoner whom the Central Prison surgeon upon being requested to certify in respect thereof, shall decline certifying to be capable of performing an ordinary day's labour through physical or mental causes or defects, the report or certificate of such surgeon respecting such capacity or incapacity to be final and conclusive.

It is further agreed that as long as ten hours are computed as the ordinary day of labour in similar industries, ten hours shall be computed as a day's labour under this agreement, but in case the ordinary labour day is reduced below such number of hours, then nine hours and a-half shall constitute a day's labour under this agreement, and the prisoners shall be employed by the said company for nine hours and a-half during every day. Six days' labour shall constitute a week, and out of every week the company shall allow to the prisoners two hours per man out of such working hours, the same to be paid for to the Government as if the prisoners worked during such time. Prisoners who at any time may not work for want of materials, tools, or proper instructions shall be charged for full time.

It is further agreed that the Government of Ontario shall have the right to use the exhaust steam in heating the said workshops, but if the heat thereby furnished is insufficient for heating purposes, that they will supply other means of properly heating the same.

The company further agree that they will not erect any buildings or erections, or building additions whatever, upon the said premises, without the written consent of the Inspector. Any buildings which they may erect upon the said premises, and the removal of which will in no way injure the other buildings or any portion thereof they may remove, putting everything in the same state and condition as they may be in when they are first allowed to use the said premises or may be subsequently put by the Government.

In case any buildings or constructions are erected, or building additions are made upon the said premises contrary to this agreement, the same shall be the property of the Government of Ontario, whether affixed to the freehold or not.

It is further agreed that in case the Government find that they are able to furnish a greater number of prisoners than two hundred and sixty, notice thereof shall be given to the Car Company, and the company shall be required within a week thereafter to state whether they are willing to accept the labour of such additional number of prisoners; if such company, within a week thereafter, intimate in writing to the Inspector their willingness to accept the same, they will be entitled to receive the labour of such additional number of men, and in such case the number which the Inspector is required to supply, and also the number which the company are required to take shall each be increased by the amount of such additional number as aforesaid, to be paid for at the rate aforesaid.

It is further agreed that, in case the said company shall, in all things, faithfully and fully carry out the provisions of this agreement, in accordance with the spirit and intent thereof, they shall have the right to a renewal of a lease of the labour of a like number of prisoners for another term of seven years and-a-half, upon such terms as, by the Government of Ontario, shall be deemed fitting and just, having regard to what experience may show to be fair and requisite.

It is further agreed that the said company may, from time to time, remove such machinery as they may have caused to be put at their cost in the said buildings, or upon the said premises; but shall have no such right while they are in default in their payments upon this agreement; and Her Majesty, and the Inspector of Prisons on her behalf, shall be entitled to a lien upon any such machinery for any moneys payable or recoverable by virtue of the provisions of this agreement.

In case of failure to supply the number of prisoners which is agreed to be furnished, then the company is to be at liberty to employ and introduce a number of ordinary labourers equal to the deficiency, and payment of the difference between the wages of such labourers and of prisoners shall be made by the Government to the company, and the same shall be a full satisfaction and discharge of any damages or claims for any default of the Government in this respect, and may be so pleaded, such labourers to be discharged in one week after the Inspector or Warden shall have notified the company of their readiness to furnish the number required.

It is further declared that it shall not be necessary, in order to constitute a tender of service under this agreement, to bring the prisoners actually into the workshop; but it will be a sufficient tender if the prison authorities intimate that such prisoners are ready to be furnished whenever requested, provided the same are immediately furnished upon such request.

It is further hereby declared that these presents shall not be construed to be a demise of the said Central Prison premises, or any portion thereof, nor to give the said company, or their employees, the right of going upon the said premises, except at such times as may have regard to the purposes of this agreement, and the safe custody of prisoners, be reasonable and proper.

And it is further hereby agreed and declared to be an essential condition of this agreement that, upon the report of the majority of three arbitrators, two to be appointed by the Lieutenant-Governor in Council, and one by the said company, in order to inquire in respect thereto, that there has been a failure on the part of the said company to keep and observe any of the covenants other than the covenants for the payment of moneys to such an extent as to be seriously detrimental to the discipline of the prison, or in case the company is in default for a period of one calendar month in any payment by them required to be made, it shall be lawful for his Excellency the Lieutenant-Governor of Ontario in Council, by order, to declare this agreement avoided, and the same and everything herein contained shall be forthwith at an end as far as any undertaking on the part of the Inspector or the Government of Ontario is concerned; but the Inspector shall nevertheless be entitled to recover damages in respect of any breach thereof that may theretofore have taken place, and shall also be entitled to recover from the said company; and the company hereby agree, in such case, to pay to the said Inspector the sum of ten thousand dollars as and for liquidated damages in respect of moneys expended in making such buildings and premises suitable for the use of the said company, and loss by the disarrangements thereby occasioned.

Neither the Inspector of Prisons, nor any one employed in connection with the Central Prison, nor any officer, shareholder, or employee of the company, shall, unless by consent of both the Government and the company, be named as arbitrators.

In case the company fail to appoint some person whose attendance can be forthwith secured, and notify the Inspector of such appointment for three days after they have received notice of the appointment of two arbitrators by the Lieutenant-Governor, and have been requested in writing to appoint one on their behalf, or in the case of the failure of any arbitrator to attend, after reasonable notice, the others may proceed without such third arbitrator.

In witness whereof, &c.

The supplementary agreement entered into between the parties was read, as follows:—

This agreement, made the twenty-seventh day of January, in the year of our Lord one thousand eight hundred and seventy-six,

Between the Inspector of Prisons for Ontario, for and on behalf of Her Most Gracious Majesty of the first part; the Commissioner of Public Works of the said Province, also for and on behalf of Her Majesty, of the second part; and the Canada Car and Manufacturing Company (limited), of the City of Toronto and Province of Ontario, of the third part.

Whereas, acting under the authority of the Government of Ontario, the Inspector of

Prisons did heretofore enter into an agreement with the said Company, then carrying on business under the name and style of The Canada Car Company (limited), dated the second day of March, in the year of our Lord one thousand eight hundred and seventy-three, with reference to the hiring by the said Company of the labour of a number of the prisoners of the Central Prison of Ontario, and for providing certain buildings, works, machinery and plant, for the use of the said Company:

And whereas subsequently thereto, and on or about the fourteenth day of July, one thousand eight hundred and seventy-three, the Commissioner of Agriculture and Public Works, acting for and on behalf of Her Majesty, did enter into another agreement with the said Company with regard to certain works which the said Company then agreed to perform for the Government of the Province of Ontario, at the Central Prison:

And whereas various disputes have arisen between the said Company and the Government as respects certain matters arising under the said contracts, and also in respect of certain work alleged to have been performed for and on behalf of the Government by the said Company, their contractors, servants, or workmen:

And whereas the Government admit the performance of certain portions of the said work, and their indebtedness in respect thereof, but as to other portions of such alleged work dispute their liability:

And whereas it is desirable that all the matters in dispute between the Government and the said Company should be settled, and it has been agreed that the same shall be determined in the manner hereinafter provided:

Now it is hereby witnessed, that the said Company hereby admit that they are indebted in the sum of fourteen thousand and ninety dollars and twenty-four cents ($14,090.24) to the said Inspector for the hire of labour of prisoners furnished under the said first mentioned agreement to the said Company, and the said Inspector hereby relinquishes any claims which he may have against the said Company in respect of the hire of the labour of prisoners tendered under the said agreement but not employed, and agrees to accept payment of the aforesaid amount in full settlement of all claims for and on account of all Central Prison labour supplied or tendered to the said Company from the date of the said agreement up to the day of the date of these presents; such sum, with interest from the date hereof to be paid as follows: one half in one year and the other half in two years from the date of this contract.

And the said Company hereby abandon any claim which they may have for any alleged breach by the Inspector or the Government of any of the covenants or agreements in the said agreement first above mentioned claimed to be by the said Inspector or the Government performed, and the said Company accept the buildings, workshops, tracks, roads, plant and machinery now being in and upon the said Central Prison grounds and workshops as finished and complete, in accordance with the terms of the said agreement as varied subsequently at the request of the said Company. And the said Company hereby acknowledge that all the covenants to be performed by the Inspector with reference to the erection, preparing, building or providing of buildings, workshops, tracks, roads, plant or machinery contained in the said agreement have been fully performed according to the terms of the said agreement, except where other buildings, workshops, tracks, roads, plant or machinery have been substituted at the request of the said Company for buildings, workshops, tracks, roads, plant or machinery mentioned in the said agreement, and the buildings, workshops, tracks, roads, plant and machinery so substituted are hereby declared to have been and to be accepted in lieu of those called for by the said first mentioned agreement.

The Commissioner of Public Works, on behalf of the Government of Ontario, hereby agrees that the Government of Ontario shall upon the same being voted by the Legislature forthwith pay to the said Company the sum of fifteen thousand five hundred and seventy-six dollars and seven cents ($15,576.07), being the amount which is admitted to be owing by the Government to the said Company for work performed, and materials provided by the said Company at the request of the said Government under the said agreements.

And the said Company admits that, except its alleged claim for the work and materials aforesaid, it has no claim whatever upon the said Government.

It is further agreed that the Inspector shall not require the said Company to pay for the labour of more prisoners than they may desire prior to the first day of May next, upon and after which day they shall pay for one hundred, if so many be furnished or tendered them, and that the Inspector shall not require the Company to pay for the labour of more than one hundred prisoners, unless they desire to employ them, until the first day of August next, upon and after which the Company shall pay for two hundred if they be furnished or tendered to them, and that the Inspector shall not require the Company to pay for the labour of more than two hundred prisoners, unless they desire to employ them, until the first day of January, one thousand eight hundred and seventy-seven, upon and after which they shall pay for two hundred and sixty if they be furnished or tendered them.

It is also agreed that the Inspector shall not be required to furnish the labour of any more prisoners than the Company is required under this agreement to accept, it being, however, understood that in case the Prison arrangements in his opinion allow him to do so, that he will provide as many as the Company may require. Provided also that the Company shall pay for the number of prisoners they employ, although it exceeds the number they are required to accept.

The Commissioner of Public Works, on behalf of the Government of Ontario, hereby agrees to permit the said Company to employ the said prison labour upon such industries as may from time to time be agreed upon between the said Company and the said Government.

It is further agreed that hereafter the amount owing for the labour of prisoners shall be paid on the first days of July and January in each and every year during the subsistence of this contract, instead of at the times mentioned in the original contract.

It is hereby expressly understood and agreed that the said Company shall not assign or sublet the said contract for the hire and labour of prisoners without the consent of the Lieutenant-Governor in Council, who shall have the right absolutely to decide any application in this behalf.

It is further agreed that the said original contract shall be and the same is hereby varied in the following respects:

1. The term of hire of prison labour extends from the first day of January, one thousand eight hundred and seventy-six, to the thirtieth day of June, one thousand eight hundred and eighty-three, divided as therein provided into three periods of two and a half years each, and the rates to be paid for the labour of as many prisoners as under the provisions of this agreement may be furnished or tendered shall be for the first of such periods fifty cents per prisoner per day, for the second of such periods fifty-five cents per prisoner per day, and for the third of such periods sixty cents per prisoner per day.

2. The provision in the said contract as to a renewal of the said lease for a further period of seven and one-half years is applicable to this contract, notwithstanding any breach of the covenants, conditions or provisions of the said contract heretofore committed by the said Company, and such renewal shall date from the date lastly above mentioned.

3. So far as the Government find it conveniently practicable, and in the public interest, prisoners sentenced to imprisonment in the Common Gaols will be transferred to the Central Prison in the following order of preference:—

First.—Able-bodied prisoners having long periods to serve, whether skilled workmen or not.

Second.—Skilled workmen, having shorter periods to serve.

Third.—Able-bodied prisoners not coming within either of these classes.

And whereas the said Company allege that the price agreed to be paid in the said original contract for prison labour is in excess of its real value, and without admitting any right of claim on the part of the said Company to a reduction in the said price ; but for the purpose of satisfying the Government and the said Company as to what is under all the circumstances of the case, and having regard to the value of the works, machinery, and plant provided by the Government, a fair price to be paid therefor by the Company, the said Commissioner of Public Works, acting on behalf of the Government, hereby agrees to name either one or more Commissioners, not being officers of the Government, to enquire into the whole subject and report to the Government the result of such enquiry ; and the price hereafter to be paid for such labour is to be considered by the Government, and, subject to ratification by resolution of the Legislative Assembly, regulated or readjusted according to what the Government shall consider fair and just ; but unless, and until a readjustment is made and ratified, the Company shall continue to pay for the labour in accordance with the terms of this agreement subject to the right to be credited with the amount (if any) which, upon the readjusted terms, they may have overpaid.

It is further expressly declared that nothing herein shall be construed to vary any of the covenants in the said agreement contained, unless so far as the same are hereby expressly varied, and unless, as so varied, all the covenants and conditions in the said agreement contained shall be and remain in full force and binding on the Company and the Government, and nothing herein shall be construed in any wise to release the lien which Her Majesty, or the Inspector of Prisons on her behalf, by virtue of the provisions of the said aforesaid agreement, and on account of the default of the Company heretofore made in its payments or otherwise, now has upon the machinery of the Company for the moneys hereinbefore declared to be owing.

It is here further agreed that everything herein contained shall be void and of no effect whatever, and that every right which is now vested in the Inspector or in the Government to claim damages and terminate the said agreement, shall revive unless on or before the first day of February next, fifty thousand dollars of additional capital be *bona fide* subscribed for the said Company by persons of good financial repute.

It is expressly declared that the condition giving power to the Lieutenant-Governor in Council to declare the said agreement void is continued in force, and is hereafter to apply to the first mentioned agreement, as varied by this agreement, and that the same shall be applicable to the covenants herein contained in the same manner as if such covenants had been contained in the said agreement.

The provisions of the said original contract shall be deemed to be incorporated with this contract, so far as they are not inconsistent herewith.

This agreement is subject to the express condition that the same and everything therein contained shall be void, unless the said agreement is ratified by resolution of the Legislative Assembly of the Province of Ontario at the present Session thereof.

In witness whereof, the parties hereto hereunto affixed their hands and seals.

The Commission then adjourned to visit the work-shops at the Central Prison.

The Commission re-assembled at three o'clock.

Mr. WELLS said:—I might as well indicate the course which I think we shall pursue. I suppose the issue to be inquired into is settled by agreement and by the Commission—rather by the Commission, viz., the value to the Company of the prison labour, taking into consideration what has been supplied by the Government in the way of works, plant and machinery; and I suppose the true way of testing that value would be to fix the labour at such a price that the Company would not be in a worse position than they would be if they were employing free labour outside the Prison; in other words, not to have the disadvantage of paying more for the labour, according to what they get out of it, than other manufacturers engaged in the same business outside of the prison are paying. That I understand to be the true test of the value of this labour to us. I propose to examine, in the first place, the Secretary of the Company, who has been returning to the Company, for several weeks past, a statement of the cost to it of the actual work turned out, and the value of that work, showing the balance of profit or loss. I may say that these statements, which we shall put in, were not prepared for the purpose of this investigation, but prepared at the instance of the Company, for their own satisfaction, to see exactly what their position was. I think these statements have been so carefully prepared, and are so full in details, that they will show those facts very clearly. I then propose to examine certain foremen engaged in the different industries, for instance, Mr. Brandon, who superintends the pails, tubs and washboards department, with a view to showing what the comparative value of the prison labour is with free labour; he has had considerable experience now of both, and no doubt will speak intelligently as to the comparative value of the two kinds of labour, and also as to what he considers to be the cause of the discrepancy, as he will show, between the two kinds of labour. With the same object, I will examine the foreman of the brush department, and also the foreman of the broom department. In the first place, I will call Mr. Smith, the Vice-President of the Company, to show how it came about that these statements, which I am about to put in, were prepared.

The CHAIRMAN said the Commissioners would have to consider the question of taking evidence on oath

Mr. HARDY.—I may mention that at a conference with the Attorney-General on this point, he expressed the opinion that all evidence, in the nature of official evidence, which would be in the nature of the evidence of experts, of returns, of reports, of statements of officials in connection with other prisons,—that in matters of that kind the Commissioners should admit the evidence without oath ; also that, for the convenience of the Commission, and all parties, the opinions probably of all men connected with like institutions in a business way, where giving evidence, not of a particular fact, but of general results, obtained by experience, might go without oath. But where there was specific evidence as to a fact—that was to say, of probably the value of particular work, or evidence given by men not in a position to speak with authority, whose reports are not received by the Government—such evidence should be on oath.

Mr. WELLS.—With regard to the reception of the reports of Superintendents of other Institutions, of course there is no doubt that they are perfectly accurate ; but at the same time, I submit that the Commission ought to adhere rather strictly to the terms of the Act under which it sits. I take this ground, because otherwise the Company will be placed at a very considerable disadvantage. For instance, a bare fact may be stated in a report, but that fact may admit of considerable explanation ; yet, of course, we are utterly un able to explain it. We may take the report of the Inspector of Prisons at Albany. It may be that a certain sum, large or small, is given for prison labour there ; but how it happened to be given, whether the party who has the contract is in some peculiar circumstances by which he is able to get more out of it, by having been long in the business, or by having a contract with the Government for the supply of certain goods, and thus is in an advantageous position compared with us—all these and a great many other things we are utterly unable to show. And, besides, the circumstances of the two companies are so entirely different ; what might be very moderate or very good consideration there would be wholly inapplicable here. I think we must, therefore, insist on the importance of having witnesses here, so that we may learn from their own lips all the surrounding circumstances of the case in cross-examination. Of course, under the letter of the Act, the Commission has no power to examine except upon oath, and it has power to compel the production of books, papers and documents, such as are ordinarily produced in an ordinary court of law.

Mr. HARDY.—I do not concur in my learned friend's view of the law. The power to take evidence under oath is an additional power, conferred upon the Commission. To say that persons should be brought from the United States is entirely out of the question. The ground which my learned friend presents as a reason for not accepting the bald statements of various reports does not attack the truth of them. The object of taking evidence under oath is to ascertain the truth, but not one word of my learned friend's argument goes to cast suspicion on the accuracy, the entire truthfulness of the reports—the only object of the oath. He might desire to bring out some additional facts not disclosed by the reports ; but that might be very readily taken into consideration by the Commissioners. My view of the Act is, that the Commission is not confined to taking evidence under oath, but may lay down its own rules ; the Commissioners have power to examine under oath, but are not compelled to do so. Formerly Commissions had not the power to take evidence under oath. The Attorney-General was very clear on these points.

Mr WELLS.—The power of the Commission is entirely regulated by the Act, and the instructions of the Commission, namely : " May, by the Commission in the case confer, upon the Commissioners or persons by whom such inquiry is to be conducted the power of summoning before them any party or witnesses, and of requiring them to give evidence on oath." I think that even if the Commissioners had the power, the absolute power, it would be an unfair exercise of power to simply receive reports, not because the statements are questionable, but because they are not full enough.

Mr. HARDY.—You may take them for what they are worth.

Mr. WELLS.—That is all very well. They are worth nothing, unless we have a full statement.

Mr. HARDY.—Send out circulars with such questions as you desire. We have no power to deal with witnesses from the United States ; we would, therefore, not be able to get the advantage of the opinions of others. I have no objection to have all the parties placed on oath who are here or may be got here.

The CHAIRMAN.—Has the Government any objection to have all parties who are here examined upon oath ? The difficulty with me would be to discriminate ; it would be rather unpleasant.

Mr. NOXON.—We might have all oral evidence on oath, and admit documentary evidence for what it is worth.

The CHAIRMAN.—If the Commission should think it agreeable in the course of the inquiry, in order to satisfy themselves, and enable them to come to a proper conclusion, to go to the United States and visit institutions where such labour is employed, while they would not have the power to take evidence under oath, it might yet be competent for them to inform themselves in that way. Our conclusion would be with the reservation that we would not be bound by any decision come to now absolutely ; but still I should think that, practically, if there is not some serious objection, it would be better to adopt a general rule here.

Mr. HARDY.—The Government has no objection to every person produced being sworn. What I would desire, however, is, that in taking that course, the question as to receiving documentary evidence and reports should be left open for consideration by the Commission hereafter.

Mr. WELLS.—I suppose the question may be left in abeyance now, because when it arises on some document being tendered in evidence, we can discuss whether it is admissible If documents are admitted, the Government have a very alarming advantage, because, of course, they have read these reports and we have not.

Mr. HARDY.—Then we have information—no advantage.

Mr. WELLS.—They have these reports and we have not. They may select such reports as may be favourable, which may state bald facts, entirely useless as evidence, even in the United States, unless there is proof of the surrounding circumstances, much less here, where there is not only no proof of the surrounding circumstances, but where the circumstances of the country are entirely different. Thus very difficult questions, indeed, are involved.

Mr. HARDY.—Any reports Mr. Langmuir has are quite at the service of my learned friend. He has not failed to take advantage of them in the past in working up his case ; he has had almost a monopoly of them, and they are quite open to him ; any information we have is perfectly at his service.

Mr. BROCKWAY.—We had better proceed and take the testimony now offered, and leave the question to be determined afterwards.

ALEXANDER M. SMITH, sworn :—

BY MR. WELLS.

Q. You are Vice President of the Car Company ? A. No ; I am a Director.
Q. You caused certain statements to be prepared for you, by your Secretary, I believe ? A. Yes ; they are here, I think.
Q. How long is that ago ? A. Some eight or ten weeks.
Q. What was the object you had in view in having the statements prepared ? A. My object was this—there were got from the different foremen very often memoranda of large quantities of stuff being turned out, and I found that we were not getting returns for that quantity. They stated that they turned out certain amounts, and I suggested to Mr. Bailey the preparation of the statements which are now in his possession. We have been working at them and trying to get them into reasonable shape since. They are now in such a state that they can be understood—at all events by myself.
Q. They were not prepared for this investigation ? A. No ; I had no idea of it.

BY MR. HARDY.

Q. You say that they are now in such shape that they can be understood. Were they in a different state previously ? A. They were not made out at all. We had no such statements. Our Manager made certain statements as to what he had turned out and, after making certain allowances, there appeared to be large profits ; but when the goods went into the hands of the agents, the quantities did not at all come up to those mentioned in the statements. I found that instead of having turned out, as we had been previously told, perhaps three hundred dozen pails a day, the quantity was not more than one hundred and fifty dozen. Then I suggested that this form of return should be prepared.
Q. Had you no returns—nothing in writing to show what number were placed in your agents' hands? A. Yes ; I may state that the fixing of the prices rested pretty much upon me as

one connected with the sale of that class of goods. From my business I knew what I was in the habit of paying for a similar class of goods.

Q. Then, were the statements which were made to you incorrect? A. Decidedly.

Q. They were verbal statements? A. Yes. Mr. Warren was Manager then. He is gone now, I am happy to say.

Q. Did his returns and vouchers correspond? A. No.

Q. Who had the supervision or checking of the returns during that period? A. The Secretary.

Q. Who was he? A. Mr. Buchan.

Q. Where is he now? A. In the city.

Q. He is not in your employ? A. No.

Q. Who took the place of Mr. Warren? A. Mr. Brandon.

Q. How long had he been there? A. From the beginning.

Q. How long has he been Manager? A. Since about last January.

Q. And who took the place of Mr. Buchan? A. Mr. Bailey took his place as Secretary.

Q. At the same period? A. Yes; but I think a little later on.

Q. Then the present Secretary and Manager are comparatively new men as such? A. Our Manager is not a new man in the works.

Q. But he is a new man as Manager? A. Yes; still he has been in the works from their commencement.

Q. You did not make up the returns with the view of submitting them to the Commission? A. Certainly not.

Q. You were aware that the Commission would be eventually appointed? A. The Commission was not then appointed.

Q. But it had been the subject of discussion for a year? A. I am not aware of it; it had been seriously considered how we were to go on unless we got the price of our labour reduced; I am not aware that the question of the appointment of the Commission had come before us in any shape; I may, however, be mistaken.

Q. Have you financial charge of the Company's affairs? A. No.

Q. Have you examined the returns and the books? A. I examined the returns and fixed the prices.

Q. These statements which were prepared, had nothing to do with a design of making an exhibit for the purpose of this Commission? A. Certainly not; I never thought of it.

Q. How long has this system of making such returns been in existence? A. About eight or ten weeks.

Q. Would you think that a fair test to employ in connection with a large concern of this kind as shewing what the results are? A. Yes.

Q. Would you think a period of eight weeks a reasonable time to make such a test? A. It is a test which satisfies me. I consider it a pretty clear test.

Q. How long has your business been in operation there? A. I suppose that this class of business has probably been in operation for about a year. The time when we began the work was in May a year ago.

Q. With how many men did you commence? A. I cannot give you correct information on that point.

Q. The statement made out is one which satisfies you, at all events? A. Yes.

Q. And the old one was unsatisfactory? A. It was very unsatisfactory to find that while apparently a large quantity of goods were turned out, the quantity was really very small.

Q. Books were kept, I suppose? A. Yes; and the books will show what the turn-out was.

Q. You said that you had fixed the prices? A. Yes.

Q. Upon what system do you go in fixing prices? A. We sell in our own business almost everything that the Car Company produces.

Q. What business is that? A. We are in the wholesale grocery trade.

Q. In the city? A. Yes.

Q. What is the style of the firm? A. Smith & Keily.

Q. And you sell nearly every thing that such a manufactory produces? Yes,—except churns, and such sort of goods. We sell pails, tubs, and such articles as are usually sold in a wholesale grocery store.

Q. Where do you get your supply generally? A. We procure it generally from Mr. Nelson, but sometimes we bring it from the United States; we get it sometimes from one place and sometimes from another.

Q. Do you deal with Mr. Eddy, of Ottawa? A. Mr. Nelson is the agent of Mr. Eddy here.

Q. Do you fix the prices of the goods turned out by the Car Company with reference to their prices? A. I have invariably followed their price list as nearly as I can.

Q. Do you make the same quality of articles? We do, and we try to make them better.

Q. Are your articles identical with the class of articles which Mr. Eddy turns out? A. Yes.

Q. Do you not consider your pails stronger than those manufactured by Mr. Eddy? A. I do not think that they are so strong; I think that they are rather on the weak side. We make them a little thinner, and we have had complaints about them.

Q. Does that apply to churns? A. I do not deal in them. It applies to pails and tubs.

Q. Do you speak as a matter of fact on that point? A. Yes; I think that ours are a shade lighter in the material.

Q. Have these goods you manufacture any advantage over those which Mr. Eddy manufactures? A. They have advantages over the latter; we have been very careful to turn them out as good as possible, and for this reason: there is always a little objection to goods made in a place of this sort, because the idea is entertained that the men so employed have no special object in view in turning out good work.

Q. Are they not better articles than Mr. Eddy's? A. We try to say so; but I could not guarantee them any better; we sell them side by side; sometimes we sell the one make, and sometimes the other.

Q. How do you fix the prices? A. They are exactly the same as Mr. Eddy's for the same class of goods.

Q. Delivered at his own place? A. No; delivered here; he delivers goods here probably as cheaply as he sells them at his own place; I am not sure but that they are not sold cheaper here.

Q. Is there any other large manufactory besides Mr. Eddy's in that line in the country? A. No.

Q. How do you learn Mr. Eddy's prices? A. By getting his price list and by buying his goods.

Q. Do you allow any discount on these prices—do you throw anything off from them? A. No; but if Mr. Eddy allows ten per cent. we do the same.

Q. Have you not been under-selling Mr. Eddy. A. No.

Q. Has not this been the case in brooms and pails. A. No.

Q. Mr. Eddy has gone through Insolvency two or three times? A. Yes; but that is no benefit to us.

Q Have you been marking goods down to his bankrupt prices? A. No; neither Mr. Eddy nor ourselves have the power to keep the prices up because they are pressing these goods into this country from the United States, and they come from Michigan and from several points the names of which I cannot remember now.

Q. These goods were made there? A. They were made in the United States.

Q. Were they manufactured by any of these institutions? A. No; but by free labour.

Q. Then you say that the American prices for these goods have been rather low? A. They have been lower than ours.

Q. Your prices and Mr. Eddy's prices have been low? A. You have got to sell near the market price, or you cannot sell at all.

Q. Prices have ranged low on that class of articles in these hard times? A. Yes; they have been lower than when the times were good.

Q. You started your business about one year ago—in May? A. We commenced to get ready before that, we began to get the machinery together.

Q. Beginning operations in May, a year ago, you have run during a year of bad times, and obtained the same prices as Mr. Eddy. Has he lowered his prices very much since his bankruptcy? A. I do not think so; I do not think that he lowered his prices on account of his bankruptcy; but he had to lower his prices, or he could not sell his goods, because of the American goods being pressed upon our market.

Q. When did he fail? *A.* I think that it was last Fall; and probably he reduced the price of his pails about that time.

Q. Did you follow suit? *A.* Yes.

Q. How much did he reduce them in price? *A.* I think that it was about ten cents a dozen, or somewhere about that figure.

Q. Then you did the same? *A.* Yes.

Q. Who are your agents here? *A.* Messrs. McMurray & Fuller.

Q. Exclusively? *A.* Yes.

Q. Do they simply act as agents for the Company, or do they take a risk? *A.* They take the risk of their sales; they guarantee their sales.

Q. Do you find a pretty ready market for all your goods? *A.* Yes, we have been able to dispose of all that we could make.

Q. Have you orders in advance? *A.* Sometimes we have, and sometimes we have not; sometimes we accumulate stocks.

Q. Have you for certain classes of goods large orders in advance? *A.* Sometimes.

Q. Do you consider the present or last year a good year to establish a large business of this kind, in view of the state of the market? *A.* No; I do not think that last year was a year when you could calculate on making a great deal of money on anything; at the same time, it was a good year to test whether you could live or die in that kind of business.

Q. Had you anything hanging over you from the old Car Company the first year you started? Any old debts, or anything, which in a financial way, could interfere with the new Company? *A.* How do you mean to interfere?

Q. Did any large indebtedness exist? Was there any want of credit? It has been supposed that the old company very nearly failed? *A.* We settled up all the debts without any compromise, I believe. I was not in the first company.

Q. And you are not responsible for their debts? *A.* I am not responsible for their sins; I mean to say that the gentlemen now acting at all events upon this Board, are not in any financial distress. They need not be, and they have not allowed the Company to suffer in any shape, even where their own personal credit was necessary to prevent it. But there can be no doubt that the original Company lost a great amount of money, and I think that we are going to lose the balance of it from present appearances.

THOMAS BAILEY sworn—

BY MR. WELLS.

Q. You are Secretary of the Car Company? *A.* Yes.

Q. How long have you acted in that capacity? *A.* Since the first of March last.

Q. Your office is on the premises, I believe? *A.* Yes, on the prison grounds.

Q. You have prepared certain statements? *A.* Yes.

Q. At the instance of the Company, I believe? *A.* Yes.

Q. Are these the statements? (Statements produced.) *A.* Those are some of them.

Q. Will you explain to the Commission what is the nature of them? and state when they commenced? *A.* They started from about the first of March. There are eight here. The first of these starts from the 19th of April and extends to the 6th of June. Those which were made at the commencement were in rather crude form in regard to their being put together, but about the 19th of April the returns commenced to be more complete. The returns were made out for each week and divided up, representing separately each department—pail and tub; box; broom and whisk; brush; and wash-board and churn. These account for all the prisoners employed, and for the free labour distributed among the different departments.

Q. From what material are those statements prepared? *A.* From the actual returns of the goods produced during the different weeks in question.

Q. What does this return, for the week ending the 19th of April, show? *A.* That 1617 boxes were made during that time.

• *Q.* How many prisoners were employed that week on this work? *A.* Twenty; one foreman was also employed.

Q. What did the wages amount to? *A.* To the sum of $62.40.
Q. Then you allowed something to cover running expenses. What does that amoun to? *A.* To ten per cent. This relates to expenses for which provision is not otherwise made.
Q. What is included in that percentage? *A.* The wear and tear of the machinery, oil, and several other matters, with the wear and tear of tools.
Q. Is that the recognised percentage? *A.* Yes.
Q. I understand that in all such business ten per cent. is charged to cover running expenses. As a matter of fact, that is taken into account by manufacturers engaged in your business? *A.* Yes. It is the custom of manufacturers to do so.
Q. You have the cost of the material; what is that? *A.* An average of six feet of 4½ inch stuff at $13 per 1,000 feet is used for each box; the lumber costs $8.50 per 1,000 feet, but after it is re-cut, cross-cut and planed the value of it is brought up to $13 per 1,000 feet, then there is the cost of the nails to be considered.
Q. You made 1,617 boxes during that week. What was the net cost of the work? *A.* The net cost is $187.60.
Q. What was the net value of the work—that is the price you got for it? *A.* That was $160.94, showing a loss of $26.69.
Q. Then you have a statement of the goods in hand at the end of that week, will you read it? *A.* There were 2,000 caddies; 600 crystal; 1,400 biscuit boxes; 1,000 Morse's soap boxes; 800 Queen City; 1,600 common soap boxes, and 1,200 miscellaneous.
Q. The next department is the pail and tub department? *A.* Yes.

Mr. WELLS,—I will read the returns for the week mentioned. The total number of prisoners employed was 78, and of foremen 4; the total amount of wages paid was, $276.05; the ten per cent. allowed to cover running expenses amounts to $54.29; the material valued at cost amounts to $195.45; the total cost is $525.79; the net value of the work, $542.92; and the profit, $17.13. In the broom and whisk department 31 prisoners were employed, and one foreman; the wages paid amounted to $104.50; and the ten per cent. allotted to cover running expenses, to $38.90; the cost of the material is valued at $220.44; the total cost, at $363.84; and the nett value at $388.92; the profit amounts to $25.08. In the brush department, 10 prisoners and two foremen were employed; $54.65 were paid in wages; the ten per cent. covering running expenses amounts to $13.17; the total cost was placed at $126.48; the net value of the work at $131.70 and the profit at $5.21. In the washboard and churn department 29 prisoners and three foremen were employed; $195.75 were paid in wages; the total cost amounted to $542.26; the net value of the work was $534.89; and the loss amounted to $7.37.

Q. All these statements are made up on that principle? *A.* Yes.
Q. Can you tell us what was the net result of those eight weeks work? *A.* The net result was a profit of $251.66. The outlay was $12,795.16; and the profit realized was about two per cent.
Q. Do you consider that these eight weeks furnish a fair test? *A.* I do.

By Mr. Hardy.

Q. Suppose you deduct the 10 per cent., what would be the amount? *A.* $1,541.07.
Q. On what principle do you make that 10 per cent. allowance? *A.* It is 10 per cent. on the net value of the goods.
Q. For a week? *A.* It is for a week, because we take the amount for a week.

By the Chairman.

Q. In your statement you say "the net value"; do you mean to say that is the cost of the goods, or the value of them, the amount for which they would sell? *A.* The net value we receive for the goods—that for which they are sold.

By Mr. Noxon.

Q. The net value is fixed by the wholesale prices? *A.* Yes

By the Chairman.

Q. In this statement for the week ending April 19, you commence
with wages, $62.40; then you add ten per cent. for running expenses, $16.09; then the cost of the material, $92.97; nails $16.17, and carry out the total, $187.63. Does that include all the items? *A.* The wages, ten per cent. for running expenses, and material.
Q. Then you put down the quantity of material, 1,617 boxes? *A.* Yes.
Q. You put down the net value at $160.94? *A.* Yes.
Q. That has no reference to its cost? *A.* No.
Q. That is what it would sell for? *A.* Yes.

By Mr. Noxon.

Q. I understand you put the material down at $13.00 per thousand feet? *A.* Yes.
Q. I understand the first cost of the material is $8.00? *A.* Yes.
Q. Cross-cutting, planing, and resawing brings it up to $13.00? *A.* Yes.
Q. But the same labour required to do this you have already charged for? *A.* No; in all these returns yard-men are not included—they do not figure in the return at all.

By the Chairman.

Q. Is the planing and preparing done by some other department? *A.* Yes; it is not shown in that statement.
Q. Is the material brought to the shop? *A.* Yes.
Q. Have you charged to the shop the cost of preparing it? *A.* Yes.

By Mr. Langmuir.

Q. Where is it prepared? *A.* Upstairs.
Q. By prison labour? *A.* Yes.
Q. Do you account for 215 men in that statement for that particular week? *A.* No.
Q. How many men are accounted for? *A.* That statement on the face of it shows 205 men.
Q. How many men were charged to the company at that time? *A.* 205 men.
Q. The labour of 205 men is charged in the cost of the goods? *A.* No, there is not a return of the whole 205—there is only a portion embodied; we cannot classify yardmen, who are going about carrying timber from place to place; there is no return of them.

By Mr. Hardy.

Q. What do you include under the 10 per cent. allowance? *A.* The principal items are wear and tear of machinery and tools, oil, salaries of secretary, office men, night-watchmen, insurance, which is a very heavy item.

By the Chairman.

Q. None of these things were charged in the statement? *A.* No. There is also interest on the outlay. Tools are a very heavy item.

By Mr. Hardy.

O. That charge of 10 per cent. is a usual charge? *A.* Yes.
Q. Is that usually charged when the buildings belong to the parties? You have not made it any less because you are not paying rent? *A.* No.
Q. You are taking the charge of 10 per cent. on ordinary things, when parties are paying rent; it is what ordinary business men allow? *A.* Yes; but I have added on for the extraordinary position we are in there.
Q. How much have you added for that? *A.* I have considered that as an offset to the

buildings being ours; not quite an equivalent. There are a great many drawbacks—some minor ones—but in the aggregate they amount to a great deal.

Q. What has been your expenditure per month? *A.* $12,000.

Q. What is the estimated outlay during this year? *A.* From $75,000 to $80,000; it would not have been that for the year ending now.

Q. How long have 215 men been employed? *A.* I should judge from three to four months, but the number has been gradually increasing up to that.

Q. During the eight weeks, ending June 6th, you have expended $12,000? *A.* Yes.

Q. Is that the outlay for material and wages? *A.* Yes.

Q. You put your own price on the material in this statement? *A.* Yes, what it cost.

Q. How do you get at what it cost? *A.* We know what it cost.

Q. How do you get at it exactly? *A.* It is so much per foot.

Q. Is pail lumber by the foot? *A.* It is by the foot.

Q. How do you get at what it cost you? *A.* We know what a certain quantity will produce.

Q. You say a certain quantity will produce so many pails? *A.* Yes.

Q. How much does it cost to prepare the lumber, say for pails? *A.* You will see by the returns; we figure the labour only on this basis; we take 78 men engaged on pails, the pail in its finished state cost so much; we don't go into the extent of work each man does.

Q. You put down the lumber for the pails, at what? *A.* The cost is not made up here; the amount is 46¼ cents for a dozen pails.

Q. How do you arrive at it? *A.* By figuring up the lumber and estimating the work done on it.

Q. How much did you put down for that? *A.* I cannot recollect.

Q. Did you say that so much wood would make so many pails, and the cost was so much? *A.* The cost is figured up; it is figured on the basis of a cord.

Q. What do you pay when it is delivered in the yard? *A.* Six dollars a cord.

Q. What does it cost you to put it into the shape of pail lumber? *A.* I should judge it would be about $10 a cord finished.

Q. Who made up that estimate? *A.* Mr. Brandon in conjunction with myself.

Q. You prepare that sort of calculation? *A.* Yes.

Q. In what state is it finished at $10 per cord? *A.* It is cut into small pieces, and matched into right sizes.

Q. That probably is worth $10 per cord? *A.* Yes.

Q. You don't know that that is the figure? *A.* Yes.

Q. The labour during the time of its preparation you have charged for? You have charged all the labour in these? *A.* But we don't charge it twice over.

Q. You have charged the labour while preparing it? *A.* Yes.

Q. At so much per day for the men? *A.* Yes; we have not put it in twice.

BY MR. LANGMUIR.

Q. You have charged in statement for April 19th twenty nine prisoners in washboard and churn department, ten in brush, thirty-one in broom and whisk, seventy-eight in pail and tub and twenty in box. You have nine men adjusting machinery in hammer shop. Was that an abnormal expenditure? *A.* They were removing machinery to the hammer shop. That comes under the 10 per cent.

Q. Do you require to be constantly removing machinery? *A.* No.

Q. Having removed it, you will not require to move it again? *A.* No.

Q. These nine men could be utilised in another shop? *A.* Yes.

Q. Then that expenditure is abnormal? *A.* Yes.

Q. Then there were four men relaying pipes in dry-kiln. Could not they be afterwards distributed in other departments? *A.* Yes.

Q. Do you not save money by having them lay the pipes? Would you not otherwise have had to bring in outside labour to do it? *A.* Yes; it was repairs.

Q. Then there is clerk and shipper, are they constantly employed? *A.* Yes.

Q. Then fourteen are entered as on cars? *A.* They are put in for the purpose of making up the 205 men. None of these returns take in the car works.

Q. Were those fourteen men not employed on finishing cars ? *A.* Yes.
Q. Those prisoners were fully utilised ? *A.* Yes.
Q. Five men were employed as engineers and firemen ? *A.* Yes.
Q. Three men as machinists and blacksmiths, constantly ? *A.* Yes.
Q. You have charged all that labour ? *A.* No; there is no return of these.
Q. Although not returned here as products, was there not a product—say from the prisoners relaying the pipes ? Was there not so much money saved ? Had not the prison labour been used, would you not have had to call in outside labour ? *A.* Yes.
Q. And the same with regard to removing machinery from the north shop into the forge ? *A.* Yes.
Q. Is not that money saved to the Company ? *A.* Yes.
Q. Should not that be put in as a product ? *A.* It is an unforeseen expense. It is an expense that is covered there.
Q. On 19th April, fourteen men were working on cars : why is there no car product given ? *A.* No product is given.

Mr. A. M. SMITH.—We are finishing these cars, and we are keeping the work entirely outside of Mr. Bailey's department, or pretty much so. There are men employed under different foremen by Mr. McBean, who is supervising it ; you will notice no return is brought in, in any of these statements, of that work, because we are not sure it is going to be permanent work. We are simply finishing it, and not carrying on regular work, though using prisoners for it ; we are not building cars as work which is certain to be permanent ; we are finishing cars there. I merely make this statement with the permission of the Commissioners.

Examination of Mr. Bailey resumed.

BY MR. LANGMUIR.

Q. In statement of April 19, you have thirty-two men entered, leaving out the engineer and firemen who were not productive ? *A.* Yes.

BY MR. HARDY.

Q. Have you put in here the results of work when completed and ready for shipment to market, or after shipment ? *A.* After the day's work is laid aside a young man takes charge of it, and enters it in his book, and brings his book in at the end of the week, and the result is made up.
Q. Do you commence on Monday morning with the raw material and finish the work up that week ? *A.* That has more special reference to brooms.
Q. Is that the way you make up a statement ? Do you take it right through from the beginning through a whole week, and say, " We have made so many pails complete, including hooping and painting, and getting them ready for market " ? *A.* The return of the pails is as they come out of the paint-shop complete.
Q. You complete a whole series of pails each week ? *A.* No.
Q. Then how do you get at your statement ? *A.* The statement is of the pails turned out this week complete. It may not be what has gone in during the week in a rough state.
Q. Then during the eight weeks you might turn out very few or very many ? *A.* No, because we keep the men constantly employed.
Q. It would depend on how far the work was advanced when you commenced ? *A.* We have a stock-book and credit everything in hand. When the returns were started on March 4, they were incomplete for three or four weeks, until we got them checked and in running order. At the very start a lot came out, and I did not know how many there were in hand We had returns incomplete for some weeks. We made, on April 19, a fair start, and took each week as a period that would include everything that was at the commencement of that week in a raw state.
Q. It is a mere estimate you start out with ? *A.* No, we took stock of everything on hand.
Q. If you had a great deal on hand when commencing those eight weeks, you would turn out a large quantity of goods ? *A.* We credited what was on hand.

Q. Why did you want to make the return complete for eight weeks ? *A.* We took eight weeks because it would better illustrate the business than a shorter time.
Q. Why did you want to illustrate it? *A.* For your satisfaction.
Q. Then the returns have been brought here for the purpose of the Commission ; they have been made up expressly for the Commission ? *A.* Nothing of the kind ; I brought them from the office to furnish any information you might want as to the return.
Q. Have you a statement made up for last week ? *A.* It is not complete.
Q. You have none prior to 19th April ? *A.* Not in as satisfactory a state as these ; on account of the amount in hand I did not know the exact quantity.
Q. How was it different a week afterwards ? *A.* Because a week after we took stock of what was in hand.
Q And took stock again at the end of each week ? *A.* We could do it, but we did not.
Q. Did you do that in order to ascertain these figures ? A. Certainly.
Q. These represent what is actually turned out ? *A.* Yes ; we took stock to shew what goods we had in the hands of our agents ; these statements shew what were actually turned out complete from the paint shop.
Q. The quantity of stock made ready to deliver must depend on how much you had partly manufactured before you commenced operations during the period mentioned in the returns ? *A.* We kept track for about six weeks before we got things into proper shape, and took stock of what we had in hand.

BY MR. LANGMUIR.

Q. When you took stock at the end of the week, did you charge the raw material for the churn and broom shop in hand ? *A.* No.
Q. Do you only charge it as it goes into the shop ? Do you send in only one week's supply of the raw material ? *A.* No, we send in as occasion requires.
Q. How do you make a charge for raw material until it is used up ? *A.* We don't distribute it as stated times ; we charge raw material only on goods turned out.
Q. All the prisoners are charged you say ; sometimes you have a break down ; the wages of the men are going on ? *A.* Yes.
Q. Have you ever had to stop for want of raw material to be supplied by Mr. McBean or others ? *A.* Not to my knowledge.
Q. You have heard of Mr. McBean not having furnished you with material, and of the men being delayed on that account ? *A.* Not to my knowledge.

BY MR. HARDY.

Q. Do you think that eight weeks' work would be a fair test of the business of the year ? *A.* Yes ; I would consider it a very fair test.
Q. I see you have entries "Goods in hand ;" who took stock ? *A.* The clerk.
Q. Who is he ? *A.* George McKenna.
Q. Is he a prisoner ? *A.* No.
Q. Does he take just the finished stock? *A.* Yes.
Q. Then anything that would be in course of manufacture, all the partially manufactured goods would not be taken into account ? *A.* No.
Q. Not until the end of the next week ? *A.* Not until they are completed.
Q. How long does it take before the work in the wood shop to-day comes out painted ? *A.* About three days for pails and tubs.
Q. Are they put through with that rapidity regularly ? *A.* Yes ; unless an accident occurs.
Q. When do you remove them from the paint shop ? *A.* Just as occasion requires.
Q What does that mean ? *A.* Sometimes more frequently than at other times. They are taken every day ; sometimes twice a day.
Q. Was what we saw there to-day the work of to-day ? *A.* They may have been through one process and waiting for another.
Q. How long do they remain in that state in the shop ? *A.* I am not positive.

should be charged $13 per thousand ? *A*. It is not the labour alone that brings it up ; there is the machine work too. For boxes, some material has to be cut more than once. $8.50 per thousand is the price of lumber used for the common soap boxes, but for biscuit boxes the lumber costs $10.50 and $11.00 per thousand, and it has to be kiln dried too. This return is two months old.

Q. If there is one dollar more expended, point out where it is shown ? *A*. The material for biscuit boxes goes up to close upon $13 in its raw state.

Q Do I understand that you depart from the original statement that the lumber cost $8 per thousand ? *A*. Some cost $8 per thousand.

Q. Can you show in any case where you have charged for lumber costing $8, $12, or $13, any return of the work in the preparation of it ? *A*. I should judge that some of that must have cost close upon $13.

Q. Do you mean that if it cost $12.50, you put it down at $13 ? *A*. There is the kiln drying. This was figured out at the time, but I cannot at this late date remember how it was made up. I can get the figures. The return books of the foremen show the stuff used.

Q. Who fixes the prices you have here upon which the calculations have been based ? *A*. There is a price list arranged by Mr. Smith.

Q. I see in the statement you had at one time a lot on hand. Were they marked for sale and the prices fixed ? *A*. We don't make any boxes unless the prices are agreed upon. We don't make them for speculation, we only make them to order. They are special boxes.

By Mr. Noxon.

Q. The value of the statements will depend entirely on their accuracy. It is stated that the charge for the lumber for biscuit boxes is $13 per thousand. Is $4\frac{1}{2}$ feet the actual quantity in a box ? *A*. The plan we adopt is to measure the box as it stands and allow a shade over to cover cutting up.

Q. The lumber you buy is inch lumber and you have it resawn, making double the quantity ? *A*. Yes.

Q. The lumber would cost you $11 per thousand by being resawn and doubling the quantity, still making it worth $13 in the box ? *A*. Yes.

By Mr. Wells.

Q. Were these statements and estimates from details made by you for official reference ? *A*. Yes.

Q. And as accurately made as you could make them for the purpose of informing the Company, and for that purpose only ? *A*. Yes. The quantities were known before the returns were made out ; every care was taken to make them as accurate as possible.

Q. Do the whole of these returns show the total turn out for that period of all the prisoners you employ ? *A*. Yes, with the exception of those in the car works.

Q. Mr. Langmuir has pointed out that a number of prisoners in one of these statements were not embraced in the particular return ; were not these prisoners employed in what you consider repairs and removing ? *A*. Yes.

Q. That is going on always ? *A*. Yes, always in a place of this kind.

Q. In the extra price you have put on the lumber in these statements you have included the price of the prison labour upon that lumber ? In estimating the cost of the material for boxes, for instance, you put it at a little more than the actual cost per thousand feet. The difference between the actual cost of that material and the price which you put it at represents the prison labour put upon it ? *A*. Yes.

Q. You put it on because the price of the prison labour is not included in this statements at all, otherwise than by increasing the price of the material by that labour ? *A*. When I made the statement as to $8.50 per thousand for lumber, I presumed it referred to soap boxes. It must have been lumber for biscuit boxes, which has to be kiln dried, to be clear stuff, and labour has to be put upon it.

By the Chairman.

Q. I understood you to say that you estimated the lumber would cost $8.50 per thousand ? *A*. Yes.

Q; But you charged it at $13? *A.* Yes.
Q. I understand you to say that the reason you add the difference between $8.50 and $13 is because the cost is increased by the work done upon it previously?. *A.* Yes.
Q. Is that so? *A.* As all the men are included it cannot be so in that case.
Q. Does this statement include all the labour put upon the manufacture of the boxes? The first process is to plane the lumber and saw it into the requisite size? *A.* Yes.
Q. Does this statement include that labour? *A.* The statement does not show the total number of men employed in connection with the work, but it includes the total cost.
Q. I mean the twenty men put down in the statement as at that time being occupied in that particular work. Does their labour perform the work of manufacturing these boxes? *A.* No.
Q. What portion is done elsewhere or by other men? *A.* First, the lumber is increased in value when it is piled. There is also the carrying of the lumber to the shop, and after it has been prepared, to be carried to be nailed up, and a certain proportion to be kiln dried. These 1,617 boxes, without referring to the books, I may say, doubtless include eight or ten different materials, some kiln dried and some not. In a statement such as this it could not be attempted to carry them out in detail.
Q. None of these men would be employed in kiln drying for instance? *A.* No; and those men known as yardmen are also not included in the return.
Q. You have given a statement of the employment of 205 men, the whole men employed; do these statements you have handed in of the work done comprise the whole result of the labour of those 205 men, with the exception of those employed in the car shops? *A.* It does not give a return of those men employed in necessary repairs, and one thing and another, also the stokers and machinists.
Q. I understand there are men employed in the yard moving in timber and piling lumber and various things of that kind; but was there any other specific work to which their labour has been applied except this that you produce statements about? *A.* No.
Q. And the men in the car shop? *A.* The idea was to get out returns of the work meeting with ready sale and that which we could put into a return in a practical shape. Of course, there is some work with which it is almost impossible to do so, and that has been left out.
Q. The other point which Mr. Hardy asked you about was the method you took to arrive at these results, and I did not quite get your explanation of it. We were in the shops to-day, and we saw a very large number of tubs and pails in various processes of manufacture. You want to arrive at the result of what has been done. I should like to know what system you have of arriving at that. If we are to go there to-day for the purpose of arriving at it, we would have to take stock, it appears to me, of all inside that shop in its various stages of manufacture as it stands now. Then there would be great difficulty in determining the results of this labour, how many boxes and pails were made by this labour; and when the time had expired for which you intended to prepare the statement, you would have to do the same thing again. Did you do that? *A.* No, we did not; we took stock at the commencement of what was on hand, and we deducted that, and took a statement of all the goods that came out complete every week.

BY MR. HARDY.

Q. Here are fourteen men at cars; you have returned them amongst the 205, and you have given no account of the product of their labour? *A.* We don't charge their labour.
Q. You charge them—you make up the full 205, and make it part of your outlay? *A.* In what way?
Q. Here are 37 men, of whose work you give no account at all. *A* That to which you are referring is not an analysis of the written statements; it is a memorandum for the Board of Directors to show what the men are doing.
Q. There are 37 men of whom you give no return in the work you charge in the week ending April 19? *A.* Yes.
Q. During the week ending May 3, there are 60 men employed of whom you give no account? *A.* But we don't charge their labour.
Q. How did it happen that about the period when the Commission was expected to sit you adopted that new system, commencing in April, and took out results for eight weeks?

What induced you to do it? A. It was a request of the Board of Directors to adopt some ystem; we had no system before.

Q. No system at all; had you not your books? A. We had books for the goods manufactured and delivered; there was no system of this kind; the other system was the ordinary book keeping.

Q. Don't you keep those books yet? A. Yes; we have not changed them.
Q. You continue them on the same system as before? A. Yes.
Q. This, then, is something additional? A. Yes.
Q. Do you keep them now with the aid of an assistant? A. Yes.
Q. Who is the assistant? A. George McKenna.
Q. Who kept them prior to your taking charge? A. W. T. Mason.
Q. When did you commence to keep them? A. April 1, 1876.
Q. Have you been keeping them ever since? A. Yes.
Q. Do you mean to say the books are not correct? A. They are correct.
Q. They would give you a pretty good notion of things? A. Yes.
Q. Did you balance up the books for last year? A. Yes.
Q. Showing the results of last year's work? A. Yes.
Q. Have you got it here? A. No.
Q. What did it show as the result of last year's work so far as profit or loss is concerned? A. It showed a loss on the new industry of $10,000.
Q. How do you mean a loss; do you mean an out and out loss? A. This was entirely on the new business; the old business was kept separate.
Q. Is it kept separate now? A. Yes.
Q. Is there a separate statement in the books? A. Not a separate set of books.
Q. How is it kept separate then? A. It is divided in the books.
Q. Placed on separate pages? A. Yes; the old business is so entirely different from the new.
Q. I am speaking entirely of the new business. Do you remember how many men, on average, were employed last year? A. From May 1st I suppose the average would be about 130.
Q. What wages did you pay last year for prison labour? A. Fifty cents a-day.
Q. How much during the whole year? Do you remember what the entire wages account was last year? A. Between $10,000 and $11,000.
Q. The Government have been paid nothing really as yet? A. Yes.
Mr. LANGMUIR.— Eight thousand dollars have been paid by the new company.
Mr. HARDY, to witness,—Q. The amount of from $10,000 to $11,000 all told was paid for prison labour last year? A. Yes, as far as I can recollect.
Q. What items did you lose on? How do you fix the loss at $10,000? A. I shall have the books here in the morning.
Q. How was it that the statements you have submitted were commenced to be prepared at that period? A. We could not arrive at the cost of the goods without getting out such a statement; attempts have been made to find the cost of those goods, but the moment we approached the question of labour we were nonplussed, and it became an absolute necessity before we could put the goods in the market to get out a statement of what the goods actually cost.

BY MR. LANGMUIR.

Q. You commenced in May with very few prisoners? A. Yes.
Q. And you gradually increased the number? A. We had some before May.
Q. You really commenced the new industry about May? A. Yes.
Q. And you increased the number from those you employed at first until you reached 215? A. Yes.
Q. During May, 1876, and six months forward, what was about the number of prisoners employed? A. I don't remember accurately.
Q. What was the proportion of free labourers to the number of the prisoners? Did not this largely increase the cost of manufactures—that you had a large number of free labourers and very few prisoners? The proportion of prison labour is very much greater now than in June, 1876? A. I cannot answer the question without referring to the figures.

Q. How many more foremen have you in the shops now than there were then? A. We have close upon three times as many now.

Q. Can you give a statement showing the number of free labourers in your employ from the commencement of the new industry and the number of prisoners? A. Yes.

BY THE CHAIRMAN.

Q. When were the branches of industry commenced of which you have given statements? A. About May, 1876.

BY MR. BROCKWAY.

Q. When did you close up the books to make a statement? A. On 1st January, 1877.

Mr. BROCKWAY—I think this whole line of enquiry will be exceedingly unsatisfactory, if proceeded with, and occupy any amount of time we may have to bestow upon it. It would be much more satisfactory to me if the Company would now take an inventory and make up a statement from 1st January, when the last statement was made, showing the whole operations, and whether there has been any profit or loss—if it is desirable for us to ascertain that fact. I am not sure that it is. Suppose it should be shown by that statement or any other that the shop has made a loss, does it follow that it is because too high a price was paid for the labour? It may be one fact that should govern us in deciding the value, but how much I am not prepared now to say. We can judge much more correctly, I think, by a general statement covering a few months—that would be almost six months—than we can possibly do by taking up a statement of this sort and analyzing it in this way.

The CHAIRMAN—My idea, of course, was to allow the Company and the Government to make any statements or representations they thought desirable for the information of the Commission. After we get such before us, then we might see what further we should order, so as to satisfy us in regard to the labour.

Mr. A. M. SMITH—The books of the Company were audited on 1st January by men outside. We took stock before the statements were made out. We took outside men to go through the old works, and report for the new undertaking.

BY THE CHAIRMAN.

Q. Was not the Company reorganized at a time previous to that, and an investigation made, and the whole affairs brought up to a certain point previous to that? A. In 1876 we went through the same process, and made up a statement of the new affairs of the Company for the information of the stockholders. That was when I had the misfortune to be roped in.

Q. Was the statement made up to 1st January, 1876? A. Yes; it was made up to 1st June as near as I can recollect; at all events, there was a statement laid before the stockholders at their annual meeting and a change made in the directors.

Q. And since the period I first spoke of—that up to which you made up the statement for 1876—you have been engaged in the present kind of manufacture? A. They commenced after that; they got Mr. Warren (I was not here at that time) to come over here to establish these works.

Q. I understand from your Secretary that everything appertaining to the old business has been kept separate? A. They have not been mixed up with the new industry; the affairs of the Canada Car Company proper have been kept separate as far as possible; of course, we had to remove some of the machinery of the old Company to put in some of the new machinery.

THE CHAIRMAN.—We had better have the books produced.

THOMAS BAILEY, re-examined:—

BY THE CHAIRMAN

Q What number of hours of prisoners' labour do you count a day? A Ten hours.

Q. What hours do you actually work? A. Ten hours, except on Saturday, when the time is eight hours.

BY MR. HARDY.

Q. From when to when? A. From seven to six, with one hour for dinner.

BY MR. BROCKWAY.

Q. You have a memorandum showing 23 citizens and 215 prisoners employed? A. Yes.
Q. You have four citizens in the pail and tub department, what do they do? A. One is a turner, one a painter, one is a man who has charge of saws, and another who has charge of the lumber and drying kiln.
Q. What number of men do they have to direct? A. 82 men.
Q. You have three foremen in the erecting department? A. Yes.
Q. What are their duties? A. That includes wash-boards in the upper shop. In putting up wash-boards and churns.
Q. Three mechanics and four prisoners are employed with them? What do they do? A. They are now engaged in putting up new lathes.
Q. You won't need so many when the lathes are up? A. No.
Q. One mechanic will be sufficient? A. Yes.
Q. Can you run the engine by prisoners? A. No.
Q. Fourteen prisoners are engaged on cars, what do they do? A. There are four working on the erection of cars in the Company's premises.
Q. You have two men in the office and one prisoner—three clerks? A. Yes; the shipping clerk is outside.

Mr. SMITH made the following additional statement:—

The order the Secretary had from me in regard to the statements (and I claim to be responsible for them) was not to take the stock in the process of manufacture, but to take what was turned out one day with another; some articles would fall a little behind one week and go a little ahead another. My instructions were to give me a return every week; and it was entirely for myself. I claim that their production here is without any desire on my part. They were entirely to guide me in regulating the prices of the goods. I could not tell by any possible way otherwise what the goods were costing, and if you know anything about business, you are aware that it is necessary you should know the cost of the goods before selling them, to keep the right side up. They were entirely got up for my own information. I said to Mr. Bailey: "Every week give me a return of what you have finished, and one week with another the results will be about near enough to guide me in the object I have in view." That was what I wanted to explain.

BY MR. WELLS.

Q. If this Commission is adjourned, the more accurate will these returns be if continued? A. Yes.

BY THE CHAIRMAN.

Q. In regard to the sale of these goods: have you any difficulty in finding a market for all the goods made there? A. No, we have been able to find a market for most of them. When we find certain goods accumulating we stop the manufacture and go to something else. Our agents are very enterprising and have been trying to ship to outside points. They have tried shipping to Australia; I have not heard the result, but I am afraid it is not a good one. They are now trying to ship to England some particular goods. They have worked very hard to introduce the goods into the United States.

Q. I understand you to say that the prices you obtain are about the same as those of other manufacturers? A. I follow as closely as possible Eddy's or Nelson's list. Nelson is a broom manufacturer on his own account and I follow his list; as my firm buy his brooms I have no difficulty in comparing prices.

The Commission adjourned to ten o'clock to-morrow.

THURSDAY, June 21st, 1877.

The Commission met at ten o'clock.
\RLES T. BRANDON, sworn—

BY THE CHAIRMAN.

Q. What position do you occupy in the works? A. I am the superintendent of the mechanical departments.
Q. How long have you occupied the position? A. I have occupied that position ever since we first commenced.

BY MR. WELLS.

Q. Mr. Brandon, what has been your experience in this line of business, prior to the time when you entered into the service of the company? A. I have had experience in general wood work.
Q. Where? A. I have been engaged in the manufacture of machinery and of goods of the same description, such as water pails, etc.
Q. Where? A. In Acton, Ohio; I have also been engaged a good deal in the manufacture of furniture.
Q. For what number of years? A. For about five years; between four and five years.
Q. And then? A. I was engaged for about one year in the manufacture of wooden and iron haems.
Q. What position did you hold? A. I was foreman in the shop.

BY MR. HARDY.

Q. You were foreman in a furniture shop? A. I was foreman of the furniture shop, and also a member of the firm.
Q. And this was the case during the whole five years? A. Yes, sir.
Q. And after that Mr. Brandon? A. I was then engaged in a manufactory where was made wooden ware, haems, and other articles.
Q. At Acton? A. At the same place.
Q. In what capacity? A. I was engaged in erecting machinery.
Q. And after that? A. I was with Messrs. Turnbull and Shelley, manufacturers of agricultural wheels, waggon and carriage hubs, spokes, &c., and of the Ohio Patent Carriage Wheel.
Q. Where was that? A. In Napoleon, Ohio.
Q. And after that where were you employed? A. I was with the Union Improvement Company at Toledo, Ohio.
Q. What business did they carry on? A. The manufacture of wooden ware, sleighs, children's sleighs, coasting sleds, butter-tubs, wash-boards and boxes, and kitchen ware.
Q. And of pails? A. Yes.
Q. In fact it was the same industry that is carried on here? A. Yes.
Q. Then you were employed here? A. Yes.
Q. In fact Mr. Warren came from there? A. Yes.
Q. I think Mr. Warren brought over with him specimens of their manufactured articles?
A. Yes, more or less.
Q. And in that way he got this industry established? A. Yes.
Q. Did you come with him? A. I came with Mr. Warren for the purpose of erecting this machinery and of doing mechanical engineering work generally.
Q. I believe that one or more improved machines are used in the works of this company? A. Yes.
Q. What are they? A. Machinery connected with the manufacture of wash-boards.
Q. Well, now, what was your experience in Toledo—say with regard to what is specially made the business of the company here? I understand that as a matter of fact you use here the same machinery, the same style of machines generally that you did in Toledo? That you use the same machines generally not only in the wash-board department, but also in

other departments? A. Our machinery here is much improved compared with the machinery we used there. It is better, but still it is of the same general character. It is of the same model, and the same labour is required.

Q. Well, with reference to a turning lathe—a pail turning lathe, how many men does it require to work each machine? A. It requires six men and boys.

Q. Well, how many men and how many boys? A. We generally consider young men as men at eighteen years of age—at seventeen, eighteen or twenty years of age, while the ages of boys are from twelve to fourteen and sixteen.

Q. How many of each are employed at each machine? A. You mean, Sir, how many that are able to do a man's work?

Q. How many persons of each class are so employed—how many men and how many boys? A. Four boys and two men are employed on each machine.

Q. Four boys of ages varying from twelve to fourteen, and two men, aged eighteen years and upwards? A. Yes. However, some boys at the age of sixteen are able to go through the whole process.

Q. How many persons did it require at each machine in the industry at Toledo? A. What it requires anywhere.

Q. Well, it requires the same number of hands there? A. Yes.

Q. Six to each machine? A. Yes.

Q. Four boys whose ages may vary from twelve to sixteen, and two men, aged eighteen and upwards? A. Yes.

Q. Well, what is the average number of pails that you could turn out upon a single lathe per day? A. I might state here that the common water bucket was not manufactured there (at Toledo); the pails they manufactured were made of hardwood lumber, besides butter tubs and tobacco pails; a larger number of tobacco pails can be made per day than is the case with water pails.

Q. Are they made of hard wood? A. No; of soft wood.

BY THE CHAIRMAN.

Q. How many of them can be made in a day? A. Five hundred.

BY MR. WELLS.

Q. Can that number be made per day by each lathe? A. Some days more can be made, but that number is considered a fair day's work.

Q. How does that compare with the common pail which we turn out here—as to the ability of the machine to turn them out? A. There is not a great deal of difference. The number is about the same. The tobacco pail is only a trifle larger.

Q. Now as to tubs, do you know the capacity of the lathe for making tubs for turning out work? Does it differ from the pail lathe? A. It is of the same construction, only heavier.

Q. Does it require the same number of persons to work it? A. Yes, the same number.

Q. It requires the same proportion of men and boys? A. Yes, the same.

Q. What was the average capacity of that machine? A. I may state that during my experience with the Union Manufacturing Company, we manufactured no tubs. The average day's work of the tub lathe is, for the largest sized tubs, about 130; of the next size, about 150; and of the small size from 175 to 200.

Q. Well now, what has been the average number of pails turned out here? You employ six men, as I understand, to each lathe? A. Yes.

Q. What has been the average capacity of each machine here? A. You mean the average capacity.

Q. What does each pail lathe turn out daily? A. Do you mean what it should do?

Q. I mean what it does, and what it has been doing? A. The turn out has been something near 250 probably.

Q. I do not make that out from these returns here. What it your practice each day as to the taking of the stock which you turn out? A. The work of the morning is left until noon before it is removed. The pails are left as they come out from the lathe, piled up beside the lathe, and they are not removed until noon. This relates to what are made in the morning.

The foreman takes these pails from the lathes, Nos. 1, 2, 3, 4, et cetera, and gives all lathes credit for the quantity of pails they have standing near them, and these are then removed before the men commence work at one o'clock. The count is again taken in the evening by the foreman and also by the clerk in the Secretary's Office. The number is checked by him.

BY MR. LANGMUIR.

Q. The return is made to the office every day? A. The return is made twice a day.
Q. Of the product of each lathe? A. Yes.

BY MR. WELLS.

Q. What do you find to be the capacity of the large tub machine, such as I suppose the machine which makes the large tubs that you have spoken of? A. It varies considerably. The average I suppose would not be much over fifty.
Q. Fifty: and the next size? A. Fifty or sixty; but I am not quite sure about that; some days the production is considerably lower than that, and some days it is more.
Q. Well, you are in the shop pretty nearly all the time, Mr. Brandon, are you not? A. I pass through the shops, and am there as I am called upon.
Q. Do you think that these machines and the present labour upon them are now being fairly tested? A. Under the present manager of the Prison, and the discipline &c., I think that they are.
Q. You think that the yield has been all that the circumstances permit of, and that the manager has been efficient? A. I think that the yield has been all that could be expected under all the circumstances connected with it.
Q. The machines have been running, I believe, to their full capacity for some time now, have they not—for several weeks? A. They have been running just as usual.
Q. Now, to what do you ascribe this very remarkable difference in the turn out, and between the free labour that you have been accustomed to see and this prison labour? A. The chief difficulty is that the prisoners we have had in this department have been there for very short terms; another difficulty has been owing to their inability to take hold of the work when first brought in, making it a necessity to have a portion of green labour, as we term it, distributed through the shops on these lathes.
Q. How does that work out practically—having one green hand say upon a lathe—one or more? A. If there be five experienced men on a lathe, and one inexperienced man, it retards the product of the entire lathe—that is, their day's work.
Q. Well, what other disadvantages have you noticed? A. Their defiance of all the authorities as to the performance of a certain quantity of work; their breakage of tools; their carelessness in reference to the cutting of material; their lack of discretion in many points, and their want of mechanical skill; consequently many accidents occur which might otherwise be avoided.
Q. Does it ever happen that men employed in this manner are called away from their work? A. They are called away for various purposes; frequently on account of the doctor, a man engaged on a lathe is called away. If it happens to be the man who sets up or joints the staves, the lathe is idle until he returns—or nearly so.
Q. Are there any other purposes for which they are called away? A. They are also called away for shaving, and for hair-cutting, et cetera.
Q. I suppose that the orders are imperative? When a man is called away he must go? A. Yes, Sir.
Q. Men are taken away for punishment? A. Yes; they are taken away for punishment, and not only for breaches of the rules of the shops, but also for breaches of rules that occur while in the buildings.
Q. Well, how does that affect the work, the ability, or the capacity of the man? A. He is certainly unfitted for labour—for performing his daily labour after being confined during the night.
Q. It unfits him for work to some extent, no doubt? A. Yes.
Q. Do you find it a difficult thing to teach men that are given to you promiscuously in that way? A. We find some difficulty in teaching men of advanced years; but in most

cases there are a great many of them that are apt. They learn very quick, but it requires some length of time, even with the most willing. to give them practice enough to handle the machinery as a person used to that class of work would do.

Q. Well, you speak of boys being employed in Toledo—is much of your work here of that light character to which the labour of boys is applicable? A. Our work, with the exception of the preparation of the raw material, is almost universally so.

Q. With the exception of the raw material. What do you mean by that? A. Such as the handling, bolting, cording, piling loads, cross-cutting. It is the handling of the material; the bolting requires heavy, able-bodied men.

Q. The work is generally of a light character, adapted to the capacity of boys. A. Yes.

Q. Can you give us any idea of the percentage or proportion so adapted? Does the preparation of ordinary work require men, or is it a work in which you might use boys? A. The work requires men in but one department—that in which the raw material is prepared, where a very large proportion of the employees must be men; however, some few boys might even be employed in that department; but aside from that the proportion of men to boys employed would not be more, I think, than one in ten.

Q. Could you give any sort of idea of what the gross proportion would be? or have you thought of it? A. I have not.

Q. Would you make that up for us, and have it ready? A. I think that I could give it to you, but not thoroughly; you might take any particular branch—say wash-boards—and make it; I am quite familiar with that department.

Q. How would it be in that branch? A. The proportion there requires some eighteen or twenty men; that is, eighteen to twenty to perform the labour, but out of that eighteen not more than two men are absolutely required for the purpose of making wash-boards.

Q. When you speak of boys, you mean boys of the ages already spoken of? A. Smaller boys can be employed in that department—boys of ages as low as between nine and ten years of age.

Q. The work is particularly light in that department? A. Yes, sir.

Q. Take another department; take the pail department; what would be the proportion there? A. I should judge that there would be about one-third required there.

Q. One-third of the employés here should be men? A. Yes.

Q. What is the case in the tub department? I mean, taking tubs, pails, &c., all through, it would not require as many men on pails. One-third men and two-third boys would do the work? A. Yes.

Q. You mean boys of the ages mentioned before—from twelve to sixteen? A. Yes; however, some boys may be employed on lathes for one portion of the work.

Q. Well, have you any knowledge of the other industries? What are the other industries? A. Painting for instance.

Q. Painting : how is that done? The painting is done almost altogether by machinery, is it not? A. The graining is done by machinery, but the other part is all hand-work.

Q. What is your estimate of the proportion in question in this department? A. This work does not require in fact the employment of any men, other than the foreman to instruct them.

Q. What other department is there? A. There is the Erecting Department where the work is driven up. and the nailing of the boxes is done.

Q. How about that? A. This is what we call the Erecting Department. The finishing room is where the work is driven together, and where churns after the machine work is done are set up. In fact, this relates to the erection of all the work performed with the exception of tubs and pails, which require to a certain extent the services of mechanics.

Q. The proportion of men employed in this department would be somewhat larger than in the others? A. The proportion would be somewhat larger.

Q. What would it be in your judgment? A. It would require about seven men. Thirteen or fourteen, I think, is the number which we have; but only about seven men are needed.

Q. That makes the proportion of men necessary to be employed here, one-half? A. Yes, of mechanics and general wood-workers.

Q. Are those whom you call mechanics, prisoners? A. Yes, sir.

Q. And the other seven among this number of employees might be boys, you think?
A. For box-nailing, that might be cheaper help. I am speaking with reference to outside labour.
Q. You mean by erection, the putting together of articles manufactured? A. That is what I would call skilled labour.
Q. The putting together of churns, sleighs, and ladders, table-cleaning and anything of that kind would require the services of about seven men and of six boys? A. Perhaps.
Q. And as to the box department, how about that? A. Both boys and men are required here. However, it is not considered as skilled labour. Box-nailing may be done with comparatively cheap help as to both boys and men.
Q. What proportion of boys to men should be so employed? A. That would depend very much on the kind of boxes. If the work to be done consisted of small boxes, boys could do the work to better advantage; but if it concerned very heavy boxes, men would do the work to better advantage.
Q. You could hardly give a proportion applicable to the whole department? A. No.
Q. You heard Mr. Bailey's evidence yesterday? A. I did.
Q. It bore principally upon the statements furnished here; have you had an opportunity of seeing these statements? A. I have never examined them.

BY MR. HARDY.

Q. I suppose that these are what you might call the irregularities you speak of, Mr. Brandon—such as men being called away; the breaking of tools; the defiance of authority; and carelessness in the cutting of material; causing accidents. I suppose that these are but the surroundings of all prison labour; it is so, I suppose, wherever prison labour is employed?
A. I presume so, but I have not had experience in prison labour before this.
Q. This is not singular as regards this particular prison? There is nothing in this particularly worthy of mention under the circumstances? A. I would suppose that it would be the natural consequence of the employment of prison labour.
Q. The natural consequence—yes. You did not intend that we shall understand anything more when you mentioned that to be the case up here, than what you would suppose or presume was to be found elsewhere in this business and under these circumstances? You did not intend to make us understand that, I suppose? A. No. I could not say that. I made reference to prison labour and to free labour.
Q. You say that it requires, for instance, at a pail lathe, one or two men and several boys. Will you tell me—and probably the Commissioners would like to know it—what the process is and what is the duty of each particular man? A. There is the number of the staves and the machine; the staves are piled up and sorted, the culled staves being thrown out.
Q. In what character are they brought to the men, and how far are they then prepared as staves? Are they kiln-dried? A. Yes, sir; one man brings the staves.
Q. One man brings the staves, what does the second do? A. He equalizes them, and cuts the ends off.
Q. With a machine? A. Yes, sir; this is done by a part of the machine.
Q. And they are sawn, I suppose? A. They are sawn and cut at both ends at the same time.
Q. What does the third man do? A. I have taken the lathe as it stands; however there is the jointing of the staves. When they are sawn, they are passed to the equalizer. The man who joints the staves, would come second. However this is further on in the machine.
Q. Do I understand you to mean by jointing, the putting of them together? A. No, sir.
Q. What is it? A. In jointing the stave we saw it and cut it to the proper taper.
Q. Are they piled up for him? A. They are carried to him, a man joints them and lays them down beside him, and a man who sits on a stool, takes them up and passes them over.
Q. To number four? A. This is number three.
Q. What is number four? A. That is the matcher, and the staves are passed from the equalizer to the matcher.

Q. What is that process? A. The putting of them together. This is fitting the grooves properly.

Q. What does the next man do—number five? A. Number five is the setter up.

Q. And number six? A. He is the outside turner, and number seven is the inside turner.

Q. Then there are seven persons employed in the operation instead of six? Explain. A. Where you have only got to turn out the quantity they do here, the equalizer has quite sufficient time to carry his staves and do the equalizing himself and pass them over. If we turned out a full complement of work he would not have that time.

Q. How long does it take an ordinary man—supposing that he is not a mechanic at all—to learn outside turning? A. That will depend greatly on how he was pushed forward. In the ordinary way, he would probably turn for a year or two before he became an outside turner.

Q. I mean with regard particularly to the making of tubs and pails: how long would it take such a man to learn that character of turning, and for that purpose? A. It is a simple thing to learn how to do it, to be shown the process and to understand it.

Q. But how soon could he learn how to do it, and be able to be employed at it? A. It would probably require three months or four months; some require a longer time than that.

Q. And for a mechanic how long would it take? A. A mechanic in that line of business?

Q. Take a blacksmith for instance. A. He would probably never make a good pail-turner.

Q. What class of men are put on? A. We put on young boys.

Q. Having how long to serve? A. As long as possible.

Q. The other parts of the work can be learned, I understand, by a prisoner who is not a mechanic about as quickly as by any other person? A. Yes.

Q. The other four do not require to be mechanics at all, as I see? A. No, sir, leaving out the turning.

Q. Ordinary men will answer about as well as if they were skilled labourers when they went in? A. Unless they were in that line of business.

Q. Well, now, I suppose that to the making of tubs the same thing applies? A. Yes; however, this is a little more difficult. A little more skill is required in turning a tub; owing to their size, the workman has to be more careful with his tools.

Q. As to wash-boards: are they made in the same department? A. No.

Q. They and wheel-barrows are made together? A. All the machine work is done in the upper flat.

Q. For the manufacture of washboards and wheelbarrows, you do not require mechanics? A. We require what are considered machine hands.

Q. Of what kind? A. To run the wood-working machinery.

Q. That is work of a very general character. A. Very general. It is the mere operation of machinery. However, it is not expected, in prisoners, that they should set—or at least very few of them, are capable of setting their machines; in fact, they can never be trusted to set them.

Q. What is setting? A. It relates to the setting of knives and guages to the proper sizes for the work to be performed.

Q. How do you operate in that respect? A. The foreman does that; he takes care of the machinery in general.

Q. As a matter of fact, I do not see any particular work you have, wherein skilled labour would be of any very great advantage to you? A. It would be this advantage: men would be able to take care of the machines. Accidents occur frequently because the prisoner does not understand his machine; it frequently occurs that work is thus spoiled. In fact, the prisoner does not know whether his machine is in order or not, and goes along with the work until the foreman happens to call attention to it, or notice that the work is being turned out wrong.

Q. How many foremen have you in the pail and tub department? A. There is a foreman in each room.

Q. And how many men are there in that room? A. Twenty-three.

Q. Twenty-three prisoners? A. Yes, sir.

Q. Well now, as to this work of turning out pails—after they get a little under headway, it does not appear from what you have said, from anything I can gather, there is any particular reason why there should be any very great difference between free labour and prison labour. Taking the quantity turned out, you say that it will probably average from fifty to sixty a day in tubs, and from 130 and 175 to 200 with free labour. I have not heard any very specific, or definite account advanced in this respect. In what respect—where is the drawback? Where is the difficulty? You have full-grown men to operate with in the first place. They are not disobedient, I apprehend, to any great extent in the shop, are they? A. They are disobedient to a certain extent. This always will be so. They have not the interest there is to work for that a foreman has; that is very well understood.

Q. Still they keep together? A. Oh yes; but still a man spends an immense amount of time in trifling. Their object is principally to put in the time and nothing more.

Q. What object is it to them to put in the time? They are about as happy there as they would be in the cells? A. You generally find that a lazy man who can either sit or lie down, prefers it to working.

Q. Is there much of that feeling? A. The general sentiment and tendency is that way.

Q. It is not then for want of skill particularly that the deficit arises, or from want of ability on the part of the men to learn? A. After they have been in there for a sufficient length of time,—this requires from three to four months, it depends greatly on the character of the prisoner—they begin to be useful; it is not from lack of ability that they do not perform a day's work; but taking into consideration the fact that men who are able to do this work on a lathe, may be called away without any notice whatever, and that we are obliged to replace them on the gang by men who are not acquainted with the work at all, the result is not surprising.

Q. They have got to learn? A. Under these circumstances, these men cannot be held responsible for a day's work; but if a lot of these men could be taken and kept for two years without being disturbed, and if the prison authorities would require of them and see, that they took no advantage of their positions, there is no doubt that they would do a great deal more work.

Q. Now, as you did not turn out any tubs while at Toledo, nor any of the common water pails while there, from what source do you derive your experience as to what a lathe will turn out with two men and so many boys? A. They did not manufacture water pails at Toledo; but they made tobacco pails; and if taken and compared mechanically, it will be seen that they are about one and the same thing.

Q. Are they painted? A. That has nothing to do with the turning of them.

Q. I am going to get out what the difference is. I ask you—is a tobacco pail turned out completely like a water pail? A. It is not painted.

Q. It is plain? A. Yes.

Q. Has it the same shape or is it straight, up and down? A. Yes,—it is of the same shape. It is the same as the water pail.

Q. As the ordinary water pail? A. It is the same as the ordinary water pail.

Q. Why do you call it a tobacco pail? A. Simply because it is made of a different kind of material.

Q. Of what kind of material is it made? A. Of either cotton-wood or of bass-wood, as being cheaper and better adapted for the purpose.

Q. It is a cheaper pail than the ordinary water pail? A. The material used in the making of the pail is cheaper, but at the same time, the workmanship is of a higher price.

Q. The work is dearer? A. This pail demands a higher price for the making of it than the ordinary two-hooped water pail, because it is larger than the latter.

Q. How much larger is it, speaking by quarts? A. I cannot tell you exactly what it would hold, but I will give it to you in dimensions. It is probably about an inch larger in the bottom, an inch higher and an inch wider, than the ordinary water pail.

Q. And it is made in the same manner? A. It is made in the same manner.

Q. They did turn out tobacco pails at Toledo? A. Yes.

Q. Is it easier working on these kinds of wood—Cotton and Bass, than on other kinds? A. It is about the same.

Q. Is there any recognized difference? A. There is no recognized difference.

Q. There is no reason why they should turn out more tobacco pails than water pails? A. No sir; the difference is in favour of the large pail, in reference to the quantity.
Q. With regard to tubs, where do you get your information? You do not give much information about pails, but a good deal about tubs; as to the number they are turning out in Toledo by means of free labour? A. I told you that they made there no tubs at all.
Q. And where did you get your information as to the number of them which they turned out with the lathe? What experience have you had in this respect? A. As to the quantity turned out by the lathe, I got my information from the foreman of the pail department.
Q. Where? Here? A. Here, in the city.
Q. You say that the average number of tubs turned out would be of a good sized tub, one hundred and thirty; of the small tub one hundred and fifty; and of the small sized ordinary tub one hundred and seventy-five, or two hundred by free labour. Where do you get that information? A. As to figures, I got them from the foreman in that department.
Q. What department and where? A. The pail and tub department; and a very practical knowledge of that class of work.
Q. That does not answer my question. You have given figures as to what was turned out at Toledo by free labour—how do you know that? Where do you get information as to what was turned out while you were not there? And that was not your business before you went there. You give a contrast; you say that from fifty to sixty were made per day here? A. I say that this is the case.
Q. Where do you get your information respecting free labour at Toledo concerning the manufacture of 150 and 200 tubs per day? A. I never said so. This was not the average there. I said they manufactured there no tubs but pails.
Q. And who, then, turned them out? You said that a lathe should turn out that many? A. Well, that — you say that —
Q. Now, no hair splitting. A. If you want a correct statement ——
Q. I have taken the trouble to so explain myself, that any man of ordinary understanding would understand what I have stated. You gave testimony to the effect that of any ordinary tub, one lathe should turn out of the larger size 130 per day, of a smaller sized tub 150, and of a still smaller size, the ordinary tub, from 175 to 200—am I right? A. Yes; and I told you distinctly that I got my information from our foreman now acting up here.
Q. Ah! that is it? A. I told you so from the first start.
Q. This is not, then, from your own knowledge at all of what a lathe would turn out? You have no personal knowledge of what a lathe will turn out, from your own working at it, and from superintending it worked by free labour? A. That is—as to tubs.
Q. Yes? A. No.
Q. Very well. Do you know what they pay? Take, for instance, pails; do you know what they were paying for this work while you were in Toledo, where you were working? We will commence with the payment of turners? A. No, sir, I do not.
Q. Do you know what was said to be paid in this regard? A. No, sir.
Q. Do you know what was paid for the grooving and tongueing business? A. No, sir.
Q. You do not know anything about it? A. I know nothing about it.
Q. Do you know what was paid a boy of fourteen or fifteen? Had you any boys employed when you were a member of the firm that has been mentioned? A. No, sir.
Q. Do you know what a boy of fifteen or sixteen years of age got in the place where you were working? Had you any such? A. Over one-half the boys in Toledo average in wages from 25 to 75 cents per day.
Q. What would a boy of 14 or 15 years of age get? A. He would receive seventy-five cents a day, and if possessed of extraordinary ability for that kind of work, he would get as high as $1.25 per day. Payment ranges according to abilities.

BY MR. WELLS.

Q. From twenty-five cents a day, upwards? A. Yes, sir.

BY MR. HARDY.

Q. Now, being Superintendent, I suppose you know whether any of the men, since the first of last January, have been engaged in making any tools, or machinery used in the shop? A. Yes, sir.

Q. Has this been the case regularly? A. Nearly so.
Q. How many of the men have been so employed? A. On the average, two or three of the prisoners have been engaged in this work.
Q. What kind of tools are they making? A. All kinds of turning tools, or cutters for turning pails and tubs; in fact, the lathes in general.
Q. Turning tools and lathes; anything else? A. Knives, machine knives of every description used in this relation.
Q. Is there anything else made? A. Have you reference in this regard to new machinery they are making, or simply to repairs?
Q. I refer to men that are engaged in that class of work—either in making repairs or tools? A. That is about the average.
Q. Two or three men are employed in making turners' implements, knives, lathes, et cetera—anything else? A. They are engaged in making repairs on machines.

BY MR. WELLS

Q. Repairs on tools? A. Yes.

BY MR. HARDY.

Q. What kind of men are these? What are they described as? Blacksmiths and machinists? A. As blacksmiths and machinists.
Q. What are the eight men who are engaged in adjusting machinery in the hammer-shop? What class of men would they be? A. These men would be, some of them, carpenters, such as put up counter-shafts and timbers for securing machines; the counter-shafts are very considerable. The others are employed in putting up shifters for the purpose of starting there machines, and the foundations of a set of planers, under the instructions of a foreman.
Q. Now as to the work put upon the building. Has the work on the shops where they have been lined, and the buildings which you say have been boarded, been charged into the ordinary expenses of the Company? A. I could not say how it is charged there: it has, however, been kept separate. The time has been so kept.
Q. All the time has been so kept by you? A. Yes.
Q. Who is the time-keeper? Who is responsible to the secretary as time-keeper? Has it been done altogether through you, or does each foreman make his own returns? A. Each foreman of the department makes his returns; they have books, and these are taken up; they correspond of course with the prison books.
Q. Now, for how long a period are you speaking when you say that these tub-lathes turn out from fifty to sixty tubs per day? What proof, what evidence, what memoranda, have you on that point? A. Well, I have none at all.
Q. How do you know that this is the case? A. I know it from my supervision of these machines; and, in fact, this is the case not only one day, but every day.
Q. Do you yourself pay sufficient attention to know that this is the fact? You do not count them yourself, I suppose? A. No.
Q. You take your information from the foreman? A. There are no duties that lie in the road as to making myself acquainted with this fact. There is no disarrangement in the machinery through these shops but what is laid before me, and I have to adjust them.
Q. Have you daily returns? A. No.
Q. As to the produce of each machine every day, have you returns? A. No; my business has reference to the management of the machinery, and to the keeping of it in working order.
Q. Oh; that is it? A. I have quite an object in keeping track of what is being turned out; I am responsible for the machinery, for the manufacture of the goods, and for the process of manufacture.
Q. You do not, properly speaking, keep accounts of what the machines turn out? A. Not as Manager.
Q. Returns are not made to you to that effect? A. The returns do not come to me.
Q. How do you get your information? A. I told you.
Q. You say that they turn out on an average I think, fifty or sixty tubs, did you give the average of pails?

3

Mr. Wells—It was two hundred and fifty.
Q. How do you get at that? Where do you get your information? A. If you were to co..e into the place any day you like, and ask me how many pails do you get off that lathe, I would probably be the most competent man—excepting those who counted the work, and had actually counted them one by one—to tell you what was the amount of work they were getting off, as it is part of my business to know it; I am connected daily with it, and that gives me an idea of what is being done all the while.
Q. A general idea? A. Owing to my position, of course, it would be incumbent on me to enquire into these matters and know it.
Q. I would say that you have not enquired into them; the men who count and remove them do not make returns to you, and you are not called upon to do it, and I do not see why you should have more than a very general idea of what is being done, according to your own showing of it? A. I am called upon to enquire into these matters, and into everything connected with the manufacture of these tubs and pails, and to see that the men are not working at any disadvantage; that there is no break-down or anything of that kind as far as possible; and to obtain the greatest amount of work on these lathes and from the other machinery there; and if I did not know what was being turned out, how could I properly perform my duties as Superintendent?
Q. So long as they are not turning out work up to their highest capacity, if they have a capacity for turning out five hundred a day, that leaves something to be done? A.' Certainly.
Q. But you do not keep an account of that and see what is being done? A. As to this keeping count, you do not for a moment think that I have time to go in and count the pails.
Q. No, I quite understand that, and that is why I say that better evidence can be had on this point—the evidence of persons who have accurate information respecting it. It is not your business to have accurate information regarding these matters. You have nothing more to do than to maintain a general oversight; who attends to the removal of the goods? A. The foreman does that; I have also taken account of that for a term of almost three weeks.
Q. Have your men frequently been found—and I ask you this in the presence of some of the officials of the prison—standing waiting for hours, or for a long time without having material for work supplied to them? How is that? A. My men waiting for two hours?
Q. I happen to have a return by me; it is made up by the Guard, and I will put it in comparison with the return of the foreman here. I will see how accurate you are in reference to your general knowledge. It is only from general knowledge that you have spoken, of course; while this Guard was there the whole time. Here is May 1st; he reports as to No. 1 lathe, that six men were employed on the lathe; and the Guard has it that No. 1 lathe that day turned out five hundred pails.
Mr. Wells.—One day they did that. Here is the day.
Witness.—We have the same figures.
Q Then you ought to give us the benefit of them and not conceal or keep them back in any way whatever? A. We have not done it at all.
Mr. Hardy.—On May 1st, No. 2 lathe turned out 400 pails.
Mr. Wells.—That is right.
Mr. Hardy.—And No. 3, 380 pails.
Mr. Wells.—That is right.
Mr. Hardy.—And No. 4 lathe, 250 pails You have given it as about one hundred and fifty pails? A. That is the average, go along through.
Q. On May the 2nd, No. 1 lathe turned out 360 pails; "delayed two hours for want of staves." This entry is made opposite the figures; and No. 2 lathe—how is that? Do you remember being delayed for want of staves? A. Probably you will find it remarked.
Q. I did not ask you that. Have you any memory of that? A. No, sir, I do not remember it?
Q. You do not remember it? A. No.
Q. Do you remember any cases of delay? A. Yes, I do.
Q. Do you remember any conspicuous occasions of it? A. I am not prepared to give day and dates.

By Mr. Hardy.

Q. No. 2 lathe turned out 370 pails on May 2nd ; delayed two hours for want of staves. No. 3 lathe turned out 360 pails ; delayed two hours for want of staves. No. 4 lathe turned out 300 pails; delayed two hours for want of staves. Again the entry is made. On the 3rd idle all day for want of staves?
WITNESS.—Idle all day? That is not correct.
Q. It is not correct? A. No, sir, it is not.
Q. Idle all day—that is his report. A. That is, no pails turned out; idle all day is incorrect.

By Mr. Langmuir.

Q. Why were they idle? A. I say that they were not idle.
Q. What were they doing? A. They were changed from pails to other work.
Q. But there were no staves there? A. I will admit that there were no staves there ; that I will admit; but I say that they were not idle.

By Mr. Hardy.

Q. On May the 4th, one lathe turned out 240, and was idle then for two hours; another lathe turned out 200 ; one turned out five tubs, and another 150; but all were idle for two hours for want of staves. Again, on May the 8th, No. 1 lathe turned out 290 pails ; and with green hands on lathe No. 3, 90 tubs. I understood that the average turn out of tubs was 50 ; and yet, we see that with green hands they have turned out 90 a day.
MR. LANGMUIR—Is that the return ?
MR. WELLS—Yes.

By Mr. Hardy.

Q. May 8th : Nos. 1 and 2 lathes 480 pails; No. 4, 250 pails. May 10th, Nos. 1 and 2, changed from pails to churns ; No. 3, 280 ; two bottom hoopers idle all day for want of hoops is another entry ; still they turned out 280 pails, and lathe No. 4, 240 pails. May 11th, 840 pails; three men idle all day for want of hoops. Every day there is something of that kind down ; and yet they seem to have turned out a pretty good quantity of goods ; I just draw your attention to that matter, you do not appear to remember it ; did you not set a regular task up to three hundred—making three hundred a day's work ? A. At eight hours a day, we did.
Q. Did the men perform the task ? A. They did : but we cannot say positively that they did do it.
Q Can you say that they did not do it ? A. No ; we cannot say positively that they did not do it, and I will tell you why : the system of keeping count there was very incorrect.

By Mr. Langmuir.

Q. Whose fault was that ? Who is responsible for it ? A. The foreman was at that time ; if the men had performed that amount of work it would have been satisfactory ; but we have nothing to assure us, that three hundred pails were then made a day.
Q. If everything is at fault, how can you be certain ? When we come to actual facts, you say that you have nothing to assure you ? A. I do not think so ; when you take a man from his general line of business, and bring me from the general supervision of this place into figures upon certain days and dates, you see you would confound anybody.
Q. I am not endeavouring to confound you ; but I am trying to convince you, merely that you are giving evidence which is not the best evidence on this point; did you raise that task, and to what figure ? A. Raise the task ?
Q. Did you raise it from three hundred up ? A, It was raised.
Q. You resumed the ten hour system, and then you put it at what figures ? 375 was it not ? A. It was put at 375.
Q. They did that, did they not? A. No.

Q. Then what did they do? A. They ran down to a loss.
Q. How much of a loss? A. They ran down to 120; and the number had been put at 375; previous to that, the same lathes were turning out a very small quantity of work.
Q. Did they not rise up to 350 and 360 a day? This foreman reports that this was the case? A. Let me explain. When I went among these men, and told them at what we set a day's work, we were then trying to make some arrangement, in order to get a standard day's work; and in order to do so, we used some means to give them some chance, and to induce them to do that day's work and be recompensed for their labour besides, after they went out; for two days this was done; but then the Captain told us that we had no right to do anything of that description, and we had to drop it.
Q. You offered the prisoners a cent a pail over and above how many? A. Over and above 375.
Q. But they did not make over 375? A. Yes; they made over 375.
Q. And in order to increase the number turned out, you offered a cent a pail? Remember you told us that 350 pails was the daily average. A. I said that the average was 250; and I think that this would be found to be the case if you go back and take the general run, not using this special instance.
Q. Then this plan was dropped; the Warden discontinued it, and what did the men then turn out? A. They came down to ——
Q. To 350 and 340? A. Yes; and lower and lower.
Q. Our foreman reports 350 and 340; and for tubs he gives the number at 250? A. 250 tubs.
Q. From 100 to 150 according to size, instead of doing what you required of them; how much did you require in tubs? A. I required 110 No. 1 tubs to be made; will you allow me to refer to a book?
Mr. HARDY—Oh, yes.
WITNESS—I have returns of some of this work as well.
Q. We won't press that further; you say that you fixed the number at 110, for No. 1 tubs, and the others I suppose, in proportion? A. They ran up to 160 I think.
Q. They did that work? A. No sir, they did not.
Q. How much did they fall short of it? A. They turned out that number, I think, for one day; but as I tell you, it was got up for the purpose of demonstrating, for our own especial benefit, what the lathes might be made to turn out if the prison authorities exerted themselves, and were ready to push these men; the turn out was raised to 500 through my own exertions; it would have never been raised to that figure, but for the purpose of demonstrating to Captain Prince what could be done there; I made it up for the purpose of demanding more work out of the men.
Q. When Captain Prince ordered you to discontinue the payment of the bounty, did he not go and address the men? A. The day before yesterday, or two or three days ago, he did.
Q. Did you not in the trimming shop, give rewards in the same way? A. No, sir; we did not.
Q. Did you not offer a reward? The men were taxed there? A. They were to do so much work, that is, the ordinary day's work. Capt. Prince went in and assembled the men— I was not present at the time but so the foreman informed me—and told them that they would be obliged to do what he required of them.
Q. And they did it, did they not? A. They have, that is in a general way, they have done so.
Q. Under pain of punishment, I believe he told them? A. These returns were kept for the purpose of reproaching the Captain in reference to more work being possible—as was required.
Q. How do you account for so much idle time as appears by the returns? The men remained idle for hours each day, and for many days. This is the case right through. It is so for the month of May, and up to the end of May. Have you not yourself represented to the Company the want of material? A. No, sir.
Q. Have you not felt it to be your duty to do so? A. No, sir.
Q. You never made a complaint of that kind to the Company? A. I never said anything more in this respect than would be done in the ordinary course of business.

Q. Have you not drawn the attention of Mr. McBean, the foreman, to it—to the fact that the men were idle a good deal of the time for the want of material to work upon ? A. I have not drawn Mr. McBean's attention to that fact, for the reason it was something beyond the control of either Mr. McBean or myself.

Q. It was beyond the control of the Company ? A. Yes.

Q. How would that be when the Company had always enough stuff on hand ? A. We commenced in that shop with only one pail lathe, one tub lathe and a churn lathe. We also commenced with all the stave saws in that one department, which you saw yesterday was so crowded when you passed through. We had the cylinder saws, the cross-cut and the stave saws and everything of that description in that one building, with only one room ; and its capacity for sawing, for cross-cutting and for getting out staves was limited ; and when we took to enlarging on the churn, it was so small that we could not get the staves out. We always ran at a disadvantage there until the new shop was started outside; and at times then, we would not be able to cut with the pail saws, but we had room to operate in this small building without extending the turn out into any great quantity of other promiscuous work.

Q. You had not enough means to prepare material ? A. Not to put it through, nor to catch up with the work.

Q. Is it improved now ? A. It is now improved. As soon as we started the outside shop and got in there, we ordered two or three new cylinder saws to prepare staves. This was done when we had a place to operate.

BY MR. WELLS.

Q. When was that? How long ago was it ? A. I think that it was about six weeks since we have been in that building.

Q. You do not contend against these difficulties now, and have not for some weeks ? A. Oh, no.

BY MR. LANGMUIR.

Q. You were speaking, Mr. Brandon, about the difficulties surrounding the utilization of prison labour, and you mentioned, as one of them, the employment of short-date men—now as a matter of fact, are short-date men always the worst class of men that you meet with ? A. No, sir.

Q. Not always? A. No.

Q. Invariably it is not the short-date men who are the worst class ; is the labour of some short-date men just as good as long-date men under certain circumstances ? A. That is where you can employ them for yard service, or for anything of that kind.

Q. That is an ordinary labouring man that you mean ? A. For ordinary labour.

Q. They are quite as good for that class of work as long date men ? A. Yes.

Q. Well, take the man who comes in as a carpenter, and he is imprisoned for two months—if that carpenter is sound physically, would his work and services not be available at once ? A. Certainly.

Q. And would he not be as serviceable to the Company as any other, except for the time when he is going away, and it is required to replace him ? A. Well, he could be utilized on a portion of the work ; we could manage to place him so that he would be useful ; however, we have men on some parts of the work—say for instance the setting up of a churn ; it is according to the amount of practice that one makes a good churn ; the longer a man works at it, the more proficient he becomes ; in six months, a man is able to go on and becomes an adept ; and we are well satisfied that what he turns off will give satisfaction.

Q. Is not that the case with ordinary labour ? Did you not find at Toledo that the longer a man was with you, the more serviceable he became, although you paid him the same price as at first ? A. Quite so.

Q. It is the case every day in connection with labour ? A. Yes.

Q. With regard to short-date men, have you noticed very closely whether it has not been a fact that short-date men are more cheerful, and do their work with greater willingness than long-date men ? Have you observed that to be the case ? A. No ; I do not think it.

Q. Have you got your mind's eye now on short-date men who are very serviceable, and equally serviceable as are two years men ? A. To what have you reference ?

Q. I am talking about the value of short-service men compared with long-date men; we are talking of prison labour? A. We dispose of our short-term men as a general thing, —unless they are tradesmen—in the yard gangs, and they work well so—that is, probably as well as even long-term men; in fact, we do not consider it necessary to be very particular about selecting men for that purpose, or taking men from that work.

Q. When a man comes into the prison and is tendered to you, are you not also made aware of his previous occupation at the time? A. We have a list sent to us.

Q. By the authorities of the prison; do they not tell you what he did before he was committed? A. Yes; a list is sent to us, and we are informed of his occupation.

Q. Do you avail yourselves of that information? If a prisoner is put down as a worker in wood, do you utilize him as such? A. Yes, sir.

Q. And if he is a good mechanic or a worker in wood, &c., and you find that out, whether he is a six months' man or not, is he not as serviceable as if he was sentenced for two years? A. He might be as serviceable at the time on certain kinds of work, if sentenced for six months, as if he were sent down for a longer time.

Q. There are many things that a good mechanic or a good worker in wood, or a good carpenter, may not have become proficient in, as in connection with the manufacture of pails and tubs; and it is the same outside. is it not? A Yes, sir.

Q. What I want to get at is this: whether having regard to a two months' sentence, a carpenter is not, as a matter of fact. just as valuable to you as a man sentenced for one year —say after one month's work on the lathes? A. No; I could not say that he would be so.

Q. Tell me why? A. From the very fact that the longer a man works, and the more he is acquainted with shops, and the general work that he has to do about a shop, the more valuable he becomes; this is the case with free labour.

Q I quite understand that? A. I could not say that he is as valuable as indicated; but I would say, that I would prefer a carpenter committed for six months, or for two months, to a labourer committed for two years, and would take him on in preference, if we had work for him to do.

Q. Then you get the trades of prisoners from the prison authorities as they are tendered by the latter to you? A. Yes, sir.

Q. And therefore you use that information for your advantage, and place them accordingly? A. Yes, sir. However, we do not always find the information thus furnished to be correct.

Q. Why do you not find it correct? Where are the inaccuracies? A. Say for instance that a man is put down as a cabinet-maker, he is tendered to us as a cabinet-maker. When a man is required for the shop where the benches are—in the bench department, we naturally wish to use such a man there; but when we come to get him into the shop, we at times find that he is entirely unacquainted with that line of business.

Q. You find that to be the case? A. Yes.

Q. On the principle you speak of, is it not just as likely that a man who was a carpenter would say that he was not a carpenter, to avoid a shop, or a blacksmith deny that he was such for the same reason? A. You will find, as a general thing. that tradesmen are very apt to come to us, if they have not handed in their proper occupations; and they are always more willing to work at a trade than at anything else, as a general thing throughout; that has been my experience.

Q. Well, then, you have demonstrated to yourself, from your own experience, that prison labour is capable of getting a large amount of work out of prisoners, when you offered a cent a pail to them? A. I demonstrated that to obtain the figures for the purpose of—

Q. Of showing the capacity of the lathes or of the men? A. The capacity of the men; so that in case of any dispute this might be appealed to. to let Captain Prince thoroughly understand, that he might not be punishing a man for not doing what would be an exorbitant day's work—and for Captain Prince's proper information; some days before this day's work was done, I called his attention to the fact.

Q. Are you aware that Capt. Prince has punished prisoners for not doing a proper day's work? Are you aware of that? A. I am aware that a few parties who have not been connected with these lathes, but with other departments, have been punished for some misdemeanor with reference to their work, but as to so treating the prisoners as a whole in the shops, I think that this has not been done.

Q. Of course they have been punished for every infraction ? A. What I mean by that is this, that the authorities allow the prisoners to fool their time away on a much less quantity of work than they might turn out ; and such measures as those in question, were not taken until Capt. Prince, a few days ago, assembled the men as mentioned.
Q. When did you commence testing the advantages and trying the capacity of the lathes and the men ? A. I think that I have it here : it was on April 18th.
Q. It commenced in April ? A. Yes, sir.
Q. Did you represent to Capt. Prince prior to that time, that the men were not doing what you thought was right that they should do ? A. Prior to that time, the facilities which we have had for getting material, were not as good as might have been expected.
Q. There were delays experienced ? A. Yes, and there was nothing definite that I could place before him.
Q. And as soon as you placed the matter before him, did he take steps : say in the broom shop, to remedy that state of things ? A. In the broom shop he did.
Q. Are you aware that he went to the factories in the town and ascertained what work other men were doing ? A. No.
Q. But you do know that he did task the men in the broom shop ? A. Yes, sir.
Q. And did they accomplish that task ? You mention that they did it generally ? A. They did in a general way.
Q. Did you increase that task ? A. I have not complained to the foreman with reference to the making of the brooms since.
Q. Did you increase that task afterwards in the sewing department, et cetera, from what was supposed to be fair, reasonable work to a higher amount ? A. I think not, I am not aware of it. I am not aware of any such thing being the case.
Q. As a matter of fact, did you not increase the task in the pail department, and did you not say that it was owing to the increase in the working hours of the day ? A. After what was remarked, the foreman, with our permission, tried to make up that amount of pails, but it was never assigned to the prisoners directly as a task. It was given to the foreman as a basis on which he might work the prisoners.
Q. Then you say, Mr. Brandon, that you could not commence this system of taxing or of telling what was the capacity of the lathes, or what the men should do, because you had not the facilities for getting the material ? A. Yes.
Q. And now you have such facilities ? A. We have them at present.
Q. Are they very good ? A. We have facilities for extraordinary supply.
Q. And, as a consequence, are the works going on better than was the case three or four months ago ? A. You will now find what was never seen before—the quantity of staves and material of that description piled up in the shops, which was absolutely necessary to be there. There is no lack of staves now.
Q. What was the number of pails that was produced to-day for one lathe, working with the full complement of men—six men ? A. My attention has been drawn to the matter, and I find that they were averaging from 180 to 240 per day, or something like that. I passed through the department during the last two days, and I found that the average has been rather fair. but I do not remember the figures at the present time.
Q. We will revert to another point—the long-sentence men ; have you refused men in the shops sentenced for a long period ? A. Refused men ?
Q. Have you refused men sentenced for long periods ? A. Yes, sir.
Q. Why ? A. We refused one party for inability to perform the labour on account of his being crippled in the hand.
Q. That was in the brush shop ? A. No.
Q. In what shop was it ? A. That was in the place where they thought that we could employ the man ; it was in the tub and pail room.
Q. You have a right to reject ; and you reject such men as you find are maimed or incapacitated physically or otherwise for work ; you have the right to reject ; do you exercise it ? A. We understand that we have that right.
Q. And do you exercise it ? A. We reject these men, but no quicker do we do so than they are shoved back on us.
Q. The same rejected men ? A. The same rejected men

Q. How many such instances have you on record ? A. We have not had a great many such instances.
Q. How many have you had ? That is rather a serious thing to charge. It is against the rules. How many such instances have you got on record ? A. I could not tell you without referring to the book.
Q. Have you four ? A. What ?
Q. Have you four such instances ? A. No, I do not know that we have.
Q. Have you three ? A. No—probably not.
Q. Have you two ? A. I think that we have.
Q. You say that no sooner are they sent away than they are returned; and now you say that you have but two instances of it. When you reject a prisoner the doctor calls; is not that so, Mr. Brandon ? and then they are sent out. The doctor is one who is there, and you are bound to the doctor's opinion. Do you point out why you reject, or that it is because of illness that you do so ? A. We have not rejected a great many.
Q. You rejected one two-years man ? A. We did reject one two years man.
Q. Do you know a man named Brooks ? Why did you reject him ? he was a two-years man. Have you any knowledge of that case—Mr. Brandon—of the Brooks' case ? And do you remember Charles Stephens, a two-years man ? Have you a record of these cases ? A. Brooks, I think, is a man who was sent to the hospital on account of diseases in one of his limbs. He was set to draw brushes, but he said that the work was very painful to him. He was not really an able-bodied man. However, would you allow us in these cases, where men having two years terms were rejected, to make an explanation as to what kind of men they were. I do not recollect the cases clearly.

Mr. LANGMUIR.—I state it because you have the first choice of the men, and you can utilize your advantage.

WITNESS.—Would I be allowed to state a certain fact ? Some time ago I made application for a man and was refu-ed him ; he was to be employed in a particular branch.
Q. I would be very glad to hear this information for the Government ? A. I had a man tendered on our list. He was a painter by the name of Orr. He was tendered to us, and when I went for him, I was refused that man on account of his being employed for domestic purposes.
Q. His name was Orr ? A. Yes. We also had a painter tendered to us. He had been an old hand in the shop. His name was Greely. He was tendered to us, and he was also refused.

BY MR. HARDY.

Q. He was a painter ? A. A painter. The explanation which the Captain gave, when I said that the men were tendered to us, was that men employed for domestic purposes never should be tendered.

BY MR. LANGMUIR.

Q. These are two men you asked for, and wanted to get, and could not get ? A. Yes.
Q. And they were refused you ? A. Yes.
Q. Did Capt. Prince give you reasons for doing so ? A. Yes ; he said that these men were wanted for domestic purposes.
Q. You have 215 prisoners engaged at work—what proportion of that number do you suppose or know, can be employed in ordinary labour—in the yards or shops, in the ordinary labour of clearing them out and doing the work which has been mentioned ? What proportion of them need be skilled labour—among over two hundred persons, including the labour in the shops, with the ordinary men and hands that have the proper capacity and can do the work required of them ? What is about the per centage ? How much do you think ? A. You mean to say——
Q. Out of two hundred persons, what can be, and what cannot be worked with advantage, under the most favourable circumstances, and utilized for ordinary labour ? What proportion of the men so employed should be composed of mechanics and skilled labour ? A. Probably about one-third of them.
Q. That is—two-thirds of them may be labourers ? A. I would not calculate that any great proportion of them would be really labourers, but young men and boys.

Q. For instance, for a yard man, the very commonest labourer would do, I suppose? A. Oh, yes.
Q. Then there are other men—sailors, farmers, and men of that kind—would you place them at a sort of thing that you would call a little above ordinary labour? A. Oh, yes.
Q. And altogether you would employ about one-third of 260 men for running full time, and the remainder need not necessarily be skilled workmen? A. That would be about the average—either outside or in.

BY MR. WELLS.

Q. You speak of having plenty of staves now on hand; how long has that state of things existed? A. It is just gradually working itself into perfection.
Q. Has that been the case for two or three or four weeks back. A. Yes.
Q. For the last two or three or four weeks the statements furnished would he fairer on that account. A. Yes.
Q. What has been in your judgment, Mr. Brandon, the results during the past two or three or four weeks? Of course the statements would show it more accurately? A. It would be well to make a statement in explanation of this lack of material, where stoppages have taken place; this was not due to the lack of material in the yard. The material was on hand, but owing to the changes of machinery from one shop to the other, and also to the accident which occurred to the drying kiln, this was the case; to these facts the delays are to be attributed, and not to the score of material being lacking in the yard for the purpose of making pails.
Q. I see by the return for the 6th of June, that the return for No. 1 lathe from the 31st of May, and for the six days ending June the 6th, 230, 240, 180, 220, 240, and 260, the aggregate being 1370; and showing a daily average of 221 pails turned out. I also see that the return for the fourth lathe, on the same days, is 110, 110, 240, 230, and 280 aggregating 1,230, and showing a daily average of 215 pails:—are you able to say whether or not this is a fair average? A. That is the average.
Q. Was there any accident to interfere with the production for these days? A. I cannot say that anything of the kind occurred. In reference to the average, it is only from the time we have commenced to take these statements, that we have a record of the products of the lathes for each day.
Q. Do you know whether any accident happened to interfere with the turn out during that week? Do you remember anything of the kind occurring during the week ending the 6th of June? A. I do not remember of any for that week.
Q. You do not know that any accident then took place? A. I think not.
Q. Well now, with all this before us, do you still adhere to what you said, apart from the accidents which you have just alluded to, concerning, and what, in your judgment, is now the average capacity of the machines which are being worked in proper order and on full time? Do you still adhere to your opinion as to the average capacity of your machines and the average yield? A. Yes.
Q. It is what? A. Two hundred and fifty pails per day. It might be more some weeks, and some weeks again, it might be less.
Q. These returns of course continue? Are you aware when they end? Do they end on Saturday? A. No; they end on Wednesday.
Q. For instance during last week—the week ending the 20th, has any accident of any kind occurred to interfere with the proper yield of these machines? A. No; I think not.
Q. Well, do you think that the return when it comes in, if it is a true return, will give a fair idea of what the yield of these machines is?—with regard, for instance, to the return for the work ending the 20th of June, which was last Wednesday? A. I think it will, in reference to quantities.
Q. The men mentioned are engaged in repairing tools. I suppose that this is necessary in any establishment of the same kind? A. Oh, yes.
Q. This is requisite? A. Yes, sir. There are chisels and things of that kind to be sharpened and ground daily.
Q. That accounts for the blacksmith as I understand it, and for the machinists, does it not? A. That accounts for some three men.

Q. Who are employed in performing this kind of repairs? A. Yes. We have not more than three machinists in the shop.

By the Chairman.

Q. I understand that you are not employing prisoners in the whole of the works? A. No, sir, we are not.

Q. With regard to those whom you do employ, do you exercise the right of selecting them? A. We do; that is as to what is left outside of those employed in the prison buildings. The authorities seem to retain the right of selecting their own men for such purposes.

Q. Then as to the balance, do you exercise the right of selection? A. They are tendered to us for selection.

Q. In case of a man being taken off for illness, or any other cause, under the orders of the prison authorities, from your work, of course you do not account for his time any further? A. No; and they send us a man who is wholly inexperienced in the work, to fill his place.

Q. In the first place you do not account for the time in question? A. We do if he is taken away a short time; and during that time we are compelled to take a man on for one or two or three hours, as the case may be, to fill that man's place, until he is ready to come back again.

Q. That is regularly so? A. Yes.

By Mr. Langmuir.

Q. Now how often does that happen? A. It happens as often as a man is taken off for any ailment.

Q. How often does it occur? How often did it take place yesterday? A. I was not there yesterday.

Q. Well, the day before? A. It does happen as we can show. I make the statement.

By the Chairman.

Q. The practice then, is that if a man is taken off from sickness, or from any other cause, under orders from the authorities of the prison, they send another to fill his place? A. Yes, sir, this is invariably the case.

Q. I suppose that there is a set of rules in this relation which are regularly followed? Mr. Langmuir.—Yes, sir, there is.

The Chairman.—I hope that they will be put before us—the rules they have to obey, contract itself, and the rules of the prison.

Mr. Langmuir—Yes; this shall be done.

Witness—I may also state here that we have one instance where we had a man, and were expecting to employ him in the office; but they made a demand for him, and without any sanction whatever on our part, removed him, and sent us another man in his place.

Mr. Langmuir—There will always be exceptional things occurring in a prison of this kind, and there must be.

Q. What is the name of that man? A. Irish.

Mr. Langmuir—I venture to say that excellent reasons will be given for this having been done.

Witness—I do not know.

By Mr. Hardy.

Q. What was he employed at? A. He was employed out in the yard.

Q. Was he a yard-man—a labourer? A. He happened to be in the gang, and he was used to figure up and run up columns, being a scholar, and the foreman there used him in measuring lumber et cetera; that is the reason why he was a yard-man.

BY THE CHAIRMAN.

Q. What has been your practice in this regard? If you find a man that is not desirable for your purposes, do you get the prison authorities to take him off your hands and send another man in his stead? A. We try in every case to do so; sometimes we accomplish our object, and sometimes we do not.

Q. But it is the understanding that they shall do so, as a rule? A. Well, it was so; this was the case for some considerable time—yes; I am not speaking of any particular time; but for a long time since I have been there, this has been the general run of the management of the place; for a while it was done; but then when a man was taken on, they would not condescend to change him, under any consideration, unless the man in some way was wholly unfitted for the place, owing to disease, or to something of that description, or was an unsound man; I believe that we have some men of that description, or have had them.

Q. Say a man was taken off for sickness, and laid up for a week, or for two days, would they substitute another? A. Yes, sir; this is done if a man is taken off for three hours; if he is taken off in the morning for instance, owing to the fact, that they do not feel disposed to send him to work without the doctor's sanction, one man is sent in his place until the doctor comes, or we send him out and take him back at that time.

BY MR. NOXON.

Q. I might just state that the impression which this evidence has left on my mind is, that for a considerable portion of the time, since the first of January, owing to the want of proper organization, the machinery, or the men could not be worked to advantage: that is, your machinery was not in the proper place to keep up the supply of material, in order that you might be kept running? A. This has not been the case since the addition was made to the premises; we have enlarged our facilities, and we enlarged the inside for turning purposes previously; we gradually enlarged it before the other shops got into full operation, in order to supply the material; we started on with lathes, and the delays that occurred, were due to the inability we experienced with regard to the getting out of enough material to supply these lathes before this new shop was started and brought into successful operation.

BY MR. LANGMUIR.

Q. It was the same with the drying-kiln? A. Yes, sir.
Q. You are aware that as soon as it was brought to our notice as to its want of capacity for drying, we went to work to make a new drying kiln? A. Oh yes, I understand, of course, the kiln was all right, and is to day; there is no trouble in drying in it; but there was great trouble experienced with reference to the supply of material.
Q. It was a great drawback until it was placed there? A. Yes; and would be more serious now as it has been enlarged; but these delays were not caused by the want of material in the yard; they were due to the fact that we did not have sufficient room in the shops to set up extra machinery to prepare the material which was necessary for our purposes.

BY MR. NOXON.

Q. I understand that the organization has been out-grown, and that sufficient room, or sufficient disposition, was not provided to meet requirements as business increased; there was constant change, and this has been undergone almost ever since the removal of the machinery to the new building? A. With reference to the removal, that is one thing; the stave business was moved.
Q. A period extending from the first of last January does not afford a really fair test of the capabilities of the business, owing to the want of machinery, and of the room in which to work it.

MR. WELLS.—Matters are now properly disposed, and provision has been made for some time.

BY MR. HARDY.

Q. This state of things continued until the last of May? A. It existed until some time about that period.

By Mr. Langmuir.

Q. When did you occupy the new building? A. It was somewhere about the 1st of May, but it took some time to get a quantity of material a head, of course.

Mr. Noxon.—The whole scope of the enquiry, as far as the business is concerned, seems simply to bring out the fact as to the profits that might have been made in the business; but it was not thoroughly organized.
Mr. Wells.—It was not the fault of the Company.

By Mr. Wells.

Q. How long did it take after you got into the new shop before you got into settled order? A. When we first started we were delayed some time there.
Q. At all events, you have been working successfully and continuously for some three or four weeks? A. We were somewhat behind in staves, and as a consequence ran out at the new lathes. The supply of staves was not adequate.
Q. But for the last three or four weeks you have been settled? A. Operations during the last three or four weeks would be a fair test.
The Commission adjourned until 2.30 o'clock.

The Commission met at 2.30 o'clock.

Mr. Langmuir.—I beg to fyle the Rules and Regulations. There are many orders which were made after the Rules were printed, in order to meet cases that arose, and I have asked the Warden to prepare all these orders that have a bearing on the industrial departments, and submit them to the Commission.

Charles Greenwald, sworn :—

By Mr. Wells.

Q. What is your occupation in the Central Prison? A. My occupation in the Central Prison is foreman of the Broom Department.
Q. What previous experience in broom-making had you before you entered the service of this Company? A. What is my experience in the broom business? I have never done anything else all my lifetime. Since I left school at the age of fourteen, I have been engaged in this business.
Q. Where were you engaged in it immediately before coming here? A. I was in the employ of E. D. Brunston and Company, at Amsterdam, N. Y. I was in his employ for ten years; and was there just before I came here.
Q. I believe that you make brooms by machinery? A. By steam—yes. This is not wholly the case here, because we employ hand labour as well as steam labour; it is mixed.
Q. How many machines have you? Four? A. We have four for making brooms by hand and two for making them by steam.
Q. You have two steam machines? A. Yes.
Q. And then? A. We have four machines for making brooms by the old way; and the broom sewing is all done in the old fashioned way.
Q. Is it done by hand? A. Yes, sir; the sizing of the corn we do here by steam.
Q. Well, are the machines which you use in the prison of similar description to those that Mr. Brunston uses? A. They are not; that is you mean the hand machines.
Q. No, I mean the steam machine. A. The steam machines are the same of course. They come from Mr. Brunston.
Q. The steam machines are precisely the same as those used in Mr. Brunston's establishment? A. One was made here in the prison, but the iron work was brought from the other side; and one was sent here. They are from that establishment. E. D. Brunston is

the patentee; he is the inventor of this machine. I was sent here to have such work done; and I was engaged to set up his machinery here.
Q. Who own the patent rights for this machine in the Dominion? A. The patent right was bought by Messrs. McMurray and Fuller.
Q. They are as a matter of fact the owners of these machines; One of these machines is the property of the Company; the machine itself was made there? A. I could not say, sir.
Q. Well—what can you tell us of the yield—the daily yield of a machine of this character in Mr. Brunston's establishment? A. Yes, sir, I can, I have the running of one of them myself.

BY MR. LANGMUIR.

Q. Steam has been used for about nine months? A. Yes. We calculate on turning out from three to five hundred a day with a man and a boy.
Q. He works the machine? A. Yes; the man is so employed; he becomes a skilled workman after working at it probably for a month, at the highest for two months; brooms are turned out according to the quality; for the best quality of brooms, a turn out of three hundred is a day's work—that is twenty-five dozen; of the second quality, the making of four hundred is a day's work; and of the common, cheap brooms, five hundred is a day's work. That is the capacity of the machine; a small boy of about thirteen or fourteen years of age feeds the machine at the rear end of it.
Q. As I understand it, this is what you call a Winding Machine? A. Yes.
Q. And that machine is attended by a man and a boy? A. By a man and a boy.
Q. And that machine turns out in Mr. Brunston's establishment three hundred first-class brooms, four hundred second-class brooms, or five hundred of the common brooms? A. Yes.
Q. The other machine is a sorting machine? What will it do? A. A sorting machine is calculated to run through—we have two of them here, one brought from the other side, and the other built in the prison—one thousand pounds of corn in a day.
Q. How many brooms does that represent? A. The make on the average depends on how heavy you make the broom; that quantity would make about five hundred first-class brooms, allowing two pounds to a broom.
Q. And the machine, you say, runs through one thousand pounds of corn a day? A. Of course, we employ a boy to do that over there; but here, of course, we have to employ men. We haven't boys.
Q. Will you tell us what work is actually done in Brunston's establishment in a day? A. Mr. Brunston turns out at present, or did when I left him, from one hundred and fifty to one hundred and seventy-five dozen of brooms in a day.
Q. How many men did he employ? A. As nearly as I can figure it up, he employed altogether about thirty-seven or thirty-eight; may be thirty-nine.
Q. He employed thirty-seven, thirty-eight, or thirty-nine persons? A. Yes; I think that there were in his employ twelve boys, engaged in sizing, boring, sorting, &c.; and then six more boys to feed the machine; that makes eighteen persons. Then there were six men employed in winding brooms—heading on the machine, as it is called here, and twelve men in sewing; one man in bunching and one man for labelling the brooms; that is about all who are employed there, with a superintendent.
Q. How many persons does that make? A. That makes thirty-nine.
Q. Thirty-nine including the superintendent? A. Yes.
Q. Of whom eighteen are boys? A. Yes.
Q. What do you call a boy? What are boys' ages? A. Boys' ages vary from thirteen to fourteen, fifteen, and sixteen, and run up to seventeen.
Q. Eighteen boys and twenty-one men, including the superintendent, turn out from one hundred and fifty to one hundred and sixty dozen of brooms completed per day? A. No. If these men did first-class work they would turn out twenty-five dozen by working on piece work. There is not a man employed but who works by the piece. They are making twenty five dozen—three hundred. Workmen on these machines will turn out 150 first-class brooms, and if of second class, they will probably turn out 175; and if of common brooms, so much more.
Q. How much more? A. He would probably run two hundred.

BY MR. WELLS.

Q. Two hundred dozen brooms a day? A. Yes. The product will run from three to four and five hundred. It depends on the quality of the brooms.

Q. From three to four and five hundred, or from 150 to 175 dozen; how many men have you employed in your department? A. I have twenty-six men.

Q. Twenty-six? A. Yes, sir. The number, including myself, is twenty-seven.

Q. What is your daily yield? A. My daily yield has been, I guess, from thirty to thirty-five dozen brooms; during the last two weeks the average has been forty dozen a day. We are compelled to keep an account of the turn out, and give a weekly return to that effect. I guess that would be the average for the last two weeks.

Q. Now, you are able to come up to forty dozen a day with twenty-six men? A. Yes. I did yesterday the best day's work that has been done since I have been there. We turned out forty-five dozen, I think.

Q. To what do you ascribe the difference in the yield between the employment of prison labour and of free labour? A. The difference is this: I will suppose, in the first place, that the men in the establishment where I come from are sewing brooms—by the piece. They get for common brooms seventy-five cents a hundred; for the others, $1; and for the next size, $1 25. Now, you see that the men there are averaging in wages from $1 50 to $1 75 per day; and you can judge how many brooms a man has got to sew in order to make wages. A man has got to sew, on the average, about 125 brooms; and of the common brooms they should sew 160; I did the first year I started in there.

Q. I would like to know rather, what you are doing now? In the first place, I assume that your department is in good working order—as well as you can put it? A. Yes.

Q. There is still a discrepancy. Your last work has been forty-five dozen a day, and forty dozen a day has been heretofore the maximum? A. Forty dozen was the average for the last two weeks.

Q. I want you to tell me as well as you can, to what do you ascribe the difference between the working of forty dozen brooms a day with twenty-seven men, and the number you have given in as having been turned out at Amsterdam, N. Y., by thirty-nine men? A. I do not believe that as much work can be got out of prison labour as out of free labour.

Q. You do not think that as much work can be got out of prisoners as out of free labour? A. I do not. In the first place, as I have been there since the 19th of March—I think that when I first came here it was on the 19th of March—I put up the steam machinery, stayed a week—returned—stayed three weeks and came back, and I have been here ever since. In the first place, to attempt to compel a man to do a certain amount of day's work, is to endeavour to obtain an impossibility, in my estimation; and to coax a man to do a certain amount of work is about the same thing. It might work with one man but not with another.

Q. You speak of prisoners? A. Yes, I speak of prisoners. For instance, I have got a man in my department who will sew sixty brooms of one kind in a day. We make three different styles, sixty will be his day's work of the best, and eighty of others; but we also make common brooms. The consequence was that when I wanted sixty from the man that sewed sixty of the best kind, the man who stood beside him would not sew more of the common than this man would sew of the best brooms. They all hobbied on the sixty, and the consequence was that I explained the difficulty to them, the difference between the brooms and everything else; and now they have started this week, sixty, eighty and a hundred brooms a day without any difficulty. That is the sewing part.

Q. Is there any other causes of difference besides what you have mentioned? A. That is where they are behind a good ways on free labour. Now, as to the winding machines and winding by hand. I have wound brooms by hand for Mr Brunston for 8½ cents each; but when steam machines were provided, we used to get for the best brooms that we made there one and half cents.

Q. I want you to tell me to what you ascribe the difference between the results? A. The short way of telling the story, in my candid opinion is, to put it this way: No live man taking charge of a gang of prisoners, can get as much work out of them as he can out of free labour. If any one can do so, he can do more than I can.

Q. You consider that the work which you are now getting out and which you have been doing for the past two or three weeks, of which you have spoken, is a fair test of what you can get out of these prisoners? A. I do not think that I could get more work out of them if I was to be hanged for it, than what I get out of them now. I have tried to run the product up to fifty dozen per day, but I doubt very much whether, with the present gang of men, I can accomplish it ; I may, however, do it in a week or so.

Q. Are the men changed? A. Yes. I think that we lost two men this morning.

Q. How will that affect you? A. I will tell you. In the first place, when I first came there with the steam machinery, a man who was working from the time I came there, was turning out twenty dozen brooms a day and doing good work ; and may be there was another man I had with me, who was also a good workman ; they were the only two in the whole gang who shewed any energy for work. He runs twenty dozen to-day and then he is taken sick. The Warden, I suppose, has seen him. He is unwell and as a consequence he is taken off. I had then to go to work and put on a new man. I have a man now in his place who makes ten dozen brooms a day ; and the consequence is that it will take probably three months—and he will probably enough fail to do so—before he can be as expert as the man lost.

Q. So you know it to be a fact, that you lose capable men and have green hands put on in their stead? A. And this very man who was put on this machine to take the place of this other one is reported sick and was kept in to-day; and so I have lost him.

Q. What do you consider will be the effect of taking off two experienced men and putting on two new and green hands in their places? A. The effect will be that it will make a difference of some ten or twelve dozen a day in the turn out of my work.

Q. Your average is also decreased? A. Certainly.

Q. For how long do you think that this would be the case? A. That all depends on how the man who is so put on, picks up skill. It may take a man a month to do so and it may take two months. I have lost a man, a winder on the steam machine, and another man who is a broom sewer ; and I calculate that it will take at least a month to break a man into sewing his sixty brooms a day.

BY MR. HARDY.

Q. I do not know that I have got exactly your statement of what men would do under free labour and what otherwise, but I understand that you had machine work over there? A. Yes.

Q. While up here the work is partly done by steam partly by hand? A. Yes.

Q. You have but two machines here? A. Yes. We have two steam machines for winding ; and we do all the sorting and sizing here by steam.

Q. It is then a composite affair—a mixture? A. At present, yes.

Q. There is no way then of fully comparing results with the establishment over there? A. Not exactly. If it was all run by hand or all by steam I could compare them better.

Q. And I understand that the steam machinery has been only in operation since the first of March? A. Yes. Mr. Brunston has run them however since a year ago last Fall.

Q. But here they have only been up since the first of March, and your men have had to get skilled with them since that time? A. Yes.

Q. You just give it as your general conviction that you cannot get as much work out of prison labour as you can out of free labour? A. No, sir—that cannot be done.

Q. How much difference is there? Can you get two-thirds as much out of prison labour? A. On the average you cannot get more than one-half.

Q. You can not get more than one-half as much? A. Not more.

Q. Prisoners will not average more than one-half as much work as free labourers? A. No.

Q. Where it is wholly hand labour, were the men new men? A. Some were new and some were men who had worked in the broom department.

Q. What wages would such men get where they are working with free labour—here or elsewhere? A. The wages that Mr. Brunston paid over there were as follows: the small boy engaged in feeding the machine received fifty cents a day. He, of course, does as much in a day as two men here.

Q. What about the others? A. The man that is engaged in winding gets sixty cents a hundred, and that gives him about $1.80 a day.

Q. Is there nobody else? Is there any other class? A. Then there is another class employed in sizing and sorting. They average probably—it is all done by piece-work—from 75 cents to $1.00 per day. They are paid ten cents a hundred for sizing corn.

Q. Is there any other class? A. There are the broom sewers; they get from three-quarters of a cent to one cent, and one and one-quarter cents a broom; and they average in wages from $1.50 to $1.75 a day; it runs up according to their worth.

Q. And then if you can only get one-half as much work out of prisoners,—take a man who is earning from $1.50 to $1.75 a day, and the prisoner who does half as much work is worth 75cts. a day, or six York shillings? A. That is something which you cannot do. It is a man that does the feeding of the machine up here.

Q. But I understand you to say that you got about half as much work out of prison as out of free labour? A. Let me explain. The boy that feeds the machine over there gets 50cts. a day, and he will do as much again of work as you have to pay fifty cents for here; and I have eighteen of such men in my department. As a consequence, if I had to pay this man, I would not pay him more than twenty-five cents a day in comparison with the boy in question.

Q. You mean to say that all round you only get half as much work out of the prisoners here as out of the boys and the men there? A. Out of a certain class, I do; I could hire men to do that class of work for less money than Mr. Brunston could.

Q. Have you hired any broom-makers in Canada? A. I could very soon make a broom-maker.

Q. How long does it take to learn the business of making brooms? A. I estimate that a good, smart, active man will learn to do as good work in three months as is anywhere to be got; and then you have him for a lifetime.

Q. Then you can learn the business in three months to a raw hand, and a prisoner is sometimes a man who is an old hand. That is about as good as learning prisoners; it is an advantage? A. I can learn prisoners broom-making, if they are willing to learn; but by the time that you get a man learned, he will report himself sick, and then you have to take another one.

Q. Have you much sickness in your family there? A. We had a case twice in succession inside of two months, on this machine.

Q. I only saw one man in the hospital yesterday? A. I had half a dozen men reported sick this morning.

Q. In your department? A. In my department alone.

Q. What did the doctor say? A. Some were sent back, and two were kept in. I had a man by the name of Allen reported sick yesterday morning.

Q. What did you say to that? A. He was sent back to go to work; but that man, as true as I sit here, is no more able to do his work than anybody.

Q. He was a sick man? A. He was a sick man. The consequence was, that he came to me and said, "Mr. Greenwald, I am not able to pull a needle through that end." You could judge from his appearance that he was not; he was as white as a sheet; accordingly I sent him back again, and the consequence was, that he was kept in the second time.

Q. The doctor examined him? A. I suppose he did.

Q. I suppose that prisoners will often put up a job on you as to sickness, if they get the chance? A. I suppose that they do.

BY MR. LANGMUIR.

Q. There you had thirty-eight men, and here you have twenty-six. They get only about one-quarter of the wages and they should do about one-quarter of the work? A. Forty-five dozen was the bast they did.

BY MR. WELLS.

Q. What do you consider to be the value of a raw hand when you take him on? A. What do I consider the value of him to be when I put him on? In the first place, whatever work he does in the first week is very poor, and insufficient; and another thing, when a raw man comes in, it breaks upon, and spoils my set.

Q. What do you consider his value? A. The consequence is, that the other men who depend on his work, have to wait until he gets his hand in.

Q. What do you consider that such a man is worth per day? A. My valuation of him is not a great deal.
Q. How much is it? A. It is not a great deal.
Q. How much would you say? A. I have men in my employ, handling broom corn, whom I do not consider worth fifteen cents a day; I would not give it to them if I had to pay it.
Q. How many machines does Mr. Brunston work? A. He works six machines; that is the number he was running when I left him.
Q. How many men have you employed on hand machines? A. Four.
Q. Here? A. They are engaged in winding.
Q. That is done on what you call hand-machines? A. This is done with hand-machines.
Q. All the rest of the work, however, is done by steam, is it not? A. All the rest of the work is done in the same manner as in Mr. Brunston's establishment, except the sewing part; the sewing is not done here the same as there.
Q. Are the brooms of the same description? A. Yes.
Q. The only difference is, in the four men you work here on hand-machines; do you separate the corn with hand-machines? A. We do all that in the bulk; it is separated in the same manner all the way through.
Q. The corn is separated by your steam machines? A. It is being done by steam machines.
Q. So that in point of fact, you have only four men that are engaged on hand work; all the rest are employed in the same way, as is the case in Mr. Brunston's establishment? A. Yes.
Q. So we have got to come as near that now as we can; that is the only difference which exists; of what kind of brooms is the daily average of forty dozen composed? A. This is a mixed class, but the major portion consists of common brooms.
Q. What is the majority, do you suppose? A. Twenty-five dozen third-class brooms are returned; and the balance was composed of brooms, Nos. 1 and 2.

BY MR. HARDY.

Q. You say you have some men in your employ for whom you would not pay fifteen cents a day; how many have you that are worth $1.50 a day? A. How many worth $1.50?
Q. Yes? A. I have not got one in the establishment at the present time that is worth so much.
Q. How many have you that are worth $1.25 a day? A. I have not one man worth that.
Q. How many have you worth a dollar a day? A. I haven't one man of that description.
Q. That is rather a broad statement; how many men have you had under your control who were worth $1.00 a day? A. I have had but one man who made twenty dozen brooms a day, and he is sick.
Q. How many men have you had there worth 87½ cents a day? A. The highest that I have got there, is one who sews sixty brooms a day, work worth 1¼ cents for each broom; I guess that is the highest.
Q. How many men have you got that will do that? A. I have five; and I have eight men sewing brooms altogether.
Q. Will they all do that much work? A. They will average that quantity.

BY MR. LANGMUIR.

Q. How many had you in Amsterdam that did so? A. The men averaged there from $1.25 to $1.50 a day.

BY MR. HARDY.

Q. What is your next best lot? A. Well, as to the next best lot, I do not know that; there is no best lot among the rest.
Q. There are several men there worth five York shillings a day? A. I would not like to pay it to them.

Q. There are the feeders and the binders? A. What is a feeder on a machine worth, making ten dozen brooms a day, at the rate of a man who makes five hundred a day.
Q. How many should a man wind by hand per day? A. A man should wind by hand nothing less than 125.
Q. How many do they wind per day, do you know? A. I have one man there that winds about three dozen a day; and that is the highest number to which I can fetch him.
Q. How many have you that wind fifty brooms per day? A. I have two men winding fifty; one winding forty, and another who winds about three dozen a day.
Q. What is the winding of each broom worth? A. Some brooms are worth three-quarters of a cent, some one cent, and some one cent and a quarter for winding.

By Mr. LANGMUIR.

Q. Has the quantity of brooms turned out in the sewing department of your shop increased lately? Has the number increased? A. We have had an average of forty dozen a day turned out during the last few weeks, and that is the highest quantity yet done.
Q. I mean the prisoners who sew brooms; have they increased the number per day and per man? A. They have run up as I have told you, to sixty brooms a day.
Q. Was it that three weeks ago? A. It was forty and fifty a day.
Q. Then it has increased? A. Now they are doing sixty brooms a day.
Q. The number turned out has increased then? A. Certainly, it has increased some.
Q. Why? Do you know the reason for it? Did you complain that the number turned out by the men was insufficient? A. That is what I did.
Q. And this is the result? And, when yesterday you told the Warden that there should be a change, what did he say? He asked you how many should each man make, and how many did you say? A. I stated sixty of one kind and eighty of another kind.
Q. When you told the Warden that they should sew sixty brooms a day—did they sew that number afterwards? A. After he left his orders, they did it on the first day.
Q. You placed the amount for a fair day's work? A. I thought that it was the best we could do under the circumstances.
Q. And have they done it since? A. Yes.
Q When they have done that, you say that they have done a fair day's work? A. Excuse me, you are figuring the sewing part, the best part of the establishment.
Q. Have you been in any of the broom shops in this town? A. I have not, sir.
Q. Do you know what sewing is in Canada, apart from Amsterdam? A. I do not know what it is here.
Q. Do you know that sewing one hundred brooms a day is considered good work here? A. It may be so.
Q. People are lazier here than in Amsterdam? A. I should judge so then.
Q. Should you be surprised to learn that sewing one hundred brooms a day is capital work here? Do you sew over there over hours? A. We do not.
Q. What hours have you? A. We have ten hours.
Q. Nothing else? A. Nothing else.
Q. You closed the works at the end of the ten hours? A. We worked only ten hours in the establishment where I was.
Q. Did you not take work home? A. No man took work home.
Q. You did ten hours actual work? We worked from seven to twelve, and from one to six, that is the way we worked.

By Mr. HARDY.

Q. Have you asked the Warden to increase the amount to 75? A. I have not. I do not think that I have.
Q. Sixty is the number you placed it at any anyway? A. That is of the best kind.
Q. Of the best kind? A. Yes.
Q. As to the other kind, how many should they do? A. They should turn them out in proportion to the number given for the best kind; of the second grade, they should send eighty a day; and of the common kind, a hundred a day. They have done it for me this week.

Q. Numbers 60, 80, and 100, are what you thought, under the circumstances, should be done ? A. The number of the common kind mentioned is about equal in work to sixty good ones; a good broom has three bands, while a common one has only two. They are light, and it is easier to sew one hundred common ones than sixty big ones.

Q. Under the circumstances you say that is what the prisoners should do, and what you have asked in the mean time ? A. It is in the meantime ; but I should not judge that it is the best they should do. The men under my charge—that is the majority of them,—weigh from one hundred and ninety to two hundred pounds ; they are fat, and they must surely receive pretty good and healthy food. They are in good condition, and they should do good work.

Q. Do you consider it desirable that the number to be turned out should be increased ? A. I think that it should be increased.

Q. Have you asked the Warden to increase it ? A. I have not.

BY MR. WELLS.

Q. The men under your charge have considerable experience in this work ? A. Yes; all of them have.

Q. How much will a green hand do ? A. As to breaking him in, it will take about a month to make a broom-sewer of him. During the first month he will probably make a dozen a day, and during the second month probably one-and-a-half dozen a day.

Q. So that when you tell us that they can do 60, 80, and 100 a day, you are telling us what men who have been broken in, and who are placed under the best circumstances, can do ; without taking into consideration the putting on of green hands and the breaking-up of your set ? A. No, sir. I have men there sorting over broom-corn by hand, but it is impossible to get them to perform a certain amount of work without standing right over them ; this is all done outside at so much per pound ; I have four men doing that kind of work up here, and these four men are paid for at the rate of fifty cents each, making in all $2, and they sort 120 pounds of hard, or fine corn, for the outside; from $2\frac{3}{4}$ to 3 pounds of it are allowed to the dozen. Mr. Brunston pays 75 cents per hundred pounds to have this done ; and these men, for whose services $2.00 are paid, are doing about the same amount of work for which over there seventy-five cents are paid.

Q. What he gets done for seventy-five cents costs us $2.00 ? A. Yes; I can explain it to any man that comes to see it. You must not figure on the best, but put one with another, and classify them.

Q. What is the proportion ? Can you give us an idea of what should form the average? A. I guess I have ten men altogether of that description.

Q. Of what description ? Of the poor trash ? A. Yes.

Q. These are fifteen cent men ? A. They are not worth much more than that ; if I had to pay it I would look at the money before I gave it to them.

Q. What do the sixteen men who are left average from one week to another, or from one month to another ? A. It would depend on circumstances ; if I had time to think over it I could tell you more about it.

Q. What would you judge it to be ? You are liable to lose your best men to-morrow, and to have new men put on in their places. What would you say that it was ? What would you be willing to give if going into business outside or inside for that labour ? A. I would not give you a cent for it, for I do not believe in it. I can take broom machinery outside and compete with that labour; and if that labour was paid for at the rate of 25 cents per man, I could run you out of the market. No man knows anything about prison labour until he gets among prisoners so employed. If the company had to hire me again at Amsterdam to come over here, they would have a great deal of trouble in securing me. I will tell you that much, it is a pretty hard situation to be trying to please somebody and to please nobody.

Q. You think, Mr. Greenwald, that if you took machines outside and ran them with free labour, you could compete with prison labour paid at the rate of twenty-five cents per man ? A. Yes, I will.

BY MR. LANGMUIR.

Q. You know Mr. Brunston's business pretty well ? A. I should think so.

Q. What do you think his running expenses apart from wages—in the way of light, water, fuel, taxes, and insurance—amount to? What would you put them at? A. I do not know anything about such things.
Q. What do you think that his taxes would be? A. I have no idea.
Q. Have you any idea of the cost of light and water? A. I could not tell you that, sir; I know nothing about it.
Q. Have you any idea of what his property cost? Of the cost of the shops when you were there? A. I do not; I could not tell you that; Mr. Brunston has got a pretty nice establishment there.
Q. Of course Mr. Brunston's establishment cost something? A. Yes, sir.
Q. And you have no idea what keeping it up—apart from wages, would cost? A. I could not tell you what that costs.
Q. Would it be $3,000 a year, with the interest on the money and capital invested; real estate, and taxes, and insurance, and putting up houses, and all such as that—do you think? Would it amount to one-half of the wages? A. He has an engineer whom he hires.
Q. He has steam power. A. Yes.
Q. Would the cost be $3,000 a year. A. No, I do not think that it would take much: forty pounds of steam runs this whole establishment—forty or fifty pounds is sufficient for the purpose; I could not estimate the value of that.

By Mr. Wells.

Q. As I understand your estimate, you are willing to take machinery and go outside and give this prison labour all the advantages they have from the use of steam power and everything else, and then keep them out of the market, though this labour were obtained at the rate of 25 cents per day? A. Yes; I will hire my own hands; just give me a show at it; prison labour stands no comparison with free labour, in any way or shape.

By Mr. Hardy.

Q. This is your first experience of prison labour? A. I guess it is.
Q. And evidently you are not very well situated where you are:—have you all the material you want on hand? A. Yes; we are always supplied with everything.
Q. You never had to lie idle at all? A. We have never lain idle since I have been there.
Q. Have none of the hands been idle? A. None of the hands are idle because I keep my hands in work; we once ran short since I have been there—on the machines, but I put the men to work at something else; since they have been under my charge, they have been employed every day, and right through.

By Mr. Wells.

Q. A good deal of your time is occupied in working on machines and in teaching the men, is it not? A. I think so myself.

By Mr. Hardy.

Q. Do you find plenty of sale for brooms? A. They seem to sell them, and about as fast as we make them.

By Mr. Wells.

Q. Do you know whether any of the old hand-made brooms have been returned? A. Yes; ninety-seven dozen came back the other day.
Q. What was the matter with them? A. They were loose on the handle, and broken.
Q. They were utterly useless as brooms, were they not? A. They were worth nothing under the present circumstances. You could not sell them. No one would buy a broom without a handle.
Q. What was the reason for this? Were the men who made them inexperienced men

—new men ? A. The man who had charge of the department before, I suppose, started with green men, and, probably, did not pay right attention to them.

Q. Ninety-seven dozen were returned at once ? A. They were returned from time to time.

Q. Have you made returns to the Secretary ? Have you made any for what you have done from week to week ? A. Yes, I have made returns every week.

Q. Have you kept copies of these returns yourself ? A. I have one here in my pocket.

Q. What is this ? A. That will show you the weekly statement of all brooms made; also I guess, every day's work up to a recent date.

Q. When was your last return made ? A. On the 20th instant. I guess that you will find it there.

Q. We will take the return for the week ending June the 6th ; what did you do during that week ? A. You mean the whole week's work ?

Q. Yes. A. We made that week $219\frac{1}{2}$ dozen.

Q. What number is that ? A. The number of brooms we made that week was $219\frac{1}{2}$.

Q. Were they brooms and whisks ? A. Yes. Brooms and whisks.

Q. How many men had you at work that week ? A. Twenty-nine.

Q. Including yourself ? A. No, sir.

Q. I have twenty-six here ? A. The number is twenty-six at present. You asked me concerning the week ending June the 6th.

Q. Ending June the 9th, I have it here ? A. I have had two men who went out after that date. I have only twenty-six men in that department at present.

By the Chairman.

Q. You gave a partial statement of the amount of work done by each man in Mr. Brunston's establishment, but I do not think that the statement was as definite as we would like to have it. Will you then just carefully consider and give us what is considered a day's work in each department in his establishment ; and tell us what is the amount paid for that work. Just commence with the first department of the work utilized in the making of the broom ? A. Will I make it jointly or separately ?

Q. Give each one separate. What is the process followed in making the brooms ? A. The first process is taking the broom corn and passing it through one of the sorting machines. A bale of corn is rolled to the side of the machine, and a boy takes it up and feeds, spear by spear, through the sorting machine. This is done in the shop of Mr. Brunston at the rate of ten cents per hundred pounds. A boy on that scale would, of course, according to the manner in which he worked, earn from fifty to seventy-five cents a day, and some boys thus earn a dollar a day. A thousand pounds of corn can be fed in a day through this machine, and the feeder is paid according to the work he performs, you see.

Q. He is paid by the piece ? A. Yes, by the piece. I have two men up here—one on each machine that are being paid for at the rate of fifty cents a day, and they run through these machines about three hundred pounds of corn a piece a day ; on some days they run through four hundred pounds.

By Mr. Wells.

Q. These feeders are paid ten cents per. hundred pounds ? A. That is what they are paid.

Q. Then these men would earn from thirty to forty cents a day ? A. Yes, I have two of them.

By the Chairman.

Q. I want to know what is done there ? A. The next process that is gone through after is the sorting ; when they are taken out of the machines there is the separation of the good corn from the bad. The machine sorts them according to length—some are short and some are long, et cetera.

Q. That is done by machinery ? A. That is done by a machine. Then a man takes it rom the machine and sorts it over, separating the good from the poor.

Q. Is it a man who attends to the sorting machine ? A. Yes, up here.
Q. What is his day's work ? A. That is generally paid for over at Brunston's by the hundred. Payment is made according to the length of the corn ; for the long corn, twelve cents per hundred pounds is paid ; for the medium corn about sixteen cents per hundred pounds; and the very shortest costs, I think, twenty cents per hundred pounds for sorting. It is according to length that payment is made. That is the way this is done there ; but I have a man here to do the sorting. Of course he is a prisoner ; one man sorts after each machine, but one can get more work out of a boy over there, than out of a man here, in this respect. A boy would probably earn seventy-five cents a day and he would do the sorting of these two men.
Q. What is considered a day's work in sorting ? A. Well, it runs from three to four hundred pounds and five hundred pounds according to expertness, and the length of the corn. I have seen long corn sorted at the rate of twelve hundred pounds. You can handle long corn so much faster than the other, and it has greater weight. One good, smart boy will do the sorting after two machines.
Q. Well, is the sorting not done by machinery ? A. No, sir, it is not.
Q. It is done by hand ? A. Yes, sir.
Q. This relates to the selection of the corn ? A. And the sizing ; as to length, this is done by steam. The sorting concerns the selection of quality.
Q. Now then, what is the next process ? A. The next process is the cutting of the hurl —the fine covering that is put over the outside of the broom. That is what we call hurl. This is done up here. We have machinery that cuts it by steam. It cuts the stalk off and separates it ; the short is carried underneath into a small box and the fine hurl is carried into another box on top. The machine cuts it off and separates it.
Q. Is that operation done in the same way over there ? A. Yes, in the same way as here.
Q. One man attends to that machine ? A. One man does up here, yes.
Q. What is his day's work on the other side ? A. That machine is calculated to run through five hundred pounds a day.
Q. And what wages are received ? A. About seventy five cents a day.
Q. So much is paid per pound ? A. Payment is made by piece-work, and it amounts to about that much per day.

BY MR. HARDY.

Q. A boy does that work ? A. A boy of about fourteen or fifteen. He will do more than a man, and make quicker work. He will handle more stalks in the same space of time, outside or in any other place.

BY THE CHAIRMAN.

Q. What is the next stage ? A. In the next process, this broom corn is picked over, and the centre stalks are taken out. Some of it is composed of heavy eared spears, and other parts are clear of them. Over there we pay thirty cents per hundred pounds for ing out the centre stalks ; and up here I have got three men to do that work. They are doing from 120 to 130 pounds a day, and that is the quantity which we use. They are the men who are worth about fifteen cents a day, as I have mentioned.
Q. This is done by hand labour ? A. Yes. There is no machine labour about that operation. It cannot be done by a machine, I suppose.
Q. What is the next process ? A. In the next process, the corn is dampened and put in a bleaching house with brimstone over night ; and the next morning it is put on the machines, each part separately, as it has been sorted in the way we work it ; we put on the handle and wind the corn on the broom.
Q. This is done by machinery ? A. It is done up here partly by machinery and partly by hand.
Q. We will take the machine work first ? As to the machine, what attendance does it require ? A. That machine requires this attendance: at one end of it there are two small stands, and two sizes of corn lay on one side of it, and two sizes on the other side. A man stands up here and over there a boy—who feeds the machine according to the requirements

of the man. The experienced man—the most experienced of the lot—stands on the front of the machine, and winds on the broom handle.

Q. There are two men attending one machine? A. Yes. We call it a winding machine.

Q. How much will they do over there per day? A. I have had done there from three to four and five hundred, according to the quality of the brooms. For the best brooms, three hundred is considered a day's work, though they could do more; and more has been done; but that is what is considered a day's work in brooms of that description. It depends altogether on the quality and weight of the broom. You can wind a small broom a great deal faster than a heavy broom, weighing from two to two and a quarter pounds, an increase in the number from three to five hundred makes quite a difference.

Q. Well then, what do they receive for that work over there? A. A boy gets fifty cents and the man on the front gets sixty cents a hundred for the best.

Q. Fifty cents a hundred is paid? A. Fifty cents a day is paid for feeding the machinery; and the man, when he is working the best kind, averages sixty cents per hundred. That gives him $1.80 a day when he makes 300; and for the four hundred kind, he gets from 40 to 45 cents per hundred brooms, which amounts to the same thing; and for the five hundred kind, we used to get 40 cents per hundred.

BY MR. HARDY.

Q. That gives a wage of $2.00 a day? A. Yes. It is made the fastest because it is the common broom and light. We average that for a day's work.

BY THE CHAIRMAN.

Q. Does that finish the broom? A. It finishes that process. It is then handed over to the sewing department. It is sewed by hand, being placed in a vice, and over a winding machine; it is then dressed into shape. We have two kinds of vices: one of them is used principally in Canada. The broom is sewed the handle up and the brush part down. Every time he sews a band across, he has got to raise the broom high enough for the other one. An improved vice is used at Brunston's, and two of them were brought up here. I advised them to get them for small brooms. With Brunston's kind, the broom is sewed with the brush end up and the handle down. It is easier done this way. That vice is worked with a lever, while the old-fashioned one is worked with a screw and crank; the other is manipulated with a lever which opens and shuts.

Q. Does one man do all that work? A. Yes, one man does it.

Q. What is his day's work? A. Over there, on the average it was from 125 to 150 up to 200, according to the quality of the brooms.

Q. It varied according to the quality of the brooms. A. Yes.

THE CHAIRMAN.—This makes it very indefinite. They pay from 75 cents to $1.25, according to the quality and the size, and this work is all done by the piece. This is the reason why I spoke as I did. There is nothing paid for by the day in the whole establishment, excepting the labour of six boys who feed the machines. The rest of the employees are paid by the piece, and all the rest of the work is done by the piece.

BY MR. WELLS.

Q. So that the proprietors are sure to get the value of what they pay out? A. Yes, sir.

BY THE CHAIRMAN.

Q. Your branch of the business has nothing to do with the preparation of the handles? A. No, sir, it has not.

Q. The handles have to be stained? A. The handles are all prepared and put into my hands; I have nothing to do with the preparation of the handles in any way or shape.

BY MR. HARDY.

Q. The brooms you make up here are not precisely like those which you manufactured over there? A. Some are not and some are about the same.

Q. You have a new patent of your own? A. I brought it over with me; it relates to the style and finish of the broom.
Q. The others over there are not made like these? A. The brooms made here have not the same finish as mine; the finish on my broom is different.
Q. Yours is the best? A. I claim it to be so.
Q. And your way of finishing the broom is the best? A. Yes.
Q. And it is more expensive? A. No; I think that as far as that matter is concerned one is about the same as the other. I claim for my broom the most solidity on the handle. In winding brooms by steam we claim that we wind a tighter article; there is the same strain of the wire on the machine, and the broom is wound more firmly. To wind tightly by hand, it is necessary to use a treadle with the aid of the foot and elbow, and the consequence is that they do not wind so tightly as is the case with the other method. As to working with the hand machine, I think there is but one process done differently to that over there; winding is done by hand up here; I have four doing it.
Q. All the rest is done by steam? A. Yes.
Q. As to winding by hand, can you tell me what was a day's work over there before they got to using steam machinery for the purpose. When you say winding by machinery, it is machinery that is used to which you refer, and not to steam machines? A. Oh, yes, they are worked either by foot power or by hand power.
Q. What was the day's work over there when these were used? A. The number turned out depended on the quality of the broom; of the best I turned out 125 a day, and of the next size probably 150, and so on up to 200 per day.
Q. What was the ordinary price that you received for a day's work? A. For the best we received one and one-half cents; for the next, one and one-quarter cents; and for the others, one cent. That is now about one and three-quarter years ago.
Q. What is the difference in value between this labour which is supplied to you and the ordinary free labour? Do you attribute it to a want of aptitude in these men to do that particular work? A. That is about the main point in my opinion.
Q. It is due to the unwillingness of the men to do the work? A. Of course, a man who is put in as a prisoner naturally does not feel like doing anything.

BY MR. HARDY.

Q. Unwillingness is the cause of it? A. That is about the amount of it. I do not suppose that there is a man in my department—with the exception of two—who would do anything were there not force behind them.

BY THE CHAIRMAN.

Q. There are many portions of the work in which the manipulation by man has very little to do with the manufacture; the machine does the work, and the man simply requires to attend to it and keep it supplied until it has done its part of the work. There are other parts again which require quick manipulation—such as sorting and the taking out of the centre piece, which need quickness and a ready eye? A We start on the sorting machine first. This is very light work, and the faster a man feeds the corn, and handles it spear by spear, the more work he will do. It has to be fed in singly, and the more that is fed the more will a machine carry away. A man may be slow, and one man may only feed one spear to another's ten; but the same process is gone through on all steam machines all the way through my department. The boy who is feeding the machine is calculated to keep the man on the front of it busy; both have got to work together, and if there is a smart active man on the front he will turn out a good deal of work. Of course, he has to handle all this corn by handfulls. It goes to him separately by handfulls, and he puts it in the broom. When you put on the treadle and start the machine it is very nice work, and very light work for anybody that feels like it.
Q. Do you keep accounts of your department? A. I have to. I am compelled to put put in a weekly statement of all the work done.
Q. To what extent do you give details of all that is done? In what shape do you give it?. Do you merely mention the number of brooms turned out? A. No, sir. I have got to give the quantity of each separate kind.

Q. Of each kind of broom ? A. Yes, sir.

Q. Does each of these departments correspond in the amount of work which they do ? For instance, if you turn out one hundred dozen of brooms a day finished, does that prove that the whole hundred dozen were prepared that day ? A. The whole process in this regard is nearly, but not quite, all performed the same day. The work is taken in at one end of the building and it comes out finished at the other end of it.

BY MR HARDY.

Q. Some men may not do their part ? A. The work is passed from one to another, and by the time that evening comes, it is about finished if the foreman does his duty.

BY THE CHAIRMAN.

Q. I want to get at the amount of labour performed by each man here in each branch of the manufacture. I desire to ascertain whether the fact of their turning out one hundred dozen brooms a day, proves that the men prepared one hundred dozen—or whether one hundred and twenty dozen were prepared, and one hundred and twenty dozen finished, and that the men did a certain amount of labour ? A. Each man is required to do certain work. It takes so many sorting machines to supply so many winding machines. For the steam machinery up here I would allot so many sorting machines, to so many winding machines, and so many sewing machines, and all would run like clock-work. One would have to do so much work to supply another, et cetera.

Q. I wish to know whether the different departments correspond in the amount of work which they will do ? Is each calculated to work with the other, and produce just what is required for the next department ? A. That is about the way we are working at at present. For the last few weeks we have done it. One department supplies another. I have equalized as well as I could, I have done so to the best of my knowledge. I am trying to do the best I know how in this direction.

BY MR. WELLS.

Q. Have you tried the system of rewards there ? A. No. I have not.

BY MR. BROCKWAY.

Q. I have memoranda precisely as to how many hands it takes to work the two winding machines. You say you have ; but what is a set of hands ? A. A set of hands consists, in the first place, of the sizer, then of the sorter and cutter, the feeder makes the fourth, and the binder, the fifth, the sewer is the sixth and the buncher is the seventh.

Q. That is all ? A. These are the different grades of labour required in making a broom, from the commencement of it to the finish.

Q. Then seven men are a set of hands. You stated in your testimony a little while ago, that one of the reasons why prison labour was worth less than free labour consisted of two facts, viz :—the men are discharged constantly, so that you have to put green men into their places, and men are taken out when sick as well as for disciplinary purposes, et cetera. Now, I want to ask you whether you have not a list of the men who are to be discharged during the next month, given you ? A. I have not, sir. I have ascertained this fact to the best of my ability among my own men, for my own curiosity's sake, and to find out how long the men will stay with me, and to place them to suit myself. That is all the statement I have ever got, or that has ever been furnished me in this respect.

Q You could have such a list by asking for it, I suppose ? A. I suppose I could.

MR. LANGMUIR.—And such a statement is given to the Company.

MR. BROCKWAY—That answers the question. Did it never occur to you, and have you had this practice in the management of your department—to select a long-date man, and learn him all these various processes, and have an extra man, instead of seven having eight men, so that when one is called away, you would have another to put in his place ? A. I will answer this question in this way : when I first went there, and came to introduce steam machinery,

I took a long-term man to be the main man of the set, and do the winding part; he had some fifteen or sixteen months to serve, and after he was broken in, the rest got along very easily, and made their twenty dozen a day; but then this man became sick, and I had to put another, a green man, on. I had only one machine, and I could not break two men in; only one person could learn at a time. When I saw this state of things, and acting on my own responsibility, I put on one feeder behind, and a broom winder; and in the same way, I put one on in front, and I calculated that if I got these two broken in and one fell sick, I could take the feeding man from behind, and let him take the sick man's place.

Q. You have not done that thoroughly? A. No; in fact, I have not been there long enough. When you take a main man off a set, it spoils the set.

BY MR. WELLS.

Q. I suppose you have no difficulty in finding out from prisoners when their terms expire? A. When they feel like telling me, they will do so; sometimes they will not; some will say that they have been sent down for a year and a half, when their time is only three months; and some will say, that their sentence is for three months, when it has been for a year and a half.

BY MR. LANGMUIR.

Q. Are you aware that you could get that information at the office of the Canada Car Company? A. Of course, when I went in there, as I have explained to the Warden before, I did not know where to get these things; and I did this on account of the machinery business, and in order to avoid inconveniences.

BY MR. NOXON.

Q. You speak of two methods of sewing brooms —one with the handle up and one with the handle down—how many more brooms could you make with the one method over what you could turn out with the other? A. In sewing the same broom with the handle up and down, whatever the shape of the broom, one being sewed straight across, and the other in a circular direction with the handle down—I suppose a man could sew very nearly three, while the other man was sewing two.

Q. That would be about one-third more? A. Yes.

Q. Are you supplied with all you require, to do the work? Are you supplied with all the necessaries and with everything that you require? A. My department, ever since I have been there, has been pretty well supplied; I generally look out for that myself.

Q. You have been getting them from time to time as they were required, and getting things into proper shape? A. Yes.

Q. Have you succeeded in getting the work organized to your satisfaction, and in having them work smoothly? A. I have tried, since I took charge of the place, to do the best I knew how to organize it for the benefit of the men who employed me; and as nearly as I could do so, for the benefit of the prisoners.

Q. It always takes time to get these things into proper order? A. Yes.

Q. You have been doing all you possibly can do in this regard? A. Yes; considerable has been done in this direction since I have been there.

Q. How long have you had it so? A. It has been the case since we have done the best work—during the past two or three weeks.

Q. Things have been for about two or three weeks running smoothly and to your satisfaction? A. Yes: under the circumstances.

WILLIAM CROSS, sworn:—

BY MR. WELLS.

Q. How are you employed? A. In the Brush Manufactory.

Q. You are foreman in the brush shop? Yes; I am foreman in the brush shop.

Q. How many men do you employ? A. I have eight men in my own shop, and one up in the north shop, near the machine shop; my labour is done all by hand, with the exception of the use of one machine.

Q. What experience had you prior to getting into the prison? A. I was with Mr. Boeck for fourteen years.

Q. Who is Mr. Boeck? A. His shop is situate on York St. opposite the Rossin House; I was also in New York during the space of time I have mentioned—for eight months; I was foreman for him during nine years of that fourteen.

Q. You make a variety of brushes? A. I only make one class of work: that is, drawn work; I do not make paint brushes. There is one thing to be taken into consideration: I made white-wash brushes, and for this brush I had a man from the outside.

Q. You make short hair brushes? A. Yes; I make scrub brushes and stove brushes.

Q. Do you make no hair brushes? A. No.

Q. How many varieties of brushes do you make? A. I think that we make twenty-five different varieties.

Q. Are these brushes of the same general character as those that were made in Mr. Boeck's establishment? A. The twenty-five varieties that we make are of the same general character, but we do not make all the kinds that Mr. Boeck does.

Q. You made more varieties in Mr. Boeck's than you do now? A. Yes; we made fifty different kinds in Boeck's.

Q. And here? A. We make ninety-six dozen on the average; of course, between free labour and prison labour there is a difference.

Q. What is the total yield of your establishment here per week? A. I told you that I think it is ninety-six dozen.

Q. When were ninety-six dozen made? A. Ninety-six dozen were turned out last week.

Q. Is that your highest yield? A. Ninety-five or ninety-six dozen is the average of a week's work; sometimes the turn-out is less and probably sometimes it is a little more; I think that it has ran up to one hundred and four dozen.

Q. It was ninety-three dozen for the week ending June the 6th? A. Ninety-three.

Q. And seventy-seven dozen at another time? A. Yes; some weeks go lower and some higher.

Q. Do you find that the yield of one week varies with that of another? A. Yes.

Q. Very much? A. Yes—very much; it varies according to the class of brush you make; sometimes a prisoner will turn out three dozen a day, and sometimes he will only make one and one-half dozen a day.

Q. This relates to different kinds of brushes? A. Yes.

Q. Do you find that the yield varies for the same brush; and that the turn-out of one kind of brush differs very much in one week and another? A. Yes; the make of one week will vary from that of another.

Q. When it relates to the same character of brush? A. Yes.

Q. Is it very much, or how much is it? A. No. I do not consider that it varies very much. The difference is not a great deal.

Q. Well now, can you give us an idea of what it is? You say that the utmost turn out was about ninety-six dozen for one week? A. No; that was not the highest; but to procure the greatest number, of course, I gave the men something. We were greatly pushed with orders.

Q. What is a fair average yield? A. Ninety-five dozen a week.

Q. Of assorted brushes? A. Of such as we see now.

Q. I see, for instance, that on May 23rd, there are different kinds, varying in value from 52 to 38, 44 and 80 cents? A. Ninety-five dozen has been made per week for a while back; but it has been only during two or three weeks that this has been the case.

Q. That is your utmost capacity? A. Yes; ninety-five dozen.

Q. According to your experience, what would be your yield of the same generally assorted brushes in Mr. Boeck's establishment? A. With the same number of men that we have got at the present time?

Q. Yes? A. Two hundred dozen brushes a week, and sometimes over that.

Q. Of the same kind of brushes? A. Yes. The same number of men will sometimes do more. All the work is done by piece work. It is according to how a man works. If the men will work steadily, with the same number of men—I have six drawers on now—they will turn out two hundred dozen brushes a week, working from 7 a.m. to 6 p.m. A brush drawer, working by piece work, generally begins at 8 a.m. and stops at 5 p.m.

Q. Will you describe the process of brush-making? A. In the first instance. of course, the lumber is brought in. It is cut into different sizes, of all qualities of brushes. We have different sizes of blocks— $\frac{5}{8}$ths, $\frac{3}{8}$ths, and $\frac{7}{8}$ths, that is the thickest; and they are of all lengths. They are lopped off, and cut to all the sizes I tell you of. The next process is to saw and cut the veneers, cutting off one-eight of an-inch of lumber; and in the next process, the bench knife is used to cut off the wings of the brush. After that, they are brought from the sawyer and cutter, and taken to the bench knife to cut off what we call the wings of the brush, to give them all an oval shape, and different kinds of shapes. From that they are taken to the machine of the borer, and he stencils them with a stencilling machine, and stamps them. After he has stencilled them, he bores them. They are then brought from the borer to the finisher, who planes them, and finishes them, and smoothes them, and takes them to the drawer. They are then placed on the drawer's bench; this gets the blocks into the drawer's hands. The next process is to procure the hair—what we call tampioca or fibre. This process is gone through by the comber. He takes the stuff out from the rough bale of tampioca, and after it is taken out of the bale, it is cut by the bench knife. We have a bench knife to cut them to the different lengths. The comber then takes that and combs it thoroughly. It is then tied up in a bundle and kept separate, and handed to the drawer, who has to take wire, and wind the wire on and over the roll. He puts it down into every hole and blocks it in a vice; the work is drawn, and as this is done, different lengths are cut off until it is finished.

Q. It seems to me that it takes a good many more than eight hands to do that? A. The brush passes through eight hands. In the first instance, it goes to the man who cuts the blocks.

Q. Now. have you got the establishment in what you consider to be good working order? A. Oh, yes, I have been now eleven months there; the time is close on eleven months.

Q. You make returns—how often? A. I make them every week - every Thursday.

Q. Your returns have been correct, I suppose? A. They have been correct as far as can see; my book is here It is always returned as correct. They take this statement. The clerk come to me and takes it down, and I take it down.

Q. Mr. Cross, to what do you ascribe the great difference in the yield between free labour and prison labour? What has been your experience in this respect? A. My experience, of course, with regard to the free man is, that I find he does more than double the amount of work that I get out of the prisoners up there. I always get my men to do a task every day. For instance, when I get a man in drawing work, he will seem surprised when I tell him "I want you to draw and get up to four thousand holes a day." He will look at me, in pretended astonishment. When he comes in he says, " that this never can be done," and it is the utmost I can do to get them to do four thousand holes a day. For the first few weeks that he is in there, I let him do as much as he can, and let him learn, and show him how to do it I let him be for the first three weeks, and then I give him a task.

Q. How long does it take to make an efficient brush-maker? A. In the old country, of course, an apprenticeship of seven years is served. In drawing it is not so much being an efficient maker as to be able to do the work quick; that is what I call a good drawer. I cannot make an efficient drawer, draw anything like a day's work in less than six months. A man may come in and say, "That is easy enough work," on seeing a man drawing. but it is not exactly putting it in the holes, as it is the quickness and expertness of a man in the doing of the work that makes a good drawer.

Q. Is it the practice to employ the labour of boys in a great deal of this work? A. Yes, and a great many women. Boys and women do most of the drawing work, unless it is very heavy work; and then they employ men.

Q. In what proportion? You have eight men at work here under your care: What proportion of boys, if you could do so-- would you employ in this number upon that work? A. I should employ about six on the whole.

Q. You would employ six boys? A. I have six drawing hands.

Q. Do I understand you to say that out of eight persons so engaged, you would employ six boys and two men? A. Yes, I would employ the boys for drawing.

Q. Do you know what boy's wages are in town? A. Yes, I know perfectly well. They average from $3.50 to $4.00 a week.
Q. From $3.50 to $4.00 a week? A. Yes.
Q. After they get expert? A. Yes.
Q. That is—after how many months? A. After six months' labour and sometimes after a longer period than that.
Q. What do they give boys from the date of their commencing work up to the termination of the six months? A. We give them the average wages of men, and they have to pay back to the man who shews them how to do the work so much per week to recompense him for loss of his time.
Q. What does it cost the employer for the labour of a boy? What would it cost the employer for the six months elapsing from the time when the boy begins to work? A. They pay the boys so much per thousand.
Q. How much do they pay per thousand? A. From sixteen to twenty-two cents—according to the class of work performed.
Q. How much can a boy make? A. Sometimes four and sometimes five dozen.
Q. A day? A. Yes, on the average, a person will not draw over two thousand holes a day during the first six months.
Q. Making twelve thousand holes per week? A. Yes.
Q. What do they pay for that? A. The makers are paid from 16 to 22 cents per thousand holes. It is according to the class of work done. These boys do not get the best class of work to do.
Q. And for the best class of work what are workmen paid? A. They average eighteen cents a thousand.
Q. And they average during the period mentioned two thousand holes a day? A. Yes.
Q. That would amount to thirty-six cents a day for the first six months? A. Yes.
Q. What do they pay men after they get expert? A. There are no higher wages than those I have stated. The highest is twenty-two cents per thousand.
Q. How much is a day's work? A. A good man, according to his work, will draw seven thousand holes a day, and sometimes a good man will draw eight thousand.
Q. What would you pay a man for the first six months? He gets expert as I understand you after six month's practice; if he is a good man? A. It is according to what he holes.
Q. What would he earn during the first six months? A. A man would not earn more than a boy during the first six months; after the six months have elapsed, he gets a little expert.
Q. Do brush makers commence to learn their trade when men or when boys? A. Sometimes they commence as men and sometimes as boys.
Q. What is the next process? A. The next is the finishing. That work I have done myself. I have never employed a prisoner in the finishing department. One man is employed to do the sand-papering. After I finish the brush, he takes it from me and to the sand-papering machine in the shop. I have always attended to the finishing department myself; and I have myself worked here from the day I went into the establishment until now.

BY MR. BROCKWAY.

Q. What are the processes gone through in the making of the brush? A. The brush is taken to the glueing department; the glue has to be prepared and the backs cut; it is put on the glueing-up bench and the back is glued to the brush; we then leave it until the next morning; we then take off the screws, and with a bench knife cut off the ends of the brushes; it is then taken to the vice and shaped with a drawing knife; after it is shaped, we take and trim it; I trim them all myself; a man then takes the brush to the sand paper-ing machine and sand-papers it; and brings it down and tacks it; after he has tacked them he brings them and ties them up in parcels and labels them; they are then ready for the market.

BY MR. HARDY.

Q. If so much work could be done by boys as you say, one might suspect that your

Company did not exercise very good judgment in entering into this branch of business up there? (No answer.)

Q. The proportion you state you would employ would be six boys to two men? A. Six boys to two men.

Q. How old would the boys be? A. I have had boys commence at eleven years of age.

Q. Is that the usual run? A. Of course, the ages of persons commencing to learn the business run from that up to manhood.

Q. What do the men earn per day generally—say for a set of drawers who make seven thousand a day? A. They would make about $1.54.

Q. What is the other important branch? A. After drawing?

Q. Yes. A. The finishing.

Q. What does your finisher make per day? A. I reckon my wages at $2.00 a day.

Q. What is another important branch of the work? A. The boring.

Q. And what do the borers make? A. Their average wage is from $1.50 to $1.80 per day.

Q. Boys do not do that work? A. No.

Q. That is putting the hair in? A. Yes—the putting in of the hair or fibre; the next process before boring is the cutting out.

Q. Do you mean to tell me that a boy of fifteen years of age can only do one, two, or three thousand holes a day? A. They do 2,000 when they get expert—after six months practice.

Q. Is six months the recognized and regular standard of time for learning? A. Sometimes you can never make a man expert

Q. That may happen in every trade? A. Of course.

Q. Is six months the recognized and lowest standard? A. We never recognize any standard.

Q. What is your experience? Can you remember many boys who got up to four or five thousand in less than six months? A. No; I cannot make out many of them; sometimes they exceed that.

Q. One-half the boys? A. No; in about three months they will sometimes do fifteen hundred a day.

Q. What do they do when they come in during the first week? A. I have known them do about eight hundred holes a day—from six to eight hundred, then they will keep at that figure for some time, and not seem as if they could get ahead of it.

Q. That is very natural; but they will make a start by and by? A. Yes; they will get a little quicker.

Q. You were turning out some two hundred dozen a week with the same number of men at Boeck's? A. Yes.

Q. Had he exactly the same number in a set of men? A. A set of men will turn out two hundred dozen a week.

Q. That was their average? A. Yes; with the men I had there.

Q. But you did not make the same kind of brushes there as here? A. Some kinds were the same, but in all kinds we did not make the same there.

Q. He made two hundred, and some of the brushes were smaller and easier made; and some you make, he don't make? A. We make the easiest brushes made, and the commonest brushes.

Q. And the easiest of his lot? A. Yes.

Q. He could not turn out a more difficult brush than those at the rate of two hundred dozen a week? A. Yes.

Q A more difficult brush? A. Yes. Of course we had faster hands there employed. In good brushes, we classified them all at Boeck's; there is the fine large brush, the good second and the common; that is the way we do. Of course, in Boeck's establishment I never kept count of the brushes; but I know the amount of brushes which we had to turn out a week. I was foreman of the same department of which I am now foreman; and we were expected to turn out a certain quantity of brushes a week, and to get that amount of work out of the men.

Q. Had you different machinery there? A. I used a finishing off machine.

Q. At Boeck's? A. Yes.

Q. And now you do not? A. No. I do all my own work by hand.
Q. Did you use there any other machinery that is employed in the processes of boring or cutting? A. We use, of course, a boring machine, as we did at Boeck's.
Q. And a cutting machine? A. That is done by hand, both at Boeck's establishment and at ours.
Q. Is there any appreciable difference? Had you any advantage at Boeck's which you have not now got? A. The only thing I see relates to the shaping machine.
Q. Is that an important thing? A. It is in finishing.
Q. Is it connected with the trimming? A. No.
Q. Whose department is it connected with? A. We generally have that done by a man who does what they call the chores around the Central Prison. He does the trimming and may do the packing up or cleaning up, and all that sort of thing. That is his Department. This is all done by hand.
Q. Then a boy who made four thousand holes a day would earn eighty-eight cents a day? A. Eighty-eight cents when he got up to that number.
Q. You have a runner to each shop? A. No, my runner belongs to another shop.
Q. Your runner has been handed over to it? A. No; he comes up at seven o'clock in the morning and does the ordinary business, but I do not see him again.
Q. Some other shop has got hold of your runner? A. Yes; I am not supposed to have any runner in my shop. He comes up and brings clean water for the men to drink, and water at quarter to twelve for the men to wash with, after working in the black tampioca. That is the only time when I see him.

BY MR. LANGMUIR.

Q. You worked at some disadvantage in the present shop before you got into the new shop? A. Of course we are now in the new shop. We wanted a shaper and we did work at a disadvantage when I first went there. I can work just as well as I could wish if I had room enough for a shaper. That is the only thing I require; otherwise, I work at no disadvantage at all.

BY MR. HARDY.

Q. Where is Boeck's shop? A. On York street.
Q. Is any steam required there? A. He has an engineer, but I believe he has now sold his engine to Kilgour, next door—the paper-bag man.
Q. What does he pay for rent? A. I believe he pays sixteen hundred dollars a year.
Q. And he had an engine, an engineer and stoker, and had to buy fuel? A. But he has done away with all that. The services of the engine, and fuel and fire, and everything in that connection he finds that he can buy cheaper outside.
Q. Instead of manufacturing? A. Yes. He can buy them cheaper outside than he can manufacture.
Q. Have you sold him any from the prison? A. I do not know.
Q. Do you find any brush-makers among the prisoners? A. I never had one—not one, sir.
Q. I find twelve, and ten the first year, put down? A. No, never had one. I had one brush-maker sent over to me, but I believe he was a Swede. The man was of no use, and I sent him back.
Q. You did not like him because he was a Swede? A. No, that was not the reason; the country has no effect with me. He was an old man and he was not quick. I could not utilize him in any way, and so I sent him back.

BY MR. LANGMUIR.

Q. Do you get the list giving the previous occupations of the prisoners placed under your charge? A. No, sir; I never had one supplied me.
Q. Is it not sent? A. I never saw one since I have been in the prison. I do not know what class of men comes under my care.

By Mr. Hardy.

Q. You turn out about one-half as much, ninety-six; and the wages paid are not over one-third as much as they were at Boeck's? A. Yes.

Q. Rent included; your department ought to pay pretty well? A. I just told you the amount we do; of course, some weeks we average more than others; during the last two weeks we have; I have got three men who are pretty expert in drawing, and they do a pretty good bit of work; the reason is, because I give them an advantage to induce them to draw quickly for me.

Q. What advantage do you give them? A. I give each man $1.50 when they get out, and a plug of tobacco a week.

Q. On · dollar and a half when they get out? A. When their time expires.

Q. And tobacco? A. Yes.

Q. Is that allowed by the rules of the prison? A. I do it after they have been discharged from the prison; I give them $1.50 when they get out, but I never give them any money while they are in prison—never a cent; I also promise them their dinner when they get out; and I help them to keep themselves for half a week, while they are looking around for a job; I never could have got them to work otherwise; a prisoner tells me when he first comes in "If I could get the least encouragement I would work." They have drawn up a statement I believe, in my shop, and handed it to Mr. McBean, I believe. I said to them, "I cannot help you at all." The men said, that while engaged in this compulsory labour, they did not feel like work at all; that is what every man among them says to me; I do not reason with them at all.

By Mr. Wells.

Q. Practically, you work yourself all the time? A. Yes.

Q. So instead of eight, nine persons have been employed in our establishment all the time? A. Yes; I think the Captain can prove that; every man in my shop sees me at my vice; and I see after the boring, sand-papering, et cetera.

Mr. Wells—I will establish from the returns, what follows :—the profits for the week ending April 19, amounted to $5.21; for the week ending April 25th, the loss was 71 cents; profit for the week ending May 2nd, $11.04; for the week ending May 9th, $12.74; for the week ending May 16th, $18.61; for the week ending May 23rd, $3.01; for the week ending May 30th, $5.01; and for the week ending June 6th, $4.54.

Mr. Langmuir.—That includes the ten per cent. ?

Mr. Wells.—Certainly it does.

Q. Are the wages of the foreman included in the $41 50? A. Yes. My own opinion is that ten per cent. does not cover expenses.

By the Chairman.

Q. Do you know anything about the cost of the material used in the making of brushes? A. I could not tell that, sir. It is always handed into the office. I do not buy the material myself. It is the manager's business to buy the stuff. I hand the order into the office, and he purchases. I inform him of the quality desired.

Q. You do not know what the material should cost for a dozen of any of the particular kind of brushes that you make? A. No, sir. The market always varies; sometimes prices are low, and sometimes prices are high, for the stuff used in the manufacture of brushes. Material is now very high in price—higher, I suppose, than ever was known before,—especially for Brazils. Some classes of Brazils you cannot get for love or money—even in New York. Wilks and Company, in New York, could not buy them. Mexican fibre has gone up, I believe, four cents per pound; and still the brushes are sold at the same price. This difference makes a great item in the cost of a dozen brushes where five pounds of material are required; and then the price of labour has gone down in the city so considerably. That affects us. It is always a great disadvantage—working in the prison. For instance, I have got three or four of my best hands who will be going out; you may say, two this coming month, one in September, and one in October. I have got to replace these men and learn the new hands the business.

By Mr. Hardy.

Q. You have ample time for that ? A. But I have to take them green. One man leaves the prison on the 12th of July, and another twelve days afterwards; these are two of the best men I have in the establishment.

By the Chairman.

Q. How do you propose doing under these circumstances ? Can you bring in a man and have him learn before these men go out ? Could you have two extra men ? A. I have six men, of course, always, and I shift them up. Lately I had one man who happened to be by profession an engine driver—a driver on the lakes. He was taken away to drive the engine; of course he could never make a good drawer, I could tell that; I had him work for me over three months—I think that it was three months. I could tell that he could not pick up and become a quick drawer. He was willing to work, but he told me himself that he would never make a quick drawer. He was put to work the engine, and a new man was sent to take his place, still I knew that he would not make a quick drawer.
Q. You must expect these changes ? A. In a free shop they never make them.
Q. Of course ? A. I have known men remain in Boeck's ever since I was there.

By Mr. Langmuir.

Q. How long have you been a foreman in the Canada Car Company's Works ? A. I was in the latter end of July that I came there.
Q. That makes not quite a year ? A. Yes.
Q. How many men have passed through the brush shop since you have been there ? A. I have eight there now.
Q. How many altogether have been in the shop ? A. I have had two who left me; no, the number was three.
Q. Then you have had eleven men employed in the shop since you have been there ? A. Yes.
Q. All the rest continue with you ? A. Yes.

By Mr. Wells.

Q. You had long-term men placed under your charge ? A. Yes.

By Mr. Langmuir.

Q. You have made no changes save three since you have been there ? A. Yes.
Q. And the result of eleven months operations is that you have turned out ninety-five dozen brushes a week ? Oh, no. I can only say that this has been the case lately.
Q. Very well; you have got up to that, and in the very highest state of organization at Boeck's, you turned out two hundred dozen a week; is not that doing pretty well to commence with ? You say that it takes six months to learn the trade; and comparing the results you have achieved with the operations of a highly organized establishment, do you not think that you have done pretty fairly ? A. Yes, it is pretty fair.

By Mr. Wells.

Q. In other words, you have been working under the very best possible circumstances ? Mr. Langmuir—Oh, no !
Mr. Wells—I beg your pardon. There have been only three changes; it takes six months to make a man efficient, and yet they have only turned out ninety-five dozen brushes a week.
Mr. Langmuir—He says that he has very bad men.
Witness:—I have the very best men in the place going out, and goodness knows what sort of men I will get in for drawing.

BY MR. LANGMUIR.

Q. You will have to make more brush-makers? A. Yes.
Q. Could you take charge of more than eight men? A. I could if there was the business to be done to require it.
Q. How many could you take charge of? A. Then I would have to leave the finishing work, and the Company would have to pay me my wages to look after the men. I would have to employ a finisher, and learn a man this department of the work. I told them that I could not employ another drawer. If I had another, I would have to employ a finisher. I b our now pretty hard. I never worked so hard at Boeck's as I do now.

BY MR. HARDY.

Q. You did not get as much there for your services? A. I got the same wages there that I receive here.
Q. Two dollars a day? A. fteen dollars a week is what the foreman gets there now, in the same department that I was in. You will find if you enquire, that this man gets the same wages that I do, and he does not do one-half the amount of work that I do.

BY MR. LANGMUIR.

Q. Do you find that brush-makers go to goal? A. I never found it to be the case but once yet.
Q. Did you ever hear of any men who were employed in Boeck's establishment going to gaol? A. Never. I never heard of one case. I never had a brush-maker who had been in prison under my charge at Boeck's; and I never had but one brush-maker in this prison here. If I could get such a workman, I could help myself along; but I never can. If they get two more men and put them in the department for drawing, I will have to quit the bench and employ a finisher.

BY MR. WELLS.

Q. When this change takes place, you will not be able to turn out this quantity of work that has been mentioned? A, I can not do it; it will be impossible.
Q. And during the year that you have been employed there, you have had only three changes? A. Yes
Q. You have been furnished with long-term men? A. The longest term-men are sent down for twelve months.

BY MR. LANGMUIR.

Q. Some are sent down for eleven months? A. I have had six-months men and five months men.

Commission adjourned until the 10th of July.

TUESDAY, July 10, 1877.

The Commission met at ten o'clock.
Hon Mr. Hardy appeared for the Government, and Mr. Lockhart Gordon, of the firm of Messrs. Morrison, Wells and Gordon, for the Canada Car Company.

H. F. PERRY, called on behalf of the Government, sworn and examined:

BY MR. HARDY.

Q. Mr. Perry, where do you reside? A. In Montreal.
Q. In what business are you engaged? A. In the business of broom-making.
Q. In what capacity? A. As foreman.
Q. By whom are you employed? A. By Messrs. H. A. Nelson & Sons.
Q. They carry on business in Montreal? A. Yes, sir.
Q. And how long have you been engaged in that capacity? A. With them?
Q. Yes. A. For six years—on just about the first of this month.
Q. Were you engaged in the trade of broom-making prior to entering their employment? A. Yes, sir.
Q. For what length of time? A. I have worked in the business for about thirty-six years.
Q. Have you ever been employed in connection with prison labour? A. I have.
Q. In what capacity? A. As foreman, I did general work.
Q. This was in the broom business? A. Yes, sir.
Q. Where and when? A. It was at Trenton, in the State of New Jersey; I think that it was in 1859, 1860, and 1861; it was during part of this period, I know; I think I commenced in June—if my memory serves me right.
Q. What sort of a prison was it? The State Prison? A. Yes.
Q. Was it a short or long term prison? A. It was long and short—both.

BY MR. GORDON.

Q. What was the name of its place? A. Trenton.

BY MR. HARDY.

Q. How short were the terms? They were down as low as ——? A. One year; men were in for one year, and some for two years; and sentences ran as high as twenty years.
Q. How many men had you under your charge? A. We were bound to employ fifteen men, but we did employ for part of the time as high a number as twenty-five men.
Q. Just at that special occupation? A. Yes, sir.
Q. Making brooms? A. Yes, sir.
Q. That was between 1859 and 1862—it was, then, before the war? A. Yes, sir; it was before the war.
Q. And it continued from 1859 to 1861 or 1862? A. Yes, sir.
Q. Now, how many men have you down at Montreal working for the Messrs. Nelson? A. We have fourteen working at what we call mechanical work—working at winding.
Q. And how large is the staff—counting all of the hands? A. The whole staff is composed of twenty-one persons.
Q. Sixteen men and five boys? A. Yes.
A. Do you employ or use machinery for making brooms now? A. No, sir.
Q. At Montreal? A. No, sir. Do you mean steam machinery?
Q. Steam machinery is used at the Central Prison? Do you use it? A. No, sir.
Q. What do you use? A. The improved hand-machinery, which has been in vogue for the last—well, for the last twenty or thirty years.
Q. Did you use machinery at Trenton? A. We used the same kind of, or similar machinery.
Q. That is, the ordinary hand-machinery? A. Yes, sir.
Q. You use a machine called a sizing machine? A. Yes, sir.

Q. Are these the same machines that are used here? A. I have never seen those that are here. Ours is run by hand. It is the small common machine.

Q. The same machinery, too, I believe, is run by steam? A. We do not use steam. We have no steam power. It is all hand work.

Q. Now, how long does it take an ordinary man to become somewhat proficient in the making of brooms? A. You mean only a certain class of brooms? or do you mean all kinds?

Q. I mean brooms generally—the general common broom of good quality and of different qualities? A. It varies. Some learn a little quicker than others; but in from a week to ten days a man gets so that he makes a good broom, which will pass in with the work of the old hands.

Q. And it will then pass in with work done by old hands? A. Oh, yes.

Q. After a week's work? A. Yes.

Q. And that includes the most intricate part of the business? A. Yes.

Q. The winding? A. That is the winding.

Q. What men do you call experienced men or skilled men? How long have they to work to become skilled men—you have such hands? A. A man soon gets to make a good common broom. Very few are made except what we call common brooms. When we come to what we call fancy work, as that is styled—with fancy braid—it takes a little longer time to learn, although one man will sometimes pick it up very much quicker than another.

Q. What work do you regard as work to put skilled men at? A. The winding.

Q. That is all? A. Yes.

Q. And in what length of time can they learn that? A. A man will make a good broom in a week or ten days.

Q. And in a month he will become an efficient workman? A. For one kind of broom, Yes, sir.

Q. Do you mean the ordinary kind of broom? A. Yes, sir.

Q. Well, then, you have fourteen of these men at Montreal? A. Yes, sir.

Q. What are the others engaged at? At what class of work? A. The smaller boys—for those in whom is required no skill at all—work at what we call sizing, the first process in broom-making; they cut the corn off and place it in different boxes, in different lengths.

Q. Does this work require skill? A. It needs no skill at all. You can show them how to do it in fifteen minutes; and after having shown them, all you have to do is to watch them sometimes and see that they do it properly.

Q. How many boys have you employed? A. We have six at the present time. That is piece work. We have to keep quite a number of small boys. They do not work very much sometimes, but we have to keep in stock enough.

Q. You have a buncher? A. We have a buncher.

Q. How long does it take to learn that work? A. That can be learned in five minutes.

Q. And a bleacher? A. That can be learned as quick as one can show a man how.

Q. It requires no effort to learn it? A. No.

Q. And the same thing is true with regard to the bleacher? A. Yes.

Q. Then, as a matter of fact, out of twenty-one men and boys you have fourteen who take from ten days to a month to make themselves thoroughly familiar with the best class of work made in prisons,—an ordinary good class of work? A. Yes, sir.

Q. This may take a month, and the rest of the work requires simply the effort of a labourer? A. Yes—with the exception of the sorter. This work requires a little more experience.

Q. How long does it take to learn this part of the business? A. From a week to ten days.

Q. It is not a question of expertness? A. No; but simply of adapting the size to the kind he wants to take out. We take the best corn—the smoothest corn—where the finest starts from the stalk, and put it on the outside of the broom.

Q. It is not a question of mechanics? A. No, sir.

Q. What do you pay these men—say the winders? A. They work by the piece.

Q. What do they earn? A. When they work ten hours their wages vary from $1.50 to $2.40. They get on the average about $2.00 a day.

Q. And what about the bleacher? A. We pay him $8.50 a week.

Q. How much do you pay him a day—can you call it to min: at once? A. It is about $1.40.

BY MR. GORDON

Q. Do they work by the piece? A. No.

BY MR. HARDY.

Q. Eight dollars and a half a week?—That is what you pay them? A. Yes.
Q. Is the bleacher a boy or a man? A. A boy or a man is capable of doing the work; but we have a man now performing it.
Q. And then there is the buncher. How is he paid? A. He is paid in the same way.
Q. And what do the boys do? A. The boys cut the hurl and assist in sorting the corn, putting on labels, &c., and doing anything that we want them to do.
Q. And you pay them how much? A. We pay them $2.50 a week.
Q. That is the lowest grade is it? A. Yes sir—with the exception of one small boy whom we pay $1.50 a week, and who does the running round and the light work.
Q. And as to the sewing? Are the sewers and the winders the same? A. N. Sewing is a different thing from winding; but our men here do both.
Q. The fourteen whom you mention, do sewing and winding? A. They do the sewing also. In a great many places however, the winders only wind and the sewers only sew; the sewing does not take as long to learn. You can show a man in an hour or two all that you can shew him about it. It requires only shewing first and then practice The machine gives the shape, and all a man has to do is get the thread around and stitch it. You can shew him all that is to be shown in very little time.
Q. When you were at Trenton, New Jersey, the men you had under your charge were entirely composed of prisoners? A. Yes, sir.
Q. What proportion of work could you get from them compared with the results of free labour in Montreal—man for man? A. Oh, all I can say to you with regard to that is this —at the time their labour was quite cheap as you recollect was the case before the war.
Q. Labour was cheaper before the war than it has been since? A. Oh yes. That is since I have been in the States. I have been now away some six years. At that time—after I gave them their task—I would have had to pay for the same work if it had been done outside, from $1.25 to $1.40. It varied. Some would work so as to get a little more, and some a little less. The price varied from $1.25 to $1.40—as regards the task I gave them to do.
Q. For the task which you gave them to do, you would have to pay how much outside? A. From $1.25 to $1.40.
Q. Is that for the same class of work which you get done here now by the men per day? A. It is similar. Every shop has a little different make of broom. We are making now only one kind of broom, that we made at the prison at that time. The same kind of broom now costs us $1.46.
Q. What did it cost you then? A. It cost us $1.25.
Q. The rate was $1.25? A. Yes, sir.
Q. And it now costs $1.46? A. Yes.
Q. Judging by that, you would get about as much work out of prisoners as out of free labour? A. I think about as much.
Q. Would you notice any perceptible difference? A. I do not know what really I could get out of them (the prisoners). I did not put them as heavy a task as they could do.
Q. What was it? A. I put them to do what I thought was right, and what I thought they could stand all the while. We gave them a chance to make over-work, and quite a number of them did so. We paid them at the same rate that we paid the prison authorities for the labour.
Q. What were you paying for prison labour then? A. We paid for it forty cents a day.
Q. Do you know whether prison labour has been higher since then? A. I have learned that it has. I have received a letter from a gentleman I was connected with then, and he

states that it is paid for at the rate of fifty and fifty-four cents in Baltimore and in Trenton; and that this is the general price.
Q. That is what he says? A. That is what he says.
Q. And who is the man? A. Mr. Chipman, of Baltimore—Mr. George Chipman.
Q. He had the contract at that time of which you have spoken? A. Yes.
Q. And you were his foremam? A. Yes, sir.

BY MR. GORDON.

Q. Do you know what you got with that prison labour? Was there any machinery or anything given in at the prison? A. We furnished our own machinery.
Q. And does the gentleman you're referring to mention this point? A. No, sir.
Q. Does he say anything in his letter about it? A. No, sir. He merely states that this was the contract price.

BY MR. HARDY.

Q. Now, speaking of twenty years men—did you take men who had been already engaged in broom-making when you were there? Had they been old broom-makers—those whom you took from among the prisoners? A. When we first went in there, we took an old hand who had been engaged at the work of broom-making, but with the understanding that we could change them whenever we wished to do so. Recollect that the men we took on unconditionally we had to keep.
Q. I see? A. That was the understanding on which we took these old men: it was agreed that we could give them up if we did not like them; I feared that we might have trouble with them as we were making a different broom from the kind that they had been making, and I knew that I could get the task required better out of men whom I had learned myself; I chose to learn the men myself as I learned them in a manner a little different from the manner in which they had been learned.
Q. You preferred then as a matter of choice to take on new men and learn them the business, to taking on old hands who had formerly learned the business? A. They left that chance for me.
Q. And you took it? A. Yes; I only kept on one of the old men after the first year.
Q. Only one? A. That is all; I replaced them by others all through the first year.
Q. You preferred new hands to the old ones? A. I did so.
Q. And one reason for this was that you could get the task out of the former easier than out of the latter? A. Yes; I could learn them to make a broom as I wanted it; it was harder to learn old hands to make the broom as I required it to be done, than new ones.
Q. What were men getting for this work outside of that period? A. Where outside?
Q. What would a man's labour after it was done, then cost outside? I understood you to say that a man now getting probably two dollars a day, would then make one dollar and a-quarter—with free labour? A. The number of brooms that I gave them to make, would there make $1.25 a day.
Q. That is among prisoners you mean? A. No—with outsiders.
Q. That is for the same class of broom for which you now pay, on the average, of two dollars a day? A. Yes, sir; but all men vary in the work they turn out; some would get perhaps twenty cents more and some twenty cents less than others—taking a fair general average.
Q. Speaking now from your knowledge of the business here in this country—I mean practically—that is, what men making the quantity of brooms the prisoners did, would receive? A. They would earn that amount of money; but what they could make is not for me to say.
Q. Speaking now from your own knowledge of the broom business in this country, and of what has been paid to men, and of what the rate of wages is, and from your familiarity with prison labour—would you consider the payment of sixty cents a day too high a rate for men,

all able bodied men, taking them at terms, running from six months to two years? A. For prison labour?

Q. For prison labour? A. I would not like to take six months men unless they had been employed at the same work; but for one year or two years men I would not consider sixty cents a day too much.

Q. I mean without anything being furnished at all—you furnishing your own machinery? A. Yes.

Q. You would say that sixty cents a day would not be too much to pay under such circumstances for one and two years men? A. I do not think so.

Q. And would you take men with an average of from eight to nine months to serve? A. Not if I could get men to fill up and do what I wanted them to do of other work.

Q. Take the unskilled department, for instance? A. Yes; in the unskilled department, of course, it would make hardly any difference.

Q. Whether the men had short or long terms? A. It takes but a few days to learn how to do that sort of work.

BY MR. GORDON.

Q. I understand you to say, Mr. Perry, that labour in the Prison in New Jersey was available for a period varying from one year to twenty years? A. Yes

Q. It varied; the highest term was twenty years, and none were sentenced for terms under one year? A. I do not think that any prisoners were confined for less than one year; I do not state this positively; however, that is my impression.

Q. You were only employed there as the foreman—you were not the contractor? A. I was not the contractor, but I did all the business there; the contractor was not there.

Q. You managed the business for him? A. Yes, sir.

Q. Had you the pick of the prisoners? A. Whenever a batch came in I could take a man, and when I took him I had to keep him.

Q. Were you told beforehand what occupation the prisoners had followed? A. No, sir.

Q. Before you made your choice? A. No, sir.

Q. You were not told what had been the occupation of the prisoners—whether they had been mechanics, farmers, or labourers? A. No, sir.

Q. But you were allowed to examine them, and find out what they knew? A. All I had to serve me in making my selections, were my eyes.

Q. You had a tongue though? A. Yes; but we had no right to talk to prisoners.

Q. But under the circumstances I suppose you were allowed to ask them what they had been engaged in? A. We were not allowed to ask them anything of the kind.

Q. Do you mean to say that you chose your men merely by looking at them? A. When we took one of them, we did so without any words—without asking him anything.

Q. And having taken him, you had to keep him? A. When we took a man we had to keep him.

Q. You were not allowed to ask him what his occupation had been? A. I never asked; I did not care for that.

Q. Could you tell from the appearance of a man, whether he was a broom-maker? A. I did not care whether he had been a broom-maker or not, I would just as soon that he had not been.

Q. How did you manage to choose the right men? Were you always successful? A. No, sir.

Q. You were not? A. No, sir.

Q. The contract was for fifteen men? A. The contract was for fifteen men, but we could take as many as we chose; we had, however, to keep fifteen, and we had to pay for them: that is, when they were well; whenever they were sick, we did not have to pay for them.

Q. Can you give any idea of the average sentences of the men you took? A. The average length of their terms?

Q. Yes? A. I do not know that I could, sir; there was one man whose sentence I do know; he was a two years' man—he was an outside man, and that did not make any difference; I do not think there was one engaged in winding, who was confined for a term less than three or five years; I think I took none having less time to serve, for that purpose; I would not be positive about that, however ; I do not recollect distinctly, whether this was the case ; it was only the winding part that I cared for ; I would just as soon have others—if they were good men—who were only staying in the prison for six months. It takes but a few moments to shew what is to be done ; in many particulars, and in a day or two, they will do as much of good work, as any one else.

Q. How long were you there altogether ? A. Two years—or about that.

Q. Why did you leave the place ? A. On account of the war.

Q. Was the contract given up ? A. We gave up the contract ; if we had kept it longer, we would have had to keep it for five years.

By Mr. Hardy.

Q. For five years longer. A. Yes.

By Mr. Gordon.

Q. Could you have kept it for five years longer at the same rate ? A. Yes, that was the contract in the first place.

Q. And notwithstanding that your employer gave up the contract, although he had the option of keeping it for five years longer ? A. Most certainly.

Q. Although he could have continued the contract, only paying forty cents a day for the labour of the men ? A. Certainly, and that was left optional with me ; I could have stayed or not, as I had the management of the whole thing.

Q. And you advised him not to continue the contract ? A. Under the circumstances, I did.

Q. Now I understand you to say, in answer to my learned friend, that as long as you had a sufficient number of good men, you would not mind employing this kind of labour— prison labour—to do the easy part of the work ; but suppose now, that you had to take a fixed number of prisoners, say two hundred and fifty, and that you had not a sufficiency of unskilled work for them to do, how would that affect you ? A. I think that you would find enough skilled workmen in two hundred and fifty prisoners, if you carried on a business large enough to employ that number—for the broom business ; and the other labour could keep the skilled workmen busy.

Q. But suppose that you had not enough of those skilled workmen, and that you had to employ unskilled men on the parts requiring skilled labour—such as twisting, &c., what effect would that have ? A. One must be a very poor man if he could not earn that much money. He would be below par, and there is hardly any one but what could do it.

Q. Suppose that the winding had to be done by a man who was only in prison for three or four months, would that fact have any effect on the work ? Do you think that it would ? A. Do you mean to say that the man would have only to stay there for three or four months ?

Q. Suppose that the winder had only three or four months to serve, and that you were always changing this man, and putting a fresh man on the work ? A. Well, if I had the management of it, I would only put on as the winders the men who had the longest terms to serve, and I would change about the others instead.

Q. That is not the question ; I suppose that you could not do that. Suppose the average term of the men to be four months, and that you had to employ one of these men as a winder, and put on a new man every four months, what would be the effect of the circumstance on the work ? A. You could not get so much profit out of it, but I think that he would pay his way.

Q. You think that under the circumstances such a man would earn fifty cents a day ? A. I think that he would.

Q. You think that such a man would earn fifty cents a day ? A. He would be a very poor man if he did not.

Q. At winding ? A. Even at winding, and at skilled work. I can learn a man in one week to make a broom, even in two days I can learn a man to make a passable broom, unless he is very stupid ; and in a month's time, if there is anything in him at all, he will earn more than his sixty cents a day.

Q. As long as you have a good man there working with him? A. I do not care whether one is there. Two foremen can look after the work of one hundred as well as of five.
Q. Could one foreman look after fifty men? A. Certainly—if he has nothing to do but to look after their work.
Q. One could look after fifty men? A. Yes.
Q. I suppose they were five months' men? A. That would not make any difference.
Q. You would undertake to manage fifty men and five different machines, with nothing but short-term labour, and still make these men earn fifty cents a day? A. With the kind of machines I am working with; Yes, sir.
Q. With the kind of machines you are working with? A. Yes, sir.

BY MR. HARDY.

Q. They would earn that from the start as I understand you? A. Not from the start It requires sometime to get a start.

BY MR. GORDON.

Q. Take a four months' man, would he make sufficient towards and during the last part of the four months to recompense the contractor for the deficiency doing the first part of the four months? A. Yes, sir—and more too. On sixty cents a day, there would hardly be any deficiency.
A. Do you know, Mr. Perry, that at the Kingston Penitentiary they advertised for tenders for labour, and that the highest tender was thirty cents a day? A. I do not know anything of the kind.
Q. You do not know that this is the case? A. No.
Q. You did not know that penitentiary labour was advertised at Kingston? A. I have not heard of it.
Q. You seem to have such a high opinion of penitentiary labour, that it struck me perhaps you might know it?
Q. You seem to have such a high opinion of penitentiary labour, that it struck my perhaps you might know it? A. I am only speaking with regard to my own branch of business, recollect. I have nothing to do with any other. I know what in my own branch I can do. I have been through it.
Q. I can understand that with fifteen men, not very many to look after, but when you come to increase that number nearly four times, and perhaps more than that, would not that make a considerable difference? A. It makes a difference to be sure, but how long is it before a man makes up this little difference, or that little difference.
Q. In supervising fifteen men, it is very easy to go backwards and forwards, but when there are fifty men to look after, it would make a great difference? A. It only makes the difference of a little more time to be spent in looking after them
Q. I understood you to say that at the New Jersey Penitentiary, these men were allowed to work over time? A. Yes, sir
Q. And that they were paid the same wages? A. They were allowed to do more than their task.
Q. More than their task? A. Yes sir.
Q. Was that the case during the whole of the time you were there? A. Yes, sir.
Q. And you found that it had a beneficial effect? A. Certainly.
Q. When you talked of what they turned out—I think you said that it varied in value from $1.25 to $1.40? A. From $1.25 to $1.40. It varied, according to the different kinds. On some kinds it would be a few cents under that.
Q. Did that include what you call overtime work? No, sir.
Q. That would be simply for their ordinary work? A. That was the task which I gave them.
Q. And until they completed the task, they could not get anything for themselves? A. Certainly not. I put them their task to do.
Q. First of all, they had to do their task, and then they could get this intentional reward? A. Yes, sir.

Q. Now, do you recommend that system with prisoners? Do you think that it forms an inducement for them to work? A. Well, all I can say is, that if I was going to take charge of prisoners, I would ask for that privilege; I think that it is an inducement for them to do their task, and that it is better for both parties.

Q. I suppose that it has the effect, not only of inducing them to make some money for themselves, but also to do their task in the way in which it is put? A. Yes.

Q. Who was it that fixed the amount which they should do? Was it you or the prison authorities? A. I did it.

Q. I suppose that you knew what freemen could do? A. Yes, certainly. As I said before, I did not put the task to the extent of what the men could do, but so as to get a fair day's work.

Q. In fixing that task, how much less did you give these men to do than you would give to freemen to do? A. We pay by the piece outside, and I gave them work to do which would cost us outside $1.25 or $1.40.

Q. What would a man make outside at this same work? A. It would rate according to how he worked. He would be paid by the piece.

Q. What would an average man make? A. $1.25 to $1.50 and $1.75 in this time.

Q. Did you give them nearly as much to do as a freeman would do, or two-thirds, or one-half as much? A. I gave what I thought would be a fair day's work for them.

BY MR. HARDY.

Q. Would it be a fair day's work outside as well? A. It would, taking one man with another, although plenty of men do more, and plenty do less.

BY MR. GORDON.

Q. It was about an average day's work? A. Yes, at that time.

Q. You said to my learned friend, that you thought a man, or perhaps a boy, could learn this style of business, or at least some part of it, in a week or ten days;—now how do you know that, Mr. Perry? Do you employ in your establishment, men who have never done this kind of work before, or do you generally employ men who have been broom-makers? A. We employ men now when we want them that have worked at the trade. I have been engaged in it my whole life. It has been my business to start shops and learn men.

Q. Are these men what you call apprentices? A. You can call them what you choose; they were grown men—some of them—and some were young boys.

Q. Some were boys? A. Yes.

Q. Had you any contract as to the period for which they were to serve? A. I was hired to teach them.

Q. Had you any contract with them, or were they bound to your employers. A. Oh, no.

Q. They were not? A. Oh, no.

Q. And did their wages increase according to the time that they were with you? A. They were paid just the same as old men were paid; those who learned in the shop were paid at just the same rate as the old hands.

Q. From the start? A. From the start, sir.

Q. I do not understand that. I supposed that new men were not so useful as experienced men? A. It is because they are, at commencing, put on the poorest and cheapest kind of brooms, and they are paid the same price as is paid for this work.

Q. They make the poorest and cheapest kind? A. For the first day or two.

Q. And when they learn that, they go a step up and are put on something better? A. After the first or second day, they are able to take hold of any kind of common broom that is made and make a passable broom, not quite as smooth and handsome as is made by more experienced hands, but just as strong a one as is wanted for winding; after that is done, the press puts it into shape, and if there are any irregularities, it removes them, and leaves it in shape to pass inspection; it is only the first part that they have to do. They are liable to get the covers so that they will not work quite in their proper place; they may get loose, and this is the only part that has to be steadied and got on true and tight around the handle so that the broom may not come loose; the man brings them into place.

Q. With regard to that work, a little time before you gave a man that work to do,—a man coming to learn the business? A. If we happen to be in want of a workman, we put them on right after two or three days' practice.

Q. Would you supervise their work to any considerable extent? A. Most assuredly.

Q. Now you are referring to free men—men employed in the Messrs. Nelson's establishment? A. To them, or to any you choose—in prison or anywhere else; I use all the same.

Q. I was asking with regard to these men,—I was referring particularly to the Messrs. Nelsons' establishment—whether it is the custom to take men there who had not learned the business previously? A. We have done so; but more before I went there than since.

Q. Then they do not do it now? A. Oh, yes; we have now one man whom I put on; he has been at work for us I guess about three months, and he earns from $10.00 to $12.00 a week.

Q. What is about the length of time the other men you have—I understand that you have altogether twenty-one employees? A. We have twenty-one, boys and all.

Q. Sixteen men and boys? A. We have only fourteen whom we call winders.

Q. Can you tell us how long these sixteen men have been with you? A. All have been there over three months; and I could not state how long some of them have been there; they have been employed in the establishment all the time I have been there.

Q. How long is that? A. Six years.

Q. How many have been there all the time you have been employed by the Messrs. Nelson? A. Six of the fourteen have not been there two years.

Q. Six of the fourteen have not been there two years? A. Yes; one has been there about three months; another about four months; and another since the first of January last, and one has come since that.

Q. Out of the six how many had learned the business before they came to the establishment? A. They were all old hands but one.

Q. Then all, with the exception of one amongst the number, have been for some time engaged at broom-making? A. Certainly; we do not put on apprentices when we can hire any other men.

Q. You do not? A. Not if we can get old and good men; we may hire others when hurried with work; we may take on a man during the hurried period, and afterwards discharge him.

Q. Do you think that it is a better policy to pay a good price for a good man than a small price for a poor man? What is your experience on this point? A. It is just according to the kind of work you have to make; if it is first-class fancy work and I wanted a man to do it, I would rather pay a good price.

Q. Don't you find that this principle is a good principle with respect to all kinds of work. A. Yes.

Q. It is better to pay a good price for a good man than a poor price for a poor man? A. Yes; I admit that.

Q. I do not think that you have told us what these twenty-one men and boys could do —their out-put each day? Could you give us that information? A. For the winders?

Q. I want the total? A. The other you can figure up yourself—at so much a week; we pay the winders by the piece; the sizers also; they made about three dollars a week— that is, at the first start.

Q. I want to know how many brooms they turn out a day out of your establishment, and what the total cost of the wages is? Can you give me that? A. I could do it in a very few moments; the winders average about two dollars a day.

Q. How many of them are there? A. There are fourteen of them; taking them on the average that is the case—some run $1.80 and some $2.30.

Q. That makes $28—what do the others get? A. Two receive $8.50 a week.

Q. These two—who are they? A. The bleacher and the buncher; they also do general work—as sorting, and painting, and anything we want them to do.

Q. What do the others receive? A. There are three more who get $2.50 a week.

Q. Well, what do the boys do? A. One of them assists in sorting and all do general work that we have around—any loose work that is to be done.

By Mr. Langmuir.

Q. And sizing? A. Not sizing; they make about $3.00 a week; they cut the hurl and help to sort the corn.

By Mr. Gordon.

Q. What are the others? A. All our sizing is done by the piece.
Q. We have now accounted for nineteen—are the other two sizers? A. There are six engaged in sizing.
Q. I understood you to say that you had fourteen men? A. Fourteen men winding—yes; there is a bleacher and a buncher as well, and four boys besides that; how many does that make?
Q. Four boys besides that at forty-one cents a day—that makes twenty? A. And then there are the sizers; they work by the piece; whatever they do, they are paid for; they make about three dollars a week, and they can earn $3.35.
Q. How many are there of them? A. There are six of them; it is immaterial how many there are; they are paid so much a piece.
Q. They get $3.00 a week? A. About $3.00 a week.

By Mr. Langmuir.

Q. There are fourteen winders, and two bunchers, and four who do general work and six sizers? A. Yes.

By Mr. Gordon.

Q. They get sixty cents a day? A. We do not pay them by the day; that work i done by the piece.

By Mr. Langmuir.

Q. But you say they can make that? A. Yes.

By Mr. Gordon.

Q. What will fourteen winders, two bleachers, four sorters, and six sizers do in a week? A. It is just according to the kind of broom that we put them on; we are averaging now, and we have averaged for the last two or three weeks, from sixty-five to seventy-five dozen brooms a day; last Friday—I recollect it particularly—as I figured it up, the number we made was eighty-eight dozen and a half; but the out-put varies according to the different kinds of brooms that we make; sometimes it is a cheaper broom and sometimes a more expensive one, whatever we may require.
Q. What class of brooms are these you mention? A. They are all kinds, mixed up.
Q. Don't you make so many of each sort? I understand that there are three qualities? A. Three qualities; we have some twenty-eight different kinds of brooms.
Q. Twenty-eight different kinds? A. That is in style; they are all made similarly; there is some little difference in the sewing, and some difference in the winding—a little difference.
Q. Well then, for $33.00 and $35.00 you average between sixty-five and seventy-five dozen a day? A. It is according to the kind of the broom that we are on, sir.
Q. Suppose you had all of the common class, how many would you make of them? A. I could not tell you, sir.
Q. Would you make double? A. Not double.
Q. Not so many as that? A. No.

By Mr. Langmuir.

Q. You said, Mr. Perry, that you were engaged with prison labour for two years? A. Yes, sir.
Q. Well, when you first went into the shop in the prison how long were you in organi-

zing the work to your satisfaction? A. I could not state that exactly, but I had everything going in nice working order in from six weeks to two months.

Q. In from six weeks to two months? A. Yes.

Q. And after you made changes—exchanging old men for young men, with young hands—you did that in six weeks? A. With part of them young hands, I did.

Q. The changes were still going on? A. Yes; at the end of the first year, I had but one old man; I kept him during the whole term.

Q. You consider that the shop was thoroughly organized in two months. A. Yes, sir.

Q. And you closed your connection with the prison in two years? Yes, sir.

Q. For the rest of the time that you were there, from the time of organization, these six weeks, up to the end of the two years, did the prisoners work satisfactorily in your opinion? A. They did.

Q. Well then, in that case does it make any difference whether they are one year men or twenty years men? A. No.

Q. They are just as valuable to you at the end of the six weeks, in either case. A. Certainly.

Q. The short term are just as valuable as if they were twenty years men? A. As far as the twenty years men are concerned, no matter if you closed your work-shop at the end of the year, they would be just as good as the twenty years men—there would be no difference.

Q. The shop was thoroughly organized, and you got as much out of it in two months, from the time of commencing, as at the end of two years? A. Yes, sir; this would be the case at the end of two months, unless one had to put on new men; we had the men changed as fast as we could; I put my full task on the men, I think, at the end of four or five months, I would not say which, and I then got as much work out of them as ever I did. As to fixing the task, I waited until I could see what I thought we ought to have, and then fixed the regular task; there was no bother.

Q. You were then fully organized? A. Only we did not have all the men taken on at the time; we changed some men after that, but only a few; I think there were some two or three that I changed after that, but they learned so quickly, that they were soon right up to the task, and made what was required.

Q. Quite so; and on the whole then, you were organised certainly in three months, and from what you say, you were fully organised at the end of six weeks or two months? A. I think that I took no new hands on after four or five months at the outside; I know that I took none on after six months.

Q. And they were under task before the end of the six months? A. Well, fourteen or fifteen were at the end of two months.

Q. And they turned out as much work before three months were over, as at the end of two years? A. Certainly.

Q. Now, you were asked the question as to whether you had knowledge of what the trades of these prisoners were before they came into the prison, and you said that you had no knowledge of them? A. I had no knowledge of them; I don't recollect of having had any.

Q. Now, if such information was communicated to you, and you had found a broommaker or a brush-maker, or a person possessing skill applicable, or nearly applicable to the trade of broom-making, would you take him on? A. Not unless I had information that he was a good workman.

Q. And if he was a good workman, would you consider it a benefit to know that? A. Yes; certainly.

Q. You speak of having taught outside men and free labourers during the period of apprenticeship; will you tell us what is the amount—the average amount that a young man or men would earn during this period, while the apprenticeship is going on, and the teaching is going on; I allude to raw hands while being learnt. What will they earn during the first six months—say you took five young men into your shop to-morrow, and taught them the broom business, what would be the average daily earnings of these five men per day? About what sum would it be—judging from your experience? A. Oh, they would earn from $1.25 to $1.50 per day.

Q. While being taught the trade? A. While being taught.

Q. You stated a short while ago that you could teach some branches of the trade in six days, or in ten days, and I want an average? A. You mean to do all kinds of work?

Q. I do. Say you take five raw hands—men who have no knowledge of the broom business, and thoroughly instruct them for four months; and that at the end of the four months they are made pretty proficient. What would be the average daily earnings of these men during the whole time they were being instructed by you? Taking the average, would they earn seventy-five cents a day? A. They would earn more than that.

Q. Would they earn a dollar a day? A. Yes.

Q. And they would earn equal to a dollar a day even during the period of instruction? A. Yes, sir.

Q. Well now, if you were asked the question again about the variety of trades, would you put on a certain number of men on ordinary labour, and a certain number on skilled labour? In the broom business, you say that out of twenty one men, you could utilize or use about eight unskilled men to a reasonable advantage. Could you not in a very short time use eight raw men, say in ten days? A. We use more than that now.

Q. That is close upon it; and it is about thirty or forty per cent. of the number you are using in your shop? A. We have six sizers.

Q. You stated that you had two bunchers and four other men doing general work, and six sizers, and that makes twelve? A. Four of the sizers would do work enough, so that I could use—six and four—ten.

Q. You could use ten then? A. Ten with fourteen.

Q. They need not necessarily be experienced men at all? A. If we had the work to do, I could use ten.

Q. That is ten of the twenty-one? A. Ten of the twenty-four.

Q. Ten of the twenty-four might be men undergoing instruction, and some of them might be quite green? A. Yes.

Q. Judging from your knowledge of other things than broom-making—where machinery is used in its perfection, do you think that the average will about hold good? A. With steam machinery, where it is used, it would.

Q. The same number of unskilled men might be engaged? A. With steam machinery?

Q. I am not talking of the broom business now. I take it for granted that you have also a knowledge of brush-making, and other trades, and bringing your knowledge to bear on this point, do you think that the same number of men, that is ten out of the twenty-four in other trades, need not be skilled men, when they are required to work machinery in its perfection? We will take the pail and tub business for instance? A. I should judge that they might be—nearly or quite that number might be; I could not state exactly, because I do not know.

Q. You have no knowledge on that point? A. In all trades a great deal of work can be done by common labour.

Q. And, of course, that state of things is increased by the employment of machinery? A. That is increased by machinery.

Q. And the greater perfection to which machinery is brought, the less work there is for real skilled labour? A. Certainly; at the time I learned this same trade, I learned it with a roller under my foot; and it took me three months before I could get wages; I can now learn a man to make as good a broom as I learned to make in nearly three months, or as good a one as I made in two months, in two days; you had then to do everything with the hands and feet; and now there is machinery to do it all; the work is all done by machinery; it only wants a little watching and a little practice.

Q. You were asked a question about the giving of rewards or rather allowing men to work over-time, and receive money for it—now who paid that money? The contractors in every case? A. Yes; we paid it, that is we paid what they earned; we did not always keep it.

Q. You kept it for the benefit of the prisoners? A. We kept it sometimes, and sometimes we gave it to the head keeper to keep for them.

Q. But it came from the contractors? A. It came from the contractors—yes; and sometimes we kept it, and sometimes the head keeper kept it.

Q. Did you ever know of a case where the authorities of the prison paid for extra time in that way? A. No, sir—never.

Q. It was always paid by the contractors? A. Always by the contractors; I asked for that privilege.

Q. And you believe it to be a good one? A. Yes.

Q. And you would ask for it again? A. Certainly—most assuredly.

Q. For instance, where the men were tasked as to the labour they were to perform, you tasked them? A. Yes.

Q. As foreman for the contractors? A. Yes, sir.

Q. And for instance, if they did not work up to the task which they had to do, had you the power to punish them? A. No, sir.

Q. You could not punish? A. No, sir.

Q. That was left entirely in the hands of the prison authorities? A. Yes, sir.

Q. Well then, you were giving the cost just now of what twenty-six men in your factory at Montreal—14 winders at $2 a day; 2 bunchers at $1.41 a day; 4 others at $1.41 a day; and 6 at about fifty cents a day; altogether, about $35 a day—now what do you consider to be the best, judging from your knowledge of prison labour: twenty-six persons employed at the rate of fifty cents a day, taking them as they come, raw men and all, or twenty-six freemen, as in Montreal, costing thirty-five dollars a day: which do you consider to be the most desirable? A. I would take the prisoners.

Q. As by far the most profitable? A. Yes.

Q. How much do you think the advantage would be, judging from your knowledge of the broom business? A. I would get it as cheap as I could.

Q. I quite understand that, but which do you consider preferable, the twenty-six free men for whom you are paying $35 a day, or the twenty-six prisoners, for whom you would pay $13 a day? Would you rather give as high as twenty dollars a day for the prisoners than thirty-five dollars to the free men? A. I think I would—would give eighteen to twenty dollars.

BY MR. GORDON.

Q. Would you be prepared to take the contract off the Car Company's hands, if they were to hand it over to you? A. If I had the money to do it with, I would.

Q. It would not require very much money? A. If I was starting and going to carry on business, I would not like anything better.

Q. They would make an immediate return? A. Yes, but to obtain an immediate return you must have capital to start with. I think that broom manufacturers are subject to the same regulations as all other trades, and they have to give from four or six months' time.

Q. As to prison labour in New Jersey, you say that you established the system of paying for over-time work? A. Certainly, I asked for it and my request was granted.

Q. Did you try prison labour without that inducement? A. I did at first. Of course we had to do it then, because I was not prepared to do it until I got started.

Q. Did you find a material difference in the turn-out at that time? A. Some men did less and some did more. Some men did their work, but all did not do their work.

Q. Well now, suppose that the men did not accomplish their task, I presume that you came to a determination as to what they should do—what they could do, and what you thought they ought to do, to enable you to earn the wages which you paid? A. We did not view it simply as a question of earning wages; we calculated to make some money.

Q. A sum of money additional? A. Yes, sir.

Q. I suppose they did not make up the task required? A. Then they had to make it.

Q. The task was what you thought they ought to do? A. If the authorities found out that I did not task the men too heavily, they would have to do it.

BY MR. HARDY.

Q. What was the alternative? A. Punishment.

BY MR. GORDON.

Q. Suppose that the men would not do their work, was it made up to the contractors in any way? A. No, sir, the men would be ordered to do it.

Q. Would they be ordered to make the work up by working extra time? A. I suppose they would be punished; but I never had a man under my charge punished.

Q. But that would not be of any benefit to the contractors, except the work was made up to them, say the next day. Suppose that on Monday a man would not do his task, that he was punished, and that on Tuesday he did his task properly, what compensation would be made to the contractor for the deficiency on Monday; would any be made? A. Nothing of the kind occurred. We had no case of that kind.

Q. They always did their task? A. They always did it; and no one complained of the task, save one man.

Q. Was there anything in your contract with the Government whereby the men could be obliged to do it? A. I could not answer that question as I do not know what the contract was.

Q. Now, you also state, that of these old men who were employed before you took the contract, you only retained one. I think you said that? A. I only retained one of them after the first year elapsed.

Q. What objection did you have to these men? A. I had no objection at first, only the thought struck me that they had been used to tying as it had previously been done there, and not having had very good instruction, they might perhaps bother me, and rather than have any bother with them, knowing that I could learn a man so quickly as this instruction can be given, I chose to take my chances with new men and learn them the work. I had it stipulated that I might change the old men provided that I chose to do so.

Q. Did you find that the men did not do the amount of work which the new men performed? A. The old men.

Q. Yes. A. One or two of them did their task; there was one man who died.

Q. And what about the others? A. The others did not do their task.

Q. How did you account for that? A. Part of them did not do their work; and I felt that I was not going to get the task out of these men as easily as I could out of new men, and accordingly I changed them as fast as I had the chance to do so.

Q. Can you account for the fact that the old men did not do their task, while the new men did their's? A. I can account for it in no other way than this—this is only my opinion however—that they had not been properly looked after, and that they had been accustomed to do whatever they felt disposed to do.

Q. And this was before you were there to look after them? A. Yes; when I got there a man did what I told him to do.

Q. The men had got into bad habits and you could not get such out of them? A. Yes; in that department it was the case. They got into bad habits owing to the fact that a task had not been put on them.

Q. But you were very stringent, and you seem to have obtained a tremendous amount of work out of the new men? A. I was not there when the old men were worked.

Q. They were worked by other parties? A. The old men I am speaking of had been worked by other parties, and not by myself. I had the old men under my charge when I first went on, and then I commenced to change.

Q. How was it that you did not estimate a task for the old men when you first went on? You had no tasks set for several months, had you? A. I had one of the old men for the full term, and the rest were new men.

Q. But you did not change them all for three or four months? A. I changed them as fast as I could do so, satisfactorily.

By Mr. Hardy.

Q. You gave up the contract at the end of two years—had you lost or made money up to that time? A. We made money.

Q. You gave it up on account of the war? A. Yes, sir.

Q. It was a question of calculation on whether the war would continue or not? A. Yes, sir.

Q. If it continued, you did not think that you could carry on the work with advantage? A. I did not think that we could work with advantage. It was all left with me, and I wrote him that I thought that the war would be a long one. The consequence was I did not think we could do anything even if we got the labour for nothing, and my advice to him was to give it up.

Q. I believe this was the case for the first two or three years? A. During the first couple of years we would not have done anything; but we could have made money after that.

BY MR. GORDON.

Q. Wages went up during the war? A. Yes.

Q. And you did not think of that, when you could have secured the contract for another five years? A. I do not know whether I thought of it or not. One could hardly tell what the country was coming to.

BY THE CHAIRMAN.

Q. How many divisions have you in your labour in the manufacture of brooms in the establishment where you now are? A. I will commence from the first to enumerate them.

Q. If you please. A. The first work which we do after we get the corn into the building is to size it. We size it into different lengths, and then it is thrown into the vaults and tied up. The next process is to bleach it, and after being bleached—it is put in at night and taken out in the morning—it is sorted. It is all sorted to separate what is to be put on the outside of the broom, from that which is to be placed on the inside of the broom. The next work done is the winding, or rather there is a work that comes between these—the cutting of the hurl, the same thing as sorting. We take the inside of the stalk and place it on the outside in making the hurl and fancy brooms, putting the rough, outside corn on the inside of the broom. Then comes the winding, and then the sewing; then the clipping and scraping, which is done by the winder and the sewer. When our winders are done winding, they sew and clip and scrape, and then the broom is ready for bunching, and for being taken down stairs and placed in charge of the shipper.

Q. That is done by one man? A. That is done by one man, although in the States, and generally, I think, it is done by two men, one doing the winding and the other the sewing; the old-fashioned way was for the winder to do both, and the men prefer it. They think that it is easier for them to tie for half a day, and then sew for half a day; they think that it straightens them up; but in the States we cannot get our men to do both, save very seldom. They would rather do all winding or all sewing.

Q. Is there any other department after that? A. There is nothing to be done after they are bunched and sent down stairs as they are wanted.

Q. There is a man employed for bunching? A. Oh, yes—for bunching and putting on labels and piling them up, so that they will not mould in this warm weather.

Q. Now, can you tell us what price you pay apiece for each different department's labour? A. Oh, yes. The men are all paid—the winders—so much apiece, according to the different kind of brooms that they make, for there are quite a number of different kinds of brooms. The prices paid for them vary, and men vary in the amount of labour that they do.

Q. In the first place, then, if you take a common broom, how much do you pay apiece, commencing with the first process? You pay by the piece all through, I understand? A. Oh, no; the sizing is done by the piece.

Q. You say that the sizing, the first process, is done by the piece? A. Yes.

Q. How much is paid apiece? A. It costs for the sizing about one-sixth of a cent a broom per pound.

Q. Well, then for the next process, do you pay by the piece? A. For the bleaching? No, that is done by the month.

Q. By the month? A. Yes, sir.

Q. What do you pay the man that does that? A. We pay him $8.50 a week.

Q. Well, now what is the next process? A. The next process is the sorting; the same man does that work.

Q. The same man? A. Yes; you see the bleaching only takes a little time at night—a couple of hours; he also does sorting and varnishes handles, and anything that is to be done in outside work: there is always plenty of outside work to do; we keep about ten out of twenty-four men doing outside work,—outside the winding and sewing. This is the mechanical part of the work, the rest is not mechanical.

6

Q. Well, then, what is the next process you mention ? A. Cutting the hurl,—that is done by boys.
Q. Is that done by boys paid by the week ? A. Yes, sir.
Q. How much do you pay them a week ? A. We pay them $2.50.
Q. You stated that before ? A. Yes, sir.
Q. Well, then, the next process ? A. The next process is winding.
Q. How is that paid ? A. By the piece.
Q. How much apiece ? A. It is according to the different kind of brooms which are made ; the prices run from a cent and a quarter to six cents and a half.
Q. From one and one quarter cents to six cents and a half ? A. Yes, sir ; there is only one kind made at the latter price.

By Mr. Brockway.

Q. That is the price paid per dozen ? A. No, for each broom ; we make only very few of the six cent and a half kind, once in a while we turn out a few dozen ; I am just mentioning the two extremes ; the most that is made of any one number or kind, is the one and a quarter cent broom, that is the cheaper broom.
Q. Then are a certain number considered a regular day's work ? A. We regulate the day's work as we want brooms ; sometimes we allow them to make one day, and sometimes two days, and sometimes half a day, and sometimes all they can make in the ten hours. They have sometimes worked from half-past five to half-past seven.
Q. Is there no limit ? A. It is all done by the piece. There is no limit. We just limit them as we want the brooms. They are making now full time.
Q. And how many do they make when on full time ? A. It varies according to the different kinds of brooms that they make. I can tell you the amount of money earned and the different prices we pay for different kind of brooms. When working for ten hours, the men will make on the average about $2.00 a-day. Some will make $1.80 a-day.

By Mr. Gordon

Q. On any class of broom ? A. On every class of broom.

By the Chairman.

Q. The prices you state here—were they the estimates you made on the value of the prison labour you employed, or were they based on the same prices by the piece which you are now paying ? A. Yes ; I based them on the prices they were paying outside at that time, before I went into the prison.
Q. Were they the same, as are now paid ? A. We are making only one of the kind that we made then, and, as I stated before that would cost us at ninety cents a day in the prison. I think that was the rate, $1.35 outside ; and to-day, that work would cost us $1.46¼ I think this same broom is one of the kind which we make to-day. Every shop differs a little in the make of the brooms, and consequently the prices differ. There are hardly any two shops that make brooms just alike ; one will put a little more sewing on ; some make a longer, and some a shorter broom, and another will put a little more braid on the broom. There is always more or less expense incurred in the manufacture of these different brooms. There are hardly two shops where they make them just alike. but they do not vary a great deal as to the amount earned by the men. This varies all over a little, but not enough to make any particular difference.
Q. Can you remember at what amount you fixed the task for these men in the different departments employing prison labour ? A. In the prison ?
Q. Yes. A. There was one kind of broom we tied there, regarding which one man tied and another sewed. We divided the work there, but here we do not divide it. In the winding of one class of broom, I gave eighty for a day's work. The winding of that class of broom would cost $1.40 outside. It was what we call a long braided and corded broom. I have not seen any of them in Canada. What we call long braided, they make

short braided—the common broom made there. Eighty was the day's work for these and some of the men made over work at that, a good deal of the time.

Q. Can you give any of the other tasks that you gave? A. And then there was the hurl broom, I gave of them ninety a day as the task. I think that this was the number. That would then cost us $1.35 a day outside, and now it would cost us $1.46 a day.

Q. For that number, for that task? A. The number I gave them to make would cost that much outside; then as for the sewing, I gave one hundred three strung brooms to be sewed round by the picket machine. We have what is called a "Yankee press," a square-shouldered press, a round-shouldered press, and a picket press; the brooms were sewed with what we call a picket press, and they were sewed three times. That work would cost us $1.25 outside; we paid fifty cents a day for the first string, and for every every extra string three York shillings, making ten York shillings, or $1.25. For one kind of broom, which was sewed a little heavier, I gave $1.50 a day.

Q. These prisoners had been employed, I understood you to say, on the same kind of work that had been carried on there? A. On the same kind of work? Yes, sir.

Q. Had it been the practice to pay them for overwork previously? A. I could not tell you that; the prison authorities worked them themselves, I think.

Q. Did the giving of this inducement, and the payment for overwork after they had done their task, have an important effect? A. I think that it stimulated the others to keep up their task without any trouble; as I said before, I had no trouble with the men while I was there; I did not have a man punished; I had no trouble except with one man, and he was one of the old men. As I went into the prison one morning, Mr. Stollwell, the head keeper, said to me, "One of the men says that the task is a little too heavy for him." I said, "Very well, Stollwell, I only ask one thing of you, and that is, for you to go a certain cell"—naming the number—" and ask those prisoners how they like me, and whether the task is too much, or any question you choose to ask, and if you find out by inquiry of them, or of any of the rest of the prisoners, that they say the task is too much for them, I will take it off." He went out, and I stood where the prisoners could not see me, and I heard him ask a number of questions as how they liked the foreman, and how they liked the work, and whether the task was too much, and whether they could do it, &c. He asked a number of questions, which I do not exactly remember, and they stated they were perfectly satisfied with it, and that they had no fault to find. They said they were allowed to make over-work, and got paid for it at the same price that we paid the prison authorities for their labour. When he had satisfied himself there, I opened the other cell, and he went in and asked this prisoner a number of questions regarding the work, &c., and the fault he had to find, and then told him what the other prisoners had said to him. He told the man that he must do his task, and that he certainly could do it, for if the new hands could do it, the old hands could also. The man was ordered to do his task.

E. B. EDDY, called on behalf of the Government, sworn and examined:

BY MR. HARDY.

Q. What is your business? A. Lumber manufacturer.
Q. What kind of implements and instruments do you manufacture? A. Wooden ware and matches, sashes and doors.
Q. Pails? A. Yes.
Q. Tubs? A. Yes.
Q. Washboards? A. Yes.

BY MR. BROCKWAY.

Q. At what place? A. Hull, opposite Ottawa.

BY MR. HARDY.

Q. That is in the Province of Quebec? A. Yes.
Q. About across from Ottawa? A. Yes.
Q. You have been engaged in that business for some time? A. For 25 years.

Q. Speaking with regard to tubs, pails, and washboards, and wheelbarrows—do you make wheelbarrows? A. No; nothing but wooden ware.

Q. Speaking with regard to tubs, pails, and washboards, does it require skilled labour to carry on that trade? A. Some portions of it.

Q. What proportion of the whole? A. Finishers, head turners and head painters.

Q. The work is done by machinery? A. It is done by machinery largely.

Q. How many men are there to a machine? A. That is according to the expertness of the man at the head of the lathe; some can run more than others—2, 4 and 8.

Q. At one lathe A. Yes.

Q. Is there only one man at a lathe—the head man—who requires to be an expert? A. One man will take charge of two lathes, sometimes three.

Q. How many of the four, six or eight men require to be skilled men—more than one? A. More than one at the first instance—at the first commencement; I get from your questions that you are speaking about prison labour—unskilled men, green men; you put on eight or ten green men and you would require more than one skilled man for the first ten days, but after you have ran them thirty days, one skilled man will run eight.

Q. What do you desire that we should understand by the use of the phrase one skilled man; must he be a man who has had long experience and served an apprenticeship? A. A man who has served his apprenticeship and been accustomed to turning out pails for years; it is a regular trade.

Q. Taking the mixed character of the men, coopers, machinists, blacksmiths, &c., such as is found in prison, with a foreman who is a skilled man in the business, how long would it take the prisoners to learn the business, turning and all? A. To become an expert turner and finisher would take some little time; but a man can soon learn to turn a lathe, and do as much work as the turner himself in the different stages, from the commencement to the finish; he can learn to butt as many staves in a week as a man who had been working at it for ten years, if there is any sharpness to him at all.

Q. What other branch does he require to learn? A. He has to edge them, butt them, and make them, and set them in a hoop; a green man, who has never seen a pail before, can in five minutes learn to set up a pail, ready to put on the hoops.

Q. The work can be taken up very easily? A. Largely so.

Q. In a few days? A. Largely so. The way we run our works is to have one skilled man to five or eight unskilled men; our labour is similar to the prison labour: that is, we take the common French Canadian, a green man, and we put him in with a gang of five, six or seven others; they are overlooked, and worked by a skilled man, and they do immediately—within one week—about half the work of the old turner; that is just about what it is.

Q. What do you pay these men per day? A. They cannot keep their lathe in order, but they will perform the necessary butting, edging, and setting up.

Q. How do you operate to keep the lathe in order? Does the head man do that? A. Yes.

Q. What do you pay these common men? A. From $1 to $1.10 per day.

Q. And what do you pay the head men? A. From $1.50 to $1.75; sometimes $2. Sometimes they work by piece and furnish their own strikers.

By Mr. Gordon.

Q. What do you mean by that? A. Green men.

Q. They furnish their own green men? A. Sometimes they do.

By Mr. Hardy.

Q. Then the class of men you introduce into your factory are very largely composed of common labourers? A. Yes.

Q. They are not mechanics or skilled in any way? A. Common labourers as a rule.

Q. I understand it requires one skilled man to six or eight unskilled? A. To every five or eight. I am speaking now of when they first commence. As you heard Mr. Perry explain, one man can look after a great many more men after they have got fairly started; I am speaking now of it at the worst stage.

Q. Judging from your large and wide experience in manufacturing of this kind where you employ men, paying $1 or $1.10 to common labourers, and $1.50 or $1.80 to skilled men, would you consider 60cts. per day too high a price to pay for prison labour? A. I would say—as I have always said when talking about it—that prison labour here is worth from 75cts. to 80cts a day; if you will give me the prison labour, and bring it to me, I will pay that and consider I get it very cheap; that is, I mean to say that no free labour can compete with prison labour in the manufacturing of my goods at 75cts. a day; that is at the rate of wages for the last two years.

Q. That is, that free labour, with the wages you have to pay, cannot compete with prison labour even at 75c. or 80c. a day? A. No, sir.

Q. Now, as to the prison here—perhaps you have not been through it? A. I have not. I have been refused admittance. I should have liked to have gone through, but I was not admitted.

BY MR. LANGMUIR.

Q. To whom did you apply? A. I applied to the Clerk at the gaol, and he sent for Mr. Warren, who sent out word that I was not to be admitted.

BY MR. HARDY.

Q. The machinery furnished there consists of all the steam boilers, engines, shafting pulleys, very elaborate; fuel for heating premises, very large shops, water and light; all these are furnished together with exemption from taxation. That would increase the value of the men considerably? A. Yes, it would to me.

Q. Are you able to say how many men are engaged in the tub, pail, and washboard branch in your factory? From 60 to 75; some are boys.

Q. Could you tell me what proportion of your capital per annum would be represented in providing engines, pulleys, shafting, and those things I have mentioned, in your branch with 60 men? Do you make brushes and brooms? A. No.

Q. Sashes and doors? A. Yes. Each department is entirely to itself. The pail and tub factory, and the match factory. Each stands alone.

Q. How many are employed in manufacturing matches? A. Six or seven hundred.

Q. Manufacturing matches? A. Yes, and the boxes.

Q. Men? A. No, hands; altogether children.

Q. Take the machinery, engines and boilers, shafting and pulleys, buildings, shop-room, work-room, railway branches running in connection with all the railways of the province, drying kiln—what fair percentage per annum would be allowed upon the outlay for the erection of such works. Or you may take the shops by themselves, and then take the machines by themselves, subject to wear and tear? A. As I have never been through the works, I am not capable of judging what the works are worth and what the per centage would be. At my own works the building for the manufacture of pails and tubs is worth from $2,000 to $2,400 per annum rent.

Q. You use water power? A. Yes.

Q. What per centage should be allowed for the use of machinery, engines and boilers, per annum? A. I don't know; I am not a steam man.

Q. You represent that your building for pails and tubs for 60 men is worth $2,400 per annum? A. Yes. Of course, our pail and tubbuilding and power is a very small portion of our works.

Q. What proportion of boys do you employ in the manufacture of tubs and pails—boys under 16 years? A. Very few. We don't have many boys employed in turning out pails; there is only a small proportion of boys in the turning shop. Perhaps there is one boy to a lathe; I could not tell the per centage.

Q. Do you make agricultural implements? A. No.

Q. Can green men more readily pick up, learn, and adapt themselves to the manufacture of pails and tubs and that kind of goods, than to the manufacture of agricultural implements? A. I should judge so, although I have never been in an agricultural machinery manufactory still I should judge so by the look of the machines.

Commission adjourned until 9.30 o'clock to-morrow.

WEDNESDAY, July 11th.

The Commission met at 9:30 a. m.

E. B. EDDY continued his evidence.

BY MR. GORDON.

Q. I think you said yesterday that you were in the pail and tub business, or at least the pail business, at Hull? A. Yes.
Q. You are a competitor with the Canada Car Company in business? A. I am their competitor or they are mine. I don't know which you may call it.
Q. I think you have lately signed a petition to the Government with regard to this matter, have you not? A. I did, sir.
Q. To the effect that this prison labour was injurious to those working with free labour —that is the effect of the petition, is it not? A. We do not object to prison labour; we were objecting to prison labour if obtained for nothing.
Q. You thought it was an improper thing for the Government to allow the prison labour to come into competition with your business? A. Not at a fair price.
Q. Well, you have signed a petition to the Government to that effect, have you not? A. No; I did not consider it that way.
Q. What did you consider it? A. We considered they were giving the labour for less than it was actually worth, and that it was not fair to give labour to joint-stock companies at an under valuation, to compete with free labour.
Q. Is not the gist of your petition, that it is unfair of the Government to use prison labour to compete with free labour? There is no question as to price? A. I am ready to compete with any kind of labour at a fair valuation.
Q. There is nothing about the price in your petition, is there? A. I am not positive, but I think there is; that was the impression, and the expectation, and the understanding that petition was based upon.
Q. You and others have presented a petition to the Government, requesting them to discontinue the leasing of prison labour to companies or private individuals, so as to compete in your business? A. I do not think so. I think the petition asks that the price of labour shall not be reduced to the Canada Car Company.
Q. Were you subpœnaed to come to give evidence here? A. No.
Q. You volunteered your evidence? A. No.
Q. How did you come if you were not asked to give it? A. I understood they were holding a Commission here to take evidence, and that very likely I should receive a subpœna when I got home; I was passing through the town and did not wish to come back again, and so I thought I would not lose the time.
Q. Mr. Langmuir did not send for you? A. Not that I am aware of.
Q. You came up to Toronto of your own accord? A. I sent a gentleman to Mr. Langmuir, to say I was here, and to see if I was required.
Q. To see if your evidence would be useful to the Government? A. No; to see if I would be required.
Q. You have no particular good-will towards the Car Company, have you? A. Yes; the best of good-will towards them, in a business point of view.
Q. A little prejudice against them? A. Not at all.
Q. Probably we will be able to judge of that? A. Perfectly friendly.
Q. You told us yesterday you employed between 60 and 75 men and boys in your pail business at Hull? A. I should judge we did; I could not say positively to a man or two.
Q. Could you tell what proportion of men to boys? A. I could not.
Q. Have you any idea? A. No.
Q. No idea at all? A. I think I said yesterday we worked in a boy or so at the lathe, and some of the boys are used in making pails and so on, but I could not say the proportion.
Q. Could you tell us whether there are 20 or 25 boys? A. No; I said I could not give the proportion; if I said 25, you would have the proportion.

Q. We want to know as near as you can tell us? A. It is no use answering the question unless I could give the percentage.
Q. Is your knowledge so slight that you cannot say whether you employ five boys or 25? A. Yes, because a man employing so many people cannot say how many boys there are in this business.
Q. Your knowledge is so slight that you cannot tell whether you have five or 25 boys; can you tell me how many lathes you have in your establishment? A. Pail lathes?
Q. Yes. A. I think I have 13 altogether.
Q. How many hands are employed upon each lathe? A. These lathes do not run all the time.
Q. But when they are running? A. You can employ all the way from two to eight.
Q. When you are running full time, how many do you employ? A. Sometimes when we are running full time, some lathes have two, some three, some four, some five, and some six; I cannot say exactly how many there are when we run full time.
Q. At the present time how many would be employed on each of these lathes? A. We are running now, I think, about 1,000 or 1,200 pails a day.
Q. How many men and boys are employed on each lathe to turn out that? A. I do not know how many lathes we are running now.

MR. HARDY.—He explained yesterday that something would depend on the expertness of the men.

MR. GORDON.—I presume he knows a good deal about it, and I cannot understand why he should not give us the information. It gives me the impression that he would be glad to give all the evidence unfavourable to the Company.

WITNESS.—Not at all; anything I state here I can establish; I am not here in opposition to the Canada Car Company or any other, whether private or a joint stock company. All I think is it is very unfair for them to have labour for nothing to compete with persons who have to employ free labour.

Q. You are turning out how many pails at the present moment? A. 1,000 to 1,200.
Q. With 60 to 75 men? A. I would not say we had so many men now; I think the question yesterday was how many men we generally employed in the pail factory.
Q. How many have you now? A. I cannot say; we have a capacity of 4,000 to 5,000 pails a day; we have a capacity for drowning the Dominion as far as pails and tubs are concerned.
Q. How many pails would a lathe with eight men and boys on it turn out in a day? A. It would depend on how many strikers were working with the expert man; two expert men would turn from 240 to 300 pails a day.
Q. And how many boys? A. I am merely speaking of two expert hands.
Q. On one lathe? A. Two expert hands on one lathe will turn from 240 to 300 pails a day; it depends altogether on your timber.
Q. And these expert men get from $1.50 to $1.75 a day? A. Yes; from that to $2.00.
Q. Supposing you had eight men and boys on that lathe, how many would they turn out? A. That would depend upon how many experts you had.
Q. With two experts? A. One is about all you want on a lathe.
Q. Take one expert? A. Take two green strikers and one expert, and they will, as a rule, turn out fully as much as two experts.
Q. That is between 240 and 300 pails a day? A. Yes.
Q. The green men you would pay from $1 to $1.10? A. Yes, to the green strikers, that is common labouring men; sometimes we have got them for 90c., but as a rule for the last four or five years we have paid what I have said.
Q. Supposing you had six men working there,—one an expert? A. They would turn out about the same proportion; he can handle four or five or six strikers just as well as two.
Q. How many would they turn out? A. The strikers will turn out fully half what the experts will do.
Q. Take five green men and one expert on one lathe, how many would they turn out a day? A. They ought to turn out from 450 to 500 pails,—all the way from 425 to 500.
Q. Now do you ever run two lathes with one expert to the two? A. Yes.
Q. Green men on the two machines and one expert to supervise them? A. Yes.
Q. How many would they turn out then on one lathe, take the case of two green men?

A. We are speaking of green strikers, taking it in its worst form. Take these prisoners coming in every day or every week, who will commonly work ten or fifteen days; as a rule, the green man will turn out half as much as the expert; in a month he will do more.

Q. Will he do half the first day? A. In about ten days, that is if he has any gumption about him at all; running on for four, five, or six months, he will get to be as good at turning as an expert, that is as to turning the pails, only they cannot keep the machine in order; it is quite a trade to keep a pail machine in order; that is what an expert is for.

Q. Have you ever worked a machine with only green men on it, and an expert only supervising four or five different machines? A. I have; and I have worked with two experts and no green men.

Q. How many is the greatest number of machines you have run with only one expert? A. I could not answer.

Q. As many as four? A. I would not be surprised, but perhaps not more than three; a great many of our men work by the piece.

Q. As a rule, do you have one man to one machine? A. We are working now by the piece; one man runs three or four machines with strikers.

BY MR. HARDY.

Q. One expert? A. Yes.

BY MR. GORDON.

Q. How many strikers would he have under him? A. Six or eight.

Q. Over the three machines or on each machine? A. He can scatter them over three or have them on two or only one; if we had all experts in our shop, and found our orders coming in faster than we could supply, I should say, "You must put on some green men;" You can increase or decrease as you like when you have these strikers.

Q. As a rule one expert has six strikers under him? A. He can work all the way from that or even more.

Q. What is the rule? A. There is no rule about it; it is just according to a man's ability in taking care of a machine.

Q. Surely you know the ordinary state of things in your establishment? A. I have men who could not look over five; I could look over forty just as well.

Q. Have you known a case where a man has looked over forty? A. No, I do not think I have.

Q. Or twenty? A. That I could not answer, because we have men there sometimes running half of our turners in the shop; I do not think that has anything particularly to do with this.

Mr. GORDON.—I want to understand how you carry on your business—how many experts you have to the green men.

Mr. HARDY.—You assume that Mr. Eddy ought to have all the details which his foreman would have.

WITNESS.—The sum and substance of it is to know whether people can make with this labour here goods cheaper at 50cts. a day than we can who pay more.

Q. Have you had any experience in prison labour? A. No; I have had green labour, which is the same thing.

Q. Is it the same? A. I don't know why it is not.

Q Are these men disabled physically and constitutionally by their previous habits? A. Well, prisoners are not disabled, are they?

Q. I do not say they come there with one hand or one eye, but I suppose these prisoners, these loafers about the streets, who get in there from their dissolute habits are not the same men as these strikers? A. I think they are something similar; of course they will do all the work they are obliged to do; we put them into the saw-mills and they are obliged to keep the saws busy; the machines run the men, instead of the men running machines.

Q. You employ French Canadian labour? A. Largely.

Q. Do you find they readily acquire the art of making these things? A. I don't know whether they are quicker than any one else, but we live in a French locality, and take what we can get. I think English-speaking people are more expert.

Q. What is the average length of time these men stay with you ? A. It is hard to say. They are very impatient. A month or two months. They are travelling birds.
Q. Among the sixty or seventy men, how many changes would there be in six months ? A. A good many.
Q. How many ? A. I could not say.
Q. Twenty per cent. ? A. I could not say how many would be dropping off. They are dropping off a good deal, but I could not come down to twenty per cent. or ten per cent. I say pail turners are a very unsteady lot of men.
Q. Have you lately reduced your prices on pails and tubs—prices of selling ? A. A very small percentage.
Q. When did you last reduce them ? A. On the 1st or 2nd of July.
Q. And before that ? A. I don't think we have had any reduction since last Fall. I cannot tell you exactly the day.
Q. How many times, and how much, have they been reduced within the last year ? A. I do not think there has been any reduction but twice in the past year, and that is very small.
Q. How much did these two reductions amount to in all ? A. Ten cents a dozen, I think. The last was ten cents, and I think the one before was ten cents, but I am not sure.
Q. It amounted to twenty cents then ? A. I think so.
Q. How do your selling prices compare with the Canada Car Company's prices ? A. I do not know. I believe they have been selling at our prices. I understand so.
Q. Then you have no complaint against the Company in consequence of their underselling you ? A. They have undersold us. That is the first cause of the reduction in the prices. Of course, it was not altogether their reduction. We have competitors on the other side that we have to take care of.
Q. Can you give us a case when the Car Company undersold you ? A. Well, they were running about town here.
Q. That is a general statement. You make general statements—are they founded on anything ? Do you know an instance ? A. I am, of course, a wholesale manufacturer, and sell 100 dozen or 500 dozen lots in carloads. They know my prices in carloads, and give prices in small quantities, which is jobbing. Because they could not get all the trade they required, they have gone to taking the small trade, and sell five or ten dozen pails at the same price at which I sell 500 dozen.
Q. Tell us a case where that happened ? A. I only know parties tell me so.
Q. Who ? A. Mr. Fitzgerald, of St. Catharines, says he can buy five dozen pails from the Canada Car Company as cheaply as he can buy a carload from me.
Q. Have you any other case ? A. Not specially.
Q. You know of no other case ? A. I know of many but not the names ; but I have heard people make this remark to me by hundreds.
Q. Can you give me the name of any other ? A. No.
Q. You have reduced your prices twice within the last year ? A. Yes.

BY THE CHAIRMAN

Q. Do you pay your men engaged in this particular manufacture by the piece or by the day ? A. We have paid them by both, but generally by the piece. Parties will take one or two or three lathes to run, as the case may be.
Q. Would the one man undertake that, and supply his own assistants ? A. Certainly. He furnishes his own strikers. He pays from $1 to $1.10 a day, and gets his profit on it, of course.
Q. When you speak of three men or five upon a lathe, what are they severally engaged in—not all in the turning ? A. You can work six or seven or eight men on a lathe if a man can stand it.
Q. And each man engaged in turning ? A. No, but there are different processes to go through on the same machine. You commence at one part to go all round, bitting and edging, and matching and setting up, putting on the spindle, taking them off, turning out the inside, and so on. They just move right round that table. Two men can work, or four men, or five or six or seven.

Q. You must at all times have one man who is expert in keeping his machine in order and understands it? A. Oh! yes.

Q. What is the average result obtained from the labour of green hands compared with those who are expert? A. The green hands who have not worked more than ten or twelve days count at about half what the expert hands do, and of course the longer they work the more they do. In three or four months, they will do two-thirds or three-fourths and almost as much as the expert himself in the manual labour, though not in keeping the machine in order.

Q. A good deal depends on the facility with which they manipulate? A. Yes. The machines run the men; not the men the machines. Mr. Hardy was asking me yesterday what I considered the labour of a green hand was worth. I merely based it on the worst side. Take two green men out of the street and put one expert and he will make those two men earn as much as he himself. Are they not worth seventy-five or eighty cents a day when he is worth $1 70 or $1 75? A joint-stock company getting labour much below the value, and competing with our domestic manufactures, injures us very much. I do not object to the Canada Car Company if they pay a fair sum for their labour in proportion—even half, though I think it is worth more. If the Government of Ontario is to run a pail and broom factory, they will wipe out all the small manufacturers in the country.

Q. Have you had any employment of prison labour? A. No, but I judge by a green man off the street; old countrymen come in there sometimes, and do not know any more about a pail lathe than the prisoners, but in eight or ten days they will earn as I have stated before; then this company have all the plant furnished beside the labour, they have a monopoly.

BY MR. BROCKWAY.

Q. What proportion of the cost of a dozen pails is labour? What percentage? A. I would not like to answer that, as far as my private business is concerned.

Q. You say you are not running your factory to its full capacity? A. No.

Q. Half? A. No, we have not been able to.

Q. Your business now is in what proportion of the capacity of your factory? A. About 25 per cent.

Q. Could you increase your business if you were to sell pails for less money? A. No not at all times, because people throughout the country are selling pails below cost, because too many are made for the demand.

Q. Could you run your factory to its full capacity if you sold at less than cost? A. No; I have run to the extent of 4,000 pails a day; there are not so many pails sold in the present depressed state of the country; we are only running 1,000 to 1,200 a day.

Q. Then the slowing up of your factory is owing to the general depression, not to competition? A. To competition as well as the depression; I have not reduced my pails particularly on account of the Canada Car Company until very lately.

Q. Do you know why Americans can put in pails at less prices than you can make them for? A. Yes.

Q. Why? A. Because if I had a door open on the other side of the lakes, I would run my shop up to the full capacity of 5,000 pails a day; if I could only sell 3000 in Canada, I would put the rest at a reduction of 4 per cent. on what they cost me on the American market, in order to get them out of my market, because you can run 5,000 cheaper than 3,000 and it is on that principle that the Americans come here.

Q. Do they get labour cheaper than you do? A. No, I don't think as cheap.

Q. It is, then, because they have a larger market? A. Yes; of course 40 millions are more than four, and they have a surplus they do not want in their own country and send it into Canada.

BY THE CHAIRMAN.

Q. Would it not be a more profitable operation for the American manufacturer, saying he makes 5,000 pails a day, and his market only absorbs 3,000, to reduce his manufacture to 3,000, than to sell the surplus at a loss? A. Not at a loss of three or four per cent.; by that three or four per cent. loss on the surplus, he would make ten per cent. profit on the others; the fact is, the people round here do not know what pails cost; they are selling goods for less than cost.

By Mr. Brockway.

Q. This Canada Car Company ? A. Yes ; they are selling at less than ;cost and have been losing money every day since they started.

By Mr. Gordon.

Q. You have been selling at less than cost ? A. I do not think so.
Q. Have you not lost money at this business ? A. No.
Q. Have you not lately compounded with your creditors ? A. Yes.
Q. How much did you pay them ? A. When all is paid, about 55 per cent. ; that is more than the Canada Car Company will pay if they keep on.

Mr. Gordon.—They have to compete with a man who only pays 55 per cent.

Witness.—It has nothing to do with my compounding with my creditors; I am not ashamed to say that I have compounded. I do not blame the Canada Car Company for going into the export trade, but the more they export the less they will have ; I know many people go down to me; they think I must be making money; they rest entirely upon my prices, and I do not think they knew whether pails cost $1.00 or $2.00 ; they based their prices on me entirely.

By Mr. Hardy.

Q. You lost very heavily on lumber transactions ? A. Yes ; I think $125,000 in bad debts and other calamities, which I do not consider I am to blame for ; I do not feel delicate in saying I have compounded, because I have made very serious losses.

The Chairman.—I do not think it bears on the question at all.

Mr. Hardy.—It is a public affair and a public calamity as a matter of fact, but I did not understand you to attribute your losses to your pail business ?

Witness.—No.

Mr. Gordon put in petition of the witness and Mr. Nelson to the Government.

[Petition put in and marked Exhibit " B."]

By Mr. Langmuir.

Q. You stated that you had from 60 to 75 men at pails, and that you considered the rental of the pail factory worth about $2,400 a year, including the water power ? A. Yes.

Q. Can you give me an average of the number employed in the premises altogether, apart from the match factory ? A. In the past four or five years we have been running over 2,000, sometimes 2,200 or 2,300 ; now I think the number is about 1,650.

Q. How many shop buildings have you altogether ? A. Six manufacturing shops.

Q. What is the size of the pail shop ? A. The pail factory—the main building—is 120 feet long and 60 feet wide, three stories high, besides the basement.

Q. That is, you have four flats ? A. We only work on three flats. The upper flat is for belting, and so on.

Q. What is the size of your sash factory ? A. It is still larger—180 feet long by 54 feet wide, three stories high.

Q. What is the next building? A. The machine shop—the machine and box department.

Q. What is the extent of that building ? A. That building is about eighty feet square, three flats.

Q. What is the next ? A. The match factory.

Q. What is the size of that building ? A. I cannot give it to you exactly. The main building of the match factory is 160 feet by forty feet. The three wings are about twenty-four feet or thirty feet wide and sixty feet long, only one flat. The main building is two and a half flats. Then the box department is 109 feet by fifty-four feet, two stories. Then there is the machine shop.

Q. For the iron work ? A. Yes.

Q. One storey or two ? A. That is two stories, but the upper flat is for bottoming pails.

Q. What is about the area of the machine shop ? A. About fifty feet long by thirty-five feet wide.

Q. Have you any more in the way of shops, not storehouses? A. We have a drying kiln.
Q. How many drying kilns? A. Twenty-three.
Q. Are they lately constructed? A. They are run by steam pipes underneath.
Q. Have you railway communications going into these shops of yours, or do you cart to the rails? A. We cart. Of course, I move my lumber by rail.
Q. That is by tramway? A. Yes.
Q. There are six shops proper, excluding the drying kilns? A. Yes.
Q. Have you knowledge of the entire superficial area of your shops. You have never made it up? A. No.
Q. If it is a fair question, what do you consider the cash value of your shop property—these six shops? Are they brick or are some frame? Is the pail shop brick or frame? A. Stone. The pail shop and machine shop and machine and match-box shop, and match shop and wings are stone. The sash factory and the regular box factory are wooden.
Q. What is the machine shop? A. Stone. They are all stone except two.
Q. What do you value these buildings at, or what did they cost, including the drying kilns? A. At a rough estimate about $125,000.
Q. What do you consider the rental of that property worth? A. At 10 per cent.
Q. That is the interest on the capital, to keep up the buildings, and all? A. Yes.
Q. Do you think that is a fair thing for a shop property where a number of hands are employed, and there is wear and tear on the property? A. That is the general rule.
Q. That is what it ought to be put at—10 per cent.? A. Yes.
Q. What is the tear and wear on belting? A. More than ten per cent.
Q. If a man offered to furnish you with your belting and pulleys, and connections and motive power, what would it be worth on the capital outlay? A. Taking the deterioration on belting —
Q. Take pulleys and all? A. Pulleys last a long time; belting is wearing out every moment. I think belting depreciates about twenty per cent. per annum, unless in the case of a large main belt. I am talking about common belting—four and six inches.
Q. Taking the running gear all through, pulleys and belting and shafts, would you say that fifteen per cent. would be a fair thing, or twelve and a-half, taking the average of all your running gear, apart from the water-wheels? A. I should say ten per cent. outside of the belting, but it would not cover the belting. It is always wearing out.
Q. What do you consider your belting and running gear to be worth in all your establishments? You value your buildings at $125,000. What is your running gear worth. A. I could not give you that so closely. Of course, I could if I had my books.
Q. Can you give the Commission an idea of your taxes on shops and drying kilns? A. Our property is all taxed together.
The CHAIRMAN.—Taxes are very different in Hull from what they are here.
WITNESS.—I should say from $600 to $700. My whole taxes are about $1,400.
Q. What are the taxes in Hull? A. One-half per cent.
Q. On the rental? A. On the assessed value.
MR. GORDON.— The prisoners must be employed in the prison.
Mr. LANGMUIR. —The Canada Car Company made a requisition on the Government of Ontario for a certain shop area. That was built and another. They kept making requisitions for shop area and running gear and machinery. There is some value attached to that. Is not the Commission to inquire into that as well as the value of the labour?
MR. GORDON.—We might have had shops erected out of the city limits cheaper. do not see any advantage in working in stone and brick buildings more than in wooden buildings.
MR. HARDY.—The question is what advantage did you get over and above the labour? Generally a private contractor has to furnish himself. If the buildings are more expensive than is requisite, that would be taken into consideration.
THE CHAIRMAN.—It is perfectly right so far. It is a question of what the labour is worth with the appliances given with it. Anything that shows the value of the appliances is a proper thing to enquire into. As to the taxes, you can find it much more readily. The taxes in Hull are very different from the taxes here.
MR. GORDON.— We have to use the labour in these buildings.

Mr. LANGMUIR.—The buildings are modelled according to the desire of the Canada Car Company.

Mr. GORDON.—If we could use the prisoners out of the prison, we could have less expensive buildings.

Mr. LANGMUIR.—They were built according to the model of the Canada Car Company, and their design altogether.

Mr. GORDON.—They cost $200,000 or $300,000. We do not want buildings like that.

Mr. LANGMUIR.—For a shoe factory, we should require different buildings.

Mr. HARDY.—We do not urge that you should be accountable for anything belonging to the prison proper.

Mr. GORDON.—We would not have put up buildings like that for ourselves.

Mr. HARDY.—In the United States prisons, as a rule, they rent shop room, and give only bare walls,—no appliances.

Examination continued.

BY MR. LANGMUIR.

Q. Would you consider it of considerable value to your premises, if all the railway systems in the Province ran into your shops? A. Yes, it would be a great saving.

Q. Would you consider one expert with five raw hands, turning out 400 or 500 pails a day, pretty fair work? A. Pretty fair work; about an average, I should say; they ought to do that easily, and very green hands at that.

Q. Have you ever tasked your experts, and your raw hands? A. No; we sometimes task our painters.

Q. Have you ever paid by piece-work? A. Yes, we do a great deal of piece-work.

Q. Did you ever try the system of giving a bonus? A. No.

Q. What do you think, as a manufacturer, would be the effect upon prison labour of giving a bonus. A. I think it would make a great deal of jealousy among the hands; I do not think much of it.

GENERAL WILLIAM HUMPHREY, called on behalf of the Government, sworn and examined:—

BY MR. LANGMUIR.

Q. What is your position? A. Warden of the Michigan State Prison.

Q. How long have you held that position? A. Twenty months.

Q. What is the number of prisoners you have now in custody? A. About nine hundred.

Q. What are the periods of sentence, a minimum to a maximum? A. The shortest time is six months,—from that to life.

Q. What portion of prisoners do you think you have under two years, about? A. Somewhat less than half of the number that are received there; the average term, leaving out the life is about 3¼ years; that is the average term of commitments. The average term of the convicts in the prison to-day, is different from the average term of commitments; the average term of men in the prison to-day is somewhat above four years.

Q. How do you explain that difference? A. The longer-time men run over.

Q. Have you many life men? A. We have now between 60 and 70, I think.

Q. What trades or industries do you carry on in your prison? A. We have in there a waggon contract and manufacture.

Q. How many men in that? A. I would like to make a statement first. We have men in all the industries there that are under contracts, and in all of the contract shops there are other men that are put on at special rates, subject to being withdrawn by ourselves when we see fit, or thrown off by the contractors when they see fit.

Q. You have certain men under a fixed contract, and then other men whom you can put on? A. Yes, temporarily.

Q. What is the number of men under fixed contract for waggons? A. Fifty men at $1.00 per day.

Q. Have you any temporary men in that industry? A. Yes, there are now 70 men, for whose labour we get $25.00 per day.

Q. That you may throw up to-morrow if you wish? A. Yes.

Q. What is the next industry? A. The next is what we call a farming-tool contract— a shop in which they make pitchforks, steel and iron rakes, and hoes.
Q. Farming implements? A. Yes, that class of farming implements.
Q. How many men are engaged in that contract? A. There are two contracts with these parties, one for 100 men at 65cts. per head.
Q. That is a fixed contract? A. Yes; and there is another for 50 men at 72½c. per head. On that contract they take all the men they want, and all in excess of that number they pay for at 50c. per head.
Q. What is the average they employ temporarily? A. Up to the 1st of July during this season, say up to this time, they have had about 35.
Q. Employed over and above the 150 on permanent contract? A. Yes.
Q. What is the next industry? A. The next is cabinet—100 men at 55c.
Q. Any employed temporarily? A. Four or five, but nothing special. If they have had any extra they have paid contract price.
Q. What is the next? A. The next is a shoeing contract—50 men at 55c. No surplus men. A cigar contract is the next—50 men at 55c. They have had 25 extra men at the same price.
Q. That was optional for them to take and for you to give? A. Yes. They have just thrown the surplus off.
Q. Any other trade? A. No, sir; no other that we contract, but we have one business of our own.
Q. What is that? A. Making brooms.
Q. How many have you employed in making brooms on your own account? A. It varies; we use in the shop men the contractors do not want, and we have now about 25 able-bodied men that do the winding and sewing, and then, as to the other men—the cripples and disabled men—we do not keep any account of them; we keep an account of the days of labour put in, but if we have such a man we send him there without any regard to whether he is wanted or not; we place him under a keeper, so that apart from the winders and sewers, we keep no record; the number varies.
Q. Do you carry on any other business on your own account? A. No, except to do our prison work.
Q. Then you have 400 men under contract? A. We have 400 men under contract.
Q. How many had you when you left, temporarily employed on the same contracts? A. Probably 150.
Q. When were these contracts entered into? A. The waggon contract in 1873.
Q. And the farming tools? A. In 1873; one in May for 100 men, and one in October.
Q. The cabinet? A. In 1872.
Q. The shoe? A. In 1875.
Q. And the cigars? A. In 1875.
Q. These same industries existed prior to these dates, did they? A. The waggon, the farming tools and the furniture; there had been a shoe contract in there; these three were old industries.
Q. Carried on in the prison for how long? A. For from 10 to 20 years.
Q. Have the contractors changed often? A. No; the same contractors run the waggon shop now that were in it 15 years ago at any rate, perhaps 20.
Q. Is it a corporation or private individuals? A. It is now a corporation, but the same parties ran it as individuals before; they incorporated in 1873, I think.
Q. What was the name of the firm? A. It is now the "Austin, Tomlinson & Webster Manufacturing Company," and it was Austin, Tomlinson & Webster, before, as private individuals.
Q. Have they made money? A. They have got rich out of it—all of them.
Q. Are they residents of Jackson? A. Not all of them. They are not rich to-day; they took the money they made there and scattered it round.
Q. But they have done well with their contract in the prison? A. Yes.
Q. In the farming tools, who had the contract prior to 1873? A. The same parties.
Q. How long have they had their contract? A. I cannot answer very definitely as to that; that contract has changed, though all the time the changes have been dropping out a partner, instead of changing the contractors.

Q. Substantially, have the same been in for 10 years? A. Yes; I should say the same men had been there for 10 years.

Q. From general knowledge and hearsay, how have they done? A. They have done well.

Q. Have they made money by their contract? A. Yes; they are making money now.

Q. Was the cabinet-ware contract in existence prior to 1872? A. The same parties have run that for 15 years; they have had three 5 year contracts, and the third is just expiring; it expires next September.

Q. How have they done? A. Part of the time well; part of the time not so well; I do not want to be understood that these are the prices they have paid for the labour all the way through; they are only the prices under the present contracts.

Q. Then, in regard to the shoe contract; you have 50 men on that? A. Yes.

Q. Does that change often—the firms or the individuals in the firms? A. This is a contract that commenced in 1875.

Q. A new industry? A. Not a new industry; there was a contract years before, and up to a year of that time there had been a shoe contract in the prison; the parties failed; this is a new firm that came in under this contract.

Q. Well, how is this firm doing? They have been in existence two years? A. They have been in the prison two years. It is an old firm. It is a Detroit business house. They are doing well with their work.

Q. As a general thing, is prison labour let for shoe purposes, not let about the lowest of any? A. I don't know how it is outside there.

Q. In your own prison it is let lower than the waggons and farming tools, but the same as the cabinet ware? A. It is a better price than the cabinet ware price.

Q. Have you any knowledge of it in other prisons? What is it let for in Albany or Auburn? A. I do not know.

Q. Was the cigar contract in existence before 1875? A. There was a cigar contract that went into the prison in 1871. That failed in 1875. These parties in contract now went into the prison in 1875, and took part of the men who had been employed under the other contract.

Q. How have they done? A. The present parties are doing very well I should judge:

Q. Can you tell me whether these prices entered into for waggons were in advance of the contract prior to that? A. Yes.

Q. And the farming tools? A. Yes; they are all in advance.

Q. You are getting a better price than under the old contracts? A. Yes.

Q. And as far as you know, they are doing well? A. I judge that they are doing well, some of them better than others.

Q. What is your experience as to the applicability of prison labour to these various industries? Do you find in your experience of twenty months that it can be well used in these industries—used to advantage? A. That is a pretty general question.

Q. Of course, but you are just the man who can give that information to the Commission. A. I suppose that with us it is better adapted than it would be up here, to make a comparison; for this reason; that, as I understand, up here they are using all the men they have, and with us not half the men are on contracts. That gives the contractors better opportunities for selecting.

Q. You have a considerable number of men idle now? A. Yes; and our men are longer term men.

Q. Do you think now that your contractors have an advantage owing to the fact that you have a considerable number of men idle? A. Yes, they certainly have.

Q. Therefore the selection is better? A. Yes.

Q. How do they select the men? A. One of the first questions the contractors ask is as to the length of term; they look a man over as to his physical qualifications and enquire after his occupation outside previous to commitment.

Q. Do you furnish them with a statement of that when the prisoners come in, or do they come to your office for that? A. We furnish that as given us by the prisoner.

Q. How do they get that knowledge? A. We take it from the convict when he comes in and make it matter of record in the office.

Q. Have the contractors the right to look over the records ? A. We allow them to do it.

Q. You do not give them a list of the prisoners as they arrive for each contractor to look over and make a selection ? A. No ; they come to the office and get the information.

Q. How do they settle between themselves ? A. That is a matter of mutual agreement.

Q. The waggon-maker is supposed to get a prisoner if he was in that trade before ? A. He goes in and is supposed to have the preference as between the contractors ; we do not manage that matter, and do not attempt to.

Q. Are all these—waggons, farming tools, and cabinet ware—carried on by machinery ? A. Yes ; all.

Q. Is the shoe contract by machinery as well ? A. Yes.

Q. Cigars ; how is that ? A. Hand and moulds ; the same as outside.

Q. The most improved principle ? A. Yes.

Q. Have you machines in your broom-shop ? A. The ordinary winding and sewing machines.

Q. The sizer ? A. No.

Q. The winder ? A. We have the hand machine.

Q. That is, by foot power ? A. Yes.

Q. Which of these are the most intricate trades—the most difficult to learn ? A. It takes the longest to learn the most intricate parts of the farming tools, but, as between the whole of the work, I do not know any great difference ; there is a part of the waggon shop, in which, if a man is not a blacksmith, he has to learn the blacksmith's trade—a part that is done by hand.

Q. Now, in regard to the waggons—you take a prisoner, a green hand ; do they put him on certain kinds of work first to let them work up to another machine or part of the work ? A. I have never paid much attention to that matter, but I should judge it depended on the length of term ; they put a long time man with a convict on a piece of work that requires some skill to learn that part of the work.

Q. How long does it take a waggon-maker to become conversant with the trade ? A green prisoner going in—after three months will become a pretty useful man ? A. He will be more useful than in ten days.

Q. In ten days, has he any knowledge of the trade of waggon-making ? A. I do not think he knows any more than the machine he works with.

Q. Does he work the machine well ? A. Their waggon-axles, for instance, are all turned by machine from the pattern. They are wood. A man will take up that piece of timber, and put it into the machine, and set the machine going, and run over the axle properly—he will learn in one day to do that, but he won't know anything about the machine, or if the axle did get out of shape, but he can handle the timber. That is the simplest machine. Some of them take more time.

Q. Do the prisoners become efficient in two or three weeks, so far as feeding the machines are concerned ? A. I think they do all through on the simpler machines. Some require more time.

Q. Out of the fifty men engaged on the waggons, how many do you think require great experience in order to be useful men ? A. As they run the contract now with 120 men—they have not run less than 100 men since I have been there—I should say the fifty men ought to be men of some considerable experience.

Q. And the seventy might be the raw hands ? A. Handling the material, putting it into the machines, and that kind of work.

Q. Would six months give that experience to some of the fifty men ? A. I should say six months on an average. Some of them are blacksmiths and come there all ready, and can go right in. I should say six months would be the average.

Q. Would that make them experts ? A. Yes.

Q. Does the same thing apply to the farming tools as far as you have observed ? A. I should say six months is the average, but in some of the work a year or eighteen months.

Q. In some of the intricate parts ? A. Yes, the fork drawing.

Q. Can the same proportion of green hands be put on at once and become available in a short time, or not ?   A. Not so many, I think.

Q. How with the cabinet ware ?   A. Like the waggon—perhaps a little more favourable to the green hands.

Q. In the shoe contract, how is that ?   A. That is not a very difficult one.

Q. It is very easily picked up, is it ?   A. Yes.

Q. How long does it take to pick it up ?   A. I should think in six months a man would do the work as well as he ever would, except for the experience.

Q. But a large proportion would pick it up in ten days, as in the waggons ?   A. There are only two machines to do the work of the shop for 50 men ; the lasting and fitting and so on is hand work.

Q. How many brooms do you turn out a day with 25 men ?   A. We have not worked up to full capacity ; with the men we have in the shop, we think we can turn out 100 dozen a day if we wished to ; we have a capacity for 1,200 brooms, but we have never done it ; we have never been able to sell the products.

Q. You speak about the advantage that your contractors possess by having a large number of idle men at present ; is that a usual thing ?   Under the old contracts, prior to 1873 and 1875 were there as many idle men ?   A. No.

Q. This is then exceptionally favourable to the contractors ?   A. Yes ; at that time there were not men enough to fill the contracts.

Q. More demand than you could supply ?   A. Yes.

Q. Is it likely to arise again ?   A. Not likely.

Q. In the event of the supply exceeding the demand, you would let another contract ?   A. When the time comes that the contractors must take every man that comes, without regard to his qualification or length of sentence, it will be against the contractors.

Q. Do you not consider where one Company is running the whole, instead of six contractors, it would be an advantage to the allocation of the men in the various departments ?   A. No ; a disadvantage.

Q. Why ?   A. Well, take in your own prison ; the blacksmith requires heavy, strong men, while a man with one leg can be just as good a cigar-maker as one with two legs, and the boys and young men would be good for nothing at other trades ; so with the shoe department, they take the young and lighter men ; they want a man that is quick.

Q. But in the Canada Car Company they are carrying on the manufacture of pails and tubs, washboards, brushes, sleighs and tables, painting, and the manufacture of cars—altogether nine or ten or twelve different articles ; could not one Company, having the choice of 260 men from the prison, divide these men among these different industries to better advantage than where there were six contractors supplied ?   A. An industry of that kind gives the same advantages ; if they were running a waggon contract, they could not do it.

Q. One particular industry ?   A. Yes.

Q. But where they are so divided, as I mention, is not the advantage of one company doing the whole, instead of six different contractors, on the side of the company ?   A. I rather think it would be against them ; if their industry were car work entirely they would work at a disadvantage.

Q. But with three or four or five other industries ?   A. If they require to work all the men of the prison, and their work was all heavy work, they would have a disadvantage ; now with their work both light and heavy, some requiring attention rather than strength, I do not see it would make any difference whether there one or two contracts in the yard.

Q. From your knowledge of the 550 men used by contractors, how many are required solely for manual labour in the yard—moving material and such work ?   A. I don't know that I can give you any percentage ; about five per cent.

Q. For purely manual labour ?   A. Yes, carrying and moving stock ; perhaps it would be 10 per cent. ; I don't wish that to be understood as an answer that is worth much, for I never stopped to inquire or look into the matter.

Q. As a matter-of-fact, for that labour an able-bodied man would be at once as good as if there for twenty years, under proper discipline ?   A. A strong, able-bodied man who comes into prison for a year, is just as good for the work as men there twenty-five years ; they take able-bodied short time men for that work usually.

Q. As a matter-of-fact, three months men would do just as well as one year men, if able-bodied? A. Yes, nothing is required but strength of body.

Q. Now, in regard to the prison labour, do you find the prisoners generally do their work well, that they do it reasonably willingly; or is it altogether controlled by discipline? A. It is a matter of discipline.

Q. Can you make the discipline such as to be able to say they do their work well and properly? A. We calculate to do it.

Q. When that is exercised, prison labour is of course, more valuable than if any want of organization or looseness exist? A. Yes; the value of the labour depends more on the discipline than anything else.

Q. Do you allow contractors to give a bonus, or allow for overtime, or anything of that kind? A. It has been allowed, and is now to a certain extent; but we are working it out of the yard as fast as possible.

Q. Why? A. It has a bad effect on the labour.

Q. In what way? Will you explain? A. If the convicts have the idea that they can get extra pay for extra work, they will make extra work necessary.

Q. I presume you would task the men when you gave them extra pay? A. Yes, that is now done.

Q. You say they will see that extra work becomes necessary; how is that? A. They will start out with the idea of beating the contractors in regard to their work, doing a small quantity, keeping the quantity down.

Q. I presume the task must be performed before there could be any claim for extra pay? A. The day's work now is considerably more than when I went to the prison and took charge of it. It was based then on what they supposed the convicts could do, and, of course, what the convicts said about it had, more or less, to do in determining the amount. It could not be avoided very well.

Q. You are now running out the system of payment for extra work? A. Yes. In regard to that—perhaps it has no bearing on your question, or the point you are making—but two years ago, before two years ago, this matter of extra labour was one of arrangement between the convicts and the contractors. Since then the arrangement has been between the contractors and the Warden, and the money is paid to the Warden instead of to the convicts, as it used to be.

Q. The Warden is to be a party to the arrangement? A. Yes.

Q. Does the contractor in every case pay the bonus? Do the prison authorities ever pay it? A. No.

Q. The contractors always? A. The contractors always.

Q. You calculate the amount for the convicts, and afterwards disburse it among them? A. Yes, according to the work they do. In our own shop, as we have never wanted a full day's work, the question has never come up, and probably never will.

Q. That is in the broom shop? A. Yes.

Q. In these contracts, what do you furnish the contractors besides the labour? A. We furnish keepers for the men, or guards as you term them here.

Q. Are there so many keepers for each contract, or how? A. It depends on the shop. Some have two, some one—always one. Our shop, a very large one, has two keepers. We furnish the contractors the shop.

Q. And one or two keepers? A. Whatever keepers are necessary, we determine that ourselves. Whatever number is necessary for the discipline of the prisoners.

Q. Any motive power? A. No.

Q. Any running gear? A. No.

Q. You just give the walls of the shop? A. The shop.

Q. Do you heat it? A. No.

Q. Do you light it? A. No; we never need any light there; we never run except by day light.

Q. You simply furnish the labour, a keeper or two to look after the men, and shop-room? A. Yes. They furnish their own store-room outside.

By Mr. Hardy.

Q. They take away the material so soon as it is manufactured ? A. Yes, and store it outside.

Q. Have you any railways running into the yard ? A. No ; none running inside ; there is one close by, just outside the walls.

Q. Is there more than one line of railway passing that prison ? A. No ; not there.

Q. It is not a railway centre ? A. Not at the Prison.

Q. Is it in the city ? A. Yes.

Q. You have, nevertheless, only one connection ? A. Yes.

Q. With one road ? A. Yes.

Q. What road is it ? A. The Michigan Central.

Q. What other roads are there ? A. The Michigan Southern, the Fort Wayne Road ——

Q. There are no switches to those? A. No ; all are connected. We can get cars over those roads, but we have to pay for it. From the Michigan Central we have free passage ; it is really three roads.

Q. How much land is attached to your labour yard ? A. We have about eight acres walled in.

Q. And you have no railways running within the walls ? A. No ; one is close by our walls, outside.

Q. Take the same class of men outside of the prison as you have spoken of, men not inclined to do much work, rather loafing fellows, but men who are labourers, and the men in prison ; would they do more under discipline than outside ? A. Yes ; they would. Men who are convicts do more work inside than they ever did outside, as a class ; of course, there are exceptions.

Q. Discipline occasions that ? A. It has something to do with it.

Q. Take a long term man and a short term man, do you find a man sent for two years or one year or two years and a half preserves his faculties and his interest in life and in work more keenly than a man in for 20 years ? Would he do better, stronger work ? A. You have taken the two extremes.

Q. Well, take a two years' man and a ten years' man ? A. I don't know but that a ten years as a rule would take most interest in his work.

Q. He would preserve his faculties, physical and mental as bright ? A. Yes, as a rule I think so.

Q. Do you impose silence or permit conversation ? A. Silence.

Q. Solitary imprisonment or gangs in cells ? Have you a separate cell for each prisoner. A. As far as cells go, we have 640 cells for 900 men.

By Mr. Gordon.

Q. I understood you to say that the term of imprisonment varied from six months up to life sentence ? A. Yes.

Q. That you had about 900 prisoners in the prison at present ? A. Yes.

Q. I have one of your reports for 1876, and I see that the number of men in prison on September 30th, 1876, under two years' sentence, was 98. I suppose that is correct ? A. That is, the number of men who are in prison without regard to the year of their sentence.

Q. Does not this table (table in report exhibited) shew the length of the sentences ? A. It gives the number of prisoners on 30th September, 1876, without regard to the year in which they were sentenced.

Q. Then the sentences of these men set out in the schedule would be longer than that ? A. If I understand your question—no. This table gives the number of men in prison at the close of the day September 30th, 1876, the number of each age, or rather the number at each trade. Of course, the proportion of long time men is greater in this table than in the table showing the number of men received during the year.

Q. But on 30th September, 1876, there were 98 prisoners out of 830, who had less than two years to serve ? A. Yes ; I suppose you have footed that correctly.

(Report of Michigan State Prison for 1876 put in, Exhibit " C.")

Q. About one-tenth of the men had less than two years to serve ? A. Yes. If you include two years men, those who have come in for two years, the number is increased. Anything I have said in regard to the number of men has been from memory ; the report will show the facts. Of these 98 men, 87 were received during the year closing September 30th, 1876.

Q. But my question is—on 30th September, 1876, how many men were in your prison who had less than two years to serve ? A. About that date.

Q. Yes ? A. I cannot answer it.

Q. Does this table in the report show ? A. No. This only shows the length of sentence, what the original sentence was, without regard to how long the men had been there at that time.

Q. Then, on 30th September, 1876, how many men were in prison whose original sentence was less than two years ? A. There were 98.

Q. Out of how many ? A. Ninety-eight out of 841. That is one-ninth or about that.

Q. Now I think you said in reply to a question by my friend that there were between 400 and 500 prisoners, under permanent contract. Were you speaking of the number at this period, or in September, 1876 ? A. At that period ? The numbers are given as at that time, but since then some have gone out.

Q. Could you give us any idea of the average length of sentence of the 430 men ? What was the shortest ? A. Some one year men are on contracts, but they are exceptional men.

Q. As a rule, do the contractors choose long-term men or short-term men ? A. They take the long-term.

Q. Do they take the longest term men they can get, as a rule ? A. The contractors prefer men whose terms of sentence are about seven or eight years. I may say that men who are sent there for seven or eight years will go out in about six. So that five or six years men, who are required to serve the full period, are the men whom the contractors will usually select.

Q. That is if they make full time ? A. Yes, that is the rule ; but for some of their work they choose the longest term men they can get ; exceptional jobs.

Q. Is it not an excepion for a contractor to choose a one year man ? A. An exception.

Q. Or for a contractor to choose a two years man ? A. It is about an even thing ; it is not exceptional because they have certain kinds of work a two years man can do as well as a five, ten, or fifteen years man ; there is heavy work that depends more on the physical ability of the man than on his skill.

Q. Do you mean that except with regard to heavy work, it would be the exception for a contractor to choose a two years man ? A. Yes ; he would take a two years man when he was a tradesman.

Q. How can you form any opinion as to how it is that the contractors prefer long period to short period men ? A. The same rule applies there as applies outside.

Q. What rule are you referring to ? A. You require a skilled workman ; a long time man would become skilled ; prison labour contract labour is entirely mechanical.

BY MR. HARDY.

Q. By machinery you mean ? A. Yes ; it is manufacturing.

BY MR. GORDON.

Q. What is your experience with regard to the difference between a one year man and a three years man ; what would be the difference in value in your opinion between the labour of a one year man and a three years man on the same machine and same kind of work ? A. I don't think I can give you that.

Q. Would there be any difference ? A. Yes; the three years' man would do more than the one year man, other things being equal.
Q. Would he be worth more than twice as much as the one year man ? A. At some work he would be, at other work he would not.
Q. On such work as the Car Company is carrying on, the manufacture of pails, tubs, wash-boards and wooden work generally of that class, do you think he would be worth twice as much as the one year man ? A. I don't know enough of that business to give an opinion worth anything.
Q. Take the case of the cabinet work in your prison; would a three years man be worth twice as much as a one year man on that ? A. I think not twice as much; he would be worth considerably more.
Q. Worth one-third more? A. I think so; it is a matter of opinion, a matter on which I have no positive knowledge.
Q. Can you give us, generally, anything to show what the value of free labour is in your neighbourhood in these different industries—cabinet-making, waggon-making and agricultural implement manufacture ? A. I can only say generally, that mechanics are getting from $2 to $3 per day, from $1 50 perhaps to $3 per day—the ordinary class mechanics.
Q. In the waggon department, of prisoners you have said there were seventy men in temporary employment at $25 per day. That would average something less than thirty-three and one-third cents per man ? A. Thirty-three cents and something over.
Q. Do you find that those seventy men are usually employed, the full number each day ? A. Except so far as they are sick.
Q. Taking all the year round, those seventy men added to fifty men would reduce the price paid by the waggon-makers ? A. To sixty-three cents and a fraction.
Q. Was it part of the contract that they should get these seventy men at that rate ? A. No.
Q. That was made subsequently ? A. Yes.
Q. How soon after the contract was made ? A. I don't know. There were fifty extra men on the waggon contract when I went into the prison. Twenty of these seventy have been added within the last three months.
Q. Had the contractors the same privilege in the previous contract ? A. I don't know. It would not amount to anything if they had, because there were not enough men to fill the contracts until the last contracts were let. Sixty-two and a half cents is the average.
Q. Could you tell us without much difficulty the average sentence of those 120 men ? A. I could not tell you anything about it.
Q. Or with regard to any other contracts ? A. I don't know anything about it here. If I was at home I could tell you in a few minutes.
Q. You have told us two cases where contractors have failed. One was the cigar contractor and the other was the shoe contractor ? A. The case of the shoe contractor was some years ago. I don't know anything about what their prices were.
Q. Have you made another shoe contract since ? A. Yes.
Q. What is the price now paid ? A. 55c.
Q. Have you made another contract for the men employed on cigars ? A. For part of them.
Q. At the same industry ? A. Yes.
Q. At what rate ? A. 55c.
Q. How many men ? A. 50.
Q. Is there any rule as to the number of freemen the contractors may employ with their prisoners ? A. On their own account ?
Q. Yes ? A. No; they can employ any number as overseers.
Q. For instance, in the waggon factory, could they employ a hundred freemen if they chose ? A. No.
Q. Why so ? A. We are not furnishing shops for freemen.
Q. But supposing the contractor said he required those men to supervise the 120 prisoners employed, would there be any reason why he should not have them ? A. Yes; we know ourselves, and everybody knows, he does not require them; he is allowed a reasonable number of men to oversee the convicts.

Q. How many men are there at present? A. I cannot tell you, but perhaps six or seven in the yard; they have other men outside.

Q. That is in the shop? A. In the shop I think they have seven freemen.

Q. And how many guards or keepers for those 120 men? A. The prison furnishes three.

Q. In the agricultural implement department, how many freemen are employed? A. I think there are seven in the shops.

Q. That is to 100 men? A. To 150 men.

Q. In the cabinet factory can you tell how many freemen are employed? A. Five, I think.

Q. That is to 100 men? A. Yes.

Q. And in the shoe department how many? A. Two; and in the cigar shop two.

Q. Have you had any difficulty or complaint on the part of contractors as to material being lost; either raw or manufactured material? A. We have some complaint occasionally from the cigar contractor.

Q. Do you compensate the contractors for any such loss? A. No.

Q. What steps do you take to conteract the difficulty? A. The convicts are subject to punishment for that offence as well as for any other.

Q. You have the men searched in order to ascertain the fact? A. Yes; as far as we can; it is not very easy to find the tobacco by making a search.

Q. Who is it that fixes the task for the prisoners to do? A. The contractor, subject to the approval or disapproval of the prison authorities, of course.

Q. And have these men to perform their task each day? A. Yes.

Q. Supposing they do not perform it, what is the result to the contractor? A. He loses the work.

Q. Is he not compensated in any way by the prison authorities? A. No.

Q. Are the men not compelled to make up their task on the following day, or at some other time? A. No.

Q. I do not quite understand the answer to the question asked with regard to the system of rewarding extra work. Do you think if a man has a fixed task, say to make 100 cigars, and for every hundred over that amount is allowed so much—first being compelled to make the task—there would be a good or bad effect? A. That question does not bring out the matter; the determining of the task is the first point.

Q. I mean the task being determined between the prison authorities and the contractors? A. Then you wish to know if extra pay would be injurious.

Q. Whether the extra pay for anything above the task would be beneficial or injurious? A. I think on the whole it would be injurious.

Q. Could you give us your reasons for holding that opinion? A. It gets up a dicker between the contractors and convicts, which is injurious in itself, without regard to the money paid.

Q. How is that if they have to do the task? A. It leads to the prisoners claiming the right to their time; any such claim inside a prison yard is injurious to discipline. But that does not reach the difficulty.

Q. What is the difficulty? A. One portion of the theory of prison labour is, that convicts will not do as much work as men outside. They are not so selected, and of course, will not do as much work, for they are not working in their own interest.

Q. Do you think there is any force in that? A. Yes; it cannot be avoided; now, in determining the amount of work a convict should do, you get the amount he can do in the first place. They (the prisoners) are on the other side of the question, beating you if they can; if they understand they are going to get extra pay for what they do over the task, they work all the time to get the task done, and they will keep it down and you cannot avoid it.

Q. If they have to do their task and don't do it, they cannot get any extra pay? A. The first thing to be determined is the task.

Q. Their task having been determined by experience? A. The point of determining their task is the difficult one. A bad effect of over pay is that it supposes a certain right on the part of the men to their labour In determining the task you have, in the first place, to get to know what it is reasonable for them to do—you have to get it by results inside the prison; if you are going to do it otherwise, your prison labour is worth as much as labour outside.

Q. You cannot base your calculations on outside labour ? A. No.

Q. Prison labour is different from outside labour ? A. The theory is, and the fact is, that it is different. Outside labour has always some skilled men to take charge of it and manage it, and that commands its value. Prison labour may or may not have some skilled labour among it—it is a matter of circumstance. The system of extra pay for overwork is more injurious, or as injurious, to the contractors as to the prisoners.

Q. Do you think that prison labour, with such discipline as you have in your prison behind it, is equal to free labour of the same class ? A. That question does not permit of an answer in its present form ; the men who are convicts are worth more inside the prison than outside.

Q. They would do nothing except inside the prison ? A. Nothing, except forced to do so.

Q. Having got inside the prison, and having discipline to compel them to do certain work, do you think under those circumstances the work is as good and efficient as the voluntary work of free men outside the prison ? A. No; some of it is, but as a rule it is not.

Q. Could you form any idea of the quantum of the difference ? A. Take the same class of men outside—they are the same inside as outside, except so far as discipline affects them ; the same class of men inside are not worth as much as the same class of men who stay out. The prisons are filled (of course there are exceptions) with men one-half of whom, perhaps, you would not employ outside, whom you would not employ at any price; they would not work ; you could not trust them ; it is only by the discipline inside the prison you are able to bring them to labour.

Q. What effect has that discipline and restraint in prison ? Does it make this bad labour, this labour that is worthless outside, equal to free labour ? A. No.

Q. Could you form any opinion as to what the difference would be in the value ? A. No ; I could not do that. There is another matter which lies outside all this, which has its effect on prison labour, and which is not covered by your question.

Q. What is that ? A. When a manufacturer outside finds his stock of manufactured articles piling up he discharges his labourers. Inside the prison he must go on, paying for the labour and for the stock put in the goods.

Q. Take the case of a young man, fifteen or sixteen years, who went to labour in the cabinet business as an apprentice, and that of a young man of the same age who went into prison and was put to work which he knew nothing about; do you think the work turned out by the boy in prison at the end of one year would be as good and in quality the same as the work turned out by the apprentice ? A. I think not. If a boy goes to work of his own choice to learn a trade he has a direct interest in it; the man in the prison has no interest in it, as a rule. Some interest themselves enough to learn trades, with the idea of following them when they go out; but, as a rule, they have no interest except to get through the day.

Q. The same rule would apply with respect to men as to boys, and probably with greater force. Do you think that is the case ? A. I think that is the case.

Q. Going back to your contract labour at the prison, can you tell us if there is a rule among the contractors, that the oldest contractor has his choice of the prisoners ? A. The contracts all specify that the oldest contractor takes precedence in selecting the men when he has less than the contract number. If he has the contract number, the oldest contractor has no precedence in the matter. By courtesy among themselves, if any mechanics come in, the contractors each take those adapted to the business ; the waggon contractor, for example, taking the blacksmiths. This is a matter of courtesy between the contractors, and is a matter with which the prison authorities do not interfere.

Q. Thus it would be some advantage to be the senior contractor ? A. Yes ; it is no advantage with us.

Q. I am talking in regard to your prison. A. It is no advantage because we have a surplus of men all the while.

Q. If there was not a surplus of men would it be an advantage ? A. It would be an advantage.

Q. The oldest contractor is the contractor for the waggon-business ? A. The cabinet contract is the oldest, and next the farming tool contract. I see the waggon contract is dated Oct. 1, 1873 ; that for farming tools, May 1, 1873 ; the furniture contract is dated Oct. 1, 1872.

Q. I understood you to say in reply to a question by Mr. Langmuir, that you thought it would be a disadvantage for all the labour to be employed on one contract, if the work was of one kind ; but if with an assorted kind it would be an advantage ? A. That is so.

Q. Take the class of work on which the Car Company is employed,—pails, tubs, churns, wash-boards, and work *sui generis*, the only other industry they have up there being brooms, brushes, and cars,—do you think it would be no disadvantage to the company having to employ all the labour in the three industries ? A. It would be an advantage to the company. I am not specially posted up in regard to the pail and tub business ; but I should think that in that business the lighter class of convicts could be profitably employed on the lighter work.

Q. Do you think it is an advantage or a disadvantage to the Company to have a contract for the whole prison labour as compared with its division amongst contractors ? A. One man could divide the labour better than half-a-dozen. Take our own case. If we had only the waggon contract in the yard, we would have a good many men who could not be employed, but who now work on other contracts ; but if the work of the contractors was as diversified as that of the Company here so as to meet the physical requirements of the men, perhaps it would make no difference. There are some parts of the pail business which boys could do—that is the point I am making—and the lighter and stronger could be worked to advantage.

Q. Do you make the division into two classes—light and strong men ? A. Yes.

BY THE CHAIRMAN.

Q. Some of your cigar-makers would not do for blacksmiths ? A. No ; our shoe-makers would not do for blacksmiths, which trade requires the strongest and heaviest men, while for other branches of light labour they do just as well.

BY MR. GORDON.

Q. Is it not the case that long term men take more interst in their work than short term men ? A. Not the longest ; neither the longest nor the shortest term men are those who do best. They are the medium term men.

Q. What is about the term ? A. Five years' men, as a rule, work the best and are considered the most valuable men by the contractors.

Q. Do you think of two equally good men, a one year man and a five year man, that the five year man would take more interest and do more work than the one year man ? A. I think as a rule he would. I base that answer more on the opinions of the contractors than on any knowledge I have of the matter.

Q. I see in the report of the Inspector to the Government under the head of " broom contract," the following : "The men employed in the broom shops are generally maimed, feeble, superannuated, and short-time men" ? A. The broom shop is our own affair. The able-bodied men who are there are men whom the contractors don't want and are as a rule short-time men.

Q. Probably for what term ? A. Probably for one year, eighteen months, or two years. Then, as to the other men, we have got three or four times as many in the shop as are needed to keep the able-bodied men going. We keep them there to have them under a keeper and under discipline.

BY MR. HARDY.

Q. How frequently do your contractors pay ? A. The contracts require them to pay every month.

By Mr. Gordon.

Q. I see on page 49 of your report you say : "The brooms made prior to the date of the contract as above were apprentices' brooms, and had necessarily to be disposed of at low rates." Do you mean the brooms made by men who had not been long at work ? A. Just commenced.

Q. How long ? A. They commenced work in the broom shop in November, and this refers to the brooms made between November and January.

Q. For the first three months ? Unless the time is stated in the report, I should say about two months.

Q. You found that the brooms made during the first two months you had to dispose of at lower rates ? A. Yes, though part of them were good brooms. We sold them altogether.

By Mr. Hardy.

Q. Having heard the statements of Mr. Perry yesterday, and of Mr. Eddy, as to the large proportion of unskilled men who can be employed in the broom, pail, and tub manufacture, do you think the question of long or short term prisoners would be of so much importance, as it would be in the manufacture of furniture or agricultural implements ? A. I don't know enough about the works here to give an opinion worth anything. I should think not ; but I don't give the opinion as worth anything, because I have no knowledge of this work. I have never been where the work has been carried on, and I know nothing about it.

By Mr. Langmuir.

Q. In the report referred to, the Inspector states that the broom business has paid its way ? A. Yes.

Q. Even under the great disadvantage of all sorts of men ? A. Yes ; if you will turn over to the page referred to, you will see there was a stock on hand, and including those brooms at the invoice prices, it appeared there was something made in the shop.

Q. The statement generally speaking was correct—that it has paid its way ? A. Yes.

Q. You have stated that only the shops and keepers are provided for the contractors ? A. Yes.

Q. If the labour was again to be leased and you were to put in boilers, engines, running gear, railway tracks and a large amount of plant and fixtures, and then invite competition, would the labour not lease for a great deal more than at present ? A. I think it would.

Q. Could you fix the percentage more ? A. I don't think it could be let at a better price ; I think it would be let at somewhere near the price we are getting.

Q. Because labour is reduced in value ? A. Yes.

Q. But would they be taken largely into account ? A. Yes.

Q. And looked upon as substantial advantages ? A. Yes.

Q. As a matter of fact, your contractors have to supply their own motive power ? A. Yes.

Q. It would then be so much money saved ? A. It would be so much investment saved ; it would be worth 10 per cent. on the expense.

By Mr. Brockway.

Q. Ten per cent. added to the value of the labour ? A. The value of the labour would be increased 10 per cent. on putting in power and shafting ; I should think it would be ; I take it that the wear and tear of machinery, together with the saving in interest or investment would be worth that to the contractor ; it would make that difference. Money is worth 10 per cent.

By Mr. Langmuir.

Q. There is unusual wear and tear ? A. Yes. If the fixtures cost $10,000, the interest on that investment at 10 per cent. is $1,000 ; that leaves out of account the wear and tear. They save their interest and the wear.

Q. In making a comparison between long and short date men, if a waggon maker was sent to your prison and the waggon contractor was made aware of it, would not the contractor take the waggon maker, even though he were a one year man, in preference to other prisoners who had five years to labour ? A. Yes, I should think he would.
Q. And that principle would follow generally ? A. Yes, I think it would.
Q. You are aware there is an Industrial Prison in Detroit called the House of Correction ? A. Yes.
Q. Have you visited it ? A. Not very recently ; I have been there several times, but I know nothing about it.
Q. Do they receive there prisoners under sentences varying from ten days to five or six years ? A. Yes, they do.
Q. The average term of sentence is very low ? A. I would rather not answer any questions in regard to the House of Correction.
Q. You know it is a short-date prison ? A. Yes.
Q. Have you seen the returns of the prison ? A. Yes.
Q. It is said to be self-sustaining ? A. It is said to be.
Q. About the employment of free men : who determines the number of freemen employed, the prison authorities or the contractors themselves ? A. So far there has never been a question about it ; the contractors have determined it.
Q. Would you allow a greater number of free men than is actually necessary for the supervision of the prisoners ? A. No ; the prison does not furnish shops for the labour of free men.

BY MR. BROCKWAY.

Q. Will you give us an average per day of all existing contracts ? A. The average contract price per diem was on Sept. 30, 1876, $66\frac{18}{100}$ c.
Q. How many idle prisoners have you now ? A. Do you mean how many are not now in the contract shops ?
Q. How many persons would you like to contract for, exclusive of persons temporarily employed ? You have shown there are only 400 or 500 persons employed out of about 900 in the prison ? A. 500 ; out of such a prison as that, which has been running so long, there will be 75 or 100 persons old and incapable, which would leave 400.
Q. As the number you would like to contract for ? A. That number would include men inside our own works ; 150 would be all we would like to contract for now. We shall have more when the cabinet contract runs out, probably 250.
Q. Why are they not under contract ? A. Nobody wants them.
Q. At any price ? A. We can get nobody for them, and we have advertised.
Q. Have you had any offer for the labour on contracts which have expired or are about to expire ? A. We have for the men in the cabinet contract.
Q. What is the offer ? A. Thirty-five cents ; it is made by the same parties who now have the contract.
Q. Is there any competition ? A. No, there is only one party bidding.

BY THE CHAIRMAN.

Q. For what period are the contracts made ? A. The waggon contract was for ten years. Of the tool contract, one part for 100 men, was let for five years and two months, and the other part was for four years and nine months, and this arrangement was made so that the contracts might expire at the same time. The cabinet contract was for five years. The shoe contract was for five years, with the right given to the contractor to throw it up on six months notice being given.
Q. Has that time expired ? A. Yes ; they have given us notice to throw it up on the 1st January. The cigar contract is a five years' contract. In regard to the shoe contract, the parties would not take it at any price. They wanted to get out of the business ; circumstances had so turned.
Q. The privilege of using extra men is a condition of the contract ? A. No ; it has no reference to their contracts.
Q. Had they any reason to expect that that would be a privilege they could exercise

when they took the contract? A. I think not. When they took the contract there were no surplus men. They even took men who were not considered able-bodied.

Q. Under the circumstances, must it not be a valuable privilege to them to be allowed to take men and put them on as the work may require? A. Yes, it is.

By Mr. Brockway.

Q. It is a privilege to the prison to have them put on? A. Yes; but it brings prison labour by that much into competition with free labour.

By the Chairman.

Q. What is the position of the contractors in regard to these men; if there were any extra men would the contractors have the option of changing men? A. No; it is done sometimes, but with the consent of the prison authorities.

Q. It is no right? A. They have no such right; if a contractor takes a man he is his man; the prison authorities cannot take him from the contractor and he cannot throw him off; he is the contractor's man.

Q. Has there been any change in the value of labour since the contracts were taken? A. Yes.

Q. What has the change been—a reduction? A. Yes.

Q. What quality of brooms do you make; we are told there are a great many different qualities made, and, of course, great difference in value? A. We calculate to make the first quality broom of the kind we make; we don't make so large an assortment as a party who was here yesterday designated—we make seven or eight grades; but the large portion of the brooms made in our shop, or any other, come within about four grades, and those made outside of these are exceptional.

Q. Is there any further information that occurs to you, General, which you can give the Commission in regard to the value of prison labour as compared with the other labour that has not been stated? A. I don't know that there is anything further of any special value.

Q. It is your opinion, you say, that the giving of a bonus or paying for extra labour over and above the task to prisoners is a disadvantage, both to the contractors and to the discipline of the prison as well? A. Yes.

Q. You think experience proves that? A. Yes.

Q. Under your present regulations, that bonus is governed by the authorities of the prison, and the ill effect does not follow? A. Not so largely; yet you see it in the same direction.

By Mr. Brockway.

Q. I suppose, General, you don't mean to be understood as against giving a portion of their earnings to prisoners? A. That was abolished by the Legislature last winter. The law was a bad one, but the principle was sound.

By the Chairman.

Q. How could you apply that? A. As it was in our laws, the prisoners had a percentage on the contract price—on the average contract price of the prison labour. For instance, the average price is 66c. and something per day. The prisoners who were at work were entitled to five per cent.; it is very small, but they thought considerably of it.

Q. But you say they have decided to discontinue that? A. The law, so far as regards that, has been repealed. It is left out, so far as regards both Institutions.

BENJAMIN WALTON, called on behalf of the Company, sworn, and examined:—

By Mr. Gordon.

Q. You are a contractor, and have been so for a number of years, and reside in Toronto? A. Yes.

Q. And have done a great deal of Government work, I believe? A. Yes, from time to time.
Q. You built the Custom House and several of the Government buildings? A. Yes.
Q. I think you had something to do with the Central Prison? A. No; I merely tendered for it. I had nothing to do with the work.
Q. You have had great experience of labour of that class? A. Yes. I have been in business twenty-five years.
Q. In the masonry business? A. Yes.
Q. In the building business? A. Yes.
Q. Not with prison labour? A. No; free labour.
Q. Have you in your time employed apprentices and taught them the business? A. I usually keep a number of apprentices.
Q. What kind or class of work do you put them on? A. Always on the plainest kind of work to begin with.
Q. What work? A. Stone-cutting and brick-laying.
Q. Carpentering work? A. No; I do not carry on carpentering work.
Q. What usually has been the period for which these apprentices were bound to you? A. Four or five years.
Q. What was the average wages you used to pay them? A. I generally used to give about $2 per week to begin with, and raised half a dollar a week a year.
Q. Did you find that from the commencement they earned their $2 per week? A. I never calculated to get anything out of the apprentices for the first year, except perhaps on bricklaying a smart boy would work up to be useful in a year.
Q. Have you visited the Central Prison lately and seen the industries carried on there? A. I have been through it.
Q. From your knowledge as an employer of labour, can you form any opinion as to whether the class of men employed there would become efficient within any given period, and what period? A. That is a very hard question to answer; some of them would take a great deal longer than others; it would take some time before any of them were efficient; there is great difference as to their capacity, as to taking up any mechanical idea.
Q. You saw that the most of the work done there was performed by machinery? A. Yes.
Q. Now, if you were employing labour of that kind, would you feel any confidence in putting those men, that class of men, on these machines? A. I should consider it would require great supervision, and I would expect to have it at a very low figure indeed compared with free labour outside.
Q. What amount of supervision would you consider was necessary to make that labour efficient? A. I couldn't say—I am not sure.
Q. Do you think that, taking the pail shop, one man to fifty would be sufficient? A. No, I should think not; it would take two in fifty; it might be sufficient in some circumstances and not in others.
Q. There are about eight men on each machine, do you think it would be safe to run two machines with only one foreman to supervise them? A. Well, it might be, if there were no other men to look after; that would be one over only sixteen.
Q. You think one foreman could do more than that? A. Not a great deal more, I should think; it depends a great deal on how the men are to be placed; it is hard to speak definitely about those things.
Q. How long do you think a man of that class in a pail factory on those machines would be before he could earn on that kind of work 50cts. a day? A. Well, that is a question that requires to be answered conditionally to my mind, taking into account the surroundings, because there must be a standard by which you must measure the value of every piece of labour. I should say he would be a long time compared with outside labour, taking the surroundings into account.
Q. Would he be worth more or less than 50cts. a day? A. I should think he would never be worth more than 50cts. a day, no matter how long he was there.
Q. When do you think he would begin to be worth 50cts. a day? A. It would vary according to his capacity, beginning at twelve months likely.

Q. In the blacksmith's department, how long do you think it would be before such a man would pick up the trade so as to earn 50cts. per day? A. Two or three years, likely.

Q. What was your chief difficulty with your apprentices the first year they were in your employ? A. I don't know we ever considered it a difficulty, only they were inexperienced and did not know their work; they had to be watched and put on the very plainest work; they could never scarcely finish a piece of work, they could finish only certain portions; the very plainest of the work they might finish.

Q. You yourself have had no practical experience in the employment of prison labour? A. No.

Q. I suppose you could scarcely give an opinion as to how far they could work in competition with free men? A. I could not give you an opinion beyond one formed on the little experience I have had in looking at the thing; I could not give an opinion based on experience further than that.

Q. Did you notice on inspecting the industries to-day whether the men appeared to understand their work and do it as if accustomed to mechanical work? A. Some I thought did and others did not. But as to the value as between prison labour and free labour, I thought taking all things into account (of course, it is a matter of opinion based on a cursory review) that I could not rate prison labour higher than one-third of free labour outside. I think I would sooner take free labour than prison labour at more than one-third.

Q. Will you give us your reason for that? What is, in your opinion, the disadvantage of prison labour? A. Their inexperience is one point. There is no incitement for them to work. Prison labour is not expected to work with the same faithfulness as free labour. I hold there is another difference. With free labour, you can not only keep your men as long as you want them and then discharge them, but you can calculate the number you require, and get men better adapted to the kind of work for which they are engaged. Of course, there is a great loss if you cannot keep your machinery going; everything is standing there (Central Prison) at a great expense if anything goes wrong with the men. I noticed a whole machine standing, for one man seemed to be short.

Q. You noticed that to-day? A. Yes.

Q. Do you think those men capable of noticing if the machine was not turning out the proper kind of work? A. Not as a rule, I should say. It requires some time to get that particular knowledge. A man may tend a machine very readily, but to attend to one when it is out of order and know when or where it requires attention, requires much larger experience.

Q. Do you think that constant change of men would have a bad effect on the work? A. I think that is a very serious drawback.

By Mr. Langmuir.

Q. You say you have had no experience with prison labour? A. Yes.

Q. Has your experience in the employment of labour been confined to the contracting business? A. Yes.

Q. In the building trade? A. In the building trade and slate quarries.

Q. Have you had anything to do with public works, such as canals and railways? A. No; with city works.

Q. What do you pay a day for ordinary labourers, able-bodied men? A. From $1 to $1.25.

Q. What do you pay good carpenters? A. From $1 50 to $1 75 per day; a great many $1 50.

Q. What do you pay a good bricklayer? A. You may rate them from $1 75 to $2 25; some $2 50.

Q. You have stated, after observation at the Central Prison, that in your opinion prison labour is worth only one-third of free labour? A. Yes.

Q. Prison labour reckoned at one-third, and taking the ordinary rate of pay at $1 and $1 25, how much would that be worth? A. I wish to point out that the class of labour employed in the prison and the trades you quote is quite different. In regard to the carpenters work, the comparison will hold good ; but it is not a class of labour that will compare with that of bricklaying or stone cutting.

Q. Did you observe the men brick-laying at the prison to-day ? A. Yes.

Q. Did you observe how well they did it ? A. I was not near to them.

Q. You think that prison labour would be worth only one-third free labour ? A. I think about one-third ; that is my candid opinion.

Q. You have stated that under any circumstance, no matter how long a prisoner might remain, he would be worth only 50c. a day ? A. Not at that class of work.

Q. Did you see them working at the lathes ? A. Yes.

Q. If six prisoners turned out as many pails as a similar number of men in Mr. Eddy's factory would do, would they only be worth 50c. a day ? A. I could not say.

Q. As a matter of fact if they were tasked up to an equal amount and they performed it, would they not be worth as much as Mr. Eddy's men ? A. No, not as prison labour.

Q. If they work their task and did as much as six of Mr. Eddy's men, would they not be worth as much to the Canada Car Company as freemen, if they did as much ? A. Yes, if they did as much.

Q. You say you saw a number of men idle ? A. I said I saw one machine lacking one man.

Q. Do you know whose fault that was ? A. No.

Q. That was not the fault of the prison labour system you suppose ; would not men be idle in your works if they were not supervised and furnished with material ? A. They would be decidedly so.

Q. Do you know whether in this particular case the men were furnished with material ? A. No.

Q. Then your statement with respect the lathe being idle has no importance ? A. I merely mentioned that there was one man lacking.

Q. When was that—to-day ? A. I am merely supposing that was the case ; I did not say it was the case. If one man can be taken away and the contractor has not the power to put another man in there immediately, he is losing the work of the other five men of the machine ; and I thought that would be a drawback.

Q. As a man understanding the utilization of free labour, do you not organise your work and make the most of the men ? A. Yes.

Q. Don't you think the same principle applies to prison labour ? A. It ought to do.

Q. You have stated the value of apprentices ? A. Yes.

Q. That for the first year or two they were of little service ? A. Little service in select work.

Q. You don't use machinery in stone laying ? A. No.

Q. Do you think that would apply if you did use machinery ? A. Perhaps not so much, because machines help a great deal.

Q. Where machinery for the manufacture of certain work is in a high state of perfection, is the labour not reduced after to a matter of handling ? A. It is so far as the run of the work is concerned.

Q. So that a man may become an expert in handling ? A. In a much shorter time than he can become an expert by hand labour.

Q. Do you think where machinery is largely used, prison labour might be applied better ? A. Yes, but machine labour is always cheaper than hand labour. Just in proportion as you can use machinery and do away with skilled labour, so you lower the class of that labour.

Q. In regard to supervisors, you state you require a greater number of supervisors for prison than for free labour ? A. Yes.

Q. Did you observe how many supervisors they were in the pail shop. ? A. No.

Q. Did you observe the amount of machinery furnished to the Canada Car Company ? A. No.

Q. Were you asked by Mr. McBean to look at that ? A. I was asked by Mr. McBean to go and look at the operations.

Q. What did he ask you to look at ? A. At the working operations.

Q. You have no knowledge of the amount of machinery furnished ? A. No.

Q. Would not $100,000 worth of fixtures and plant increase the value of the labour ? A. Just in proportion ; it might be very small, still it would be a proportion.

By Mr. Gordon.

Q. With regard to the machine you say was standing idle, supposing instead of a man being lacking the prison authorities had furnished a new man, would that have had an effect ? A. A very serious effect, because it would bring the other five men almost down to his level.

Q. Could you give us any idea as to the time it would take for the machine to be got again into working order ? A. It would depend on the class of work that was being done.

The Commission took recess.

The Commission re-assembled at 3 o'clock.

Thomas Mitchell, called on behalf of the Government, sworn, and examined :—

By Mr. Hardy.

Q. Mr. Mitchell, what business are you engaged in ? A. At present I am engaged in the manufacturing business, but up until quite recently I was engaged in the manufacture of brooms.

Q. Manufacturing brooms—where ? A. In the City of Hamilton,

Q. For how long a period ? A. Well, I was engaged in the manufacture of brooms for some sixteen years. I might say that I have been connected with the broom business for nearly twenty-one years.

Q. How many men did you employ in it latterly ? A. Latterly, very few.

Q. And when were you last engaged in it ? A. When I was last engaged in that business largely, I had some twenty or twenty-five hands.

Q. How did you manufacture them—with the aid of this new machine ? A. No. I used the old machine. Its character was explained yesterday ; it is what we call the foot machine.

Q. When you had twenty men so employed, how did you divide them up ? A. Well, I endeavoured to have them divided up as equally as possible, in order to have about the same number of what we call journeymen and the same number of apprentices. My object in having them equally divided was to prevent the men taking advantage of me and making strikes, which they sometimes do, and to be able to fall back on my apprentices in case they should make a strike.

Q. How long would you take to indoctrinate or introduce a man to the business so as to make him—say, a winder, or sewer ? A. We would take a boy for a couple of years sometimes, and sometimes for two and a-half or three years, as we made the arrangement, according to the age of the boy.

Q. I do not understand that you are, and perhaps you are not answering my question. I ask you how long it takes a man or person to learn the business ; I do not wish to know how long it takes to make a boy into a man ; I do not mean waiting till the boy grows up, but I desire to know how long it would take—say, one of the prisoners, seventeen, eighteen or twenty years of age to learn the broom business—the most intricate parts of it ? A. We took them for a term of two or three years.

Q. Did you commence young with them ? A. We commenced young. I think, that perhaps the question which you want me to answer is to know how long it takes to make them remunerative ?

Q. I do not want to know how long it takes to make a boy into a man, and remunerative ; but how long a man,—a person, a boy or man, to learn the business, so as to be a good workman or a fair workman ? A. We could make them in three months' time, so that they would do a fair man's work.

Q. They could learn to do a fair man's work in three months' time ? A. That is on ordinary work.

Q. You mean, in winding, tying and sewing ? A. In winding, tying and sewing—that is complete work.

Q. Did you take men in or had you boys altogether coming in, in regular order, and that sort of thing, or was it skilled labour that you employed all the time, or was this the case more or less except as relates to apprentices ? A. I did not.

Q. What I call a skilled labourer is one who has learned the business ? A. I think that perhaps what I stated first would answer that question : when we knew that we had an equal number of boys and men at work, we felt ourselves independent of the journeymen, and that we could work without them ; but I did not mean to indicate that we had men among our boys, but rather that we had boys sufficiently competent to take hold of any part of the business in broom-making.

Q. Yes—in numbers, you had about one half men and one-half boys ? A. Yes.

Q. How young would the boys be ? A. We took them at ages varying from fourteen to eighteen

Q. What would you pay them—the boys ? A. Well, their wages varied from two and a-half to three and a-half dollars per week.

Q. That is during their terms ? A. We would give them perhaps two dollars and a-half per week during their first year.

Q. How long would it take them to learn sorting ? A. We look upon that in the old fashioned way of making brooms as one of the most important parts of the business as it requires a little judgment, to be able to separate the corn suitably for the various kinds of brooms made. We always put a pretty fair hand at it or otherwise kept a man on it steadily right through ; we have, however, taken apprentices as sorters only, and bound them for a term of years to learn that business.

Q. Well, now, you have not answered the question how long it takes to learn a man or boy to be a sorter ? A. Well, he would pass pretty well in three months.

Q. Did you hear Mr. Perry say yesterday that he used to learn them this part of the trade in three or four hours ? A. Of course, every broom-maker has his own system of arrangement in this matter ; but I could not understand exactly how it was that a person could learn it in twenty-four hours unless it was with one of those machines on which I have been told recently in a very short time to become proficient in it.

Q. That is, on the machine ? A. Yes.

Q. And what about the sizers ? A. The sizers do the same thing ; sizers are what we call sorters ; their duty is simply to select the different sizes of corn, which comes promiscuously, for the different styles of brooms that we make ; they select the largest for the best brooms and the next size, for the second quality, et cetera ; the rule we have is very simple ; it is to mark on the bunch the size.

BY MR. LANGMUIR.

Q. Does not a machine do that business here ? A. I believe that as a matter of fact—of course I cannot speak from personal knowledge on the subject—their facilities here for broom-making are very great.

BY MR. HARDY.

Q. Bunching and bleaching require no special training ? A. Bunching and bleaching any man can do ; a man fresh from the street will do it as well in two or three days as perhaps a man who has been at it for years ; it is the same with bleaching.

Q. What wages do you pay the men ? A. The wages range according to the quality of the broom the men make ; we have paid as high as five and a-half.

Q. Five and a half what ? A. Five and a half cents a broom.

Q. What do the men average in wages per day ? A. Some will run as high as fifteen dollars a week, others will earn from nine to ten dollars a week, et cetera. The boys would, we calculate, from the very start, make from twenty-five to seventy-five cents.

Q. Per day ? A. Yes.

Q. That is for boys from the very start ? A. Yes.

Q. Take a man with all the particulars about him, what do you calculate that he would make at most; say a man of twenty-two or twenty-three years of age ? A. A man right off after the first two or three days' showing—he is shown by the foreman right through every department when he comes in and he stands by until he understands running the machine and wiring—ought to earn from three to four shillings a day; that is after he has been there a week.

Q. Take a man as they average in the Central Prison, where they are all able-bodied men—should he earn fifty cents a day or sixty cents a day from the beginning ? A. I should think so. Perhaps this would not be the case from the very first beginning, but after the first week or about that time I should say that he would earn that fully. He ought, according to our calculation, to earn twenty-five cents, more than that. I should calculate that a prisoner—and prisoners are generally men—if an ordinary man of judgment, should earn as much at any rate as a boy of sixteen or seventeen in these matters.

Q. Have you compared the selling price of the Canada Car Company with the selling price of other wholesale broom-makers ? A. Such as I was, you mean, I suppose ?

Q. Yes. A. Well, I can only speak on that point from what I was told by one of their agents who called upon me. He quoted the prices, which I do not now remember, but I took a note of them at the time; and we, ourselves, concluded that it would be cheaper to buy our brooms from the Canada Car Company than to make them. We wondered, in fact, how they could manufacture brooms so cheaply. It was a matter of astonishment to us.

Q. How long was this ago ? A. It was, perhaps, six months ago.

Q. In what kind of mercantile business are you now engaged ? A. I am engaged in a general mercantile business; I sell willow-ware, brooms, brushes, et cætera; I am not manufacturing now.

Q. Why did you give it up ? A. Because I could turn my money to better use; the business got run down so that there was no money in it; as I said before, I could buy brooms cheaper than I could make them.

BY MR. GORDON.

Q. Have you had any experience with regard to prison labour ? A. I have had none at all, sir.

Q. You do not know, I suppose, the difference between prisoners and freemen, as to the way in which they respectively work ? A. I do not think I can say that I do.

Q. You do not know anything about it from personal experience ? A. Not from personal experience, surely.

Q. With regard to the prices—have you compared the prices of the Canada Car Company with those of other houses and other manufacturers ? A. Yes, sir.

Q. And how do the prices compare ? A. I think that those of the Canada Car Company are cheaper than the others.

Q. Can you give us an illustration on this point ? Tell us with whose prices you compared them, and what was the difference in rates ? A. Of course, I had Wood's quotations, now that I was going out of the business; he sent me his quotations, and I had also those of the Brantford factory; I compared them with the Central Prison, or rather with the Canada Car Company's quotations; and I found that the last named were somewhat lower than the others.

Q. Have you any of the quotations with you ? A. I have not, sir.

Mr. GORDON—I intend to produce quotations, both of Mr. Eddy and of the Canada Car Company; I am sure that they are the same; you (witness) are mistaken with regard to that, as we will see when they are produced.

WITNESS :—With regard to the qualities of broom, we used to manufacture four or five different kinds. We always, however, found that the cheaper quality of brooms sold much in advance of the better class of brooms.

Q. Mr. Mitchell, did I understand you to say that you, as a rule, trained apprentices in order that if there should be a strike among the men, the apprentices could take the place of the men ? A. Yes, sir.

Q. Have you ever worked altogether with boys ? A. Yes, sir.

Q. You have done so ? A. Yes.

8

Q. How many boys were you working with at the time? A. I think that I had some ten or twelve.

Q. How many brooms did these ten or twelve turn out? A. Each day? You mean by the whole number?

Q. By the ten or twelve? A. I could not just now say from memory; but I could give it so that it could be soon figured up. The lowest coming in made twenty-two brooms a day.

Q. Each boy? A. Each boy. They commenced with twenty-two brooms a day, and those who had been in the shop for perhaps a year or eighteen months, would make three dozen and a-half or four dozen.

Q. They would range from thirty-six to forty eight brooms per day? A. Yes, sir.

Q. Those who had been in for a year or eighteen months would make that number, and those who had been in for a less term than a year would make twenty two brooms a day. A. Yes.

Q. For what term? A. I should say that a boy who had been engaged at the work for two or three months ought to make twenty-four or twenty-five brooms.

Q. And at the end of a year he ought to make from thirty-six to forty-eight brooms? A. Well, I would not say so before that period; before their time was up, they would range up to that number. We were accustomed to set a task for the boys to do according to their term. We would give, of course, to start with, twenty brooms to make per-day during the first week, or the first two weeks perhaps; and then we would raise the number a step, five brooms, et cetera.

Q. How often did you raise it? A. Every two or three months.

Q. And did you pay these boys by the piece or by the day? A. By the day, sir.

Q. How much did you pay them by the day? A. We paid them from $2.50 to $3.50 according to the time that they had been there.

Q. That was per week? A. Yes; some, of course, during the first portion of their term received $2.50; to others, larger boys, we had to give $3.00 a week perhaps from the start; and then we would advance their wages half a dollar a week every year as their term progressed.

Q. Then with ten new boys who had been there for two or three months you could turn out two hundred and twenty brooms a day? A. I have not figured it up.

Q. You said that at that period they would make about twenty-two brooms a day? A. Yes, sir.

Q. And that labour would cost you about $2.50 a week? A. I should suppose that the average would be more than that, sir.

Q. That would be about forty-one and one-third cents a day? A. For the lowest grades of boys—yes, then to one who was perhaps on his last year we would pay $3.50.

Q. Then for about $4.10 you would get two hundred and twenty brooms?

Mr. HARDY.—That is for the mere making.

Mr. GORDON.—That is for the mere making—the labour; the ten boys paid at the rate of forty-one and one-third cents a day each would turn out about two hundred and twenty brooms a day? A. Yes.

Q. And a boy who had been there for two or three months would make ——? A. At what figure do you reckon the price of a boy's labour per day?

Q. At about forty-one and one-third cents. A. That is for the lowest grades; you have not taken the highest.

Q. And I have taken the lowest number of brooms. A. Of twenty-two a day—Yes.

Q. And that number would be increased by about five brooms per boy every two months? A. Yes, sir.

Q. Did you find that the boys, as a rule, picked up the business of broom making quicker than men? or did you often take green men on, so as to gain experience on this point? A. Well, no; we never took green men into our employ as apprentices; but we have taken men on as sewers; that is just to work in that one department; we would learn them how, in the course of a week or so, to sew very well.

Q. Did you find that men picked it up as well as boys? From your experience as an

employer of labour, do you find this to be the case ? A. As to experience, I never tried men, save simply in one department.
Q. In that class of labour ? A. I never tried boys in sewing.
Q. You never tried the two in the same class of work ? A. No, sir. The sewers were generally men who were out of work, and whom we could employ cheap, and put in to work for us, but not to learn the trade.

BY MR. HARDY.

Q. Yours being entirely hand work, of course one can learn to do machine work probably easier than hand work—in feeding, sizing, and sorting ? A. Our's is not machine work.
Q. Yours was hand work entirely ? A. Yes, I think that it is much more difficult to learn hand sorting, than machine sorting.

BY MR. GORDON.

Q. How do you find the Car Company's brooms ? A. In what way ? In quality ?
Q. Yes. A. I believe that they are very good, sir.
Q. Have you ever tried them ? A. No.
Q. Have you done anything in them? A. No, but I have seen samples, and on comparing them with others, I found them as fair as quality was concerned. They were about equal to those of other makers, while the prices were less.
Q. Did you not give an order for them when you found that out ? A. No ; we had an ample stock of brooms of our own manufacture on hand. That was one reason why we retired from the manufacture of brooms.
Q. Are you purchasing brooms now ? A. I have not bought recently.
Q. Have you purchased any since you ceased manufacturing ? A. No. I have not purchased any brooms since then. I should say that we have a large stock on hand which we manufactured ourselves.
Q. You have not purchased from outside parties ? A. I have not bought very many.
Q. And of course when you do want any, you will give the Car Company an order ? A. Most likely. I might state for the Commissioners' benefit in one respect, that of course we bought the handles which we used for the brooms, and of course paid the profit made in the manufacture of handles, and I understand that the Car Company make their own handles. This is, of course, something which we had to pay for.

Mr. FARQUHAR, called on behalf of the Canada Car Company, sworn and examined :

BY MR. GORDON.

Q. Mr. Farquhar, you are engaged in business I believe in the City of Toronto at the present moment ? A. Yes, sir.
Q. You are in the stone business ? A. I am in the stone and lime business.
Q. And I believe previously that you were employed in the Kingston Penitentiary ? A. I was, sir.
Q. You were one of the overseers ? A. Yes, sir.
Q. How many years were you employed in the Kingston Penitentiary ? A. I was employed there for three years and a half, sir.
Q. At what period was it that you were employed there ? A. I left there twenty-five years ago last May.
Q. At that time, was any of the Penitentiary labour let to contractors. A. Oh, yes, sir.
Q. Will you tell us what kind of industries was carried on there ? A. The industries were shoe-making, tailoring, and cabinet working.
Q. Can you tell us the price that was paid by the contractors for these different industries ? What were the prices paid at that time? A. I think that it was about thirty cents that was paid for the labour by the contractors.

Q. Thirty cents a day were paid by the contractors, you say? A. Yes.
Q. Now, what were the periods for which these men were confined? A. The periods varied, sir, from two years to life men. There were many life men confined in the Penitentiary. The terms of the other prisoners were for two, four, five, seven, and fourteen years.
Q. How did you find that these prisoners did their work? A. Do you mean with regard to learning the work?
Q. Yes, and when they were learned? A. With those that I had, I had no trouble after they were learned. Most of my men were long-sentence men. Stone cutting and building was my branch.
Q. This was the industry you had in charge? A. Yes. I always found that the short-sentence men were good for nothing with respect to learning how to be masons and stone-cutters. They had to be mere labourers.
Q. What did you call short-sentence men with you? A. Men sentenced to be imprisoned for two years.
Q. And you found that the men who were sentenced for two years were hardly of any use? A. No; they were of no use.
Q. When did you consider a man came to be of use to you? A. From that period on; the longer the term for which a man was sentenced the better he was.
Q. The better he was? A. Yes.
Q. From your experience with free labour in that and about the same time, do you find any difference between prison labour and free labour? Is there any difference in point of efficiency between prison labour and free labour? A. At the prison?
Q. Compare the two. Speak from your knowledge of free labour now? A. The free labour then was worth about sixty cents a day.
Q. I am talking of the efficiency of the labour. Did you find that prisoners sentenced for terms of two or three years did their work as well as free labourers who had been two or three years in learning their business? A. Oh, no, sir.
Q. They would not do their work as well? A. No, sir; they could not do it.
Q. Was there any great difference? A. Oh—a great difference.
Q. There was a great difference? A. Oh yes; a great difference.
Q. In favour of whom? A. The long sentenced men.
Q. The question is—can you compare prison labour with free labour? Was the labour of prisoners who had been sentenced for three years and who had been learning a business for three years, as efficient as the labour of free men who had been learning the business for three years? A. I think it would. I think that they learn as fast or faster than in the penitentiary, than what they would if they were apprenticed outside:—that is the most of them would do so.
Q. You think that this would be the case? A. Yes.
Q. And do you think that the prisoners would do as good work as free men? A. If they are put to it, they would.
Q. If they are put to it? A. Yes, sir.
Q. Then would you as soon have a prisoner as a labourer as a free man? A. I cannot say that, sir.
Q. You cannot say that? A. No, I would not at the same price.
Q. Not at the same price? A. No, sir.
Q. Well, why? A. A free man is more controllable. You can work a free man to more advantage than a convict, perhaps.
Q. You can work a free man to more advantage than a convict? A. Yes.
Q. To what greater advantage would you work a free man than a convict? To what extent? A. You know that men vary very much as to the amount of work which they will perform.
Q. On the same class of work? A. There is a good deal of difference found between free men and prisoners engaged in labour, when you compare one with the other. I could hardly however draw a proper line between these two kinds of labour. Out of most of my men—I just speak of them as I found them—I got just about as much work as I could have obtained out of free men. I always endeavoured to keep them in good spirits, and

I was never down upon them as some were ; and I therefore think that they worked with as much energy as if they had been working at piece work for themselves.

Q. What was the length of the sentences of the men to whom you are referring ? A. They varied, sir; they were all long sentence men that I had in the work I am telling you of ; their sentences varied from three and four years ; there were none for terms under three years up to life ; of life men there were a good many.

Q. Do you think that you could have done as well with short term men as with those mentioned ? A. No, sir.

Q. You could not ? A. No, I could not.

Q. Well, why ? A. Because you had not time to train them into the work ; besides the class of men that is sent to prison, is generally composed of men of loose moral habits and of an unsettled character ; they have to get settled and then it takes some time to get them to learn the work at which they may be put.

Q. I see that you are speaking of men who have got over all that ? A. Yes, I spoke of men who had become settled.

Q. You think that this would make a material difference ? A. It does make a material difference.

By Mr. Hardy.

Q. How long does it take a man to learn stone-cutting, or a boy or apprentice—a free person ? A. It takes him from three to four years, sir.

Mr. Hardy.—From three to four years—that will do.

Mr. Cook, called on behalf of the Canada Car Company, sworn and examined :

By Mr. Gordon.

Q. Mr. Cook, you are carrying on business now in the City of Toronto, at the Car Works, are you not ? A. Yes, sir.

Q. And before that you were with Mr. Eddy, were you not ? A. Yes, sir.

Q. What did you do when you were with Mr. Eddy ? A. I was a foreman there.

Q. In what branch of the business were you engaged ? A. I was in the match shop, and I oversaw the pail shop and the blacksmith shop. I was also sometimes in the mills. I was wherever I might be needed.

Q. Now we had some evidence from Mr. Eddy this morning with regard to the business done there—can you remember how many men he had employed when you were with him ? A. I could not exactly say how many there were, because they would be off and on ; the number engaged at work would be sometimes more and sometimes less.

Q. When were you with him ? A. It is now going on four years since I left him.

Q. It is now four years ? A. Yes.

Q. And how long were you with him ? A. I think I was there for nine or ten years ; the period was not longer than this. I do not, however, exactly remember it to a year.

Q. Were the men engaged in the pail business constantly changing ? A. The old hands stayed on most all the time ; some of them were changed, however. Three or four who were there when I went, were there when I left. They always keep the turners. They always wanted to keep them, and to keep the old hands as well.

Q. Say out of sixty men, how many changes took place in six months ? A. Out of sixty ?

Q. Yes. A. He never had so many changes as that in the pail shop.

Q. How many changes took place in six months out of sixty men ? A. I do not know that there would be many.

Q. How many ? A. That would be a hard thing to say.

Q. Can you not give us an idea of the number ? Were there one, two or three ? A. You might say perhaps that they were a dozen or so, out of sixty.

Q. In the period of six months ? A. Yes . but then I could not give the number exactly. Some would be going and some coming. The old hands, however, generally stuck on ; they all did so.

Q. Can you give us an idea of how many new men there were that entered his establishment during the nine years that you were there ? A. No.

Q. Now, how many lathes were used in his pail business? A. There were seven, I think, when I left the place.

Q. There were seven lathes ? A. Yes.

Q. How many men were employed on each lathe ? A. Sometimes two men and then perhaps boys ; and sometimes only one man and two boys. The work was all done by the job.

Q. It was all done by the piece ? A. All by the piece.

Q. What were these men paid ? A. I could not exactly say, I do not remember.

Q. Could you tell us how much work they turned out ? A. Sometimes they turned out three or four hundred, and they have gone up as high as five hundred.

Q. What do you mean ? By whom ? A. That is by the man who took the lathe and by another man who helped him.

Q. And you do not know how much they got for that ? A. No. They often used to tell me how much they received a hundred ; but the amount has slipped my mind.

Q. Have you been through the Central Prison ? A. I have been through it a number of times.

Q. Well, from your knowledge of this kind of business, do you think that the prisoners up there are able to manage that business ? A. I do not think that they are.

Q. What do you think is the reason why this is the case ? A. The reason why they are inefficient, is that they do not care what they do. They know that they are working for nothing, and of course they do not try to do their best. When you go in, you can always see them watching their foreman. They do not watch their work. You take men who are hired by the day, and if they do not attend to their work, you can turn them out, but you cannot do this with these men. You must get along with them in the best way that you can.

Q. A freeman is paid by the piece ? A. Yes, of course he does his work, or he cannot get along ; and as to the boys he hires under him, and apprentices, he can shove them though.

Q. Is that the only reason why you think that prison labour is not efficient ? A. Another reason for it is this : you take a man and put him on a lathe, and he is there perhaps, for a month or a couple of months, or for three months ; and then you may have to turn that man off as his time is up ; and you have got to put on another fresh man. A fresh man will do much damage to the machine while learning to do half a day's work ; he will spoil his tools, and he will keep the foreman in such a state that he does not know where he is half the time ; the foreman will do all he can, and go from one of the men to the other, as the responsibility rests with him.

Q. How long do you think that it would take a man to become efficient on one of the lathes ? A. On one of the lathes ?

Q. Yes. A. If you take a smart man and put him at the work, it might take him one or two months—that is, to go right through and turn out good work.

Q. But suppose one of the ordinary class of men—you have taken the case of a smart man—and how long would it take him ? A. You cannot trust him to groove a pail ; you cannot trust him with a groover ; such men do not get the jointing right, and the pail leaks ; then there are other men who will take hold of the work and do the grooving right off, and make the matches so that the parts of the pail will come together properly.

Q. How long would it take one of the ordinary class of men to learn, so that he would become efficient ? A. He might learn in six months.

Q. In six months ? A. Yes ; if he was a good man, and if he attended to his business.

BY MR. HARDY.

Q, To learn him what ? A. To turn pails.

BY MR. GORDON.

Q. Would you be able to form an opinion as to whether the labour that Mr. Eddy has, is better for this work at the price which he pays, than the labour which the Canada

Car Company employs, at the price which they pay ? A. I do not know what the Company pays, or what Mr. Eddy pays for labour; if I knew Mr. Eddy's price and theirs, I could form an opinion on the point.

Q. Suppose that Mr. Eddy's price was a dollar a day and that their price was fifty cents a day ? A. I would rather give the work out by the job; a day's work is not done, otherwise; this work is all done by the piece.

Q. Say that the price was one dollar a hundred ? A. I would rather give a dollar a hundred than have this arrangement made.

Q. You would prefer to do that to paying fifty cents a day for labour up here? A. Yes.

BY MR. HARDY.

Q. What department were you in at Mr. Eddy's? You were not in the pail department ? A. I had just to look in.

Q. You were not in the pail department? You were not foreman there? A. Oh, no.

Q. You were not in the pail department ? A. No, I was foreman in the match department.

Q. You were in the stick and box department, were you not ? A. I was in the nicking and match department.

Q. Were you making matches ? A. Of course.

Q. You were in the stick and box department—that is what they call it ? A. I do not know what they call it; but I was making matches.

Q. You ought to know; how long were you there? A. I was there from nine to ten years.

Q. I see too that you were never foreman in the pail and tub department ? A. I was never foreman there, but I took care of the tools; if anything was broken I went to repair it; I fixed chisels and tempered them.

Q. It would not take the men—with the exception of the one man who is employed as turner—any time to learn their particular duties in connection with the lathe ? A. At the lathe ?

Q. Yes. A. The most particular part of the work is the joining.

Q. How long would it take a man to learn how to be a jointer ? A. It would take quite a spell.

Q. What do you mean by "quite a spell" ? How long is that ? A. I mean that it would take a man—a smart man—all of six months before he would become a good jointer.

Q. You do not think that you could put a man on to do it in three days ? A. You could put a man on that work right off, if you did not care whether he did it right or not.

Q. You have somewhat different views even from the foremen up there about it; your views and theirs do not correspond. Take an ordinary carpenter sent to gaol—can he not learn turning in a very little while—in a few days ? A. He might take to it right off, and it might take him a good while to learn the work.

Q. That is a different thing. It would not take a blacksmith long to learn turning ? A. A blacksmith is not in that line at all.

Q. Unless he is an iron turner; but any man who has worked in wood, as a waggon maker or a carpenter, who is in the turning line, will learn turning in a little while ? A. There are the waggon makers; they understand turning; that is turning round, but the turning of pails is different work.

NELSON FRECHETTE, called for the Canada Car Company, sworn and examined.

BY MR. GORDON.

Q. Mr. Frechette, you are working in the Central Prison, are you not ? A. No, sir; I am working in this match factory.

Q. With Mr. Cook ? A. Yes, sir.

Q. Do you come from Mr. Eddy's, too. A. Yes, sir.

Q. How long were you there? A. With Mr. Eddy? I worked there for about twelve years.

Q. With him? A. I worked in the establishment; I have done all kinds of work, filing &c. I have been employed in the sash and blind factory, and in turning pails, and in the mills.

Q. You were turning pails? A. I was engaged in turning pails for a short time.

Q. Perhaps you can tell us how they managed in his establishment? How many men, as a rule, did Mr. Eddy have employed there turning pails—that is on every lathe? A. There were four on every lathe when it had a full crew; sometimes they were taken off in the Fall, and sometimes there are only two on the lathe, and then they might be put back in the Fall.

Q. Tell us how the four men work, and what work they turn out? A. The man in charge of the lathe hires three persons—one man and two boys. The man in charge takes a day's work, and the other two do like this: I commence at noon and quit at noon the next day, and the other man commences in the morning and quits at night. I get off two hundred pails, and the other man also gets off two hundred, making four hundred for two men and two boys.

BY MR. HARDY.

Q. What time would you and the other man be at work? A. It is all done on the same day. I only commence at noon, and quit at noon every other day. I joint the staves, match them, and he turns when I commence to joint my staves.

BY MR GORDON.

Q. Would you and the other man have a different boy? A. Yes.

Q. You are not all working at the same time? A. We are all working at the same time. It is like this: one of the fellows commences to work in the morning—the four all work at the same time—he begins to joint staves and lays off at noon from that work—and I would not commence until noon. That is the way of it. The work keeps right on. I commence to joint staves and match them, and then the other joints his staves. The work goes around like that.

Q. Both work at the same time, but not at the same kind of work? A. No.

Q. One joints and the other turns? A. Others have a different way of turning.

Q. You say that two men and two boys will turn out four hundred pails a day; what would they pay for that work? A. Suppose that I had charge of a lathe, I will pay one man a dollar a day.

Q. And what would you get for four hundred pails? A. I believe that the pay is now ten dollars a thousand.

Q. One dollar a hundred? A. One dollar a hundred.

Q. And how much would you pay the man? A. I would pay him a dollar a day.

Q. The man who would be working with you? A. Yes, sir.

Q. And what would you pay the boys? A. Say thirty cents.

Q. Each? A. Yes, sir.

Q. And you would pay $1.60 in wages, and you would get $4? A. Yes, sir.

Q. And you would turn four hundred pails a day? A. Yes, sir.

Q. How many men on the average were employed in making pails in Mr. Eddy's establishment when you were there? A. When I was there, of boys and men, I think there must have been twenty-four employed. I think that four persons were employed on each lathe when I was there.

Q. And there were about six lathes altogether? A. There were about six lathes. I think that there were about five pail lathes, and the one tub lathe.

Q. Were these men changed very often? A. No; this was not the case when I was there.

Q. How long did you say that you were there? A. I was there about two years ago, but is about seven or eight years since I turned for him.

Q. How long were you in the pail business? A. I was in it for about six months with Mr. Eddy.

Q. How many changes took place during that time among the men ? A. I never saw any during the time that I was there.
Q. You did not see any changes ? A. No.
Q. The man on the machine—the head man employs his own labour ? A. Yes.
Q. And when you were head man on a machine, would you employ a man who had not been accustomed to work at the business; or did you employ a man who had already learned it ? A. I would take a green hand and break him into the work.
Q. How long would it take you to do that ? A. Do you mean to run the lathe, or to learn how to turn pails ?
Q. I mean to run the lathe ? A. It would take a man over a year to learn how to run the lathe.
Q. What would you pay a man at the end of a year when he had learned the business ? A. They get one dollar a day.
Q. From the commencement ? A. No, this is the way it is : they take on young fellows from fifteen to eighteen years of age. These may work for two years and then they may get a chance to secure half of a lathe. All those that were there have been there ever since I knew them. There were not many changes, except when I was away. I was away for six or seven years in the States after I left the employment of Mr. Eddy.
Q. He generally kept the same class of men in his employ ? A. Yes, they would take a young fellow on and keep him.
Q. Have you seen them working in the Central Prison ? A. No, sir.
Q. You were never there ? A. I was never there.
Q. They place there six men on a machine : now, suppose a man was taken off and a new man had to be got to take his place, what would be the effect of the change on the rest of the gang ? A. I do not believe that it would occasion much trouble. If I had six boys on a lathe, and the one that was turning the inside of the pail was taken off, I would put the fellow who was turning off, on the work, and employ the green hand turning off; you can learn a man in two or three weeks to turn off probably about fifty or sixty a day ; that is, turning the outside.
Q. And when can you learn him to take charge of the machine ? A. To be able to take charge of a machine would require, as I said before, about a year ; and some men have worked for four or five, or even ten years at it, and yet have never been able to make a good pail.
Q. And others put at the same work will learn in a few weeks ? A. Yes, in a few weeks.
Q. Would you say that a man could learn in three or four weeks to do this work quite as well as any other man could do it ? A. He could do the work, but the difficulty lies in the taking care of the tools ; I mean that a man can learn how to run the lathe properly in the time mentioned ; the mere running of the lathe and the turning are not much.
Q. The turning is not much ? A. You can break a man in three or four weeks to do that well.
Q. Provided that you are there to take charge of the machine ? A. Yes.
Q. And one foreman can oversee the operation of half a dozen lathes ? A. Yes.
Q. Well then, are you working with Mr. Cook ? A. Yes.
Q. You 'are not working at the Central Prison ? A. No. I am filing and have charge of the planing room.
Q. And he is not working at the Central Prison ? A. No.
Q. Then the mere fact of substituting one man for another on these machines—which is done up there—does not amount to very much ? A. No.

BY MR. LANGMUIR.

Q. What sum do you say that a green man would get after being on for a time as turner ? If you wanted to engage a green man, what would you be required to pay him ? A. In turning as in the States, all who are employed are boys. The one who butts the staves is paid about twenty-five cents and the one who sets them up in the big iron hoop to

turn off, is generally paid twenty-five cents; the one who turns off is paid about sixty cents; and the one who turns the inside of the pail—you only require to employ one man.
Q. And what do you pay the man who has charge of inside of the pail? A. About seventy-five cents or one dollar a day. Down here they do the work in a different way from the manner in which they turn in the States. Suppose that I have charge of a lathe at Eddy's. I hire one man to run his side, and I run my side. We all run together. One turns and another matches, and so we go right round with the work.

By Mr. Hardy.

Q. What time would you have to work to turn out these four hundred pails? A. We would commence work about half-past six o'clock in the morning and stop at half-past three or half-past four o'clock. Some get through at half-past three and four.
Q. In the afternoon? A. Yes.

By Mr. Langmuir.

Q. Was your work confined entirely to pails, churns or tubs? A. We only made pails.
Q. Do you know anything about the changing at the lathes up here? You do not know anything about the work up here? A. No, sir.
Q. Well then, in Mr. Eddy's establishment where there were seven or eight lathes would ten or fifteen skilled men be able to employ the rest; and would all the rest be green men? If you had ten skilled men to take charge of the lathes and look after the machinery, would it do to have the others green hands? A. Well, I do not know.
Q. What proportion of green hands could be employed? A. It could be considerable.
Q. How many lathes were you running? A. At Eddy's?
Q. Yes. A. We had five pail lathes and one tub lathe.
Q. And how many people would these employ? A. There were generally four persons on each lathe.
Q. That would make twenty-four in all? A. Yes, twenty-four.
Q. Well, say that you had one skilled man to take charge of each lathe? A. One man could take care of six lathes.
Q. But one good man on each? A. Yes.
Q. And the work could be done with all the rest green hands? A. There should be one good man on each lathe.
Q. But all the rest might be green men? A. Certainly.

By Mr. Hardy.

Q. How long ago is it since you were there? A. At Mr. Eddy's?
Q. Yes. A. It is about two years; it is not quite two years.

By Mr. Gordon.

Q. Suppose that there was one foreman to fifty-seven prisoners—men whose terms varied from four months to a year--do you think that one man would be able to supervise the work of those different men on five machines—or five lathes? A. Yes. If he did nothing else save filing and taking care of the tools.
Q. He could look after them, each machine being worked by prisoners? One foreman could supervise their work? A. I could not tell you that. I would have to see the lathes before I would give an opinion on the point. Certainly, if they were all good machines, this would not necessitate much trouble, because you can learn a man in a short time to file and grind his matches, and set all his tools.

Q. Would these green men working on the machine be able to put right anything that went wrong? A. They could not be able to do all that would be required if the machine went wrong.

JOHN McBEAN, called on the part of the Canada Car Company, sworn and examined.

BY MR. GORDON.

Q. Mr. McBean, you are Vice-President of the Canada Car Company? A. Yes, sir.

Q. I think that you have occupied that position for some time, have you not? And you are General Manager besides? A. Yes; I am Vice-President and Managing Director.

Q. And you have held this position for some time? A. Yes, sir; it's some three years now since I so engaged in this undertaking.

Q. You have witnessed the working of the business of the Company from the time that the Company first started this new industry up to the present time? A. Yes; and I was there a little previous to that period.

Q. And the work has been carried on in a great degree under your supervision? A. This has been partly the case. I was there during this time. I suppose that it commenced with Mr. Warren, who was first there, and things were then situated about the same as now, so that I was pretty nearly at the head of the affairs then.

Q. Previously to having anything to do with this business, I believe you employed a considerable amount of labour during different periods in your life? A. Yes, sir, I have.

Q. As a contractor, you have employed labour of all kinds? A. Yes; in all branches of carpentering and joiner work.

Q. Now, you are acquainted with the character of the industries which are carried on at the Central Prison—in the pail, tub, and broom factory, in the blacksmithing department, in car making, and in connection with all these different occupations? A. Yes.

Q. What is your opinion of the nature of the labour that is employed up there, and how do you think it is suitable for the work that is carried on? A. I believe that if things could have continued as they were at first, and that if car-building could have been kept going as was originally intended, the prison labour would be more valuable, as it can be better employed on that than on any other work. If this could have been done, it would have paid. But every thing went down in such a way that we have failed to get any thing to do at car-building, and of course this labour under these circumstances was turned to this new industry; a large quantity of machinery that was procured for car-building had consequently to be set aside, and we had to put in a large amount of new machinery.

Q. Well, do you think that this particular class of labour for which the company contracted, is better adapted for car-building, than for the new industries at which it is now employed? A. Well, I think that this is the case: that is to say, I would rather employ the prisoners in car-building, if this could possibly be made to pay, and if we could sell what we would turn out, than on any other work.

Q. You would rather employ them in making cars than on other kinds of work? A. The reason for this is, that in car building, there is a great deal of heavy work to be done, and when you come to work on heavy timber *et cetera*, you require a good many men to handle it. Again, the machinery that is used for car building is of a very heavy kind; and if it is constantly in operation and a man is kept constantly at work on the machinery, of course he naturally comes to be a machine himself; and he can work with it to more advantage than he can on machinery made for lighter kind of work, with regard to the working of which men require to commence early in life in order to become thoroughly efficient workmen. On this sort of work, a man must start early in life to become smart and brisk at it; and, besides, these machines are more easily put out of order than is the case with the heavy machines utilised in car building.

Q. Now, do you think that if this car building industry was carried on here, this class of persons, which they confined here, with the average length of sentences that they have, could be made efficient and to repay the rate that the Company pays for their labour? A. That is a different question altogether. The question of making the work pay is about the hardest one there is to form an opinion on. In the next place, I must confess that I have been so much used to free labour that I would not have a man in my employ unless he was a first-class man. If he was not of this character, he would not remain long with me. The greatest trouble I see in the employment of this class of labour—prison labour, lies in the shortness of the sentences and the frequent changes which this necessitates. It is impossible, according to my view of the matter, to induce a man to take hold of a piece of work for a short space of time and secure good workmanship. You may make him do the work, and you may make him turn out a good piece of work; but what benefit is secured if he eats up four times its value while he is engaged in doing it? They may do it as well as they can, but it needs some time to enable it to pay. The great trouble experienced to my mind in this regard, is connected with the shortness of the sentences. When a man comes in, and you start him at any occupation, it takes so long a time to get him to work at it properly, and even if he does the work pretty well, before it can pay. That is a serious draw-back. This is one great objection. Then the changes are so frequent. Of course, if the men were there for terms of from three to seven years, it would be a different matter. When I used to take apprentices—I have employed a great number of them—if a boy presented himself and said that he wanted to serve for three years, I told him that I did not want him, for I could not make anything out of him. If, however, he said seven years, I would make up my mind that for what I would lose during the first part of his training, I would be indemnified during the latter part of his term. This, I think, is the general experience of masters with regard to the training of apprentices. Some of these men will work more quickly than others, and there will be a few mechanics among the prisoners; but even with mechanics, if you bring them into a shop and they have a change of work, you will find that good workmen will tell you—" I won't get my hand in even for a week in this shop." They are out of their ordinary track, and it will be found that in about a week afterwards, they will do a great deal more work than they did on their arrival. And if this is so with them, it must be worse with these men who come in promiscuously, right off the streets, and with no mechanical knowledge at all. Not only so, but their brains and powers have been injured by liquor; and it is difficult to get a day's work out of them, no matter how simple it may be. If a person who has never been used to it, is placed at any work, it bothers him; and he will not come to do it properly for some little time, requiring, moreover, a terrible waste of material to bring him to that point, and to make his labour pay. This is another trouble; and a further hinderance is due to the fact that we are obliged to take any number of men that may be offered us, whether they are mechanics or not, and whether we want them or not. If we only received as many men as we could put on certain work, and no more, then it might do; but, of course, if a man came to my door and said, "I have fifty apprentices here for you," I would say, "Fifty apprentices! What in the world will I do with all that number?" But if there were only three or four, I might use them. This gives us trouble. The Company will receive fifty or a hundred men, when perhaps they do not want over half the number.

Q. You have to use them whether the work is suitable to them or not? A. I know that the foreman says to me sometimes "They have tendered us these men, but it would be better to let them stay idle and pay for them, for there is nothing to do that they will do right." There is a great deal of this; of course, every body knows that there will be a great deal of it with short-sentence men.

Q. Can you tell us of any instance in connection with which these things you have mentioned have happened—such as that of one getting into the way of doing his work properly and then being changed for another man, sent to take his place? Does that ever happen? Can you tell us from memory that it has happened? Do you know of men who had become good workmen, and who, on their sentences expiring, were replaced by another and an inexperienced man? A. Oh, yes; sir.

Q. Do you know of many such cases? A. Oh, yes; the men are often obliged to go off. When a man has been for a long time in there, and when he gets used to a certain kind of work, it often happens that you could not get a man of the same class in the prison or outside of it, very well, and you have no one to put in his place; the work is consequently stopped. We hired men for two or three days; but I believe that this is against the prison rules, and when we found that out, we never did it again. Some men have to be discharged after a short time, and this is another of the troubles we experience.

Where a man becomes accustomed to a certain work, we have no man to'fill his place ; but outside, with free men, you can always have a man to fill any place, and if a man is going to be discharged, you can hire as good a workman, right away, to replace him, and consequently nothing is lost by his going.

Q. We had some evidence as to the time in which the pail business was learned by green hands, now what is your opinion on that head, Mr. McBean, judging from what you have seen in the Central Prison, and from your experience ? A. I tell you I have frequently regretted to find on entering the shop some mornings to find so many men idle ; and I have made a good deal of complaint about it. Sometimes all the men on a lathe would be doing nothing, sometimes there would be one complaint, and sometimes another. Sometimes this, of course, might be well grounded. There might be wanting something used in pail-making ; and this might occur with free labour. Again, a man who was trained to the work might be taken away and we would have to put another man in his place for a time ; then some of the men might be called out, and therefore the whole gang would be idle, and their usefulness, as it were, destroyed ; if a new man is placed among the other five. It all depends on the part of the work the new man has to do ; but still no matter how you arrange them, if a strange man who was never at the work before, is placed with the other five, they will have to wait the whole day before he is able to do anything material.

Q. Even when put at the simplest parts of the work ? A. Even on the simplest parts of the work ; I do not care where he is put.

Q. Suppose that the head man was changed, what would the effect be ? A. Of course, if the head man is taken away, the whole of the work is stopped ; you have to try men.

Q. For how long? A. If the head man is taken off and if you have no man to finish off the work, it stops the whole gang just in the same manner that a team stopping in the street would necessitate the stoppage of all the teams immediately behind them. Of course, at some time this man must go out, just in the same way as is the case with any other prisoner.

Q. Do you know of any lathe having been stopped for a day or part of a day in consequence of a new man having been put on the work ? A. I could not say for what length of time, but this has often happened at the Central Prison. I have complained very frequently about it. Sometimes stuff has even been more or less destroyed in consequence of the change. Of course, when this was the case I would go to the foreman, but he would say that he had done all he possibly could to prevent it ; he would have to show the man how to do the work, but when he had done this, and his back was turned, some work would be spoiled ; it was impossible for him to be there all the time, and this would be the story I would hear.

Q. What would you say would be the value of the work thus spoiled ? A. Of course, it would not amount to a very large sum, but perhaps half-a-dozen pails would be spoiled in a day, and perhaps more. Some other person would be better able than myself to tell you the value of it. I would not be there all the time to see the amount of work that was thus affected, but I have often seen half-a-dozen pails, even when they had got as far as the paint-shop, with their bottoms badly put on, and have had to throw them out. Of course, some such story would then be told me, as that a new man had been put on, and the foreman could not be there while every pail was being turned out.

Q. Do you think that it would be an improvement if more foremen were allowed to be in the prison than is the case at present, in order to supervise the work ? A. Well, I do not know how that would be. Somehow or other, free men and prisoners do not seem to agree well together ; of course, if you did that, you would have to put perhaps one or two freemen on every lathe. If one good freeman was placed on every lathe, it might perhaps be a benefit, but still you would have to go over the work of the lathes with them ; nevertheless somehow or other freemen and prisoners do not agree. We had one free man employed on one of the lathes, and it did not work very well ; perhaps it is only the foreman who can manage them ; of course, some other person might be better able than myself to answer that question.

Q. Take the case of the pail shop, do you think that one man over fifty-seven prisoners is enough ? A. I do not think so myself.

Q. You do not think so? A. I do not. Of course, if you had a free man to put on the lathe, in the absence of the foreman, it could be kept in operation all the time; he would not want to be there all the time; a raw man has to be shown everything connected with the work. These men have very little knowledge of the work at which they are put and some mistake or other may happen, or something may go wrong with the machine when the foreman is in another part of the place; and when he returns, it may have occurred and when he goes to see about it, he cannot discover how it came about, or who it was that did it; this is how it is.

Q. Has much loss been incurred in consequence of machines or tools being broken by the prisoners? A. Frequently some parts of the machines have been broken and sometimes this would not have taken place had free men been engaged at work, and sometimes it would be otherwise; I know that the loss has been considerable. Even a short time ago, damage was caused which cost us fifty dollars; it was all done because a prisoner became a little angry with the foreman; to repair the damage cost us fifty dollars.

Q. Was this done through ignorance? A. No, no. It was done on purpose; and only a month ago another case occurred; a tap was turned, and a whole barrel of varnish allowed to be lost. It flowed over a great part of the place.

Q. Do you know of many such cases? Has any loss been incurred in any instance owing to things having been stolen by the prisoners? A. I know that I hear every now and then of many things being stolen, but I do not remember precisely what was taken. Perhaps some other one might give you information on this point. I do not remember the quantity of goods stolen, but it has amounted to a great deal. Complaint is made to me very often on this score. Finding this to be the case, we procured locks, and we put them on various places. I do not know how it happened, but somehow or other the locks and everything else got broken. The prisoners seem to understand that business very well, and they get through locks very quickly; still, of course, there are some good fellows amongst them. They are not all of that character; but there is always certain to be men among them who will do that kind of thing. Nevertheless, I say that, so far as the men are concerned, I can get along with them very well.

Q. Can you shortly summarise, Mr. McBean, your objections to this labour and put them under two or three heads? A. Of course, I have gone a good deal over the objections to it. I have been used to free labour, men paid for their work; but even with free labour, it is not every man that would suit me; but with these men you cannot make your choice. Two of them came to me to-day, and said: "Why Mr. McBean, we have been working for you all the time we have been here and we are going out to-morrow, we have not a cent with us, and what are you going to do for us?" Up to this time, it has cost me a hundred dollars in giving trifles to such men. Four or five of the men have even come to my house for assistance. After all, how could you expect these poor fellows to work in the way they are put in there. I suppose if I was placed there, I would not care to do the work when I got nothing for it, and everybody looked down on me. I would not have much heart to work under such circumstances; but if people are praised up a little—and everybody likes a little of it—you can get along with them much better. I do not know but that a good deal more is done by prisoners, owing to this course being followed. If you give them a little and promise them, they do very well, though I have learned in some instances that it was not well to give them anything. Still, I am not so sure of that.

BY MR. HARDY.

Q. Do you not think that a little foresight would prevent a whole lathe standing because a new man was put on, and some one had gone out occasioning a change of men? Do you not think that a man could be trained a few days previously to take the vacant place? A. No. I will explain that matter. I have looked at this question, and spoken of it pretty often, trying to see whether that could not be done; but I cannot see any way in creation of doing it, unless you have two or three freemen to take the places of men who go out. The fact is, you cannot put another man at work to train him, or if you do, the other must look on.

Q. But could not the training be communicated two or three days beforehand? A. What is the use of training a man under such circumstances? What are you going to do with the other one meanwhile ? If you did teach him beforehand, what benefit would be obtained ?

Q. I ask you whether, as a matter of judgment and appertaining to the management of this business at the Central Prison, you should wait until the very day and hour that a man is going to depart—say one man out of the six employed on a lathe—to put on another man ? A. Of course not, of course you would look out for him and have him ready to take the other man's place.

Q. You would not at all events put a man who was just fresh from the country and to the work, at the head of the gang ; but rather at the easier work and at carrying the staves ? A. Certainly.

Q. I do not see why a lathe should be standing still for a moment ? A. Of course, but if you went up there and stayed for a few days, perhaps you would know a little more about it. It is rather a troublesome thing to explain the whole matter ; these men are on the lathes, and no matter what happens—if anything happens, they must stop work, and of course amongst prisoners engaged in labour there are a good many ways of securing a stoppage ; this will be particularly shown if a man has been a little fractious—will not work and is made to work—or if a man goes out and some one else comes in ; when a man falls sick, the same thing occurs; we try to put the best men on the lathe and the poorer class of men in less responsible positions. Our foreman is here, and no doubt he will give you any information you may require on this point.

BY MR. LANGMUIR.

Q. Could you not arrange matters so that a man could work up and take the place of a further advanced man ? A. Of course, but half the time we do not know a man is going out.

Q. Do you not get a list ? A. We know the time at which a man goes out, but this is not all the trouble ; there are other troubles besides this one encountered.

Q. But do you not receive a list giving the length of the sentences of the prisoners and also their previous occupations ? A. Oh, yes.

Q. Do you know exactly the time when they are going out ? A. I think we do, so far as I can tell by anything given us of that description. I think that this is generally done ; and that we get everything we could wish from the prison authorities. I do not consider that we should complain.

Q. Well, Mr. McBean, you say that you consider prison labour more valuable in connection with car building operations than with the present industries ? A. Well, I should think so, sir. At least, I should consider that if we could have kept at the work which was originally intended to be prosecuted, the results would have been more favourable.

Q. That was the original contract with the Government, was it not ? A. It was.

Q. Well, the Government was not to blame, were they, for the stoppage of the car-building ? This was due to the stagnation in trade, was it not ? A. Of course, I do not suspect that the Government were to blame for that, the same thing affected every other trade, and there has been a great deal of it. The business of car-building in nearly all the big establishments has failed more or less. And just at that time—I do not know whether it was true or not—it was said that when the Company first commenced operations, they could have secured a larger amount of work, had it not been for the fact that the prison was not ready for the work ; and that they had hence to use a large amount of free labour, or do some other work which was not so convenient or desirable ; and, by the time that all the preparations were made, and the Company obtained the services of the prisoners, it appears that the bottom came out of car-building, and that they could not get cars to make.

Q. Were you frequently in the prison while car-building operations were going on ? A. I was not there while car-building was going on except after the change took place, when we finished two hundred cars for the Canada Southern Railway Company. I did not come until after the trouble occurred.

Q. It was reported that the Car Company was aware of the fact that the prisoners were working very satisfactorily as regards car-building ? A. Evidence was taken in this regard; a good deal of complaint was made and we had a Committee of five appointed to consider the question; I was a member of the Committee, and we obtained evidence with reference to all the prison labour used around the place; it was all put in writing; a great many were against it and some were for it.

Q. It was not carried on very long, was it? A. Before that, of course, it was carried on, but it stopped altogether at that time; I suppose that we examined about fifty men and all the parties around the place.

Q. The car-building operations were not in existence very long, were they? A. No.

Q. Were the operations of the Car Company in a state of complete organization while the car-building was going on? A. I think that they were—I think so.

Q. They were fully organised? A. I think so.

Q. Were the works in capital running order? Had you been long enough in working order to do the work completely? A. I did not expect that we were long enough in operation to get into thorough working order, but I think that we had up the steam hammers, and all the car machinery, I believe, was in full blast.

Q. Quite so? A. And the foundry was the same; of course, I do not think that they understood the business of making wheels very well.

Q. You do not think that some of the men understood their business very well? A. I do not think so.

Q. Don't you consider that their operations—that is, the effective working of the concern, was interfered with a good deal, owing to the fact that some of the men were not very well acquainted with their business? A. Now, some of that sort of thing will occur in the starting of all new businesses, and there is always something of the kind happening under such circumstances; I told you that I could not expect everything to be in thorough order at the start.

Q. Very well; after they stopped that industry this one was inaugurated or begun at the request of the Company, was it not? A. Yes.

Q. They thought the matter all over, and they thought that it was best to take this course? It was the selection of the Company? A. The whole thing was going down altogether, and if this had not been done, this would have been complete so far as we are concerned; we then came to the next trouble; they obtained the services of an over sanguine man, who made them believe that this establishment was going to be everything.

Q. When operations were commenced, Mr. Warren took charge? A. Yes.

Q. Do you consider that he was a good man to get everything into good working order? A. Well, we now have the best machinery in the Province, and he was the means, in the first place, of getting in and buying this machinery.

Q. I quite understand that; but could you say that he was capable of carrying on operations to the best advantage? A. I could not say that he was. I do not think so.

Q. He is not at present in the employment of the Company? A. No; but, of course, we have another man there.

Q. Your experience of Mr. Warren, your first manager, was that he was not a good organizer, as far as keeping the prisoners well employed is concerned? A. The fault I had with him was that I never found him there. He promised to be there, but he was frequently absent from home. I never saw him near the place.

Q. That must have interfered very much with the proper working of affairs? A. The trouble related to commencing this new branch of business. We had to procure other machinery, and about $20,000 or $30,000 worth of machinery which we obtained for this other work was of no value. Besides it took longer than he said it would take, to get into operation, and he gave us prices a great deal larger than we have ever been able to make out of the work done.

Q. He misled you? A. No doubt there was a great deal of that, or I suppose that we would never have started this industry.

Q. Now when did Mr. Warren leave you? A. He left us about twelve months ago, I suppose.

Q. Have you taken charge since? A. I have been there from the commencement; but I merely took charge after he went away, and Mason got wrong in his mind, poor fellow. I had then just to step in. I did not wish to do so, but I was the only one who had any knowledge of the business, from the commencement of it. I know everything about it. The foreman, Mr. Brandon, was there also, of course; he is a very good and excellent man, I think. I believe he has a thorough mechanical knowledge of machinery, and of everything connected with it, and is able to put everything of this kind in its place.

Q. Then matters have improved since Mr. Warren left you? A. Oh yes; the thing is in capital working order now.

Q. It is now in good working order? A. I think there is nothing it wants this year to get it into right shape, save the securing of good prices for the work which we turn out, and the obtaining of the prison labour at a little lower rate.

Q. You wish to obtain a reduction in the price of labour? A. Yes.

Q. You were speaking of the lathes having stood sometimes idle for a while—did not that disorganization in your operations extend to a certain extent sometimes to the furnishing of the material? Were you not delayed in the work sometimes owing to the want of good material? A. I can tell you that very plainly. I do not think—suppose if you will that I give the praise to myself—that you will find any other man in the city who will furnish that material as well as myself. When we started there we had to begin without all the bolts we required, and I do not believe that from that day until now—with the exception of a brief period last summer, when we had a little trouble with the man who had the contract for supplying the bolts—it has been as well supplied in this particular as any place should be.

Q. Was that the case before you took charge? A. Of course, I furnished all the material before.

Q. Was any delay experienced in the furnishing of it? A. There has been no delay that I know of.

Q. There has been no delay? A. Not that I am aware of.

Q. Did any lathes stop for want of material? A. Never, except for the one or two days, and that I will explain. You remember the drying kiln. Now as to that drying kiln of ours—the big one, when the frost came we changed the engine, and when we brought the steam to the drying kiln, the man who was in charge, a prisoner or some other person, let the thing get frozen, destroying the whole kiln. We had only one other, a little one, and of course, before we got the large kiln into order again, some little loss of time occurred, I think, in getting the staves dry; but there was no want of material, because we had thousands of them.

Q. Was there any delay? Did any delay take place owing to the want of sufficient drying kiln capacity? A. Yes, that might be.

Q. When representation was made regarding this to the Government, did they at once set to work to remedy this state of things? A. The Government would do nothing for us, we had to do it ourselves and it cost us one hundred dollars.

Q. Were the Government bound to give you any more drying kiln accommodation? A. We put in the pipes.

Q. Therefore there were some delays as well as inefficient labour? You say that the delay which happened in the furnishing of material, was due to the want of drying kiln space to a certain extent? A. It was not owing to the want of drying kiln space, but to the pipes getting frozen and burst.

Q. Then you had sufficient drying kiln space? A. Yes, sir; when we began to extend our operations, we required the other one. We could not get along with it very well; we had not as much machinery and work then as now; we had about four or five lathes when we had the small kiln.

Q. As a matter of fact, were you not delayed frequently, owing to the want of dry material, if it was not due to the want of drying space? A. I cannot tell. I do not believe that the half of what was said about it was true.

Q. You think not? A. I do not believe it.

Q. Did you go to the States, Mr. McBain, and examine their prisons, with Mr. McMurray and others? A. No, sir.

Q. You were not one of the directors, then? A. No.

Q. You know nothing at all about it? A. No. I do not know anything at all about it; but I have heard something about it. With the Government furnaces, there was a great deal of machinery which the Government furnished originally, but it is not of much value to us now.

Q. That is true; but still it was furnished to the Company? A, Oh, yes.

Q. It was furnished to the Company and paid for? A. Yes.

Q. Was this machinery originally put into the Central Prison at the request of the Canada Car Company? A. The machinery was, of course, put in by the Canada Car Company.

Q. Was the steam power, the motive power, the belting, the pulleys, and the shafts put in at the request of the Canada Car Company? A. I suppose so. That was put in by the Government—the engine and boilers, the pulleys, and the main shafting, but nothing else. We have every other machine in the place.

Q. That is the machinery; but we are talking about the fixtures. We do not claim the machinery. Do you know that ovens were put in and the cupolas? A. Yes, they put them in, but they are of no use to us now.

Q. You say that no machinery was put in—but were there not two cupolas and furnaces put in? A. I don't count them as machinery, and you do.

Q. I call them fixtures? A. I call machinery everything that works as a machine with belts and counter-shafts.

Q. And these were all put in by the Government, were they not? A. No, sir.

Q. Not the belts and counter-shafts? A. The main shafts were, but the counter-shafting never was. They belong to the machines—the planers.

Q. Whatever the Government put in, was it not placed there upon the requisition of the Canada Car Company? A. No doubt.

Q. So that the Government is not to blame if this is not desirable for your purposes? A. No.

Q. This is the fault of the Company itself? A. Of course, we keep the machinery in order. We have to keep the boiler and engine, and all these things, in order.

BY MR. HARDY.

Q. Did you ever know of a man running machinery and not being bound to keep it in order? Are you going to stipulate that the Goverment should keep it in order for you? A. No; but if we made the terms with you, you might keep them in order.

BY MR. LANGMUIR.

Q. You were saying, Mr. McBain, that your great objection was to short-date sentences? A. Short-date sentences are very objectionable, in this regard—there is no doubt of that; and then we have to take more prisoners than we really want to employ.

Q. And you also object because you are not getting enough of mechanics? A. That is one great objection; there is no doubt of it.

Q. Do you think if you could get mechanics in every instance, and long-date prisoners, and could take them just exactly as you might require them, you could secure them at the rate of fifty cents a day? I do not think that you could ever expect that. Prison labour must have its disadvantages? A. Of course, I am aware of that.

Q. And when you tendered for this labour, you tendered knowing what these disadvantages were. A. No; I do not think that they did.

Q. Do you not know that some of the Directors of the Company visited prisons in the United States? A. I am aware that they did; but, nevertheless, they do not know much about the subject yet.

Q. They do not know their own business? A. I do not think that they knew it in this instance.

BY MR. HARDY.

Q. You are only paying about half as high as the rate paid for this labour in some places in the States? A. But you know that at the time labour in the States was very high; the price paid for labour was a great deal higher then than now. Times have changed since that period. What was then worth fifty cents is not worth more than half that now, with regard to the price paid for labour.

Q. Labour, you say, is not so high now as it was then? A. No. What was then worth fifty cents is not now worth more than twenty-five cents to-day, with regard to the difference that has taken place in the times, and the price of free labour outside.

Q. This is owing to dullness in business, and the depreciation that has taken place in the value of property and labour? A. Of course; if there was plenty of business it would raise prices and make everything more lively. I suppose the same thing is true with reference to shops outside.

Q. They have experienced the same difficulty? A. They have worked for nearly the same prices which we paid for the labour of prisoners; and these employers have the advantage of being able to discharge their employees at any time if they have not work for them; they need not keep their men under such circumstances, but, of course, we are obliged to pay for them under any contingency.

Q. You are aware that many iron works have been closed up elsewhere within the past year or two? A. Yes, we know that very well. It has been the case, but we hope to have better times than these some time or other.

By the Chairman.

Q. I would like to ask you, in view of your experience in superintending these works, and of the fact of your having been a large employer of mechanical labour yourself for a number of years—what you really consider this labour to be worth to you? If you were to take it on the terms on which it is furnished by the Government, what would you consider its value to be? A. If I was going to take the contract myself, no doubt I would put in a scale of prices, as to what I was prepared to do; but so far as short-time labour is concerned with relation to the performance of good mechanical work, I would give nothing for it, because I consider that a man confined for the space of three or four months, only becomes capable of earning anything when his time is out; while as to the longer term man, I would enter a scale of prices, graded up to the time when they would have learned to do something of value. Taking it on the average, I cannot perceive that this labour is worth more than one-half the price which we pay for it, as we are obliged to take the prisoners promiscuously and to accept the number of men and short-time men, which is unavoidable under the present circumstances.

Q. If you desired to carry on this same business on your own account and the question was—what kind of labour you should employ, and this labour was offered to you, would you be willing to take it and pay the present prices? A. I would not take it at any price; I would not be bothered with it; that would be my feeling respecting this kind of labour. I have been so long accustomed to free labour and free men, that I could not bother my head with the training of all these persons during the whole of the time.

By Mr. Hardy.

Q. I believe that you make no charge for your services, rendered as overseer and Managing Director? A. I do intend to make a charge for my services whenever the Company has anything with which to pay me; I am one of those kind of men that you have not to grind down. I told the Directors, "I am not going on a salary—I have not been on a salary for nearly forty years to any man, but I will give you my services and act as if I were working for myself; and when my time is out if you think that I have earned anything and have anything to give me, give me what you like." I would leave the work to-morrow if it was desirable; I do not say that I give my services for nothing altogether, but if they say that my services are worth nothing like the labour of the prisoners to themselves, I would reply—" That is all right, I am satisfied. " I offered my services because I found the Company in such a position as to render them desirable; there was no one connected with them possessed of practical mechanical knowledge, or who knew anything at all about the business. The time was when I had nothing and I made enough to enable me to have lived as an independent man during the last twenty years without doing any work at all; and I made it in mechanical business. At the same time, I am one of the kind of men, who would work for nothing rather than be idle. I offered my services on account of the position in which the Company was situated. They had no one to take hold of the work, and the man who had managed it, had been so sanguine that he thought he could obtain money out of anything, though it is still harder to secure than any thing else.

E. B. EDDY made the following supplementary statement :—
Witnesses have stated here that the men employed on the pail lathes were about twenty-four or twenty-six in number. Of course, this arose from the fact that they gave the number of hands engaged on some of the lathes while at work, but it does not comprise the men employed throughout the pail and tub department, and in the pail and bottom department and in putting in staves. I mention this because you might be under the impression that our statements conflict, but taking the number of hands over and above what are engaged on the lathes, you will find that it will come up to the standard which I have given.

BY MR. GORDON.

Q. Mr. Eddy, can you tell us whether these price-lists, which I hand you, are correct? A. Our prices are correctly stated here. They are furnished by the Messrs. Nelson.
Q. These are the prices of the goods which are manufactured by you? A. I presume that they are about the thing, sir. These relate to about a year ago or more.

MALCOLM STEWART, called on the part of the Canada Car Company, sworn and examined.

BY MR. GORDON.

Q. Mr. Stewart, I believe that you are one of the foremen employed in the Car Company's Works? A. Yes, sir.
Q. You are employed in the blacksmithing department, are you not? A. I am engaged at work both in the machine department and in the blacksmithing department.
Q. How many men have you under you? A. At the present time, I have fifteen.
Q. How long have you been employed in that department? I believe, that you have been twice in the employ of the Company? A. I was there from the time when they began operations up to the date when they shut down; and I came back some time in the month of last January. It may be that this took place a few days after the first of that month.
Q. How many of the men who work under you knew the business before they came to you? A. There are among the number two blacksmiths, who had partly served their time and two machinists, one was a fitter, as I would call him.
Q. And what about the other twelve men. A. They are for the most part ordinary labouring men. Some of them are clerks; and some have been one thing, and some another.
Q. Now is the principal part of the work which you have to do in your department, skilled work, or is it such work as a labouring man can take hold of it at once? A. One half of it is skilled work, and one-half is labourer's work.
Q. One half of it? A. Yes.
Q. Then how many of these fifteen men could be employed right away on work which you may have to do? A. You mean what men could take hold of it at once?
Q. Yes. A. If I had any work for labourers to do, I could employ them on the spot; but as far as the other half of the number is concerned, two or three weeks would be required to communicate to them the run of the business, and to make them available for the labour, which I intend them to perform.
Q. It would take two or three weeks to learn them what to do? A. This could not be done in that space of time. I served my time for seven years, and I could not tell exactly how long it would take a man to learn the trade.
Q. And how long have these men been with you? A. Some of them have been with me since I began to work there.

Q. That is, for about six months? A. Yes; I think that this is the case with four or five of them.
Q. Four or five of the fifteen you had when you first came there? A. Yes.
Q. And you have had to take four or five new hands on? A. Yes, most decidedly.
Q. Now, how many of these men who still remain with you have become efficient men? A. I have none who have become efficient men.
Q. You have not any of this class? A. No, certainly not.
Q. You also include the two blacksmiths and the fitter in this statement? A. The fitter is gone; he was there for only about seven or eight weeks.
Q. He was there only seven or eight weeks? A. That is all.
Q. Have you the two blacksmiths with you still? A. Yes, sir, one of them came in about a month after and began work here; he was sentenced for six months, and he leaves the prison on Saturday next, I think.
Q. So on Saturday you will only have under you one man who knew anything about the business? A. That is all, sir.
Q. Do you find that these prisoners learn as fast as free men do? A. Certainly not.
Q. About what would be the proportion of work which these men would turn out compared with free men? A. As far as I have learned, the prisoners, up to the present time, taking into consideration only the men who have worked for six months, will do about one-third of the work that would be performed by free men; this has been the case since I started. This statement applies to one class, but I can get nothing at all out of the other class; I cannot get them to do the work, and they might as well stop where they are.

BY MR. HARDY.

Q. This observation does not apply to labourers? A. No, it relates only to the men engaged in mechanical work; a labourer is a labourer all over the world.

BY MR. GORDON.

Q. I understand you to say, that you cannot profitably employ one half of your men? A. I have not got labour for one-half the number of men that I could employ sometimes at labouring work; and at other days again, I will not have anything for them to do; of course, I cannot employ unskilled labour all the time.
Q. And you are beginning to obtain about one-third of the work from these men who have been with you for six months, that would be done by free men? A. Just about one-third is all that I can get.
Q. For how long have you obtained so much work from them? A. For about two months, I suppose.
Q. And then what did you manage to get out of them during the first four months? A. I would not secure over one-fourth of the work which free men would do; I do not suppose that it would amount to so much, taking into account the tools they broke, and the time I was occupied in fixing them, and doing one thing and another; I do not think that I would get anything like one-fourth of the work out of them.
Q. Have you found many tools broken? A. Oh, yes, I always find tools broken.
Q. In greater number than are broken by free men? A. Most decidedly I would; free men always try to keep their tools in good order and to continue in their situations; but prisoners do not care, you cannot discharge them; and they are not anxious to keep their tools in a proper condition—none whatever.
Q. Are these tools broken by the prisoners accidentally? A. Oh, no; tools are often broken owing to carelessness; but they are broken accidentally; this will happen in the case of freemen; even machines will sometimes be broken by free men.
Q. Since you have been there, have you been obliged to report any man in your department? A. Oh yes.
Q. What was the cause for this? A. I could not get work out of them.
Q. You could not get work done? A. Oh no.
Q. How many times have you had to do that? A. I have been obliged to adopt

this course on several occasions—with some men perhaps once a week, and with others perhaps twice a week.

Q. What has been the result of it? A. Well, you cannot find any results accruing from it. A man says he is willing to work, and I cannot find fault with him; often he is willing to work and can do a day's work. As long as this is the case, what can you do?

Q. Before you worked with the Car Company, were you employed in other places in the same way? A. Certainly; I have been employed for the last twenty-four years in the same class of business in which I am now engaged.

Q. Where a large number of men were employed? A. Yes; from one hundred to two thousand.

Q. And judging from the knowledge which you have acquired of the two classes of labour, which do you think would be the most valuable—free labour at double the price of this, or this labour at about the figure which the Company is paying for it? A. I would like to take a contract with free labour at double the price.

BY MR. HARDY.

Q. At double the price? A. Yes, sir.

BY MR. GORDON.

Q. Would you give as much as one-half the price for this labour? A. I would. If the labour at the prison was paid for at the rate of sixty or seventy cents, and free men obtained $1.50, I would consider that they were worth a little more than one-half.

Q. Who were? A. That is, if they were paid at the rate of sixty cents.

Q. I want to know if you think that the labour of a prisoner is worth half as much as that of a free man? A. No, it is not. The prisoner is not worth more than one-quarter, or a little over one quarter as much as a free man. I would not give anything more than that for his labour.

Q. In consequence of what you have stated? A. In consequence of his breakage of tools and of his not being able to repair them.

Q. Would it make any difference if the prisoners were in for long periods? A. This would make a good deal of difference to the contractor.

Q. For the contractor? A. Yes, sir.

Q. Suppose that the terms varied from three to four years, what then would be the difference? A. The difference would be this: you would have time to learn a man his business or what he was intended to do, and to obtain the benefit of his skill, but with sentences from three to six months just as soon as you succeed in learning a man how to do the work at which he has been placed, he leaves you, and you are obliged to turn round and take another man in his stead.

Q. That is your experience in this relation? A. That is my experience in prison labour.

BY MR. HARDY.

Q. Let us see: the class of work in which you are engaged, is what? A. It is car work.

Q. And machinist's work, you say; do you repair machinery in your shop? A. I have got to repair the machinery because the prisoners are not able to do it, sir.

Q. Do you do that in your shop? A. Yes, I repair it myself. But they work in iron or in wood-work.

Q. In iron-work in the making of cars? A. Yes, sir.

Q. It is like a class of blacksmiths' work, is it not? A. Blacksmiths' work includes turning, boring, drilling, fitting, and binding together as far as iron-work is concerned.

Q. It requires some little time to learn that class of work? A. It takes quite a little time to learn it.

Q. What are they called? What kind of mechanics are they called, when they learn how to do it? A. They are called machinists.

Q. What wages do machinists through the city receive, when they are free men? A. Outside at the present time, wages are very low. They have dropped from thirty to sixty cents during the past three or four years. They were $2.25, and now they are $1.50; and very few men get that amount. The very best men in the town are paid one dollar and seventy-five cents a day.

Q. Their wages run from $1.50 to $1.75 a day? A. Yes.

Q. And what do labourers receive for heavy work? A. They got $1.50 a day.

Q. And what do they obtain now? A. From ninety cents to a dollar a day.

Q. Well then, if machinists outside obtain one dollar and a half per day, you pay one-third of this amount for this labour? A. But we have no machinists engaged at work.

Q. I say, that if machinists who are free men, are paid in the city $1.50 a day for their labour, you are paying just one-third of that amount, fifty cents a day, for this labour? A. Yes, sir, about one-third.

Q. And about one-half of your men are labourers? A. Just about one-half.

Q. And you require one-half of the men in your department to be labourers? A. We require one-half of them to be labourers.

Q. You get these labourers for fifty cents a day, and as a labourer is a labourer all the world round, as you say, you are, as a matter of fact, obtaining this labour for half price? A. I do not know at what price we get the labour; I only state my own opinion.

Q. You say that they are about as good inside as out? A. As far as learning is concerned, I did not say that they are as good; I said that a labourer is a labourer all over the world.

Q. Is it chiefly hand work in your department? Is not blacksmithing proper hand work. A. Blacksmithing is always hand work.

Q. Is there any machine work in your department? A. Oh, yes.

Q. Of what kind is it? A. We have machinery for turning, boring, and drilling.

Q. I do not understand you to say, that out of two hundred odd men engaged there are only two blacksmiths? A. That I do not know.

Q. Would you not select the blacksmiths among the prisoners, or do you take such men as are sent you? A. When we send for a blacksmith and suppose that we have got one, we find, perhaps, that he has been a clerk in some store instead. That is the way in which they are served out to us; but, of course, I could not say anything about it. We generally keep changing round until we secure one, but that is not very convenient. Sometimes we have a blacksmith changed from another shop into ours.

BY MR. LANGMUIR.

Q. Are you shown the lists? Are you shown the previous trades of these people? A. I am not, sir. I have never seen them. Of course, the manager or foreman generally attends to that matter.

BY MR. GORDON.

Q. Mr. Brandon selects the men most suitable for your department? A. I suspect that he does. I have no doubt that this is the case.

BY MR. HARDY.

Q. You only pay one-third of ordinary rates for skilled labour, and one-half for common labour, and you get all the machinery thrown in? A. What machinery is that?

BY MR. LANGMUIR.

Q. You get the motive power, and the boiler and engine? A. Yes.

Q. And the running gear also? A. We get the running shafting, and that is all.

Mr. McMURRAY, called on the part of the Canada Car Company, sworn and examined :

BY MR. GORDON.

Q. I believe, Mr. McMurray, that your firm are the agents of the Canada Car Company ? A. Yes, we are.
Q. And, of course, you are conversant with their prices ? A. Yes.
Q. And you are not only the agents of the company, but, I think, you also act as the agents for some other individuals or firms ? A. We do.
Q. Can you tell us how the prices of the Canada Car Company, for pails and tubs and brooms, compare with those of Mr. Eddy's and other establishments ? How do they range ? A. Well, when the prices of these goods, of course, were settled upon, this was done of course by the Board of Directors; we have nothing to do with the arranging of the prices. On entering into our contract with the Car Company, we were guided entirely by the Board of Directors. They agreed upon the prices that should be charged, and it is our duty to sell at those prices. Of course, when considering the prices at the beginning of the undertaking, we obtained the price lists of American firms all through the United States,—from Chicago to Boston and New York ; and we took the prices of the different places: as, for instance, those in existence at Winchester, in Massachusetts, where the largest wooden manufactory in the States is situated. We also secured price lists from Cincinnati —or Cleveland, at least,—and Toledo, Detroit, and Bay City. We compared them all, and of course in doing so we calculated on freights and duties, and everything else of a similar nature, that could govern us in the fixing of the prices, in order that we might govern this market. We not only paid attention to American prices, but we particularly considered those of the only Canadian manufactory against which we would have to compete,—that of Mr. Eddy. He is the principal manufacturer in this regard in Canada.
Q. How do your prices range with his prices ? A. We always follow his lists, whenever he changes his prices, which he has been doing much to our annoyance. We not only represented this matter to the Board of Directors, but we also applied to those who we knew were interested in Mr. Eddy's welfare and on his behalf.
Q. Let me ask you this question, have you ever gone below Mr. Eddy in prices ? A. I have never known this to be done on any occasion ; and in fact the Directors of the Company have been most particular on this point. They have not taken our mere verbal statements as regards the alteration in prices, and we have always been obliged to shew it in black and white, or one of Mr. Eddy's lists before the prices would be altered. This very often created great delay, for sometimes our consultation with the Board of Directors on such a point consumed as much as a week ; and this of course was largely to our disadvantage, because during that week, when Mr. Eddy had broken his prices, he would sell and above his goods on dealers all over the country, before we dropped to meet the market. This has been a great disadvantage, I can assure you ; and I can certainly be most positive in saying—and I have to deal with the whole thing—that the Car Company's or McMurray and Fuller's lists have never been so arranged as to cut Mr. Eddy's prices with reference to any of the goods which are manufactured at the Central Prison.
Q. Now do you remember writing a letter to the Directors of the Company on the 27th of May, 1876, with reference to this question of lower prices ? A. We did ; and our firm kept a copy of it in the letter-book. We had a copy addressed to the then Secretary of the Car Company. It was as follows :—

LAWRENCE BUCHAN, ESQ., Toronto, May 29th 1877.

DEAR SIR.—We handed Nelson's printed list of 26th instant, to Mr. McBean, this morning. He has lowered price of Tubs, No, 1, to $7.25, and others in proportion. Nests are quoted at old price, $1.65. Please send us amended prices, and oblige—
American Tubs are offered as low as $5.50 same number.
J. McM. & F.

Q. It was in consequence of that communication the directors at that time took into consideration the question of lower prices ? A. Yes.

Q. Was not another letter, of date May 2nd, addressed by your firm to the directors, again referring to Eddy having lowered his prices ? A. Yes. It was as follows :—

LAWRENCE BUCHAN, ESQ., *Toronto.*

DEAR SIR.—Our traveller has returned from a trip West, and reports that he has seen quotations from H. A. Nelson & Son's Agents, for Eddy offering Pine Pails, 2 hoops, $1.55 ; 3 hoops, $1.75 ; which is a cut of 5cts. a doz. on published list quotation by same parties, now before us, which quotes Pine Pails, 2 hoops, $1.60 ; 3 hoops, $1.80. Please advise us if we are at liberty to receive orders at these quotations.
Yours truly
McMURRAY & FULLER.

Q. And these are lists of the prices of Mr. Eddy's stuff and of the Car Company's stuff at these respective periods? A. At different dates.

Q. At different dates ? A. Yes, I would like to call the Commissioners' attention to this point, for if these lists for the respective dates are examined, you will see what a terrible loss it has been to Mr. Eddy and to ourselves. For instance, in my experience in business—and I have only been a year now in this line of business. I was never accustomed to it before—I find that the trade, the wholesale trade, do not object in the least to the prices ; they would be very glad to go back to the prices of the 1st of June, 1876, but it is in consequence of the constant dropping in prices that has taken place, which has brought them down to their present level. You will see for instance, on the 1st of June, 1876, that pails were selling at $1.65 and $1.90, while now, on the 7th of July 1877, they have fallen as low as $1.40 and $1.60. That is really twenty-five cent a dozen—a figure which forms a very handsome profit on pails.

Q. Well then, I understand you to say that the Company have not lowered their prices except to follow the reductions made by Mr. Eddy ? A. That is true in every case.

Q. They have never gone below Mr. Eddy in price ? A. I do not recollect of any occasion on which it was done. In fact, I am positive that we never have done so.

Q. Now, have you any experience of the American market ? A. Yes, we have had occasionally to write to the Government with regard to American goods which were coming into Canada, and we then looked up the whole of the question as to American prices.

Q. You find that large quantities of American goods are sent in here ? A. Well, since gold has gone down or rather since there has been but a small difference between gold and currency of course, it has made a slight difference in this respect. We had some American pails seized and we gave them all the trouble that we could ; but we still met in London, Chatham and everywhere west of Hamilton with tremendous competition from American manufacturers. Our best Hamilton customers frequently write to us and say, that they can do better on the other side, but that they will give us the preference, everything else being equal. And I believe that to day they can buy pails at a shade lower than the figure at which we are even now offering them. I believe that a car load can be got from Bay City for less money, but whether the difference in prices is so much as to make it worth while sending for them, I do not know.

Q. And are you aware of the price at which they are being sold over there ? A. I believe that you can buy pails in New York to-day for $1.10 and $1.20.

Q. You can buy pails cheaper in New York than you can here ? A. Yes.

BY MR. LANGMUIR.

Q. You say that you just follow Eddy's lists ? A. Yes.

Q. Do you know whether Mr. Eddy makes a difference in the price when he sells by the car load and in small lots ? A. Well, these prices that I give are supposed to be in car load lots, and of course if we we sell in small lots, we add about ten per cent to them.

Q. That is for any lot under—what number of dozen ? A. We add ten per cent to these quotations for twenty-five dozen, perhaps.

Q. How many dozen are there in a car load ? A. About three hundred dozen.

Q. Do you know whether Mr. Eddy makes a difference in car load quotations and in twenty dozen quotations? A. I fancy that he follows the same rule that we do.

Q. When you report to the company a decline in Mr. Eddy's prices, do you report a decline in the quotations for small lots or for car-load lots? A. It is in car load lots.

Q. You don't bother your heads about small lots? A. No. The fact is, that we would prefer to have nothing to do with small lots.

BY MR. HARDY.

Q. Mr. Eddy says that you sell five dozen packages at the same price as you sell a car load? A. Mr. Eddy will come here and swear that he does not do it. He tries to make out that Mr. Nelson is not Mr. Eddy. We could say the same thing—that it was not the Car Company but McMurray & Fuller who did this. The one statement would be the same as the other.

Q. He puts it on a broad ground? A. Why Mr. Nelson will deliver half a dozen brooms to any firm in this city.

Q. At the same figure? A. To any wholesale house with whom he does business, he will be very glad to send round five dozen pails to keep them going.

Q. But not at the same prices as in large lots? A. Yes.

Q. What he complains of is that you quote car load prices by the half dozen? A. He does a great deal of it. I can bring evidence to show that this is the case.

Q. But you don't deny it. You say that you do? A. I do to the retail trade, but not to wholesale houses.

BY MR. LANGMUIR.

Q. You desire, of course, to make your sales as large as possible? You are paid by a percentage I suppose? A. Yes.

Q. Now as to the quality of these goods manufactured by the Car Company, do you find that their goods are about as good as those made by Mr. Eddy? A. I think that if you take them as a whole, they are quite equal in quality to those manufactured by Mr. Eddy, if not better.

Q. Are they rather heavier goods? A. I do not think that there is much difference in that respect.

Q. Do you get up better styles? A. I think that our styles are better than his.

Q. As a matter of fact, don't your goods command a sale, when put side by side with Mr. Eddy's? Are they not preferred to Mr. Eddy's in many markets? A. It is merely a question of price; that is fact, pure and simple; you could not get one cent a dozen more for them than his goods are sold at.

Q. Style is nothing? A. The only question with the traders is how much they can make out of them; a pail is a pail, and a broom a broom; we tried style and we spent a good deal of money in protecting our styles and getting up registered industrial designs and trade marks; we did so, to prevent Mr. Eddy preparing his goods in the same way, but found that they were not worth anything.

Q. Have you shipped goods out of Canada? A. Oh, yes.

Q. You have made sales for export? A. Yes; of course, they were based on the same prices at which we generally sell, and delivered in Montreal on board ship; we do not know what they were sold for, when exported, or whether the houses abroad paid the same prices as we sold them for, delivered in Montreal.

Q. As far as the quality is concerned, you have no complaint to make with respect to the goods that are manufactured by the prisoners? A. We have had constant complaints made.

Q. What is the nature of them? A. Well, the wood in some cases has been complained of, and the pails sometimes leak.

Q. What concerns the quality of the wood? A. I do not know as to that. Complaints of leakage are made about the goods; that is the chief thing; I do not think there has been so much fault found with what you would call wooden-ware proper—pails and tubs, as with goods coming from the broom department. This has been the source of an im mense deal of trouble ; the handles of the brooms come loose ; that has occurred even in my own house.

Q. Have you heard complaints made respecting Mr. Eddy's goods ? A. I have not heard of any.

Q. Have you not heard your travellers say that fault has been found with Eddy's goods in the same way ? A. I suppose that this is the case.

Q. In all trades, the same thing occurs ? A. I suppose so ; but really the brooms were faulty, until that new machinery was procured—the patent machinery used now at the present time in the manufacture of brooms at the Central Prison ; this was certainly the case. This state of things would have still continued had not Mr. Fuller and myself taken action ; of course, the Car Company did not seem to be in a position to buy this machinery, and Mr. Fuller and myself accordingly made the investment ; we bought it ourselves. If the Car Company did not have this machinery in there, I tell you that the broom business would not be worth five cents to any person.

Q. Their brooms would have been run out of the market ? A. They would have had to shut up the broom department. It stands to reason, that if you take a prisoner, a man who is not paid for his labour, and put him at winding brooms by hand, by the time he draws the wire around the handle for about a day, he becomes pretty sick of it ; he will not tie as tightly as it can be done by the aid of machinery ; and the heads of the brooms will all fly off.

BY MR. GORDON.

Q. What complaint is made about the brooms which are returned—the brooms you speak of ? A. Take a broom for instance : a broom is sewn according to quality with so many stitches—from fourteen to sixteen stitches—well prisoners don't care, whether they make ten or five stitches ; they just rattle through and get rid of them.

Q. Would not that be the fault of the supervisor ? A. You would have to have a supervisor for every broom maker, to oversee the work properly.

Q. Were these brooms improperly tied or sewn, or what was wrong with them ? A. Oh, yes ; they were done as if all that was desired was to get rid of the work ; it was very slip-shod. The prisoners wanted to get rid of the stuff. They had no interest in their work.

Q. Have you had more than one complaint of that kind ? A. Oh, we have not only had complaints, but the heads have dropped off the brooms used in my house.

Q. Have you lost any customers on account of this state of things ? A. We have had a great many brooms returned to us.

Q. Brooms have been sent back to you ? A. Yes ; but since we secured the new machinery, the broom business is looking better again.

Q. And with regard to the other goods, the pails, et cetera, that you deal in, have they been all right ? A. Well, our customers are frequently writing letters finding fault with them. If you were looking over the stocks, you would see that the goods were not as carefully put together, perhaps, as if they were done by piece-work. For instance, if you look at most of our pails, and examine the side of the pail where the little ear is driven in, you will find that instead of the little ear having been driven in properly, and with care—it should have sunk right into the wood,—it is just about half driven in with a sort of tap ; in consequence of this, if any very considerable weight is put in the pail, the handle comes off, and the pail goes to pieces. This is, I think, all due to the fact that the men have no interest in doing their work as it should be performed. I have always said to you, Mr. Langmuir, that I thought a system of bonus of some kind should be applied to these men ; it would be a benefit both to the Government and to the company.

BY MR. LANGMUIR.

Q. It might cause them to slight their work in order to get a large number of pails finished ? A. Well, I do not know whether it would do so or not.

Q. You mean that they ought to have an interest in doing the work well ? A. I would only pay them if they did the work properly.

Q. You think they should be interested in turning out a large quantity of work? A. I would not pay them if the work was not well done. Some system calculated to elevate the men should be adopted.

MR. BROCKWAY.—A system of inspection?

MR. LANGMUIR.—Yes.

BY THE CHAIRMAN.

Q. Have you a demand for all the goods that they make? Do you find a demand to exist for all the Company manufactures? A. For staple articles we have such a demand—that is, for brooms, and tubs, and wash-boards, and all that sort of thing; so far we have never been able to accumulate any quantity of goods. Then there is just this remark which I would like to make with regard to the output of the prison; I have never yet been able to ascertain exactly what this output is. We are told by the Company that they are turning out so many a day—well, what they do with the goods I don't know, nor am I aware whether they send them to other people or not, but we don't get them; the proof of the pudding is in the eating of it.

Q. Then you can sell all the goods that are furnished you? A. We have done so up to the present time.

BY MR. BROCKWAY.

Q. What proportion of your goods do you export out of Ontario or the Dominion? A. Oh, well, the proportion of pails we have sent out of the Dominion has been very trifling. They have been for the most part small orders.

BY MR. HARDY.

Q. Have you been sending goods to Australia? A. We have sent some to be placed on exhibition; and we have been sending some this spring to Glasgow, on trial. Whether they will take or not, I do not know.

JOHN FELDCAMP, called on the part of the Canada Car Company, sworn and examined.

BY MR. GORDON.

Q. Mr. Feldcamp, I believe that you are in the employ of the Canada Car Manufacturing Company at the Central Prison? A. Yes, sir.

Q. You are foreman I believe in the pail and tub department? A. Yes, sir.

Q. How long have you been in the employment of the Company? A. For nearly a year.

Q. For nearly a year—how many men—prisoners have you under you in that department at the present time? A. They number fifty-seven.

Q. How many free men have you to assist you? A. I have none to assist me.

Q. Now, can you tell me how many of these fifty-seven men that you have in that department were mechanics when they came to you? A. Well, there was no one who had been engaged in that line of business.

Q. There were none in that line; and how many mechanics were there to work the machinery? A. I do not think that there were any. There were none that I know of.

Q. How many machines have you for making pails? and how many tub machines? A. We have five pail lathes, but only four are running.

Q. How many men are employed on each lathe? A. Six.

Q. Then you employ twenty-four men on these lathes? A. Yes, sir.

Q. How do you employ the balance of the men? A. Some are engaged in planing bottoms, and some, in glueing them, and piecing them up; some cut out the bottoms, and some put them in. Others put the hoops on the pails.

Q. Well, how many of these fifty-seven men ought to be skilled men, or do you require any of them to be skilled men in order to do the work properly? A. All of them ought to be skilled men, except probably four or five.

Q. Now, how long does it take a man who has never learned the business, to become an efficient workman at the pail-making, or the tub-making? A. It would take him at least two years.

Q. Two years? A. Yes, sir.

Q. Have you any idea of the average length of the sentences of the men who are with you? A. I think that they will average about from six to eight months.

Q. From six to eight months? A. Yes, some sentences are for longer and some for less periods.

Q. Taking that in connection with your previous answer, would we be right in assuming that at the time the men go out, they have not been made efficient workmen? A. Sometimes when they do something wrong and are reported, they are sent away, and other men are sent out to take their places.

Q. That is not quite an answer to the question asked. I asked, whether taking your last answer in connection with your previous one, as to two years required to make a man an efficient workman, we are right in assuming that when these men leave prison, they are not efficient workmen? And that none of them would be efficient? A. No, they are not.

BY MR. HARDY.

Q. Not what? A. They are not then efficient, and not capable of doing a day's work as they should do it.

BY MR. GORDON.

Q. They are not then capable of doing a day's work? A. No; they do not take interest enough in the business to learn it. They do not care about learning it.

Q. What is the present out-put of these machines? What is the average out-put of these four machines, with their six men, a day? A. I do not exactly understand you.

BY MR. HARDY.

Q. How many pails do you make a day? A. They will average about two hundred and fifty.

BY MR. GORDON.

Q. About two hundred and fifty a day? A. Yes; this has been the case since I have been there.

Q. And with six men on each machine, they will average about two hundred and fifty a day? A. Yes, sir.

Q. Now, what would be a day's work for six free men on the same class of machines? A. If they were working by the day, a fair day's work would be five hundred.

Q. A fair day's work would be five hundred? A. I have even with boys got off as many as six hundred a day.

Q. You have made even six hundred with boys? A. Yes, sir.

Q. And what wages would you pay these boys? A. I would pay them from twenty-five cents up to one dollar and a quarter a day.

Q. Will you tell us what you would pay the different boys employed on the different parts of the machine? A. The one that hands the staves would get twenty-five cents a day.

Q. How many would there be so employed? A. Only one on each lathe. Then the one who would set up, would receive thirty-seven and a half cents a day, or three York shillings, as they call it, and another one fifty cents a day; another would get seventy-five cents, and still another one dollar a day.

Q. That would make five? A. Yes.

Q. Then would there be any men employed on the machine? A. There would be myself besides.

BY MR. HARDY.

Q. You put yourself in at $1.50 or $2.00 a day? A. At $2.00; I suppose I would make what I could; we generally work by the piece.

By Mr. Gordon.

Q. You and five boys have turned out six hundred pails a day? A. Yes.
Q. And what would you get for these six hundred? A. Oh, we would get $12 a thousand.
Q. That would be $7.20 for the six hundred, and then you would get the difference? A. Yes, sir.
Q. You could make six hundred instead of two hundred and fifty a day? A. Yes, sir.

By Mr. Langmuir.

Q. You have turned off as many as six hundred pails a day? A. Yes, sir.

By. Mr. Gordon.

Q. Is that a regular day's work at piece work? A. Yes, sir, a day's work however is generally a little less than that number ; five hundred a day for the usual number.

By Mr. Hardy.

Q. You said that you have often turned out, with five boys, six hundred pails a day, and you say that a fair day's work is five hundred? A. Yes.

By Mr. Gordon.

Q. And what would a man get by the day if he turned out five hundred? A. $2.50. They generally have only one man to run the lathe, and hire boys to do the rest of the work, you know.
Q. Well then, how much would a man get? A. $2.50.
Q. And what would the boys be paid? A. They would receive just what I told you —from twenty-five cents up. The pay varies according to the skill a man has ; he sometimes obtains $1.25 a day, and sometimes only seventy-five cents. It is according to what he is worth.
Q. Now—have you any particular difficulties to meet in the employment of this prison labour? A. Yes.
Q. What are they? A. Well—prisoners get ugly sometimes, and won't do what they are told to. When we report them, they are taken in and others are sent out in their places. Of course, we have to break these men in, a green hand may come out and work for half a day or one day and a half, and then the other man may come back and so he goes out again.
Q. What is the effect of this system on the gang of men? A. They all have to lose more or less time.
Q. If the ordinary out-put is 250 a day, what would be the difference in the production if a man was taken off and a new man put in their places? What would be the effect on the machine? How many would the men turn out? A. It would be a great deal better if that man was kept away altogether, and if the rest of the gang was left to continue their work.
Q. Five men would turn out more work than six men if one of them were a new man? A. Yes. There is another thing that ought to be mentioned ; if anything happens to break, or if something goes wrong, or breaks, or wears out, the men will sit there. You cannot discharge them, or send them out, they will sit there and do nothing.
Q. You are obliged to keep them there, whether they work or not? A. Yes—whether they work or not.
Q. Are you kept pretty busy in going from one machine to the other? A. Yes, as a general thing I am.
Q. That is as much as you can do? A. Yes ; and sometimes more.

Q. Well now, are these prisoners able to ascertain a fault in the work done, if there should ever be one ? A. Some of them are, and some are not.
Q. As a rule now—how is that ? A. I do not understand the question.
Q. Suppose that a machine was working with six prisoners, have you ever known a case in which they have gone on and manufactured, say a good many tubs, which have not been approved of? A. Not that I know of.
Q. You have never known a case of that kind ? A. Some occur. Yes.
Q. Does that sort of thing happen oftener than it ought. A. They sometimes put in bad staves, knots and such like, owing to carelessness.

By Mr. Hardy.

Q. Have you kept during this month and during the month of June a list of how much they turned out per day from the lathes ? A. Yes.
Q. Have you it with you ? A. Yes.
Q. Let me see it, will you ? A. Yes, sir. On one side will be found the forenoon's work, and on the other side the afternoon's work; we have to take a record every half day.
Q. How is it that you give up from May 31st to the 9th of June ? A. That is not the case to my knowledge, the lathes are numbered one, two, three, four and five.
Q. I see delays recorded all throughout the month of June; one day the delay is two hours, and on another day five hours, how is that ? A. That only applies to certain lathes.
Q. Well—I do not know whether it refers to certain lathes, or what it refers to, but it is stated in one place "delayed one hour," and in another, "six hours idle," this is for No. four. Do you suppose that if the men were idle six hours out of the ten, they could turn out a full day's work ? A. No, that is why I marked it.
Q. I have the month of May reported by the Guard, and it is acknowledged that his report is correct. For instance, for May 1st, he states that No. 1 lathe, turned out 500 pails ; No. 2 lathe 400 pails ; No. 3, 380 pails ; and No. 4, 250 pails ? A. No. 2 lathe has not turned out any pails.
Q. This is in May ? A. But No. 2, don't turn pails.

By Mr. Brockway.

Q. What does it turn ? A. It turns churns.

By Mr. Hardy.

Q. How many machines have you all told—four ? A. We have five altogether, but only three lathes are employed in making pails.
Q. It must have turned pails? A. It never turned out that amount. That lathe is not adapted to this sort of work.
Q. But this statement is taken exactly from the books, and it is sworn to by Mr. Brandon as correct, from your own statements put in here ; and found to correspond. There may be some misapprehension. A. Mr. Fitzpatrick and I generally take the count, every noon and evening together, and my account corresponds with his.
Q. The next day the number 360 is marked down ; and 230 for No. 3 ; and 300, for No. 4. Then the report comes down to the 4th, when lathe No. 3 is on tubs ; and on the 5th, No. 2 is at tubs. I want to draw your attention to this matter. For instance, on April 3rd, Mr. Brandon told the prisoners that he would give them a cent for every pail they would make over 375 a day. Well, then, on the second, the men were delayed for two hours—this was lathe No. 1, for want of staves ; No. 2 lathe ditto ; No. 3, ditto, and No. 4, ditto. Now, you would not expect to obtain a full day's work from the men under these circumstances, I suppose ? Were they also delayed during the month of June. A. I have it marked in my book in the same manner.
Q. I suppose that they were delayed during the month of June in the same way, for they have it marked so ? A. I am not certain whether they were or not.

Q. You do not appear to get as much work out of the prisoners since the last of May, and during the month of June as you did previously? A. Well, I do not quite know.

Q. Why not? A. Because I think Mr. Brandon on that account raised the day's work.

Q. He did what? A. He raised the day's work.

Q. Then he got more work out of the men? A. Instead of that, he obtained less.

Q. He got less? A. Yes.

Q. We will see: in June, 180 pails is marked down—no date—for the morning and 180 for the afternoon; that makes 360, which is pretty good, is it not? A. That is not for June.

Q. Here it is stated that the men were idle for want of hoop iron; but notwithstanding this fact, they turned out from one of the lathes 340 pails, on another lathe, 360, and on a third 350? A. Yes; but the lathes were not delayed for want of hoop iron; the men were bad hoopers.

Q. You appear to have turned out fair work regularly during the month of June. Here are tubs—butter tubs mentioned; it is rather mixed up; butter tubs were made part of the time and pails in the afternoon. Here it is stated that 175 pails were tuned out in the forenoon, and 170 in the afternoon, making 345 in all for one lathe; again 180 in the forenoon, and 170 in the afternoon; 140 in the forenoon and 200 in the afternoon; 170, 170, and 180 are other numbers; all along you appear to be now doing pretty good work—that is when you do not stop. Have you stopped work any lately owing to want of material or anything of that kind? A. Not lately; no sir.

Q. You have not stopped lately? A. No.

Q. Now did Captain Prince speak to you some time ago when this investigation was coming on, or at least some little time ago, about his willingness to set a task for the men? Did he offer to task them for you, and did you then prefer to have it deferred? A. Well, he came round once and asked me if I was satisfied with the work which the men were accomplishing, and I told him, "No, I was not." He then wanted to know how much I required of them a day, and Mr. Brandon had told me that I should get off three hundred pails a day. He said that I should not be content with less than three hundred, and that I should have 300 or 325 at least turned out. Mr. Brandon told me to try and get that amount of work from the men, and I said to him that I would do the best I could. So when Captain Prince came round and asked me what I required of the men, I said 325. He then went round among the men, and informed them that they must do this amount of work.

Q, Well, did they get it off? A. Yes, they did.

Q. Now he would have tasked the men at any time, if he had been asked to do so, would he not? Did he not task them as soon as you asked him to do it? A. I did not request him to do so at all.

Q. That is what I am complaining of. You never asked him to put a task on the men: you only fiddle-faddled about? A. I had no right to do so.

Q. Did you ask the other man—Brandon—to task them? A. I did; I asked him what I was to do in the matter.

Q. Do you know that when Captain Prince proposed to put a task on the men, Mr. Brandon said, "Let it stand; never mind it now?" Did you never hear him say that? A. No.

Q. Did you talk over the matter, and speak about not tasking the men until after the investigation had taken place? A. No.

Q. Did not Mr. Brandon say something of that kind? A. I asked him what I should do in the matter of the men's work; I told him how things were, and asked him what I should do about it, and he said, "Never mind for awhile."

Q. That was it? When did this occur? A. I do not exactly remember; it is now some time ago.

Q. It was sometime ago. Was it about the time when the first sitting of th Commission took place here? Was it some time about that period A. I do not know when it was.

Q. It was some time along in the month of May, was it not? It may be two months ago since he told you that? A. Yes, I guess it is.

Q. Now, you say that you have been there about two years, and that the average turn-out has been about 250 since you have been there—but they were not in good working order two years ago? A. They have not averaged that number since that time.

Q. Not during the whole of the time? A. No; because during the whole of that time they have not been engaged in turning pails.

Q. I suppose not? A. I mean they do that much on the average on a lathe every day it is in use.

Q. They must do a good deal better of late? A. They do some.

Q. They do a good deal more work of late, judging from the books as far as I can make out. It seems that they had performed a great deal more work. In fact, in July and during latter part of June they have done nearly double what they used to do, or one-third, or one-half more at all events. Are the men under task at the present time? A. Yes, sir.

Q. And they perform their task? A. Yes.

Q. Three hundred and twenty-five is the task? A. Three hundred and twenty-five; yes, sir.

BY MR. LANGMUIR.

Q. You stated some time ago, that out of the fifty-seven men which you have in your department none had been mechanics before they came into the goal—how do you know that this is the case? A. There have been no mechanics, so far as I am aware.

Q. Are you told who are mechanics among the prisoners and who are not? A. No, sir.

Q. Therefore you cannot tell, and you do not know anything at all about it? A. No.

Q. Notwithstanding this you know that there are no pail-makers among them. Would you call a carpenter, or a cooper, or a blacksmith, or any men of this description, mechanics? A. Yes, sir.

Q. Now, with regard to the statement you made, that out of the whole fifty-six men, all, with the exception of four or five, should be skilled men, I would like to know what you mean by skilled men? A. I mean men who are skilled in that particular business.

Q. The fifty-seven do not require to be skilled men. For instance all the men on a lathe should not be skilled? A. You need all skilled men on a lathe.

Q. It takes two years to become what you call a skilled man? A. Yes sir.

Q. It takes two years? A. Yes sir: and a man can not become a right good turner in two years. He cannot learn it in that time.

Q. But what I want to get at is this: you are now turning out a task of 325 pails daily? A. Yes.

Q. Very well—what would skilled men, if these were all skilled men, do? These prisoners are for the most part you say, green hands—then what would skilled men do? A. They would turn out——

Q. Five hundred? A. Five hundred at least.

Q. These prisoners are then getting on pretty well towards the status of skilled men, when they make 325 pails a day? A. Three hundred and twenty-five is not five hundred.

Q. It is not five hundred to be sure, but it depends altogether on what amount of skill is possessed, to come up to the number five hundred? A. Oh, but you see, if you put the task any higher; if you raise it the least bit, they will keep up with it for a day or two, and when a green hand comes on they will drop away below, and having a good excuse for it, you cannot punish them.

Q. Have you ever reported a man for some offence, and he was not punished? A. But you would not want to report a man for nothing.

Q. But if you found that a lathe was not turning out the task, and there was no reason for the falling off, would not that be sufficient ground for a report? A. If a green hand is put on a lathe it bothers the rest of the men so much that they cannot turn out as much work as they could otherwise do; but you cannot report men under these circumstances.

Q. Well now, with regard to that, you made five hundred pails one day when the men were offered a cent a pail over a certain number, did you not? A. On one lathe—yes, sir.

Q. And did not that shew that the men were able to do this much work? A. These men who did that had worked on the lathe for about two years at that time.

Q. Did you change about from one lathe to another, to accomplish that result? A. No; but this was before they went out and were discharged; they were discharged the next day, but the number turned out fell to 325. after their discharge.

Q. When? The next day immediately after the test was made? A. Yes, sir; and three days afterwards another man was discharged off the same lathe, and we had to put on green hands.

By Mr. Hardy.

Q. I understand that you require only one skilled man at each lathe—one turner? A. Oh, but I understand the matter differently.

Q. That is what we have been told to-day, that one man, the turner, should be a skilled workman, and that all the rest could be green hands? A. No; this is impossible.

By Mr. Gordon.

Q. Mr. Feldcamp, it was on the first of May, when the three skilled men were on, that you produced five hundred pails in a day? These men had become skilled workmen? A. Yes, sir.

Q. And you say that shortly afterwards two of these men went away? A. They were discharged; their time was up.

Q. Did they work the day after that, it was the 1st of May? A. No sir, they did not work on that day.

Q. Would that account for the difference between five hundred and three hundred and sixty? A. Yes; and for more than that.

Q. On May 1st, No. 1 lathe turned out five hundred, and on May 2nd three hundred and sixty pails,—now had these two men gone on the 2nd day of May, or did they work for a part or the whole of the 2nd day of May? A. That I could not tell you.

Q. And I see that on the 3rd of May, they turned out only three hundred and forty,—could you tell from the book? A. I might do so.

Mr. Hardy.—On the 2nd of May, there was a delay of two hours.

By Mr. Gordon.

Q. On the 3rd of May the number fell to three hundred and forty, and this was the day on which the third man left the prison? A. I do not know for certain, I could not tell you that.

Q. Could you tell by looking at your book? A. Oh, no, I could not.

Q. And on the fourth day of May, the number fell to 130, so in four days the number fell from 500 to 130? A. Yes.

By Mr. Langmuir.

Q. Does Mr. Fitzpatrick check with you? A. We only go round and count the pails which have been made.

Q. Do your reports then correspond? A. I suppose so. He puts his numbers down, and I put mine down.

Q. Should they correspond? A. I think that they should do so.

Q. What is mentioned in the report of the Guard Fitzpatrick? A. Well, if he puts the numbers down correctly, it should be so; and I suppose that he does so. I know that I put mine down correctly. I have to hand my report in to the office.

Q. Then on the 2nd, you made 360, and on the third—you have no entry for the third? A. It was probably a Sunday.

By Mr. Hardy.

Q. I see from your books that on some days they turned out tubs in the morning, and pails in the afternoon ? A. There are two lathes arranged that way ; three lathes are always on pails.

Q. And two are sometimes placed on pails and sometimes on tubs ? A. Yes.

Q. Do you change the work on the same day, placing them sometimes in the morning on pails, and in the afternoon on tubs ? A. Yes.

Q. And when they are changed ? A. It is always marked.

The Commission at this point adjourned, until Tuesday, the 24th instant.

TUESDAY, JULY 24th, 1877.

The Commissioners met at three o'clock.

Mr. Gordon put in a statement showing details of working expenses of the Car Company.

[EXHIBIT "D."]

JOHN COOPER, called on behalf of the Car Company, sworn—

BY MR. GORDON.

Q. You are chief guard of the St. Vincent de Paul Penitentiary? A. Chief keeper.
Q. And you have held that appointment for some years, I believe? A. Four years.
Q. How long have you been connected with prison work? A. Thirty-two years.
Q. I think before going to St. Vincent de Paul, you were one of the superintendents or chief guards at the Kingston Penitentiary? A. Before I went to St. Vincent de Paul, I was guard, keeper and overseer at Kingston.
Q. And you were there at the time Mr. Drennan and the Canada Lock Company and Mr. Offord had contracts? A. Yes, I had charge of the convicts in Mr. Drennan's shop.
Q. In the Penitentiary in which you are employed at the present time, is the labour let out to contractors? A. No.
Q. What is the average term of the sentences? A. I do not know the average term. They range from two years to life.
Q. Nothing under two years? A. Not that I am aware of.
Q. What is the number of prisoners there? A. We had 226 yesterday.
Q. How many guards and superintendents have you? A. We have twenty-four guards, eight keepers, and six trade instructors, I think.
Q. What industries are these men employed in? A. Blacksmiths, stonecutters, tailors, shoemakers, bakers, tinsmiths, masons and farmers.
Q. In which of these industries are the largest number of men employed? A. I suppose in stonecutting.
Q. How many men are employed in the blacksmith work? A. About eleven, I think.
Q. How many in stonecutting? A. Sometimes from twenty-two to twenty five, I think.
Q. How long do you consider it takes a prisoner to learn these different branches of industry that you mention? A. I have questioned the instructors of the tailors and shoemakers before I came away. The shoemaker says it will take six months before a man is of much use at all. The tailor says five months before he is of much use; and I do not remember the time given by the blacksmith, but it is as long, if not longer than that. The stonecutter said it would take six months before a man would be of any use.
Q. Do you know from personal experience that that is the fact? A. Yes.
Q. Does the Warden return anything as the value of that labour to the Government? A. I believe so. I believe he charges every convict so much a day.
Q. How much? A. I think two shillings.
Q. Forty cents? A. Yes.
Q. That is, taking one with another? A. Yes.
Q. Do you think that is a fair price? A. I think so, taking one with another, on prison work.
Q. For these men whose sentences range from two years to life? A. Yes, some of them are worth nothing, perhaps, and others pull up for it.
Q. Was it about the same in Kingston Penitentiary when you were there? A. I think it was the same charge. I am not sure about the charge there.
Q. Have you had any experience in short term labour? A. No.
Q. Can you make any comparison as to the relative value of prison labour and free labour? A. It depends a great deal upon the prison authorities themselves. I think, if convicts are put in a proper position and well watched, you can get a full day's labour out of them.

Q. Do you mean to apply that to every kind of work? A. Every kind of work—every work you put them at. If you do not watch them, they will kill time generally.
Q. That is their disposition, is it? A. Generally.

By Mr. Hardy.

Q. Do you mean a fair day's work as compared with a free man? A. Yes, I think so. I have seen convicts do a fair day's work when put in a proper position.

By Mr. Gordon.

Q. Of their own account? A. No, I do not say that. If they are put in a proper position to be watched. Some may of their own accord, but they are few in number.
Q. Have you had any trouble with your convicts? A. No; not any trouble with the work. We do not make trouble of it. If a man will not work, we confine him. There is no trouble. We confine him and punish him.
Q. Do you give them a stint? A. No, it is not allowed.
Q. Did you try that? A. I have known it to be tried.
Q. With what effect? A. You will get sometimes more work out of them, but you do not get the work as well done—that is my opinion.
Q. They will do their work, but not as well? A. I believe that.
Q. There is a difference between free labour and convict labour in that, then? A. Yes.
Q. How do you account for that? A. Because they want to do nothing and to sit down as soon as they get through their task.
Q. Have you found that to be the disposition of the convict? A. Yes; they will ask for a stint sometimes for that purpose.
Q. Do you find they take interest in their work? A. Some of them.
Q. But the average convict? A. No.
Q. Are they men you can rely upon with casual supervision? A. No, very few.
Q. Are they careful with their tools? A. Some; very few of them.
Q. Have you had occasions where the contrary has been proved? A. Yes; we often have to punish them for destroying tools and materials.
Q. To any considerable extent? A. Sometimes.
Q. Can you remember any instances? A. No.
Q. Or to what amount? A. No, I do not know the amount.
Q. Do you think there would be more or less difficulty in the employment of short labour—six months labour, on an average? A. It would depend what you would work them on.
Q. Do you think there is any kind of work? A. They would do for farming, weeding a garden, or shovelling, or breaking stones.
Q. Nothing else? A. I do not think it. I do not think they would be worth much at anything else.
Q. Supposing you had an industry which required an amount of delicate machinery to be used, which the convicts manipulated, what do you think would be the value of short term labour on that kind of work? A. Well, I hardly know what to say on that point, but, if they advertise for contracts in Kingston Penitentiary and cannot get more than 35c. to 40c. a day for men from two years upwards to serve, the others would not be worth more than a half or a quarter as much.
Q. You have perhaps more experience than any witness we have had, and I want from your experience what you think short-term labour— six months labour—would be worth to a contractor; and at what price you can compare it with long-term labour? A. I say I consider they would not be worth half as much a day as long-term men.

By Mr. Langmuir.

Q. That is 17½c. to 20c.? A. Yes, that would be it.

By Mr. Gordon.

Q. Would you give us your reasons for that conclusion? A. My reason is that the man has not time to learn to be useful in the six months.
Q. Would that be the only reason? A. That would be plenty of sufficient reason, I think.
Q. Yes, but sometimes you have a hundred reasons? A. There are other reasons very often. The men when they come in there are of no use for three or four weeks. They come in fit for nothing.
Q. On account of what? A. From bad usage outside. Some of them are sick and under the doctor's care for a long time.
Q. That is your experience of convicts when they first come in? A. Yes.
Q. What is the average time it takes before they are able? A. I do not know that.
Q. Does it take any time for a man to become accustomed to prison life? A. Not long. He is initiated right into it.

By Mr. Hardy.

Q. He goes to you from some gaol where he has been confined? A. Yes, many of them. We have not much trouble with us. A good many of them, when they come in first, are very weakly.

By Mr. Gordon.

Q. Are they men who turn easily to the business; that is, the occupation they are put on to? A. Some of them. Some want a change every day if they could get it.
Q. It takes some time before they settle to anything? A. Yes.
Q. Do you take much trouble to ascertain what employment the convict is most fitted for? A. It does not take long to find that out, but some of them are not fitted for any employment, and will go from one to the other as fast as the authorities will allow them. They do not want to learn anything, some of them.
Q. Do you think that a system of rewards would be a good system—rewarding the men for extra work? A. In what shape?
Q. Well, either a present reward, such as tobacco, or a future reward, such as something when they left the prison? A. You do not give them tobacco?
Q. I mean an additional amount? A. We give our prisoners tobacco, and then a remission of sentence; but not until after six months.
Q. Take the case of the pail manufacture? A. Perhaps it might induce them to good conduct.
Q. So much a hundred or a dozen extra—would you recommend that? A. I do not believe in extra work at all, for the reasons I have given.
Q. The reason I understood to be that you might get the quantity but you would not get the quality? A. I think that. I have known a good deal of task work have to be done over again.

By Mr. Hardy.

Q. Have you any experience of short-term prisoners at all—of men confined for less than two years? A. No; we congregate them together and do not take one different from another.
Q. Have you any experience in the manufacture of pails and tubs and brooms and brushes? A. No.
Q. And, although you have given us what might be a reasonable time for prisoners to learn blacksmithing and the other trades you have mentioned, you have no knowledge how long it would take them to familiarize themselves with the trades I have named? A. No.
Q. Or what proportion of skilled men would be required? A. No.
Q. I understood you to say that for, shovelling or carrying or labourer's work, a short term man should be the same as a long term man? A. He should be fit for that any time.
Q. I understood also that, if he were well guarded and watched, a fair day's work might be got out of a prisoner? A. I believe that, if the prisoners are put in a proper position to be watched, and have proper officers to watch them.

Q. You mean if the guard can readily see them? A. Yes—so that they cannot skulk behind.
Q. A good deal would depend upon the guards and overseers? A. Yes.
Q. If there was a slack overseer, they would do little work? A. Yes.
Q. A thorough overseer would be able to get more work from them? A. Yes.
Q. Are the two prisons—Kingston Penitentiary and St. Vincent de Paul—the only two you have been connected with? A. That is all.
Q. You say that the Warden charges forty cents a day in his return. It is Government labour, is it not? A. Yes.
Q. He makes his return to the Government, and charges for the work done? A. Yes.
Q. Where is this prison situated? A. About ten miles from Montreal.
Q. Are you able to state what the annual results of the prison have been? A. I could give you a report.
Q. Speaking from memory, would you state whether it has been self-sustaining or not? A. No.
Q. You charge two shillings a day to Government for the men employed on Government works? A. There is no money comes from it at all.
Q. But it comes in another form? A. All the worth that can be ascertained is, what property is gained in twelve months. That is the only way.
Q. You are doing certain Government work—what work are you performing? A. Building, farming for the prison, tailoring.
Q. You have no productive labour at all? A. No contract labour.
Q. You do not manufacture anything for sale? A. If the guards or keepers want any jobbing, they do it.
Q. But nothing for the general public? A. No.
Q. You have no productive labour to derive an income from? A. No.
Q. Would you consider that such a system as that was calculated to bring out the industrial powers of the men, so that you would get a full day's labour from them. A. Yes.
Q. You are working from hand to mouth—that is all? A. I superintended the buildings required, and everybody will allow that a good day's work was got out of the convicts there.
Q. Is not your experience that, where men are working for a public contractor, for private gain, they will do more than in a general way for the Government? A. I think in this way—they would not do extra work without extra tobacco from the contractor.
Q. Have you ever worked with these men under a contractor? A. Yes—two or three contracts.
Q. Did you find that they worked better under contracts than they would if they were working for the Government in odd jobs? A. By the inducement I have told you.

BY MR. LANGMUIR.

Q. You were asked as to the value of prison labour as compared with ordinary labour, and short date as compared with long date labour. You say you think it is only worth about half? A. We take no notice of the date; we mix them up together.
Q. What do you consider the value of short date labour—men under two years—as compared with men from two years up to life? A. I think only about a half.
Q. Say 100 men are employed in piling lumber, and making roads, and loading waggons, and work of that description—is a two years man only worth half a five years man? A. I do not say that.
Q. Just as valuable? A. If in health.
Q. Then you consider a considerable number of short date prisoners are as valuable as long date men? A. Yes.
Mr. GORDON.—You are talking about two years men.
Mr. LANGMUIR.— I speak of six months.
Q. I ask, do you consider that, in certain works such as I have named, piling lumber, making roads, taking away material from the machines, or loading waggons, if the man is in good health, one is as good as another in regard to date? A. Yes, he should be.

Q. Do you know what quantity of labour of that class—ordinary labour where the one is as good as the other—is being used in St. Vincent de Paul? A. I don't know that I understand the question.

Q. You say that the short date men are only worth half the long date men. You have 226 men there. How many of those would be just as valuable if they were in for periods under a year in the various works you are carrying on there in St. Vincent de Paul? Take for instance, the farming operations—are they just as valuable, the one as the other? A. I should say so.

Q. Among the quarrymen? A. Not quite. Some of them might, but not for certain.

Q. We come to such works as road making. Would they be just as valuable there? A. Yes; if they were in health.

Q. Then it is simply the carrying on of trades you are referring to? A. Yes.

Q. You are carrying on shoemaking? A. Yes.

Q. By machinery? A. No.

Q. All hand work? A. Yes; we have a sewing machine.

Q. A pegging machine? A. No.

Q. If you had all the modern machinery, would your statement apply in reference to six months men—say for making the heel of a boot—as fully as it does when you have no machinery? A. I do not know what to speak about the machines.

Q. Have you ever been foreman of men where machinery was used? A. Yes.

Q. Do you think it requires the same time for a tradesman to learn to work by machinery as by hand? A. They can turn out quickly, but the people who work the machine must understand the machine.

Q. Must every man in the shop understand the machine? A. No; only one.

Q. May that man not produce a great deal of work for the other men? A. Yes.

Q. Then your knowledge does not extend to machinery? A. Not what I have told you before.

Q. If you had splendid machinery, first-class machinery, are you still of opinion that short date men would be only worth half long date men? A. Not if you had first-class men to work the machine.

Q. Prisoners are always the same when they come in first. I want to know, if you had first-class machinery throughout the various departments and trades in the prison, are you still of opinion that short date men would be only worth half of long date men? A. I think a man going in there is worth nothing at all.

Q. Do you know anything of the application of machinery in prison labour? A. If you have machinery, and men who can work the machine, you help the thing considerably.

Q. If a carpenter went in there, would he be as valuable as a two years man? A. Yes, or a blacksmith.

Q. Then you do not consider that portion of short date prisoners worth only half the others? A. No.

Q. You are only working for the Government—building the prison, making boots and shoes, and clothes for yourselves? You do not task the prisoners at all? A. No.

Q. They may make one or two boots a day? A. We do not task them at all.

Q. They do the best they can? A. The best we can get out of them.

Q. Are you aware there have been many complaints as to the efficiency of the guards in St. Vincent de Paul? A. Yes, there have been some.

Q. Have many discharges taken place? A. Yes.

Q. Owing to what? A. Different things.

Q. What are the principal? A. Some I do not know.

Q. Any from the inefficiency of the guards in overseeing the prisoners? A. I do not know that. Some have been discharged for being asleep on their posts.

Q. The prison has been very much demoralized? A. Yes.

Q. There was a Commission sitting there, was there not? A. Yes.

Q. Is it fair to compare that with a well organized prison? A. It is organized now.

Q. It was not a year ago? A. No; perhaps a little over a year ago.

By Mr. Hardy.

Q. What proportion of those who come in are tradesmen? A. I cannot tell.

By the Chairman.

Q. Take, for instance, the men you have engaged in shoemaking. Do you not keep an account of their work, and the value of it, with a view to ascertain how valuable it may be? A. It is kept.
Q. So that the amount of work turned out by each man is known? A. I believe so.
Q. Do you know what these results show? A. I do not.
Q. Can you give us an opinion as to the result, in your own judgment, of this labour, where it is charged at 40c. a day? How does that compare, do you think, with the result which would be obtained from other labour outside? Would it cost more to do this same work and pay the wages you would have to pay outside? A. I am so little acquainted with outside labour, that I am not fit to answer that question.

By Mr. Noxon.

Q. You have had charge of men working on contract work; what work? A. Making haems.
Q. When you had charge, the men were not stinted—you did the best you could? A. They were in the hands of the contractors; sometimes they were stinted.
Q. You were the guard in charge—the company employed their overseers? A. Yes.
Q. You had nothing to do with arranging the work or directing the men how the work should be done? A. No. One thing that I may remark is that, when there is a contract, the Government overseer and the contractor's overseer should work in unison, otherwise they cannot do business.

LEVI B. SPENCER, called on behalf of the Car Company, sworn—

By Mr. Gordon.

Q. You are a contractor, I believe, for prison labour at the Kingston Penitentiary? A. Yes, at the present time.
Q. Have you held that position for any length of time? A. I was superintendent of the Canada Lock Company for several years before they failed.
Q. It is only lately you have had the control yourself? A. A year, the first of this month.
Q. And how many years were you with the Canada Lock Company? A. Nearly eleven years—ten and a half.
Q. Is that the only experience you have had of prison labour? A. Yes.
Q. And what do I understand you to say the prisoners made? A. They made locks and shelf-hardware—all kinds of light shelf-hardware.
Q. Can you tell us what rate the Canada Lock Company paid for the prison labour? A. I cannot tell the exact number of years, but for about six years, perhaps, they paid 40c. a day. I am not certain about it.
Q. How many men had they? A. 100; sometimes they had 105, sometimes 95, but they calculated to keep 100.
Q. Is this labour short or long-term labour? A. That was only part of the time. Then they renewed the contract at 50c. a day. They kept that on till the company failed.
Q. When did they fail? A. A year ago this spring.
Q. Is this long term or short term labour? A. Nothing under two years.
Q. Up to what? A. Life.
Q. What is about the average sentence of the men the contractors took? A. What we took I have no way of saying except to guess at it, but I should say they were about five years men. We took all the long term men we could get. Unless it was some man who understood the business before, we did not take anyone under three years.
Q. Had you any particular reason for that? A. We thought it would take so long to learn the trade that it would be an advantage to take one who knew the trade.

Q. Did it take a considerable time to learn the trade ? A. There is a great difference. Some men take three months, some six months and some eight months. Some learn quicker than others.

Q. But if it takes only that time, I do not see the advantage ? A. We would have to take the three months over again with another man.

Q. Was that about the average time they took to learn ? A. Not to get their work perfect. Some locks are easy to make, but it would take a man a year to learn to make others.

Q. You mean time enough to make a lock ? A. Yes, that is it. I do not calculate that a man would learn the business in less than a year. He would do very well to learn the moulder's business in a year's time.

Q. Were you the only contractors then ? A. Mr. Drennan and Mr. Offord were there part of the time.

Q. Have you been accustomed before or since to employ free labour ? A. I worked in a shop in a large lock factory on the other side for many years.

Q. What is your opinion in regard to the relative value of prison labour and free labour. Can you get as much out of the prisoners as out of free men ? A. No. I cannot get a third as much good work.

Q. How do you account for that ? A. Because they do not work so hard, and they have not the care about them. They do not take the same interest in it. They waste tools. One thing we miss a good deal is the waste in files and so on. We use a good many files, and they waste four or five times as much as outside men. They have not the care outside men have.

Q. What are you paying, yourself ? A. 40c. since April. Before that, I paid 50c.

Q. Why has there been a reduction ? A. Because labour was so plenty we could get outside labour cheap. I hire them for a month, and I refused to keep the men longer for more than 40c.

Q. Did they want to make a contract with you ? A. I do not know. I only asked to have them for a month.

Q. You said you refused to keep them longer ? A. At fifty cents a day. I offered forty cents, and they let me have them.

Q. Is there anything you get with the labour—any machinery or anything of that kind ? A. Yes ; the privilege of using the machinery of the old Canada Lock Company.

Q. What does that consist of ? A. An engine, boiler, two or three lathes—all the machinery they required ; nearly all required for the business.

Q. What have you to provide ? A. I have to provide the fuel, and keep the machinery in good repair while I have it.

Q. Do you provide the tools ? A. Yes.

Q. Is that much cost to you ? A. Yes, it is a great cost in the files and such like ; that is the main thing.

Q. Do you think it would be a greater cost if you had free men instead of prisoners ? A. I think it costs three times as much.

By Mr. Hardy.

Q. In the article of files alone ? A. The patterns are made so that every part fits together, but often they do not, and we have to use the files to fit them together.

By Mr. Gordon.

Q. When you took this labour on, were these the old men who had been employed by the Canada Lock Company ? A. Most of them.

Q. How many men have you got ? A. 50.

Q. What is the average number of changes in a year ? A. Perhaps one or two—perhaps two a month.

Q. As many as that ? A. I should think so.

Q. Two men a month ? A. It is guess work with me.

Q. With 50 men, have you only half that number left at the end of the year? A. A great many men I took when I took on were nearly out. Take them all through, it would not average over one a month.
Q. Do you give the men a stint? A. What I can, I do. On some kinds of work I cannot give them a day's work.
Q. Why so? A. It is men who have to be changing from one piece of work to another —you cannot do it. Where they are making locks or are moulders I give them a set day's work—all the moulders.
Q. Do you find they do it? A. I find they do about a third what a man does outside.
Q. Do they do what you give them as a rule? A. They have to do it.
Q. Have you any system of rewarding them? A. Not now, I did employ that plan once.
Q. With what effect? A. I found it did not work well at all.
Q. What objection was there to it? A. If you gave them over work, they would slight their work to get on to the over work, and that was one thing.
Q. You would get the quantity but not the quality? A. Yes, that was one trouble.
Q. From your experience of your long-term labour, what do you think would be the value of labour ranging from one month to two years and two-thirds of it under ten months? A. That is according to the business. I could not judge about your business. I could tell about my own business.
Q. In your own business? A. I would not take them as a gift in my trade.
Q. Although a man can learn to make a lock in six months? A. Yes. I do not consider a man in our shop worth anything to me on an average in the first three months.
Q. Apart from the question of not knowing their work, is there any other objection to the prisoners in the first three months—any other difficulty in getting them to work? A. I do not find them as good men to work in the first three months, until after they have been there a spell. They are more independent.
Q. Are they physically capable? A. In many cases they are not; a great many are sickly and under the doctor's care, and so on. Many claim they are not able to work.

BY MR. HARDY.

Q. How long had you been foreman for the old Lock Company? A. I think about ten years. I have been there nearly twelve years in all.
Q. Then when the Company failed you took the contract? A. Yes.
Q. Did you buy any of their stock, or implements, or tools? A. I have bought some castings from the Government. They took the old stock over for a debt from the Company.
Q. They failed after the depression of business? A. Yes, about a year and a half ago.
Q. Did they not have any stock on hand? A. Considerable.
Q. What became of it? A. All unfinished stock the Government held as security for their debt.
Q. What became of it? A. It is there now, unsold, most of it.
Q. Do you find a ready market for what you make? A. Not for all I make.
Q. At fair prices or low? A. Fair prices till the last month. Now prices are down.
Q. I believe in that line of business—hardware and lock works—a great many failures have taken place in the United States? A. There has been a combination of the lock makers in the United States to keep the prices up till the 1st July, when they dropped the prices 40 per cent., and that is the reason why the prices are down.
Q. There have been a great many failures, and many places have been closed in Pennsylvania and elsewhere? A. Two and three months at a time.
Q. Did you ever work in a free labour of that kind? A. Yes.
Q. What does a journeyman get? A. $1.50 to $3.50 a day.
Q. Are there any similar institutions in Canada? A. I do not know any in that branch of business.
Q. What would be a fair average day's pay for free labour in Canada? A. At the present time, I could get all I wanted for $1 a day, but, in fair times, the average wages, I should judge, would be $1.25 a day.

Q. That would be the average for all kinds of work? A. Yes, taking it through the shop? A good moulder's wages would be $1.50.

Q. The manufacturer finding all the furnishing and the motive power? A. Yes.

Q. Taking it that men only do a third of the work, where the prison finds motive power, shafting, and belting, and heating—not fuel for driving the engine—it would, with the power supplied, be nearly three times the amount, where the prison authorities receive only fifty cents a day? A. Yes, but there is a loss in bad work which I did not speak of when I said a third of the amount.

Q. You speak pretty largely from the prison contractor's point of view? A. Yes, but I speak what I think right.

Q. You now pay forty cents? A. Yes.

Q. You paid fifty cents how long? A. From the 1st of July till the 1st of April.

Q. You went right in when the Company had failed—took the business from the moment they stopped? A. Yes.

Q. Were the hands idle at all? A. Yes, six or eight months, except the pattern makers. I took them right off.

Q. What class of workmen do you engage to make a lock—is it moulders or skilled locksmiths? A. About a third moulders.

Q. How long does it take to learn that trade? A. About a year. A man does well to learn to do a decent job of moulding in a year's time. The next largest work is lock finishers.

Q. About how many of that? A. Nearly a third.

Q. What are they supposed to do? A. Fit in the inside work—the bolts and springs, and so on.

Q. How long does that take? A. Three months on an average to learn to make the cheapest class of lock.

Q. What others are there? A. Out of fifty men there have to be three men to work on the wheels, polishing.

Q. How long does that take? A. It requires one man who understands the work thoroughly. Then there are men to learn to run the drills. That will take two or three months.

Q. Any blacksmith work? A. Only one in the whole lot. The most I use him for is tempering and working tools.

Q. Do you make your own tools and files? A. No.

Q. I do not understand you to say that prison labour would represent a third of free labour, but that the labour you have in the prison, as you get it there, would represent a third of an outside journeyman who understood his business? A. I mean about a third of the work.

Q. Is that the average prisoner? A. I mean after he has had a year.

Q. Taking one year for moulding and six or three months for the other trades, he would do a third what a skilled, practised journeyman would do outside? A. Yes.

Q. Have you had many new men come in since you had possession? A. No, I have not; very few; because the old company had about 100 men.

Q. Have you not found, among those you have had, very excellent lockmakers? A. I have found two or three very extraordinarily good men.

Q. Some others who were more than an average or quite an average? A. I think I have three that I consider very extra men, but I do not know that I can say any more than that.

Q. Do you know what other works they carry on in that Penitentiary? A. I know they have one gang of men cutting stone. They are all working for the Government. There are no other contracts, I think.

Q. No shoe shop? A. Only Government works.

Q. Any foundry—apart from yourself? A. No.

Q. Have you ever had any experience at all in such labour as is carried on at the Central Prison—tubs and pails? A. No, I know nothing about it.

Q. You can form no opinion how long it would take to learn that? A. No, I know nothing about it.

Q. Your experience is confined simply to the trade of a locksmith? A. Yes.

Q. If these prisoners could learn a trade in a month, or the business that is carried on, and there was, perhaps, only one skilled man out of four or five required, might they not be more useful than in a trade that required a year to learn ? A. I should say they would be more useful in that case.

Q. And your opinion or your judgments have not been founded on any knowledge of the work done at the Central Prison ? A. I know nothing of that—only my own business.

Q. Is not this trade of lockmaking considered somewhat a nice trade to be master of, compared with others ? A. I do not think so—so much is done by machinery. Most parts of nice locks are fitted by machinery.

BY MR. LANGMUIR.

Q. You said you have some machinery, some motive power, belonging to the Government? A. An engine, two engine lathes, and six small lathes, I think. We have all the machinery necessary for that business.

Q. All the fixed machinery ? A. Yes, all the emery wheels and shafting.

Q. You furnish all the tools ? A. Yes.

Q. Do you know whether the engine and lathes were provided by the Government for the old Company ? A. No, they furnished everything themselves.

Q. This is exceptional, then, in your case ? A. Yes.

Q. Is it because they were on hand that they gave them to you ? A. That is the reason. They had them on hand, standing idle.

Q. What do you consider the value to you in your service of the lathes, and the power, and the small lathes—what is it worth per day or year ? A. What machinery is there would cost me about $15,000 to buy.

Q. What per cent. would you consider that worth ? A. To keep in repair and all, I should say about 10 or 12 per cent.

Q. Has each piece of work in the lock trade to be finished by one man ? A. No, it goes through different hands—from three to five hands mostly.

Q. Is there much manual labour connected with a lock—ordinary labouring work ? A. No, very little.

Q. Is there much carrying to and from the machines? A. Very little. One man will do all we have to do.

Q. If you had a great deal of that, would not prison labour be more valuable to you ? A. I should judge it would.

BY MR. GORDON.

Q. Suppose a man had been only six months at work—how much do you think he would turn out ? A. We always give the plainest and cheapest kind of work at first. I would not consider a man worth half as much at three months as at a year.

Q. Suppose the authorities wished to charge you extra for the machinery, besides the labour, would you have paid it ? A. No.

Q. Or would you pay a higher price for the labour ? A. I paid for the two together.

Q. The 40c. includes the machinery and the labour ? A. Yes.

Q. And you refused to pay more than that ? A. I refused from the 1st of April to pay more, times being so slack.

Q. Supposing you simply had the motive power and belting—the fixed motive power—I do not mean the steam, but the engines and belting, and machinery to work your lathes, how much do you think that would be worth ? A. If I had nothing but the engine and belting, and the main shafting, I would rather take outside labour. I could afford to pay more than that outside.

Q. How much do you think you could afford to pay with only that ? A. I would not have stayed there at all without the machinery. That was the inducement that kept me there.

BY THE CHAIRMAN.

Q. The Company carried on that business for 10 years ? A. Yes ; about that.

Q. Do you know the terms and conditions of their contract under which they were to employ these men? Were they allowed any selection of the men? A. They were allowed to choose their men when they went in.

Q. Were they obliged to employ a certain number? A. 100. The contract originally, I think, was 280; but the Government found they could not do it, and so it was kept at 100.

Q. And they had the right of selection? A. Yes; when fresh men came in, I judged which I liked, and if I liked them I took them; but, after we had them, we had no right to get rid of them.

Q. During a large portion of that period, business was not in so depressed a state as since. What was your opinion as to the results of that labour in the conduct of that business as compared with carrying on the business with that labour outside? Do you think it was an important advantage to them to have that labour? A. I do not think it was. I believe a man with capital to build his shops—that was the only advantage they had; they had not the capital and the shops were an advantage to them—if they had the capital to build the shops, I believe free labour can compete with convict labour to an advantage.

A. In your case now, you are only employing 50 men? A. That is all.

Q. Do you have the selection of those 50 out of the number who were employed in those works before? A. Yes.

Q. You have men who comparatively have a knowledge of the business? A. Oh, yes.

Q. And you are obliged to pay for that number—for 50? A. I have kept it up, but I told the Warden I would take them—50 at 40 cents a day. There was no written agreement; sometimes I have 49, sometimes 51 men; but we keep as near 50 as we can.

Q. Have the prison authorities offered these men to contractors? A. They did advertise for tenders for convict labour a year ago this spring.

Q. You do not know what offers they got? A. No. It was for a shoe contract, I think.

Q. Do you keep these machines in repair that you use? A. Yes.

Q. To what do you attribute the failure of the Company? A. Mismanagement and want of capital. I do not lay that altogether to the convicts.

By Mr. Langmuir.

Q. Was that Evans' Company? A. Yes.

By Mr. Noxon.

Q. What system have you of employing your labour? Do you keep an account of each man to know what quantity of work he turns out each day? A. Except in a few cases of skilled labour.

Q. Is that account regularly kept? A. Yes. I am there most of the time. I always take the account when I am there.

Q. You have piece price put on the work which you estimate as being its value? A. Yes.

Q. Have you any difficulty in the men turning out a fair day's work as compared with free labour? A. I said the only difference is we have so much bad work.

Q. When a man knows how to do his work and he turns out bad work, have you no means of avoiding it? A. Under the present management, I do not know how. There is more talk than management.

Q. The discipline does not reach that? A. Not as it used to be.

By the Chairman.

Q. Is there a general disposition on the part of these men—an unwillingness to work? A. They seem to take a pride in doing as little as they can. They will not do anything honourable if they can do anything dishonourable. One man the other day cut two or three belts. He wanted to get out of the shop to work round the yard. We did not see him do it, but we knew he did it. Six of them did see him. I said "Why did you not tell of it?" They would not blow on him, they said. A few days afterwards he broke a wheel. If they do this sort of thing there is none in the yard with honour enough to tell you of it. They think it is spry to destroy anything.

By Mr. Noxon.

Q. What portion of the work, as compared with free labour, did you give your men to do? A. Well, in making moulds, when I learned the trade, I used to do 140. I gave the moulders 60. If I get two-thirds good of the 60, I am perfectly satisfied.
Q. You attribute the amount of bad work to the carelessness? A. Yes.
Q. Nearly all the labour you employ on lock making requires some skilled labour? A. Yes.

By Mr. Langmuir.

Q. You use 50 men. What is the size of the shop allowed to you? A. I do not require nearly all the room in the shop.
Q. What is the length? A. I think about 160 feet by 60 feet wide—two rooms, one below and one upstairs, and another room about 100 feet by 60 feet.
Q. What space do you use? A. I do not use over a half of it.
Q. That is 80 feet by 30 feet? A. Yes.
Q. If you had 100 men you would use more? A. Not more than I have told you is there. Two rooms 160 feet by 60 feet, and another room about 160 feet by 30 feet, I should judge. It is guess work, a good deal, with me.
Q. When the old Lock Company was in full blast, had they use of that? A. Yes.
Q. What was the greatest number of men they used? A. I think 110 or 115.
Q. One floor would do you for the shop room you require now? A. Yes.
Q. Is there any railway communication into the Penitentiary? A. No.
Q. No rails put in for the old contractors? A. No.
Q. You say that your contract is from month to month? A. Yes.
Q. Do you look upon it as a permanent thing, though you can stop if you are losing money? A. Any month.
Q. They can stop you? A. Yes, it is as broad as it is long; I wanted to get up a set of patterns and get started, and when the old company gave way they had machinery and men there, and so I hired them; I do not want to stop long.
Q. If lock business improved and you had more orders than you could fill would you stop there? A. No; I would not take them for over four months.
Q. Not any contract on prison labour? A. No.
Q. Why? A. Because I started on very little capital. As soon as I can get a shop outside, I prefer outside labour.
Q. Is the discipline in the Penitentiary very rigid? A. No.
Q. Is it loose? A. I do not know that you can say so; the Warden does all he can, but my experience is that the guards want training.
Q. Are they not understood to be very lax? A. Yes; that is my opinion.
Q. Is it not much more lax than it was three years ago? A. Yes.
Q. Were not the men made to work in the shops three years ago? A. They were kept in their places a great deal better.
Q. That is not the case now? A. Now, when the guards are from under the eyes of the Warden, they take it very easy.
Q. That is, they malinger? A. Yes.
Q. If discipline were rigidly enforced, and the men made to do the work, and if they did not do it punished, would it not be more valuable to you? A. Yes, a third more, at least.

By Mr. Gordon.

Q. Do you think the Government are likely to stop you? A. I do not know what their ideas are; if any one came and offered them more, they might stop it.
Q. Do you think that probable? A. I cannot say.

Q. Judging from what took place with respect to the tenders? A. I cannot tell. I have not found any one lately who wanted to take the contract.

The Commission adjourned.

The Commission re-assembled at 7.30 p.m.

Mr. LANGMUIR put in Supplementary Orders and Regulations of the Shop Gangs at the Central Prison.

[Exhibit "E."]

SAMUEL T. DRENNAN, summoned on behalf of the Car Company, sworn—

BY MR. GORDON.

Q. I think you have had considerable experience in the employment of prison labour? A. As a contractor in the Penitentiary at Kingston.

Q. How many years had you a contract there? A. I took the first contract in the year 1860, and was burnt out in 1874—May, 1874.

Q. Was it the same contract from 1860 to 1874? A. No; there were two contracts. In the last instance, I had no contract at all.

Q. What price did you pay for the labour under the first contract, and what were its terms generally? A. The first, in 1860, was at 35c. a day for five years.

Q. Was there anything included in that contract in the way of machinery or power? A. None, sir; no machinery at all.

Q. Had you shops? A. The shop only.

Q. And heating? A. Yes.

Q. And light? A. We never wrought in the evening.

Q. How many prisoners did you take under the contract? A. The first contract was fifty.

Q. What term men were these? A. They generally averaged from three years up to life—three, seven, and ten years.

Q. Had you none under three years? A. Very rarely.

Q. The shortest term in the prison, I believe, is two years. A. Generally speaking.

Q. Were you the oldest contractor? A. At that time.

Q. Had you any advantage in that way as to choice of prisoners? A. The oldest contractor had the choice of prisoners, as they were coming in.

Q. Then you could pick your men? A. Yes.

Q. How many prisoners were their average in the prison at that time? A. I think upwards of 800 at that time, as far as my memory serves me.

Q. Under your next contract, what price did you pay? A. The same price.

Q. For what period? A. For five years longer.

Q. Had you any machinery then? A. I had all the machinery necessary for carrying on the business.

Q. Furnished by the Government? A. None whatever.

Q. Just the same as before—shop room and heating? A. Shop and heat.

Q. How long did it last? A. Five years more.

Q. That brings us up to 1870. A. Yes.

Q. How many prisoners had you under the second contract? A. 50, and the privilege of 50 more if wanted.

Q. That privilege you had not under the first contract? A. No.

Q. What was the last contract? A. I had no contract, for I would not sign the contract in the last case. They wanted fifty cents a day for their men, and I would not give it.

Q. Why so? A. Because they were not worth it.

Q. Did you get the prisoners notwithstanding? A. I got the prisoners, and the thing went on for two or three years without any contract, just working on the basis of the old contract. They charged 50 cents—I paid at the rate of 35 cents, and there remained an account for a considerable time before it was settled.

Q. How was it settled? A. It was settled, and they had to pay me back a balance which I got from the present Government last year.
Q. Did you pay 50 cents. A. No.
Q. What was the balance you got back for? A. It was an account between us of overpay. I had paid for men when they were not working.
Q. At which rate. A. 35 cents.
Q. When they were not working? A. Yes.
Q. I do not understand that. Explain it. A. The men would not come in at the proper time. From 7 o'clock to six was their hour, and they would be taken away for punishment and sundry things, and in paying my wages I protested at the end of each month for so much short time, year after year, in the first contract and the second. In the first contract I was not allowed it. The Government would not allow it; but they had an arbitration with Evans, the lock contractor. They appointed an arbitration with that company, and the Government agreed that whatever the arbitrators decided in that I case should be compensated in the same manner.
Q. That was for men taken away for punishment, and for sick men—was there anything else? A. They were taken away—I think for the dinner hour principally; but Peter Todd, the foreman, can give that more explicitly.
Q. Did you find that was a material objection to the labour? A. Oh! yes.
Q. It interfered considerably with your work? A. No doubt of it. Of course, men would stop work when they were in the act of jointing, and the stuff that might have been jointed the night previous, and ready the next morning had to lie over.
Q. But, when taken for punishment, one would think it was for your good, because they did not work? A. No, not for that, but for breaking the rules of the prison.
Q. And you were subject to that? A. Yes. And they got into a practice of taking them to church, to confession, and to the English Church, when they should have been working.
Q. Other days than Sunday? A. Yes.
Q. Were they taken to school? A. No. That was after hours.
Q. To the barber's shop? A. They generally shaved them at meal time—during the dinner hour.
Q. You say there was an arbitration, and the Government had to pay you a balance. What amount had they to pay you? A. $2,400 or $2,500. That I was paid last year.
Q. For the last five years? A. No. That was the balance of the account.
Q. For what period would the compensation be over? A. That was for the second contract; over the five years.
Q. For fifty prisoners? A. Sometimes, on that contract, I had more prisoners. I had the privilege of 100 if wanted—if I could get good men.
Q. Did you often avail yourself of that privilege? A. No. I could not get good men.
Q. How long did you keep the prisoners without any contract? How long did you have them? A. There was a time when they were not going to give out any contracts at all. The men got scarce. You are aware the men were divided. Some were taken back to the lower Province, and the number of prisoners ran down to a low ebb. They had not got the men, and they had the contract with the Lock Company, and had to keep them going, and my contract having expired, they were not bound to give them to me. I had a very few men for two years—I forget how many.

BY MR. LANGMUIR.

Q. Without a contract? A. More than that, I was burnt out without a contract.

BY MR. GORDON.

Q. How often were you burnt out? A. Once.
Q. Can you account for that? A. No, I cannot. The investigation which took place showed that at 4.30 in the morning all was right, and at 4.45 the whole place was in flames.

Q. Spontaneous combustion, I suppose? A. There was the ordinary material in the cabinet shop. They did not prove anything.

Q. Have you formed your opinion as to the cause of the fire? A. I have.

Q. What may your opinion be? A. I have my opinion that the place was set fire to.

Q. By the superintendent or the guards? A. I would not like to say that.

Q. By whom do you think? A. I could not say that.

Q. You say you have your opinion? A. That is, in the meantime, perfectly private.

Q. We would like to know your opinion. A. I billed the Government, and it remains there.

Q. It will not interfere with any arrangement with the Government. A. I do not like to express an opinion.

Q. Did you find the labour valuable, or the contrary? What did you find to be the advantages or disadvantages of prison labour—tell us? A. It depends entirely on the class of men you get.

Q. In your own experience of Kingston with long-term men, did you find prison labour was equal to free labour? A. No, I do not think so. We had men we could not make anything out of, and tried them six months at a time, and by coaxing and sundry agreements with the warden, we got quit of them occasionally, but we had men in the employ that we could not make anything out of. It was generally Todd who selected the men, and he had a good idea to judge whether they would make good mechanics or not.

Q. Does it take long to learn cabinet making? A. Oh, yes.

Q. How long does it take a green man to learn it? A. A long time. He would be able to do common work in six or twelve months, but he would not be a good cabinet maker inside of twelve or eighteen months—not even then, probably. It is very seldom you get mechanics in—very rare.

Q. Do you consider that these men for whom you were paying 35 cents a day were worth 50 cents? A. I do not consider that they were worth 35 cents; I had the greatest fight in 1860 to get the men for 30 cents, and would have got them, if there had not been an enemy in the field; but for that, the Government would willingly have given them. I considered them worth no more, and did not all the time I had them employed.

Q. In comparison with a free man, who has been a year at the work, do you think a prisoner who has been at it a year will do as much work? A. No, undoubtedly not.

Q. What would be the difference? A. Their mind is not in their work. They have no interest in their work. A man outside has to make it to please his employer. All they care for in the prison is to get their time in.

Q. What would be the difference in the amount and quality and value of the work they would turn out—a man a year in the prison and a free man who had been at it a year? A. I am only working by the hand, without machinery, and my experience is that the men will do twice the work that they would do inside with machinery.

Q. Was that want of interest the only obstacle to the prison labour which you found? A. No; because, in the proper light to look at it, the men are generally such characters; it is the most noted scoundrels on the face of the earth that go in there, and the mischief is still in them; the best proof of that is that when they get out they get back again as soon as they can.

Q. But surely in a place like the Penitentiary or the Central Prison that cannot have much effect? A. They are much more merciful now than they used to be; prisoners are much better treated, they deal almost as bountifully with them as if they were Englishmen, bound to live on roast beef and plum pudding, and the punishment is not so severe as it used to be.

Q. Did you ever try a system of stinting them—giving them a task or a stint? A. Yes, repeatedly, but it was always a failure; I have given them extra tobacco, and tea, and sugar.

Q. That is a system of rewards, but did you find giving them a certain task was a good system? A. They would do it once, and it would not be well done.

Q. Was your system that there was a certain amount of work for each man to do. A. No. In a shop like mine the work was so varied that it was very difficult to get them tasked; you might get them tasked occasionally, but you could never get it carried out successfully.

Q. Suppose a man did not do a good day's work, had you any remedy? A. You might make a complaint, and he would get bread and water.

Q. What effect would that have? A. He would return to his old style.

Q. Would it have a good effect or an injurious effect ? A. In nine cases out of ten an injurious effect.
Q. Did you know cases in which it had a bad effect ? A. There have been several cases.
Q. What would be the consequence of a man being punished, then ? A. I recollect one case of a man breaking a valuable barrow, worth $35, all to smithereens when he was punished.
Q. Did that often happen ? A. No, but they often destroyed work and material.
Q. Accidentally ? A. No, not accidentally but willingly.
Q. Did that so often happen that you consider it an objection to prison labour, or only occasionally ? A. Yes ; and the loss of material also.
Q. In what respect ? A. I would give a man six locks to put on a barrow, and he would have only four, and could not tell where the others went.
Q. You found that the case ? A. Yes, repeatedly.
Q. Do you mean to say that, in a penitentiary like that at Kingston, stealing and purloining went on to that extent ? A. You have read it—it is well known. Even boots and shoes have been taken out by the case.
Q. Had you any arrangement with the Government to get redress ? A. No, there was no redress for it.
Q. Did you take that into consideration in tendering ? A. I consider that to be one of the drawbacks to prison labour.
Q. You say these men were worth about 35c. Would you think that men whose sentences ranged from one month to two years, two-thirds of them being under 10 months, would be as valuable ? A. No. No one would think such a thing.
Q. What would be their value, do you think from your experience ? A. It would depend entirely what work they were at.
Q. Take cabinet making ? A. It would take six months before a man would learn to make a washstand or common table.
Q. Taking that, and supposing that you were bound to take 250 men two-thirds of whose terms ranged under 10 months ? A. My instructions to the foreman were never to take any man under three years.
Q. But I want your idea from your experience as to what the value of short term labour was ? A. I would not have them at all. They would do no good in my business, because when they were capable of doing something for you they would be going out.
Q. Would they be worth 10c. ? A. It would be a very poor man that would not be worth that. He could tend a machine or anything like that.
Q. 20c. ? A. Yes. I do not think any more—not at my business.
Q. Suppose there were delicate machinery employed, and the industry they were at was pail making, do you think that men coming in for short periods would be worth 50c. a man ? A. Oh ! no.
Q. Could you form any opinion ? A. At a business of that kind they would learn sooner, because I suppose in making a pail four or five men are engaged, as in boots and shoes, in pegging or working at a heel, they learn a great deal sooner than in my business.
Q. I find from Mr. Langmuir's report that 637 prisoners passed through the prison in 1876, and that 500 were up to 10 months. and 279 up to six months. What do you think would be the value of labour of that class on an industry which would require a lot of delicate machinery, such as pail making ? A. You would not make anything out of them for three months.
Q. Suppose it was six months ? A. I would not like to take the contract and give more than 20c. for them.
Q. Not worth anything for the first three months, and for the last three months 20c. ? A. I should think so.

BY MR. LANGMUIR.

Q. You say your first contract extended from 1860 to 1865. You paid 35c. for that ? A. Yes.
Q. Did you have any motive power furnished you ? A. None.
Q. Had you only the bare walls of the shop ? A. That was all. I bought out the plant that was there.
Q. Yourself ? A. Yes.

Q. From the previous contractor? A. From the Bank of Upper Canada.
Q. That was your own property? A. Yes.
Q. Had the Government any lien upon it? A. None whatever.
Q. What did it consist of? A. Engine, shafting, and every other machine in the shop.
Q. If the Government had given you all the motive power—boilers, engine, pulleys, shafting, belting, and things of that kind—would you have been willing to pay a higher price for it? A. It would look natural that I should be inclined to pay a little more, because there is the investment of capital.
Q. What percentage would you be willing to pay on what you were saved on your own capital? A. I cannot say I have ever defined it.
Q. What is money worth on capital? A. Money now is not worth a cent in my own business, because I am not making a cent. I should be better out of business.
Q. If you were to invest $40,000 on plant and fixtures, and the Government said, "No, we will put that in," what would you have considered that worth in the way of percentage over and above what you would pay for prisoners? A. I believe the Prison charges ten per cent. itself to the LockCompany for furnishing them with a steam-engine and boiler. But I would not have liked to have given them ten per cent.
Q. Whatever the money value of the boilers, engines and running gear? What do you think it would be worth? A. There is no business man but would say it would be a very bad investment unless he got ten per cent.
Q. It would be worth ten per cent., would it not? A. I would rather pay for the machinery and have it my own, independent of the Government.
Q. Would you rather, if the Government gave it to you at six per cent.? A. Well, that is considerably less than ten per cent. If the Government would give it to me at five or six per cent., I should prefer it to having my own machinery.
Q. Had you any railways running into your place? A. No.
Q. Were you furnished with any drying kilns? A. No; I had to furnish my own. They had the building there, but they had to fix it up. They had the privilege of drying in my kiln if they wanted to. They have the pipes there yet.
Q. If you had been tendering again, with these privileges, you would have paid six per cent. more? A. I took my foreman away to Boston and other places, looking for machinery, many times.
Q. What was the size of the shop you used for your 50 or 100 men? A. Mr. Spencer gave you the size, because that was the shop I used first. I do not know the size; I never measured them.
Q. How many floors had you? A. In the first shop I had the lower floor, and then we had a wing on the same flat; and in the second shop we had the flat above the shop—the first floor and the flat above it. That is where they are rebuilding now for an asylum.
Q. You had your choice of prisoners? A. Yes, as being the oldest contractor.
Q. Was that a great privilege? A. I consider it was.
Q. Did you generally select men who had some knowledge of cabinet-making? A. If they came in, we would be sure to bone them.
Q. If you found cabinet-makers sentenced for three months, would you take them in preference to labourers sentenced for ten years? A. We never had such a thing.
Q But if one was for two years, and the other for ten? A. We would take the cabinet-maker.
Q. As between a carpenter and a labourer? A. We would take the man who was in the habit of handling tools, certainly.
Q. You would take any man who is in the habit of handling tools? A. Yes.
Q. How long would it take a man who was in the habit of working in wood to learn cabinet making—to make him useful in your shops? A. He could not make anything out of it at all in cases.
Q. Had you any good men as men under prison labour? A. Yes, some good mechanics.
Q. As good as you have found outside? A. I would not say that.
Q. From your knowledge of prison labour, do you think the character of the industry has a great deal to do with the value of the labour? A. Oh, yes; most undoubtedly.

Q. Would it not determine largely the value of the labour? A. It depends entirely what trade you want to put them at.

Q. If you had an industry which would employ one-third of ordinary labour without reference to skill at all, would not that pay more than where you could employ only five per cent? A. There is some kind of labour you can put a boy to.

Q. If you had an industry at which you could work one-third of the ordinary prisoners —ordinary labouring work —would that be more valuable to you than where you could only work five per cent. in ordinary work? A. I cannot see through that.

Q. If you had 300 men working for you in the prison, and you had an industry in which you could work 100 of them at ordinary labouring work, such as piling lumber, taking cuts from the machines, unloading waggons, and all that sort of thing, and then, if in another trade you could only use five per cent., or 15 men out of the 300, in the same kind of work, would not the labour be more valuable to the industry where you could use a third for ordinary labouring purposes? A. I should think it ought.

Q. In determining the labour which should go into a prison, is not that for the contractor to take into account? A. To a certain extent, no doubt.

Q. To a very large extent? A. I would not say that.

Q. Were you bound to cabinet-making in your contract? A. Yes.

Q. You could not introduce any other trade? A. No.

Q. If you could introduce anything that would pay, would it not be more valuable to you? A. I cannot answer that, because I never thought of introducing anything else. Several parties came to me with a patent, but I never believed in that.

Q. I ask you, as a business man, if you found cabinet-making dull, and you could turn into making sashes or anything else, would it not be more valuable? A. Yes, no doubt.

Q. Then the character of the industry has a great deal to do with the value of the labour? A. Yes.

Q. And if it is so varied by the Government that you can turn your prisoners to anything, it is still more valuable, is it? A. Certainly, it ought to be.

Q. You say that, after the second contract expired, you refused to enter into a third contract, because they asked 50c.? A. Yes.

Q. Do you know Mr. Creighton? A. Yes.

Q. Do you see a remark in his report in 1872, in which he says:—
"The rates of remuneration were, for 130 men, 40cts. *per diem* each, and for the remaining 50, the sum of 35cts. *per capita*. In consideration of the advanced price of labour, of provisions and clothing, the directors deemed this remuneration insufficient. Hence, they notified the contractors that the labour would not be supplied any longer than the 30th of June, unless a higher rate were paid. Accordingly, all the contractors have proposed to pay 50cts. *per capita*." Is that true or not? A. I did not propose to pay. I was notified in writing, but I did not offer to pay it.

Q. This is not true? A. I did not offer to pay it.

Q. You did not offer to take it, in writing? A. I did not.

Mr. LANGMUIR proposed to put in the report.

Mr. GORDON objected to using a report to contradict the statement of a witness under oath.

WITNESS continuing—

BY THE CHAIRMAN.

Q. This report is dated in 1872. Your second contract ended when? A. In 1870, and I had no other written contract after that, but I wrought under the old contract. I cannot give the date, but I was notified by the authorities that the men's wages would be 50c. a day.

Q. Did you continue the use of the prisoners from 1872? A. Until I was burnt out in 1874.

BY MR. GORDON.

Q. But you refused to pay 50c.? A. Yes; and I did not pay it.

Q. And there was an arbitration and the Government paid you a balance? A. Yes. I do not know if that was the date of the letter to me. There was a change in the Warden, and the Warden said to me to take the men for 50c., and I would not do it.

BY MR. LANGMUIR.

Q. Were there any other contracts at that time? A. The lock and shoe contracts were in force at that time.
Q. How much did Mr. Offord pay? A. I think, 50c.
Q. How many men had he? A. I think latterly 50. He reduced them down to a mere minimum, and then left altogether.

BY MR. GORDON.

Q. He has since given up the contract? A. Yes.
Mr. LANGMUIR then put in the Fifth Annual Report of the Directors of Penitentiaries

[Exhibit " F."]

WITNESS continuing—

BY MR. LANGMUIR.

Q. You made a statement about getting back a certain sum of money on the award of arbitrators on the lock matter, which carried with regard to you? A. Yes.
Q. Did you claim any moneys for over charges over 35c.? A. For lost time.
Q. Exclusively? A. Yes.
Q. No other claim but for lost time? A. No. I used to enter a protest every month.
Q. For payment when men were under punishment, or were taken to church? A. I entered a protest every month.
Q. When you signed the list? A. When I was paying. I had no book to sign. The foreman was obliged to sign the book every month, I believe.
Q. Did you pay 50c.? A. No, I paid 35c.
Q. This was when they were asking 50c.? A. No, it was long after that. This was from 1865 to 1870.
Q. The money was recouped on the transactions extending from 1865 to 1870? A. Yes.
Q. Only for the time lost? A. Yes.
Q. When men were taken away from you to be punished, were other men offered to be substituted? A. No.
Q. If you had the offer of as good men, would you consider you had a claim? A. We could not get the offer.
Q. But if you had? A. I cannot answer that, because we did not get the offer.
Q. You did not get the offer, and consequently you made the claim? A. They did not offer any others.

BY MR. GORDON.

Q. Supposing one of your men who had been there for six months was taken away for punishment, and the prison authorities offered you another man who had just come in, would you have taken him as value? A. Not by any manner of means, because if a man is in the midst of making a table, say, another man cannot go on with it.

BY MR. LANGMUIR.

Q. You say the punishment had a bad effect? A. Very often.
Q. A hardening effect, or was it retaliation? A. Well, they would not work afterwards.
Q. Have you found that punishments had a bad effect upon the prisoners? A. Well, I never remained in the prison the time of the punishment.
Q. When you say that you could not get good men over and above the number—you had 50 under contract from 1865 to 1870? A. Yes.
Q. And sometimes 100? A. No; they agreed to give 50 more if I wanted them.
Q. But you could not get good men? A. No.

Q. What do you mean by that ? A. Men my foreman would select.
Q. Good cabinet-makers ? A. No; men he could make good cabinet-makers out of.
Q. Why ? A. It will be for him to tell that.
Q. You were the contractor—I suppose he gave excellent reasons why ? A. Because, I suppose, from their appearance he could not make good workmen of them.
Q. From appearance or sickness ? A. When they are under sickness they are never put under contract.
Q. When they recovered? A. Then the foreman might or might not take them.
Q. Did you reject men owing to the shortness of the sentences ? A. Most decidedly, and if there was a man physically looking delicate, no foreman would select such a man.
Q. If you had the selection of 260 men out of 340, would you consider that a privilege ? A. Yes; you would have such a crowd. You would have a difficulty in making your selections, but it would be an advantage, no doubt, to have a large quantity. Of course, there were gangs coming in repeatedly that the foreman could not get one out of.
Q. Did you get notification from the prison authorities of the trades the men carried on before coming into the prison ? A. No; the men generally told themselves.
Q. Were you informed that a cabinet maker had come into the prison ? A. No; whenever the prisoners came in the foreman would go and see them, and in conversation with them would find out what business they would like to learn ; and, if a man had a fancy for learning the cabinet business, the foreman would select him as more likely to make a good workman.
Q. If you could not make a selection up to the 50, had you to take what was given you ? A. No; sometimes we were above and sometimes below the number ; we never had any difficulty ; sometimes we were a little above and sometimes a little below.
Q. Would they allow you to go ten below ? A. I do not think we were ever ten below.
Q. The matter averaged itself ? A. Yes.
Q. You were burnt out ? A. In 1874.
Q. Were you insured ? A. For $4,000.
Q. Did you commence business again ? A. No.
Q. Was that the reason you closed up ? A. You know the Grits would not rebuild for a Tory ; they are building for a madhouse now ; I daresay if the Conservatives had been in power I would be there now.
Q. Was that the reason you closed up in the Penitentiary ? A. Yes; it was a complete burn out.
Q. Did you do reasonably well with your contract up to the time you were burnt out ? A. Yes, I did very well ; I was very well satisfied.
Q. Is there any antagonism to prison labour in Kingston ? Is there a good deal of antagonism to prison labour in Kingston ? A. There always has been.
Q. It is very marked, is it not ? A. It always has been.
Q. Do you know whether that has influenced the Government very largely in asking tenders for labour ? Whether this antagonism by outside artisans has affected all governments in submitting tenders ? A. No; they have always advertised for tenders.
Q. But have they not been unfavourably influenced by this outside antagonism ? A. I do not think so; so far as Kingston is concerned, there has been always a cry at election times against convict labour.
Q. And sometime very marked ? A. No doubt of it.
Q. Was the discipline very strict when you were under contract in the Kingston Penitentiary ? A. For a time at the first it was.
Q. Did it get loose ? A. I cannot say it got loose.
Q. Was it relaxed ? A. I think the Warden tried a merciful treatment instead of punishing them, in consequence of the report of the Inspectors.
Q. Had that a bad effect on the work you got from them ? A. I think it had ; I think if they had been punished they would have wrought better.
Q. If they had been compelled to do their work ? A. Yes.
Q. From your knowledge as a contractor is this a fair expression by the Directors of the day :—" It is only fair to say that the contractors do not attempt to oppress their employés in any way. The prisoners can easily perform all the work required of them, and many earn considerable sums by over work ?" Did your contract men earn sums by over-work ? A. There were cases, but they were very rare.

Q. When you tasked your prisoners did they perform their task? A. Not as well as if they had not been tasked; they slighted their work.

Q. In 1871 do you think the laxity of discipline affected your operations there unfavourably,—about the time this sentimentalism appeared in the prison about not whipping the prisoners? A. I think it will at all times; it began then, no doubt of it; as long as these men were not punished—you know what these men are.

Q. During the first five years of your contract, from 1865 to 1870, did you get more out of the prisoners? A. I think so.

Q. And did better? A. I think we did a great deal better under the first contract than under the last.

Q. You said some men were worth nothing—you did not exactly mean that? A. Yes; some men have destroyed material, and the foreman has kept men standing at the bench for a week or a fortnight at a time to get the Warden to take them away.

Q. Was the destruction of material serious? A. It will happen that you will get a man without brains to make a board.

Q. Was it malicious on the part of the prisoners? A. No. I think it was incapability.

Q. Did you ever attribute it to downright maliciousness on the part of the prisoners? A. Not from my own personal observation.

Q. Would you consider, as a large operator in labour, that this detriment to prison labour, the destruction of raw material and machinery, is more serious than, say, strikes in the outside world? You are exempt from strikes in the prison? A. Yes. We have had no strikes to my knowledge in that work since 1860.

Q. Are there strikes now in the outside world? A. There are on railways.

Q. Is that an injury to trade? A. Yes.

Q. Is not that an advantage to prison labour? A. No.

Q. As to your statement that it took six months to learn cabinet-making, do you think that applies to every other trade? A. I did not say so. I said sometimes it took eighteen months.

Q. But you said it took six months to make the common work? A. And some of them—the three years men—would be going out when they had learned to do a fair day's work for you, and that was one of the objections to taking a three years man.

Q. He would not be going out in six months? A. We looked upon it that they were going out when they were beginning to make money.

Q. On common work? A. No, because it is good work you make money on.

Q. Did you not grade your prisoners, putting men who had capacity on good work, and those who had not on common work? A. Yes, certainly.

Q. You used your discretion that way? A. Certainly.

Q. Is not that necessary in all labours? A. Certainly.

Q. You found some men who would learn the common work in six months and others the finer work in eighteen months? A. Yes, sometimes longer.

Q. After the six months, what comparison would that man's labour make with that of a journeyman outside who had just got through learning his trade? A. Just this. that the journeyman outside would be anxious to give a good day's work, and the man inside only to do his work.

Q. What does a good journeyman earn? A. Some of them $1 50 a day.

Q. Does it ever go as high as $2? A. Yes, it has. Some have not earned $1.

Q. Do any earn less than $1 a day? A. No, not if they work.

Q. Then prison labour at a half would be worth 50c.? A. No.

Q. Well, explain? A. Because they do not do half their work. If I have a man who does $1 worth of work, and the man inside does only half, he is only worth 25c.

Q. Is not the shop room worth anything? A. Only for working.

Q. Does not that go far to make up the loss? A. Not very far.

Q. What would be the taxes in Kingston? A. Not much, for I get taxes ten years for nothing.

Q. Are you aware that furniture manufacturers are very common in the prisons of the world? A. I am not aware that they are.

Q. Have you ever visited any other prisons where furniture making is a specialty—Detroit Prison for example? A. I have never been in Detroit.
Q. Have you enquired into the operations of other prisons where they make furniture? A. No. I never have been in the Central Prison here, either.
Q. In regard to the manufacture of furniture, is it largely done by machinery? A. Yes. Every day it is getting more so.
Q. Was it then? A. Not so much as now.
Q. In your opinion, does that increase the value of labour where machinery is available for all purposes? A. It increases the profit to the contractor.
Q. You can make the labour more profitable? A. Certainly.

BY MR. GORDON.

Q. Suppose the Government changed, and you were offered a new contract at Kingston, would you be willing to give 40c. now? A. I would not go into the prison at all. I would not take it for 25c.
Q. Notwithstanding the shop room and heating? A. No, I would rather go to the expense of putting a building up, and I would have if the Grits were out of power; I cannot as long as they are in.

BY THE CHAIRMAN.

Q. Your experience—and it was considerable—was confined wholly, I understand, to your own branch of business, the manufacture of furniture? A. Yes.
Q. At that time and now, if you were desirous of employing labour largely for your purposes, could you give us an idea of what value would attach to the prison labour we have in the Central Prison—prisoners from six months to two years? A. I could not do that honestly without visiting the establishment, and seeing the machinery, and the kind of work they are employed at.
Q. But for the purpose of manufacturing furniture? A. I would not think of going into convict labour for making furniture again at any price. I prefer it outside. I would know what work I would get, and if I would not make as much out of it, I would be better satisfied.
Q. The work would be more satisfactory? A. Yes. I never was afraid, but many have been, and you are not safe among such a lot of scoundrels. You do not know the moment you will be set upon. I should not like to have to be a foreman, and spend my life among them.
Q. That has nothing to do with the profit and loss. Others might be willing to incur all that inconvenience. The question is, what would be the value of this labour as compared with free labour outside.
Mr. GORDON.—Under the terms of the contract, does the witness think it an advantage or a disadvantage to be bound to take 250 labourers, for five years, say, under all circumstances; whether the rate of wages outside is falling or rising, or the demand is the same as when the contract was made, or greater or less? A. I would not like to take a fixed number for such a term.
Mr. LANGMUIR.—In the event of the other party to the contract being unable to supply that number, if he was bound to pay you the value of skilled labour for what he did not furnish? A. Then the advantage would be on my side.
The CHAIRMAN.—Would your experience lead you to infer that an important advantage would result to the contractor from having a number more than he contracts for to select from? A. Decidedly.

BY MR. NOXON.

Q. There is only one difference, it appears to me, between the class of work you employ and the class here. Your labour is on a fine class of furniture, I understand? A. If we found they were capable of doing good work.
Q. A great portion of your manufacture belongs to the finer class of manufacture? A. Yes.

Q. Is it not your opinion that prison labour is better adapted to the coarser class than to the finer class of manufacture ? A. I should say not.
Q. It is more easily acquired and not so particular ? A. I got so disgusted with them that I thought Providence had burnt me out for my good.
Q. Could not prison labour be better employed on the class of goods that is manufactured almost entirely by machinery ? A. In that class, of course ; take the caning of chairs — you will see even boys can do that quicker than men.

THOMAS DAVIDSON, called on behalf of the Car Company, sworn—

BY MR. GORDON.

Q. I believe you are superintendent of the carpentering and cabinet-making department in the Kingston Penitentiary ? A. I am keeper and overseer of it.
Q. You have held that post for some time ? A. I have been nineteen years and nine months in the Penitentiary, and during most of that time I have held that position.
Q. How many prisoners have you employed under you now ? A. Fifty-one. If you will permit me, I will say what I have to look after—tinsmiths, cabinet-makers, joiners, wheelwrights, coopers, turners and painters.
Q. These are the different industries ? A. Yes.
Q. Could you say how many of each you have ? A. Three timsmiths, four or five wheelwrights, nine or ten working at cabinet-making, seven or eight at joining, and so on, just as the work comes in to do. We have a great deal of cabinet-making for the Military College and have had for the last year and a half. We have two coopers and four painters.
Q. What do the others do ? A. There are six men working in the finishing shop. Then there is a man at the lathe, a man at the planer, and two men in the engine-room. I have a clerk, and another man who does nothing but attend to the lumber, cutting it out to the different sizes.
Q. What do you call him ? A. Assistant to the keeper or overseer.
Q. He is a prisoner, though ? A. Oh yes, certainly,
Q. What is the average sentence of these men ? A. None less than two years—from two years up to life.
Q. You are not working for a contractor, but for the Government ? A. It is Government work, but we have so much for making each piece of furniture.
Q. But no contractor hires this labour ? A. Certainly not.
Q. Have you superintended the contractors' work ? A. No.
Q. You have always been upon the Government work ? A. Yes.
Q. How often do your men change, as a rule ? How many changes would you have in a year ? A. I have had only one for the last three months. I got one Beamish from the Central Prison, and a useful man he is.
Q. What was he ? A. I don't know. He used to work at the piano making in Kingston.
Q. Can you make anything of him ? A. Nothing at all. There is one good man in the Central Prison now who used to work with me.
Q. What experience have you of those who have been in the Central Prison ? A. A keeper told me there were some who were there, but they never would admit that they were.
Q. As a rule, do they turn out good men ? A. I have only seen the one and so I cannot say.
Q. How long does it take for these men to learn their work with you—these wheelwrights and cabinet-makers and joiners ? A. We prefer men coming in who are tradesmen.
Q. But men who know nothing about it ? A. We do not take men to learn, as a rule, unless they are in for five years, seven years or life.
Q. Why so ? A. It is very troublesome.
Q. Do you find they take any considerable time to learn ? A. Undoubtedly so.
Q. How long ? A. Joiners and carpenters only serve two or three years in this country. In the old country, they serve seven.
Q. I mean how long do these green men take to become useful to you ? A. When I

have to take green men who are in for five or seven years, I set them to make wheel-barrows for five or seven months or a year, until they learn.

Q. Are they worth anything at the end of a year? A. Some of them are, and some are not.

Q. Do you consider that you can turn a good man out at the end of a year? A. Certainly not, nor at the end of two years.

Q. Is he handy then? A. Yes, and useful, perhaps, but not a good man—nor in three, nor in four years.

Q. Is he useful in six months? A. No, unless he is extra smart.

Q. In the cooperage business, could you make any good of him? A. Yes; there is a case in point of a Frenchman, who has learnt cooperage to perfection in six months; but that is an isolated case.

Q. But the ordinary run? A. No. I have tried five or six in the last few months, and they could not do anything with it.

Q. How long does it take to make a good cooper? A. We have always had coopers coming in as coopers.

Q. You cannot say how long it takes? A. There is one case—I know of none other.

Q. What does the finishing consist of? A. We have finishers. We do not learn green men that. They must know it to perfection, or they would spoil the work.

Q. Then you take only old hands? A. We have three or four painters. One of them is a real finisher.

Q. How long does it take to make men painters? A. We never make them painters. They come in painters.

Q. Have you put any green men on the planers? A. A man can learn to work on the planer in a fortnight.

Q. Make a good man? A. Yes, if he has any brains.

Q. A first-class man? A. Yes, a first-class man must go there; if not, he would knock it all to pieces, and perhaps knock his brains out.

Q. Have you had such a case? A. I had one who was half crazy, and I put him from

Q. Take the ordinary run of men, how long would it take to make one a good planer? A. Any ordinary man could be taught to run a planer in a fortnight.

Q. Suppose the planer got out of order, would a man in there for a fortnight be able to manage it? A. Not at all. There is a machinist to fix that.

Q. Would he discover when it got out of order? A. Yes, very soon.

Q. Why? A. Because it would not work.

Q. Have you had any experience with shorter term labour than this? A. There is none less than two years in the Penitentiary. I never had one at two years in my shop, unless he was a tradesman.

Q. Do you get out of these men as much work as you think they should do? A. Yes, out of the majority of them.

Q. And is that equal to the work you would get from a free man? A. It may not come up to just as much.

Q. How do you account for that? A. I do not think it is in human nature to expect such a thing.

Q. Why should you not expect it from these men? You treat them well, do you not? A. Yes, they are treated well there.

Q. Why should they not work as well as a man outside? A. Well, my experience, from what I have seen, is that the majority of men will do nearly as much as men outside, but there are a great many who will not do half as much.

Q. How do you account for a great many men not doing half as much? A. I cannot account for it at all. Because convicts are a class of men utterly depraved, and probably prefer to lie in the dark cell for a week than to work—they are so lazy.

Q. That is your experience? A. Undoubtedly so.

Q. Is the real reason that there is no incentive to work? A. No, it is laziness.

Q. Cannot you punish them for that? A. Yes, frequently they are punished.

Q. Has it a good effect? A. A very good effect in the majority of cases.

Q. Do you set your men a certain amount of work each day? A. Not at all, sir. All the jobbing of the Penitentiary is done in the carpenter's shop.

Q. Do you think it is a good plan to set an amount of work? A. No.

Q. Why? A. I never saw it half done.

Q. Suppose there is punishment if they do not do it? A. You cannot punish them very well unless you see them do wrong. A man putting a piece of work together—framing, for instance—might do it very quick, and yet it might not be worth half as much as it should be.

Q. Is that the objection? A. Yes; it would not be so well done.

Q. Do you think if you had a system of rewards there—? A. So there is.

Q. Giving them so much for extra work? A. They get five days in a month.

Q. But tobacco and money? A. They get both when they are going out.

Q. An additional amount for extra work? A. That was recommended by the Chaplain, I think, to the Government. It is not carried into effect.

Q. Would you approve of it? A. Keepers and overseers are never asked such a question as that. There are cases where it would be well.

Q. If that was the case, would you get more and better work from these men? A. I certainly would.

Q. Then you would recommend it? A. Yes, in the majority of cases.

Q. Is the reason you would get more work that the men do not work up to the full amount? Do you think, if there was an inducement for them to work up to the full amount, that they would do it? A. Every man can work more some days than others, and yet appear to be working quite as hard on the other days.

Q. Take the average of a week or a month, do you think that, under such a system as that of rewards for extra work over a certain amount—a little reward in money or tobacco or something—you would get more work out of these men? A. I think I could.

Q. What do you think the value of the labour in your shop is? A. If you look at the blue-book, page 38, you will see.

Q. You have "Material, $8,565; labour, $7,648; total, $16,213." But that does not tell us the value of that labour per man per day. A. I will tell you that.

Q. What do you consider that worth? A. From 80c to 90c a day in the carpenter's shop.

Q. Do you think that is the fair value? A. I did not compute it myself. The architect and the clerk did it, and I think it is correct.

Q. Do you think it is a fair value for it? A. I should say so.

Q. You think the labour in your shop is worth 80c to 90c a day? A. I think so, on the average. There is a great deal of furniture made. If there had not been so much furniture made it would not have been so much.

Q. What do you think the work is worth as compared with free labour? What could you get free labour outside for, to do the same kind of work? A. I could hardly answer that. All in my shop are joiners.

Q. What are they getting outside? A. $1 50 a day.

Q. Do you think your men turn out half as much as they do, each man? A. I think they did this year. I mean cabinet-makers and joiners—men working at cabinet work.

Q. These are the men who either have come in as skilled labourers, or have been made so by you? A. These are the men who were skilled labourers before they came in, and very few have been made in the Penitentiary.

Q. How many were skilled labourers before they came in? A. All were more or less skilled except fifteen or sixteen.

Q. Probably thirty five, then, were skilled labourers before they came to you? A. Yes.

Q. Supposing you had thirty-five men who had not known anything about this work before they came to you, and you had them six months, what value would you attach to their labour? A. I would not be bothered with them at all.

Q. Would they be worth 80c? A. Worth what?

Q. Worth 80c.? A. I would not try to teach them cabinet work in four or six months.

Q. How much would they be worth in six months? A. I cannot say; because I am only their guard, keeper, overseer and everything else.

Q. How much do you think you could make these men worth at the end of six months ? A. I do not see what they would be worth.
Q. 20c. ? A. No, they could not be worth that. It would take four or five overseers to make them worth that—one overseer to about 10 men.
Q. But, at the end of three years, you might probably make them worth 80c. ? A. Decidedly.
Q. Are you troubled much with things being lost in your shop ? A. That is a very strange question.
Q. Why so ? A. I think it is a very strange question.
Q. I ask if you are troubled much by things being stolen in your shop ?
Mr. LANGMUIR—Are not you troubled with thieves ? A. Is not the Penitentiary full of thieves ?
Mr. GORDON—Have you any thieves inside? Q. Are there not 650 thieves there ?
Q. But are you troubled with them ? A. Certainly not. They dare not do that. They dare not steal from one another. They would be punished.
Q. Do you lose material ? A. We never calculate that anything is lost inside of the walls of the Penitentiary.
Q. But do you find that things are lost—tools and material ? A. There might be one case of a tool being lost, but it is not a frequent occurrence. There is an outside gang of carpenters, and they are in the habit of taking tools outside. They may go away that way, but to steal and thieve in any other kind of way, it is always prohibited.
Q. But has that such an effect on the men that they do not do it ? A. They dare not do it at all.
Q. But do they do it ? A. No. Not long since, one of the reporters of the *Globe* witnessed the castigation of four or five men—McLean, I think it was.

By Mr. LANGMUIR.

Q. You have been in Kingston Penitentiary over 19 years ? A. 19 years and 9 months.
Q. All the time in the same capacity ? A. Looking after carpenters and joiners.
Q. You are a carpenter yourself ? A. Yes ; I served seven years to it in Ireland.
Q. You have charge of 51 prisoners ? A. Yes.
Q. Do you keep an account of the labour performed day by day, and return it to the Department ? A. It is in the day book there. That is what we call the time book.
Q. Your name is Thomas Davidson. Is that a correct return for 1876 ? A. I could not say.
Q. Why so ? A. I do not make out the returns.
Q. Is that your signature ? A. Not written by me.
Q. Is it a forgery ? A. That is my signature, but I did not put it there.
Q. Did you not put it to the written document ? A. Certainly not. Mr. Adams, the architect, put it there.
Q. Did you put your name to the manuscript ? A. I do not keep the manuscript.
Q. Are these figures correct from your day-book ? A. That is not my business. It is the clerk and architect who do that.
Q. Then your name has no right to be there ? A. Yes, it has, because I am in charge of the shop.
Q. Do you not know that that is a voucher for the correctness of the document? A. Certainly not.
Q. Then what is that signature there for ? A. I never took it as such.
Q. Look through that and tell me how much the labour for 1876 amounted to ? A. I never looked through it.
Q. Do you not enter in your day-book every day's labour of every man ? A. Certainly.
Q. Look at that document, and tell me what is the value of the labour of these fifty-one men you are in charge of ? A. $7,648.46¾.
Q. What is the value given on the next page ? A. $1,708.50.
Q. What is this " Statement showing cash returns for articles and labour ? " Is that separate from the ordinary work done for yourselves in the way of building and improvements ? A. These are cash receipts.

Q. But the others are not cash returns? A. They shew what they are for.
Q. Then there is "Work done on permanent improvements"—is that different from the other? A. Yes.
Q. Are these returns all different—the one for the carpenter and trades department, the other for permanent improvements, and the other cash received for work? A. Yes, they are different.
Q. Then these three returns are the value of the labour, I suppose? A. Yes.
Mr. LANGMUIR put the returns in.

[Exhibit " H."]

BY MR. GORDON.

Q. I understand you to say you did not give any authority to put your name there? A. Not at all, Mr. Adams put my name there because I am in charge of the shop, but I never vouched for that.

BY MR. LANGMUIR.

Q. Then the value of the labour performed on ordinary works amounts to $7,648? A. Yes.
Q. And the value of the labour performed on permanent improvements is $1,708? A. Yes.
Q. And the value of work for which cash was received was $3,404? A. Yes.
Q. That amounts to $12,760, made out of your fifty-one men for 1876? A. Some of the fifty-one men I have reference to are classed in the blacksmith's shop.
Q. Then there is a little more revenue derived than is stated there? A. These men are in the blacksmith's shop because five or six men are in the finishing shop.
Q. The fifty-one men produced a little more than $12,000, because some of the men were in the blacksmith's shop account? A. Yes.
Q. Then your fifty-one men produced $12,760 in the way of labour last year? A. Yes.
Q. How many working days were there in the year? A. There are only two holidays—Good Friday and Christmas Day.
Q. Then you have to take 54 days out of 365? A. Yes.
Q. Prisoners are sometimes in the hospital? A. Convicts in the hospital are not put down there.
Q. I suppose you keep the number of days in the ledger? A. That is all kept in the time-book; then it is added up at the end of the month—so many days.
Q. Then the labour is worth from 80c. to 90c.? A. Yes.
Q. You consider that a fair value? A. Yes.
Q. You consider they earned it? A. Yes.
Q. Could you get that work done any cheaper by outside people than by them? A. No.
Q. They give you good value for it—these prisoners? A. Very good.
Q. Then, as far as you are concerned, your prison labour is worth to the country from 80c. to 90c. a day? A. It averages that.
Q. You say there are about sixteen men who are not skilled men in your gang? A. Yes.
Q. Still they earn that average? A. They average it.
Q. So these unskilled men do not reduce it below 80c. or 90c.? A. It is averaged all amongst them.
Q. You speak of a man named Collingwood? A. Yes.
Q. Did he learn his trade there? A. No; he is a good tradesman—an excellent tradesman.
Q. What is the matter with Beamish? A. He is without brains, I think.
Q. Crazy? A. I do not say he is a lunatic, but next door to it.
Q. You could not expect anything from a poor lunatic? A. I would not say that.
Q. What, then? A. He is so thick in the head you cannot do anything with him.
Q. Can you reach that man by whipping? A. I do not think so. He does not give offence. He is willing to do what he is bid.

Q. But he has not the capacity ? A. No.
Q. Have you visited any other prisons besides Kingston Penitentiary ? A. I visited the vestibule of the Central Prison, but I could not get any further.
Q. Any others? A. I visited St. Vincent de l'Paul and Penetanguishene.
Q. At St. Vincent de Paul, they do not do more than you do ? A. Not so much.
Q. You are speaking of the experience in Kingston Penitentiary ? A. Entirely.
Q. And you have made the men under your charge worth 80c. or 90c. a day to the country ? A. No I have not.
Q. The men under your charge are worth that ? A. Yes.
Q. You said it took seven years to learn to make a wheelbarrow ? No.
Q. Seven years to make a tradesman ? A. No.
Q. You were apprenticed for seven years ? Yes.
Q. All hand labour then ? A. Yes.
Q. No machinery in those days ? A. None at all.
Q. If machinery were largely used, would they learn easier ? A. I do not think so—not so well, because hand work is always the best.
Q. But, as to the application of prison labour, do you think the prisoners would learn to work with machinery sooner than by hand work ? A. That is just what they are doing—working by machinery in the carpenters' shop.
Q. What machinery ? A. A planer, a lathe.
Q. How long does it take a man to learn the planer ? A. I said about a fortnight.
Q. A short date man would be very useful in a fortnight? A. Yes, on that.
Q. In taking away shafting and so on ? A. Yes.
Q. What other machinery have you? A. The matching machine.
Q. How long does that take ? A. It does not take long to put the matching, but it takes longer to understand the machine.
Q. Then there are a considerable number of men it does not take very long to make useful ? A. There are a considerable number, but it is a very small number.
Q. You have mentioned a third—that is pretty fair ? Yes.
Q. You hold out an inducement in the Penitentiary to reduce the sentences if the men are industrious and keep under good discipline ? A. Yes ; 5 days in a month.
Q. Do you keep a record of that? A. Yes. A conduct and industry book is kept, of course.
Q. If they are not industrious do you make a black mark ? A. We put down an 0 against them.
Q. Did you require to do that often last year? A. No. I adopted another course.
Q. What is that ? A. Moral suasion. It is not everyone who can look after convicts. A man must be a judge of character, and very few are judges of character.
Q. You are a judge of character ? A. I do not say so.
Q. You have adopted moral suasion and a very few 0's ? A. Yes.
Q. Are you successful in your treatment ? A. I am endeavouring to be so.
Q. You do not give any inducement other than the reduction of sentences ? A. None as yet.

BY MR. GORDON.

Q. With regard to these 15 or 16 unskilled men in your department, you can always find sufficient work for that number ? A. Yes, certainly ; carrying in lumber and so on.
Q. And that is the way you make these men do work equal in value to the skilled men ? A. Certainly. Each man has his post to fill.
Q. Suppose, instead of 15 unskilled and 35 skilled men, you had 15 skilled and 35 unskilled ? A. It would not work very well.
Q. Would you be able to make these men worth 80 cents all round ? A. No.
Q. How much ? A. About 20 cents, I suppose.
Q. If you had 250 prisoners to employ, and only had skilled work to supply about 50 of them, would it be an advantage or a disadvantage to have that number ? A. I do not understand.
Q. If you were bound to take 250 prisoners, and you only had enough skilled work to employ about 50 men, would it be an advantage or a disadvantage ? A. I would put the

skilled and unskilled men together; I would pair them, put an unskilled man at a bench by a skilled man to bring him along.

Q. Would that be as good as two skilled men? A. No.

BY THE CHAIRMAN.

Q. Can you give an idea how long these men that you employ have been in the several employments you have them now engaged in? A. The greater part of them have been there for years; there is one old man—a cabinet maker—who has been 25 years in the Penitentiary; other men have been there 8 or 9 years, 7 years, 6 years, and so on—some 10, some 5. and so on.

Q. Of course they have had full opportunity to become perfect in their work? A. Yes; since the cabinet shop was burnt down, I have had all the cabinet makers.

Q. If any of these men fall out and you want to replace them, have you the selection of them? A. If any one goes in who is a carpenter, he is sent to the carpenter's shop; we prefer him to a green hand.

Q. Do you have a supply all the while of men who have been partially skilled, and have some experience in various kinds of work? A. Yes; but there are a great many men who wish to pretend they are skilled men; a man from Toronto said his grandfather was a carpenter, and therefore he claimed to be.

Q. If you find they do not serve their purpose, what do you do? A. He is still working there; I am trying to give him a chance.

BY MR. NOXON.

Q. Do you carry on a jobbing department? A. Yes; a general jobbing department.

Q. Parties come in from outside and get work performed? A. No, inside.

Q. You send nothing to the outside market at all? A. No, only to the Military College.

Q. Have you ever had charge of men outside, so as to know how readily you could make free labour useful? A. No, except myself.

Q. Of course, the work you employ these men at requires mechanical skill to perform? A. Yes.

Q. Not rough-class mechanics? A. No, not at all.

BY THE CHAIRMAN.

Q. In these statements as to the value of the work, how is that value arrived at? For instance, here is a "Return showing work done on permanent improvements by the carpenter, and trades department. Burnt building—material, $96.02½; labour, $819.50.' Is that arrived at by charging so much a day for this labour? A. Yes.

Q. It is not dependent upon the amount of work they do—it is an arbitrary charge of so much a day? A. Yes.

The Report on the Penitentiaries was put in.

[Exhibit "J."

The Commission adjourned.

WEDNESDAY, July 25th.

The Commission met at 10 o'clock.

PETER TODD, called on behalf of the Car Company, sworn.—

BY MR. GORDON.

Q. I believe you have had considerable experience in the employment of prison labour? A. Yes.
Q. At one time in the Auburn Prison? A. Yes, I was there five years.
Q. In what capacity? A. As a foreman.
Q. In what department? A. Cabinet.
Q. And subsequent to that, you were at Kingston Penitentiary? A. Yes.
Q. For many years? A. Some 24 years about.
Q. In what capacity were you there? A. As a foreman.
Q. In the same department? A. Yes.
Q. You were under several contractors there? A. I was the first that started the cabinet department there.
Q. For whom? A. For John Stevenson and a nephew of his.
Q. How long did he have the contract? A. Five years.
Q. Do you remember what rate he paid for the labour? A. 30 cents.
Q. How many men had he? A. The contract was 50, with a privilege. Sometimes we worked 60.
Q. A privilege of taking more? A. Yes.
Q. Or less? A. No.
Q. How many prisoners were there in the prison at that time? A. At that time, when the contract was first let, when I first came, there were only a little over 400. I cannot tell you the exact number.
Q. Was that long term or short term labour? A. Long.
Q. Ranging from what to what? A. Nothing less than two years up to life.
Q. Had Mr. Stevenson that contract for more than five years? A. No.
Q. Why was that? A. It was got away from him. Other parties paid a little more.
Q. Who got it afterwards? A. Mr. Morton.
Q. What did he pay? A. I think it was 40 cents.

BY MR. LANGMUIR.

Q. James Morton? A. Yes.

BY MR. GORDON.

Q. What length of time did he have the contract? A. Not quite five years, because he failed, and it went into the hands of the Bank of Upper Canada.
Q. How many prisoners had he? A. They generally ran about the same thing.
Q. Had he the option of taking more? A. Yes; all these contracts were let from the original.
Q. With that option? A. Yes.
Q. Were you with anybody else there? A. Yes.
Q. After Morton left? A. Yes.
Q. With whom? A. Mr. Drennan. I was with him for about ten years.
Q. Did you hear his evidence last night? A. I did.
Q. He paid 35 cents? A. Yes.
Q. Were you with him when they wanted to raise the price? A. I was not.
Q. Do you know anything about that? A. Nothing.
Q. Had you anything to do with fixing the price for the contractors you were with? A. No, not with putting a price on convict labour.

Q. I mean had you anything to do with their taking the contract at these prices in the way of advising them? A. Yes, I did have.
Q. What did you do? A. Of course, I was there from the original, and I was asked my opinion. I certainly gave it that, in the second contract, the men were worth a little more than in the first, because in the first they were all green hands, and had to be all learnt.
Q. At first? A. Yes. I gave my opinion on that.
Q. You thought that having learnt the business, having been there a little time, they were worth more than under the first contract? A. Certainly, for we took long sentence men and they were taught.
Q. That was Morton's contract? A. Yes.
Q. He took over Stevenson's men? A. Yes, men and machinery. He took all his stock and tools.
Q. Was there any discussion at that time whether they should pay more than 40 cents? A. Not to my knowledge. It was let by tender—sealed tenders.
Q. And that was the highest tender? A. Yes.
Q. Do you remember what was paid for the labour in the Auburn Prison when you were there? A. I do not remember exactly, but I think it was about 30 cents or 35 cents. I know that it kept gradually going up.
Q. How long did you find it would take a man to become a good carpenter or cabinet-maker? A. When you say "to become a good one," it would take some time.
Q. What do you call some time? A. Well, I suppose you could not make what we would call a good cabinet-maker in less than two years. Of course you could get him in a year so that he would be able to pay for himself, and probably a little more, by keeping him on a certain kind of work.
Q. At 30 cents. A. Yes.
Q. Do you think he would be worth more than 30 cents before a year? A. Some would, and that would depend a great deal on the foreman, on what kind of work he kept him on.
Q. And the amount of supervision he gave him? A. Yes.
Q. How many foremen had you to these 50 men? A. Sometimes I was all alone, at other times, I had an assistant.

BY THE CHAIRMAN.

Q. What kind of work were you carrying on? A. Cabinet work.

BY MR. GORDON.

Q. But after a man had been with you about ten years, he began to be a good man? A. Yes, then we begin to think we could make of him; that is generally what we calculated on.
Q. How would these men compare with free labourers; take green men—a freeman who is a green man, and a prisoner who is a green man—do you think the prisoner would do as much and as good work as the free man at the end of the first year? A. I do not know but he would; some of them would.
Q. Then there is nothing in prison life or the character of these criminals to make their work less good than the work of free men? A. Oh, yes, because in the first place, the convict is not the same as a free man; he knows he is there and has to stay there.
Q. Do you find any disadvantages connected with this kind of labour? A. Of course there are disadvantages decidedly.
Q. What are they? A. There are several.
Q. What did you find the greatest difficulty you had and the greatest disadvantages you were under? A. We have a great many, because, in the first place, a convict knows he has to stay there, and, though some of them really take an interest in their work, and are really anxious to learn a trade, others do not care one snap whether they learn a trade or only pass away the time; you have to try either to coax or drive them—either one or the other—to get a day's work out of them, and you must use your own judgment which you will do, which you think is best.

Q. Is that the only disadvantage you find with prison labour ? A. Oh, there are several other little things that I cannot think of.
Q. What kind of things? Were they as skilful in the use of their tools? A. Not till they learn. Decidedly, you take a green man that never saw a jack plane or anything of that description—it will take him three months to learn to keep his tools in order.
Q. When they had learnt, were they as careful ? A. They were not ; not as careful as a man who owned his own tools and had to buy them.
Q. Was there much difference ? A. Considerable, of course we had to find their tools.
Q. It was then a considerable item—the destruction of tools? A. Quite an item, I assure you.
Q Did you find they were as careful in the use of material ? A. Some would be, but some would make mistakes and spoil it. I would not like to say it was all wilful. Sometimes it was, and sometimes it was through carelessness or not knowing better, but we had to lose considerable material and stock in that way.
Q. Would you as soon work with this class of men as with free men, taking them altogether —all these things you have just mentioned ? A. Well, it almost becomes second nature to me to be among convicts, but, take it in another light, if you are working outside with men, if a man does not suit, you send him to the office to get his pay and send him about his business, but I have to keep a convict and make the best I can out of him.
Q. You have to keep him till his sentence is out ? A. Yes, unless he is really good for nothing, when I can manage with the Warden.
Q. That is a matter of grace? A. Yes. He is not obliged to take him back after I have once taken him.
Q. If you had to deal with prisoners with short terms—6 to 8 or 9 months—do you think you could have done as much as with these prisoners at Kingston? A. No. I would not take them, I could not do anything with them.
Q. Why? A. The term is too short.
Q. Would they not be able to earn something for you before the end of the time ? A. Six months ? No ; it would be a loss to me unless I kept them carrying lumber or tending the drying kiln, but to put them at a bench and to attend to tools——
Q. Or on a lathe? A. That would be worse still. It takes a smart man to be a turner.
Q. Or a planer ? A. You could put him at a planer in a few weeks to learn that, if it was kept in order for him.
Q. Could you form any estimate of the value of labour of that class, judging from what you know of the long term labour and the price of it ? A. Not between both, for I never had the experience. I never took a man less than three years, unless he was a man accustomed to tools, because it was no use—we would be only losing money on him.
Q. Suppose you had to take 250 prisoners, and had only unskilled work sufficient to employ 50, what would you be inclined to give for these men with 6 or 8 months' sentences ? A. It would depend upon what kind of work I had to keep them at to make their wages. I could not do it at cabinet work.
Q. Making pails and brooms and that kind of thing, with the assistance of machinery? A. There is machinery for making pails. It is all done by machinery. Then all you want is a man who understands hooping them.
Q. Do you think it would be safe to put 200 men of that kind to turn out pails by machinery of that kind ? A. I would not like to myself; I should want a foreman over every ten of them to watch them.
Q. Do you think it would be a good contract to take that number and pay 50 cents a head for them ? A. No.
Q. Or 20cts. ? A. I would not take them at that price ; however others might.

BY MR. HARDY.

Q. I understand you then to say that, in so far as you would have the work of an ordinary labourer to do, a short term is as good as a long term man ? A. Of course ; that is, keeping both at the same business.
Q. And your experience probably will have, at all events, suggested to you that these men who are sent to prison, even if they are there for a short or a long term, will do more

under discipline—the watchful eye of a keeper and guard and foreman—than if they were working out as ordinary journeymen, if they were the same class of men? A. They will do better in the prison, providing the discipline is there and is kept up.

Q. These men, you think would do more under discipline than without it? A. Decidedly.

Q. Half as much again? A. No, I will not say that.

Q. But they would do better? A. Yes, taking the very same men working outside, and put in a prison where they are compelled to work.

Q. What has been your experience that the prison authorities do in case they decline to work—humbug-shuffle; what do they do in the Penitentiary? A. I know what we used to do—punish them and make them work.

Q. What punishment? A. The cat.

Q. How many blows? A. That depends on the crime; I have seen six dozen given.

Q. But for not working? A. I have known a man to get three dozen, and then be made to work—and he would work, too; that is the way to bring them to their senses.

By Mr. Langmuir.

Q. They are getting mild in Kingston, from what you hear, are they? A. I should think they were.

By Mr. Hardy.

Q. They are not as severe there now as they used to be? A. No.

Q. How long since you ceased to have connection with the Penitentiary as foreman? A. About six years ago.

Q. And all this occurred from twenty years to six years ago? A. I came in 1850.

Q. And remained till 1871? A. About that time.

Q. What you have spoken of occurred between 1850 and 1871? A. Yes; I came one year after Warden Macdonald. He was a year ahead of me there.

Q. Do I understand you to say that the long-term man is preferable, because he can learn his trade better—has more time? A. Certainly. It is better for the contractor. We can teach a man, probably, in eighteen months, so that he will just begin to pay; but what is the use of that if, a few months after that, he is gone?

Q. But if it was work that did not require specific training, such as learning the trades you have mentioned, such as cabinet work, a very nice kind of work; if it did not require to learn a trade, the short-term man would be as good as the long-term man? A. It depends on what you put them to.

B. How nearly as good would they be as out-door labourers? Under discipline, with the lash before them, with a prospect of punishment, how nearly would they equal out-door labourers? A. Of course, they would not come near as good.

Q. Do you think not? A. Not quite.

Q. They are as strong? A. Yes, after they come in the prison and get fed up a spell; too well, I am sorry to say, better than the folks outside, now-a days.

Q. So, as a matter of fact, pushed, driven, well guarded, they pretty nearly equal an outside labourer? A. Yes; pretty nearly.

Q. If the class of work they had to do could be the same as that done by an ordinary labourer, they would not be much behind out-door labourers? A. About a quarter.

Q. Did you give them a task? A. No; I never believed in it.

Q. Probably your kind of work was such that you could not well give them a task? A. I could, but I found it would not do so well.

Q. Speaking of cabinet-work, is there a distinction between the trade of a carpenter and a cabinet-maker? A. Decidedly.

Q. And which takes the longest to learn? A. I heard one man say it took seven years to learn to be a carpenter.

Q. Is there any distinction in learning the complete work of the trade—any distinction in the time it takes? A. Decidedly.

Q. Which could be learnt the quickest? A. Cabinet-making is a very particular, a very nice trade, and not exactly the same as joiner work. There are different branches.

Here is one style of a table, and couches, and sofas, and others different altogether. You would not probably get one job twice alike, and the only way we could make our men pay was, when one could make a good job, we worked him up, kept him on one job, say tables, until he was able to make a first class table; and then I gave him something a little better. Our object was to get him on fine work. That is where it paid.

Q. The cabinet-maker who thoroughly understands his business has learnt a finer kind of trade than the mere carpenter? A. Yes.

Q. Therefore, it would take longer to do it? A. Yes.

Q. You had long term hands there, so time was not so much of an object? A. Yes, we had long sentence men.

Q. Did Stevenson make money out of his men? A. He did towards the last.

Q. Did Morton make money? A. I do not think he made much. It was his own fault, though.

Q. He was engaged in large undertakings outside? A. Yes. It was his own fault. No man knows it better than I do.

Q. Drennan made money? A. Drennan made money. I know it. The first seven years, Drennan made money as fast as any man wanted to make it.

Q. What did Drennan get along with his men, in machinery? or was it his own machinery? A. He got a shop, it was heated, and we got benches.

Q. He furnished everything else? A. Yes.

Q. s there any contract carried on to-day beside the lock-making? A. No more.

Q. You were in Auburn prior to 1850? A. Yes.

Q. Did they have contract work there? A. Yes.

Q. Auburn State Prison? A. Auburn Prison, State of New York.

Q. Is it a long term prison? A. Two years is the shortest.

Q. Who had the contract when you were there? A. Huston Parsons.

Q. How much did he pay? A. I think he paid 35c.

Q. That was cabinet-making? A. Yes.

By Mr. Gordon.

Q. You do not approve of giving men a stint or task work? A. Not in our work.

Q. What objection did you find? A. I found, in the first place, they would slight their work; I will explain—say I give a man half a dozen tables to make, and give him so many days to make them in; I say, "all over that time I will pay you for, so much a day;" he would go to work, and, unless he was watched very closely, he would, nine times out of ten, spoil half of them to get them done; I might say: "Here, I want these tables made in so many days;" if he did not do that, and I considered it was a fair reasonable day's work, I had him reported for not doing a day's work; you must be a judge; some men can work faster than others; you must judge that.

Q. You found that was a better way to do it, than to give him a task? A. Yes; because he would do the work, and the work was well done; the way I always did when I gave a man a job was—he had a pass book; I set down the day and date, and what it was; then I could see how many days it took him to make it.

Q. You said some of the prisoners were not in a condition for a few months to begin work; you refer to their physical condition? A. Yes; some of them.

Q. In consequence of their habits? A. We are not obliged to have them, every convict goes before the doctor and is examined, and if he is not fit for work, he is sent to the hospital.

Q. Did you find that many men came in that way? A. Not many. At least they did not come under my observation, anyhow.

Q As a rule, did you find a man as fit for work the first week he was in the Prison as after he had been there for some time? A. No, because when he comes in first, of course, some have feelings, and being unfortunate enough to get in there, they worry a little, and everything is strange to them. Take them into the shop, and they do not know where to look for anything or what to do. These men are not good for a couple of weeks, even at rough common work. They are good for nothing.

Q. For the first couple of weeks a convict is not worth anything? A. No, I have had them left in the shop, and the Warden would not charge for them for a couple of weeks—some of them, but not as a general thing.

By Mr. Hardy.

Q. Are there any railway connections or switches into the Penitentiary at Kingston ? A. Not into it, but round it.
Q. From the Grand Trunk ? A. No.
Q. They are not far from the lake ? A. No.
Q. They can ship direct ? A. Yes, vessels come alongside. There is a splendid wharf there.
Q. Is there any switch within the walls from the wharf, or a tramway, or anything of that kind ? A. No.
Q. How do they ship generally ? A. Some by rail and some by steamer.
Q. And get to the Grand Trunk by teaming ? A. Yes.
Q. What distance ? A. Not two miles to the depot.

By the Chairman.

Q. Did you practise giving any compensation to the men at all for efficiency and doing the work properly ? A. I did sometimes, but it was nothing more or less than that probably I would give them an extra piece of tobacco. I used to make it a practice at Christmas to give my men some cake and coffee and some apples. The Warden used to allow me that privilege.

Q. Do you think any advantage resulted from holding out to these men any prospect of getting remuneration if they did their work well and behaved themselves ? A. I think there would be if they received nothing till they were going out, but, if you give it while they are in the prison—I have known it done, not by me—they would make very bad use of it. They would have certain things brought in that had no business to be brought in, because they had the money, and that will do almost anything. I know certain shops where they gave them taskwork, and, after that, paid them for what they did, but they found that was a bad business and they stopped it, but we never did it.

Q. But if this remuneration were retained for them to have when they went out, you do not think the bad effects would follow ? A. I do not. I think, if I were a contractor, I would say to a good man, "I want you to do a fair reasonable day's work, and if you do it well I will allow you 5 cents a day," or whatever it might be. A man might be there for 5 years. He might come in a first-class mechanic. I would say, "If you do what is right, I will allow you 5 cents a day. I will place it in the Warden's hands every month, and at the expiration of your time, provided you behave yourself and do what is right, it will be there." I believe that would be the best thing that could be done in a prison.

Q. When you reported men for not having done their duty—the amount of work you thought they should have done—did the officials of the prison act upon your report—how did they decide ? A. Yes. I never reported a man without I said, "You have been too long making that work ; you should have done it so and so ; I am going to give you the same kind again, and I want you to do it in so many days or weeks (whatever it might be), and if you do not do it, I will have to report you," and then of course I reported it to the keeper, and the keeper sent the report to the Warden. The keepers and guards have no business to interfere with contractors' arrangements at all, unless you are breaking the rules, and not doing what is just and fair. They have to order the discipline—that is their duty.

Q. Is there any difference, in your opinion, in the value of labour now to be applied to such purposes as you applied such labour to, from what it was when you were employing this labour ? Is labour of the same kind for the same purposes worth less or more now than then ? A. If anything, I believe it ought to be less now, if we look at the times.

By Mr. Noxon.

Q. Are you at present in charge of the same class of work outside the prison that you were inside ? A. No, I am working for myself.

Q. When you first went into the prison, you had all classes of machinery necessary for manufacturing furniture ? A. All classes. I kept introducing new machinery ; I kept up with the times. Of course, 27 years ago, there was not a great deal of machinery as there is now.

Q. Were you using the latest improved machinery in the prison ? A. Yes.

Q. As it was introduced outside, you put it in the prison ? A. Yes, I went to New York and Boston, and the Western States, myself.

Q. What would be your opinion as to manufacturing pails by prison labour, compared with cabinet work ? Would it be more readily adapted to pails and wooden ware of that kind than to cabinet work ? A. Oh, yes. of course, because that is one thing over and over.

Q. The same thing, and done altogether by machinery ? A. Certainly it is.

Q. If there was a market for it, unskilled labour could be employed to better advantage on that class of work than in manufacturing furniture ? A. Decidedly, I think so, the way times are now.

JOHN W. LANGMUIR, called on behalf of the Government, sworn :—

BY MR. HARDY.

Q. You are Inspector of Prisons for Ontario ? A. Yes.

Q. The Central Prison comes within your jurisdiction ? A. It does.

Q. When did the Canada Car Company commence its operations—the original company ? A. The contract was made on the 21st March, 1873. The first contract was entered into on the 21st March, 1873.

Q. Do you remember exactly when they commenced operations—was it that fall ? A. No, they did not. They were to have commenced operations almost immediately, but some delay took place. They did not commence till June, 1874. I think.

Q. Did they then take their full complement of prisoners ? A. They did not. It was not provided in the contract that they should take the full complement at once.

Q. Did they take the full complement provided by the contract ? A. They never have up to the present day.

Q. Had you the number of prisoners always ready for them after they began ? A. Always ready.

Q. When did they quit operations under the first contract ? A. They closed their shops on the 20th February, 1875, and refused to take any further prison labour.

Q. Have you any information before you which will enable you to state what number of men there were then employed ? A. I can get the exact numbers from my reports bearing upon the subjects. I can give the exact numbers employed from month to month. They took a greater number in the fall of 1874, but I think after October it dwindled off, grew less until the close of the shops entirely on the 20th February, 1875.

Q. What was the alleged cause of the closing of the shops ? A. The alleged cause was the stagnation in railway affairs.

Q. They found no market for their products ? A. The general stagnation in railway affairs, which of course affected all car-building operations, both free labour and prison labour.

Q. When they closed, had they paid the Government for the prisoners they had employed ? A. Nothing whatever.

Q. How long did they remain closed ? A. For nearly a year.

Q. And then what was done ? A. During the time the shops were closed, negotiations were going on between the Canada Car Company and the Government, with a view to new operations, to new industries being introduced.

Q. Before going into the new industries let me ask you, did the Government comply with its terms of the old contract in furnishing such shops, plant and motive power as were called for by the agreement ? A. Everything that was asked for in the way of shop-room, machinery and plant and space was furnished, and considerably more than was originally agreed for.

Q. Was the additional quantity furnished upon the requisition of the Company ? A.

Always upon their requisition, and very often upon plans furnished by them. There were regular plans drawn to show the position of the machinery and the bolting and everything, and these plans were always acted upon, or if they were not, the changes were made at the request of the Company.

Q. I suppose that with these plans were presented arguments to show the necessity to complete the works, the equipments? A. Yes, they seemed to be good reasons. Mr. Baines changed his ideas about it very often, which involved a considerable extra outlay to the Government.

Q. The new industry was inaugurated under the second agreement, I suppose, or after that? A. Yes, concurrently with entering upon the second agreement.

Q. Will you tell us practically what the contractors get in addition to the mere manual labour of the men, giving, as nearly as you can, the values? A. In the first place, they get the shop accommodation. They have the use of the ten structures expressly erected and arranged at their request.

Q. For their working operations? A. Yes.

Q. Those are apart from what would be requisite for mere prison purposes? A. Entirely. That is shop space, altogether apart from the prison proper, which is for the confinement of the prisoners, and the domestic management. They have 10 structures composed of, first, the north shop, as it is called, the wood-shop. It is two stories high, and 196 feet long by 46 feet wide. There are 16,000 superficial feet area of space.

Q. Working space? A. Yes. That can be all utilized for the prisoners to work in, and for the placing of machinery.

Q. What next? A. The next was what is known as the south shop or the iron shop.

Q. That is the one they are now manufacturing cars in? A. Yes. That is the same size—196ft. by 46ft.

By Mr. Gordon.

Q. Two stories? A. Yes, and a basement. Really it is only two stories, because that shop was altered very much to suit the requirements of the Company, and I think upwards of $10,000—almost $10,000—I cannot speak exactly about it—but I think fully $10,000 was spent to make it suit the requirements of the Company as an iron shop, a machine shop.

By Mr. Hardy.

Q. What next? A. The next is a foundry—157 ft. long, by 77 feet wide. These structures are all brick. There is only one floor in that—necessarily in a foundry—and there are some 12,500 feet of superficial space for working purposes. These three shops were all that the Government agreed to furnish to the Company under the original contract, and they were not to be so large. For instance, the foundry was to be originally a store-room, but it was afterwards changed to a foundry. It was not to be so extensive a building as it afterwards turned out to be. These three buildings were supposed to provide all the space requisite for the Canada Car Company's inside operations in the prison. But, upon their requisition, another building was put up—a frame structure, called the forge building. It is octagonal, and contains altogether 16,000 feet of superficial area. Then we built an erecting shop for their cars. That is a frame building which the tracks run into—190ft. long by 68ft. wide.

Q. What is it used for now? A. It is used for the manufacture of wooden manufactures in connection with the Canada Car Company. Formerly, it was used as a broom shop, and one side of it, the length, is used as a paint shop. When originally built as an erecting shop, it was a mere skeleton to work in in foul weather, but it was all ceiled under the new industry—ceiled inside, and heating pipes put in it, and it was made a good substantial structure—that is, when they commenced the new operations. It was represented by the Company that they would not have enough space to carry on the new operations without that, so it was all made good for that purpose and heated.

By Mr. Gordon.

Q. Is it wooden or brick? A. Wooden; a frame building, afterwards cased inside.

By Mr. Hardy.

Q. The next one? A. The next is a shop that was known originally as the scrap-shop; it was a frame building erected for the use of the Company for breaking up old iron before it went into the foundry. That shop was afterwards turned into a broom shop. The Government paid for the original structure, but the Company have made considerable additions to it, at their own expense so far, though they claim now that the Government should make it good, that they should be reimbursed for their expenditure; that is held in abeyance; that shop affords 3,700 superficial feet. Then the next structure we put up was—they represented to the Government that they had not, to carry on the new industries efficiently, anything like enough of drying kiln accommodation, and, after some negotiations, the Government decided to build an additional kiln. That was done only about a year and a half ago; it is a brick structure, and the top of it I intended to use for a tailor's shop for our own purposes.

Q. On the top of the kiln? A. Yes, there is a current of air passing under all the time; but Mr. McBean was anxious to get that for a brush factory and we gave it to him

By Mr. Gordon.

Q. Are there two kilns? A. Yes, two kilns.

By Mr. Hardy.

Q. This is a new structure? A. Yes, entirely; the Company put in some of the iron heating apparatus in this kiln.

Q. Do they claim to be reimbursed for that? A. Yes, that is in a bill presented for outlay on capital account.

Q. I suppose they say it becomes part of the real estate, and therefore will be of no benefit to them after the expiration of their contract? A. Yes.

Q. That remains in abeyance along with the other? A. Yes.

Q. The next? A. Prior to the erection of that new drying kiln, we had put up a brick structure for a drying kiln. We had furnished the labour for it and the material, and they furnished the iron, the piping and things of that kind, but in the negotiations for carrying on the new trades we paid the Company for that and many other things; at the time $16,000 was paid them for the money they advanced to put the iron piping in the old kiln, so it belongs entirely to the Government now.

By Mr. Gordon.

Q. As to this drying kiln, did you furnish the material as well as the labour—the bricks? A. Subsequently we paid for the whole.

Q. Who furnished the bricks in the first instance? A. I cannot say whether it was the Government or not. I think some of our brick was used and some delivered by the Company, but everything the Company put into that kiln was paid for by the Government in the $16,000 voted by Parliament for that purpose.

Q. You paid something, but there was some dispute whether we got enough or not? A. I know that.

By Mr. Hardy.

Q. Of course there was a difference between their claim and your contention? A. Yes; they considered it satisfactory, though. These, with some other projections which may be used for shop room, make the ten structures.

Q. Can you form an estimate of their cost? Have you data for it? A. The whole thing provides about 100,000 superficial feet of shop space.

Q. Will you state as near as you can the cost of the several erections you have spoken of, or as much as you have made a calculation of? A. It is impossible to tell exactly what they cost. Owing to the failure of the original contractor, Elliott, the work was taken out of his hands, and carried on, largely by day's work, by the Government, and without reference to taking the cost of one shop or one structure over another, but there is no doubt that, taking the measurement values, which I believe were taken on one occasion, the cost of the shops and the railways and the land is over $100,000.

Q. How much land have they? A. The shops occupy, including the yards and the lumber yard, about 8 acres of land, all enclosed.

Q. What was that put at, do you remember? A. The Ontario Government bought it from the Dominion Government—it was Ordnance land.

Mr. GORDON objected to the Car Company being charged with interest on the cost of the expensive buildings erected by the Government.

Mr. HARDY said the Commissioners were authorized to enquire into the value of the labour, including the shops, plant and fixtures.

After some argument, the examination was continued.

Q. You say it cost over $100,000. Is that within the mark? A. Taking the land, and the railway tracks and switches and their connection, and the buildings, they do, undoubtedly cost over $100,000.

Q. Are you familiar with what erections are being used by this Company? A. I am.

Q. Are any not in use? A. At the present time they are all in use with the exception of the upper flat of the iron shop.

Q. Is that fully in use? A. Only partially at present.

Q. Are they employing their full complement of hands? A. They are not.

Q. Short about how many? A. 45 men to-day, I think.

Q. If these other 45 men were employed would they be using all the shop room? A. It would depend on whether they carried on the iron industry or not. They are using the shops fully, so far as the new industry is concerned, now, and they complained that, in some respects, they have not enough, and gave that as a reason why they wanted these other shops fitted up and re-arranged.

Q. This amount does not include machinery? A. Not at all.

Q. Can you tell us the privileges they have in the way of machinery? A. The better way would be to give the bills the Government paid. The character of the machinery is steam engines, boilers——

Q. How many? A. Four large boilers, two large engines, all the running gear ready to connect with the shafts to attach the machines.

Q. Belting included? A. The heavy belting, that is the top belting, and shaftings, castings and pulleys connected with that to run the main shafting.

Q. And the Government have paid the bills for that? A. For all that. Then in the foundry, they provided all the fixtures; they put in the cupolas, and the blasts and annealing pits and all fixtures generally, I think, were provided by the Government, that is where they were fixtures that went into the building and became fixtures.

Q. Have you any other class of machinery? A. Of course, the bills will show in detail what those things were, but there were a great many things in the way of smaller classes of machinery. In the iron shop there were a considerable number of things that cost a great deal of money.

Q. What kind of things? A. Some ovens, and some very expensive shafting in connection with the iron machinery, and the manner in which it was fixed, owing to its being so heavy, was very expensive; there were what they call hangers to support the machinery—almost expensive; the roof had to be raised in order to get it in.

Q. Have you made a summary taken from the bills? A. Yes; altogether the Government paid for the plant that I speak of, the machinery and these fixtures, $66,325.43, so far as I can find.

Q. If there be any reason for it—I am not aware that there is, seeing the two agreements run into each other—but rather, following the cue that they were not using some of this, can you form an opinion, from that point of view, from the knowledge you now have, what proportion of that machinery is in the car-shop? A. I could give you the details.

Q. Could you group the details? A. I should say generally that of the $66,000 at the present time, at least $45,000 worth is in active use. The boilers and engines alone and the connections cost $20,000.

By Mr. Gordon.

Q. Is that in actual use now? A. Yes.

By Mr. Hardy.

Q. Now have you made a calculation showing how much *per diem* either the one expenditure or the two expenditures, upon the building and machinery, on the building alone or the machinery alone, would average for the number of men the Company have taken or are called upon to take by their contract? A. Do you mean what it is worth *per diem*?

Q. Yes, representing the number of men? A. Taking the shop structures and railway and land at $100,000, and considering the extent of the shops and the ground, and the connection with the railway system of the Province and the country, it has required just as much space as they use for other car companies—the Ontario Car Company at London has about the same proportion of land, and all industries of that kind require as much land—and allowing 6 per cent. at least for the rental, that would be $6,000 a year. For buildings which cost far less, the rental would run from $1,000 to five or six thousand a year. In ordinary times, this, without the plant, would certainly rent for $6,000.

Q. That is less than the value placed by General Humphreys—8 or 10 per cent? A. Yes, but taking the value of the measurements of the shops alone which was done by day's work, and the $100,000 is within the mark considerably. The next class of privileges is machinery and fixtures, amounting to $66,000. Then, in addition to that, the Government is under contract to heat and light the shops and to provide water for them, for the use of the shops for mechanical and industrial purposes, and the Government have to insure the buildings that belong to them, and things of that kind. These privileges, based upon what other large factories are paying in town, are worth at least $1,000. As to the $66,000, I consider from enquiry, and from the statements of others who use machinery, having regard to the tear and wear of it, at the very least the rental would be 10 per cent. on the outlay.

Q. That would come to how much a year? A. $6,600, taking the amount of money expended for the purpose.

Q. Then, in addition to the machinery, the privileges you have mentioned? A. Taking the water, the Government was at very great expense in bringing the water into the Prison, and afterwards into the shops, specially for the Company as far as the shops were concerned. The quantity of water they use, charged at the Commissioners' rates, would be $900 a year, as given to me by the Engineer of the Government.

By Mr. Gordon.

Q. At the rates they charge the Government? A. The quantity of water the Company uses, charged at the Commissioners' rates.

Q. At the Commissioners' rates to the Government? A. The rates they charge everybody.

By Mr. Hardy.

Q. You do not get your water from the Commissioners? A. No, we furnish our own; we keep up machinery and plant and engineers at the lake. It costs us more than that really. We are now discussing whether we shall not abandon it, and take our water from the Commissioners.

Q. Then there is $900 for that. What then? A. We are, under the contract, to provide the Company with the gas. They only require it on very few occasions, owing to the fact, I suppose, that they have not been running full time, and the obstructions to their work, but we have to supply it and we have put in the fixtures in order to supply it. Taking the winter months and a certain proportion of the day, and basing it upon what other shops are run up to—seven o'clock or six in the evening—it would be $400 a year.

Q. That they have not demanded, but may? A. Yes, we have the fixtures there. Then we heat the shops. I instructed the bursar to keep an exact account of the cost of fuel, and he returns it as $1,500 for the original structures and the erecting shop. If we heat the other shops, it will cost about $2,000, but it costs $1,500 now. Then the insurance upon the buildings, for a very small portion of them, I have put down at $300 a year—a very insignificant part of the value. Then there is the exemption from taxation. It is not paid by the Government, but the Company get the benefit of it, and basing that on such works as the large foundry of Gurney and others, it would be at least $900 a year. If these figures are right; if they are near the thing, these privileges of gas and water, and fuel and exemption from taxation, and insurance, are worth $4,000 a year.

Q. Do you supply men to provide and feed the fuel? A. Yes; that is, for heating purposes. We have not charged anything of that kind, because the same engineer heats the buildings as well.

Q. What would that total? A. These privileges which I have detailed would amount to $16,625 a year. They would practically reduce the price of the prison labour for the first two and a half years of the contract from 50c. to 29c. a day.

Q. For the bare labour of the men? A. Yes, and for the second term of two and a half years to 34c., and for the third term of two and a half years, for which, under the contract, they are to pay 60c., it would be reduced to 39c. *per diem* per prisoner.

Q. Have you made enquiries as to the value of the rental of property in town for similar shops? A. I have.

Q. Give us some illustration? A. We propose to bring people to prove it; the figures I have given you are based upon not only the cost of the works in the prison, but on what other people are paying for privileges in similar circumstances.

Q. Is the charge of 10 per cent. for machinery a low figure? A. For certain classes of machinery, where there is an unusual amount of wear and tear, 10 per cent. is altogether too little—where it requires frequent renewals.

Q. A good deal of this machinery is not of that character? A. Yes.

Q. Some of it is? A. Yes.

Q. Boilers for instance? A. That is easily worth 10 per cent.; I do not think you would get any capitalist to give you a boiler for 10 per cent.; perhaps it would go as high as 15 per cent., according to the amount of wear and tear; for certain classes of belting also, and pulleys and machinery 10 per cent. would be a very low charge; then foundry articles would be very much more, owing to the unusual wear and tear; all round, 10 per cent. would be the very lowest that such plant and machinery could be furnished for, but the cost of putting it in there was very large, and is not included in this.

Q. You have made large allowances in favour of reducing the amount of cost? A. Quite a large allowance; I have mentioned nothing that the bills cannot be produced for.

Q. Reverting to the railway privilege, is it a valuable privilege? A. A very valuable privilege; perhaps no works in the Dominion are so favourably placed in regard to position as the shops at this prison; they connect with all the railways in the Province; they are almost at the angle of the Grand Trunk and the Western, and they can all switch into our premises.

Q. All teaming by horse power is obviated? A. Entirely, except to the town.

Q. Have any of the institutions which you have visited, the same amount of railway facility? A. I know of none at all that have any such facilities.

Q. You have visited most in the Northern and Western States? A. A great number of them; besides, the land itself is very valuable from that position, for manufacturing purposes; the Government sold 5 acres to the Company for $7,000, on a valuation by Mr. Hime.

Q. I will trouble you to give us the classifications of the prisoners, their sentences, their ages? A. That has been put in as an exhibit.

Q. The number of prisoners, average length of sentences, the character of the men, their trades and occupations. First, what class of men are assigned to the Central Prison, and what are their terms? A. Since the opening of the Prison on the 1st June, 1874, up to the 1st May, 1877, 1,751 prisoners have been committed to the Central Prison; I submit a copy of a statement showing the exact details, but the average sentence has been equal to 7 months, 12·24 days.

BY MR. GORDON.

Q. That is the average sentence, or the time in the prison ? A. That is the average sentence.
Q. Can you give the average stay ? A. I cannot. There is very little difference.

BY MR. HARDY.

Q. On short term prisoners there is no remission of sentence at all, is there ? A. None at all. There is a law which may be availed of by the Province, but it has not been.
Q. That includes the average from the beginning ? A. Yes.
Q. Was there a period when much shorter terms were given than lately ? A. At first. We have the authority of Parliament to move prisoners of fifteen days' sentence, the same as other short date prisoners in the United States.

BY THE CHAIRMAN.

Q. To move them from the gaol ? A. Yes, at first, upon the opening of the prison, we removed a few prisoners of two months and upwards, but when we found the Canada Car Company could not take these prisoners fast enough, I issued instructions to sheriffs not to report prisoners under three months, then four, then five, up to six months. Now, we are removing no prisoners under six months. They may be sentenced direct to the prison by judges. A few have been, under that period, but we are removing none sentenced to the gaols under six months, unless for special purposes—our own work, or in the case of an artisan at the Company's desire.

BY MR. HARDY.

Q. The result would be the lengthening of the average sentence. A. Oh, yes. It is improving all the time. Moreover, the average sentences would have been very much greater if it had not been for the stoppage of the Canada Car Works in 1875. At that time the judges were sentencing for long periods—a great number for two years. I have little doubt the average would have been over a year and a half if it had not been for the stoppage, but, as soon as the stoppage took place, the Attorney-General addressed a circular to judges setting forth the condition of things, and asking them to refrain from sentencing at that time to a certain extent, and, as a consequence of that, the two years' prisoners were sentenced to the Penitentiary, which very much reduced the average sentence of our prisoners. We are now again increasing, getting a number of prisoners over the year and up to two years again, and I have no doubt the average will soon work up to over a year.
Q. Is there any class of prisoners you take from gaols at less than five or six months ? A. We take none from the gaols now under six months unless for a special purpose. Now, for instance, we are building a good deal.
Q. Do you not take mechanics and artisans ? A. We do ; we are bringing men in from the Toronto and Hamilton Gaols to build drains for the Water Commissioners.
Q. Do you not take carpenters and so on ? A. Yes, even short sentence prisoners who have a knowledge of business.

BY MR. GORDON.

Q. How do the Company know what prisoners are sentenced to the common gaols ? A. They do not know, but the moment they come into the gaol they are notified of it ; very frequently Mr. McBean has called upon me and asked me to bring in mechanics of different kinds.

BY MR. HARDY.

Q. He does not know the individual men ? A. No.

Q. Although you do not bring in the ordinary class of prisoners under six months, yet if mechanics or artisans are committed to gaol and are wanted, you bring them in? A. Yes, it was an expressed wish of the Company, and we followed out that wish.

Q. How do you ascertain the various trades and occupations of the prisoners when they come in? A. The *modus operandi* is this: all registers are kept in the common gaols; the prisoners there are asked the first thing when committed under sentence to a common gaol, what was their previous occupation, where they worked, and questions of that character; that is placed in the register, and it is returned to me as Inspector of Prisons, so I have that information.

Q. Have you made a calculation showing the number of artisans committed during that period, and the percentage—mechanics of various kinds? A. Yes. Of the 1,751 prisoners that were committed during the period stated, 573, or a fraction under a third of the whole number were mechanics, having a knowledge of trades directly applicable to the Canada Car Company.

Q. I see Mr. Brockway, in some papers, puts down the average of mechanics as 18 per cent.; yours would be larger? A. Ours has been larger simply for the reason that we have discriminated to a large extent.

BY MR. GORDON.

Q. My number is different from 573. A. In addition to that there are a number of men, such as sailors and farmers and others, who have some knowledge of mechanical skill; a farmer may be a rough woodsman, may understand hewing and that; and sailors are very handy sometimes in the way of making brushes and so on, but they are not included.

BY MR. HARDY.

Q. So that nearly a third of these have been returned as mechanics of various kinds? A. Yes.

Q. That is a large proportion? A. Yes.

Q. Are there any other points which your returns shew, which should be entered upon the evidence? A. Apart from these 573 that you would suppose would be at once serviceable to the Company in their shops, our distribution list—we keep a distribution list of where and how they are employed for the Canada Car Company—shows that at least 20 per cent. of the prisoners—the very lowest calculation; Mr. Brandon put it at more—are used entirely, you may say, for ordinary labour.

Q. Have you any figures giving the average ages of the prisoners or the ages at any one time? A. They are all over 21.

Q. And under 30? A. Some are over that.

Q. The average? A. The average would be about from 26 to 28.

Q. So that the average is comparatively young? A. Yes. As to the value of the two classes of prisoners—I speak of the mechanics who have a knowledge of mechanical operations before they come into the prison, and the labourers—it is very easily arrived at. The value of the mechanics would be $1 to $1.50 a day outside, and the value of the labourers from 75c. to $1 a day, if fully employed, so it would only leave a vagueness about the balance.

Q. That is the other 47 per cent.? A. Yes. Take the value of the labour of these two classes of prisoners—those possessed of mechanical skill at the time of commitment, nearly one third, or 87 out of the 260 on an average, and those required for ordinary labour, comprising one-fifth, or 52 out of the 260—and you have 139 of the 260 either mechanics or labourers. That leaves a balance of 121.

Q. If they employ less than 260? A. The averages would be reduced accordingly, about.

Q. That would leave 66, the number being 205? A. The value of that sixty-six would be determined by what they were placed at, and the length of sentences.

Mr. GORDON put in statements from St. John and Halifax.

[Exhibits " J " and " K."]

The Commission adjourned.

The Commission resumed at 3 o'clock.

MR. LANGMUIR put in statement of machinery, fittings, and fixtures.

[Exhibit " L."]

MR. LANGMUIR also put in statement of yard area, &c.

[Exhibit " M."]

Examination of Mr. Langmuir continued.

BY MR. HARDY.

Q. Can you form an opinion as to the comparative values, financial results, we will say, of long date and short date prisoners? Have you given that question any attention ? A. Yes. The aim of all prisons for the last 20 years, certainly for the last 15 years, has been to make them self-sustaining, and a great number of prisons in the United States have become self-sustaining now, within the last ten years, that were not self-sustaining formerly. As to a comparison between the long date and short date prisons, it is rather a singular thing, perhaps, that many of the short date prisons are self-sustaining when the long date prisons are not. It seems to be almost altogether a question of good management as against bad management. Short date prisons, well managed in every respect, everything thoroughly well managed and organized, under a thoroughly good system, are quite as likely to be self-sustaining, from my experience as long date, provided the proper industries are inaugurated.
Q. The appropriate industries? A. Yes, those suitable to the prisoners. Take the prison known as the House of Correction, in Detroit ; that receives both men and women, and prisoners from ten days to two years, and, in a few instances, over two years. Well, that prison has been self-sustaining for many years.
Q. How large a number have they there ? A. From 300 to 400 and 500. The industries in that prison are, the manufacture of chairs, and latterly of boots and shoes. You would come to the conclusion that chairs were a very appropriate industry for short-date prisons, one that could be handled by a great variety of prisoners, and that the various works could be allocated to suit the prisoners. Then, the prison at Albany, called the Albany Penitentiary, is a short-date prison—I think from 10 or 30 days to 2 years, with some United States prisoners, from the Federal Government, over that period ; but a very small proportion of the whole are over 2 years. They are engaged in making boots and shoes, and that is one of the most successful prisons in the world. It has paid a large revenue into the treasury of the city and the county. Then, a short time ago, I visited the prison at Cleveland called the Cleveland Workhouse. It is a prison where only offenders are placed, though it is called a workhouse. There they are sent for periods of from 15 to 30 days, up to 2 years —nothing over 2 years. I think in that prison they have upwards of 300 males, besides a number of females. That prison is about self-sustaining, if not quite. It was nearly, last year, and this year they expect to make it more than self-sustaining. They manufacture brushes and paper boxes. I saw the work there. The prisoners who have been there for two weeks—quite raw hands—it is so arranged that they work in at once. I have subpœnaed that man to be here to give evidence to the Commission.
Q. Is it contract labour or Government labour ? A. It is carried on by the Government. All these prisons I have spoken of are carried on by the Government or the municipalities having charge of them.
Q. What is the capacity of this prison ? A. Three or four hundred, I think. Then there is another house in Chicago, where the same class of prisoners are committed. They

are engaged in manufacturing brooms, knitting stockings, and things of that kind. That prison has been very nearly self-sustaining for a number of years. They are all short-date prisoners. That one is the Chicago House of Correction.

Q. Are some of the long-date prisons self-sustaining? A. Many are becoming so, although for a long period, when they were not, the Albany Penitentiary and the Detroit Prison were, simply because they were admirably managed—thoroughly well managed. General Pilsbury, in Albany, is perhaps one of the best prison-men we have.

Q. Take the class of labour that we have—would there be much difference in the result? A. As to the periods of sentence and the character of the prisoners themselves, physically and otherwise, there is really no difference whatever. They are the same. The only difference, I suppose, is in the circumstances connected with the country, that is, whether the markets are as good in the one as in the other. But the character of the prisoners is quite the same. They are committed for the same offences, the average of those having mechanical skill is just about the same, perhaps not quite so great as we have, because they do not make the selection we do. They have not the authority we have to take men from all the common gaols of the country. They take them as they are sentenced and as they come. There are 700 or 800 prisoners in the common gaols of the country daily. We have a right to select from that total, except in the case of those sentenced direct by the judges.

Q. How does the class of the industry here adapt itself to the wants of that class of prisoners, upon the whole, judging from the experience you have had of that class of labour? A. In the establishment of the Central Prison, after a great deal of consideration and thought about the matter, and after visiting several prisons, particularly one in Indiana where car manufacture was carried on, I came to the conclusion that the very best industry that could be appropriated for the utilization of prison labour was the building of cars. It afforded all scope for the employment of prison labour. If a man could not be used for one thing he could be put to another. It was a question of rigid supervision and close watching to make a man most profitable to any company that would pay a reasonable rate. The Company succumbed under that, and commenced this industry. I was inclined to think at first that it was not as good as the car-building operations, but, after close observation of the past year, I am inclined to think it is almost as good as the car-building. I think it is an admirable industry for prison labour—I mean the new industries—the combination. It is such as is used in many prisons. The broom making is adopted in many prisons, and so is the making of brushes and many similar articles—sleighs and tables, and things of that kind—what they call "Yankee notions." That is adopted in many prisons, and with great profit. It seems to afford as great a variety of work for the various capacities of the prisoners as any industry that could be adopted.

Q. Something has been said incidentally as to the shops being too expensive for them. Have they said they have too much room? A. Both under the old industry of car-building and under the new, the Canada Car Company has almost constantly complained of the want of room. When the new industry was started, it was obvious that they had not enough room, so long as they did not use the iron shop, which was the only one lying vacant. Now, it is evident that they could not do with less room than they have. They have been re-arranging other shops to meet this work, and I do not see that they could do with less ground space. It seems to be all occupied.

Mr. GORDON.—I don't think we complain of too much room, but that the buildings are too expensive.

Mr. HARDY.—Is that so, excepting the iron shop? A. That is a question for a manufacturer to consider—whether a brick structure is as cheap in the long run as a frame structure. I do not believe that the Canada Car and Manufacturing Company, were they to carry on a manufacture of car-building, could have got premises with the same accommodation of yard room and railways, and so on, for anything like the money—$100,000. I venture to say other car works, which do not intend to carry on so large a trade, cost more for their buildings in proportion than that.

Q. Take the trades they are carrying on now, and leave out the iron shop? A. The buildings are not a bit too good.

Q. Not too expensive? A. The frame buildings are all of the cheapest kind. The foundry, of course, is a very expensive building, and they are not using it, but an offer was made to use it, which would have brought in a good rental. An offer of $1,000 was made, but I thought it too small, and that it was worth $2,000 a year with the fixtures. I did not encourage the offer, for the reason that the Company who wanted to take the building, did not wish to take a sufficient number of prisoners—because they wanted the privileges without the prisoners. That was Mr. Gartshore's Company.

Q. Suppose they were carrying on any other industry—say shoemaking; suppose you were originally building the works or premises or working-room for a shoe factory? A. For a boot and shoe factory, or a matting factory—which is the great industry in England in the prisons—or many similar knick-knacks, where the men can be put together, but more particularly for boots and shoes, there is no doubt we could have got shop-room enough for the 260 men for, at the outside, $20,000. That is, the four walls, with the three story building. You can put at least 200 shoemakers in a room of 160 feet by 40 feet; whereas for the same space in some trades they have only 40 or 50 men. The machinery will take it up.

Q. How is the discipline of the Central Prison? A. I look upon the discipline of the Central Prison as being as good, if not better, than any prison I have visited on the continent.

Q. How in respect to compelling the men to work? A. There we have aimed at making them, if we could arrive at what a task was. I have frequently spoken to the Warden about it, and asked him to consult with the officers of the Company to arrive at what a task was, to compel the men to do it, but we never could get the Company to come down to what a task was. They evaded it on several occasions. We have set tasks, and they have invariably been performed. Wherever we have set them, it has been reported to me officially that they have been performed.

Q. Speaking now of the system of rewards of which something has been said, upon what policy or principle do you act? A. I think that, in a short-date prison, rewards are most desirable. I do not know that they would have the same force in a long-date prison. In the latter case, where a man is in for from three years to life, under any system of shortening sentences, he will still be there for many years to come, and it has not the same effect upon him. The man is hardened and does not care.

By the Chairman.

Q. The reward is too far off? A. Yes. But take a short-date prison, it is a very great thing. He knows it is within his power and he will be able to attain to it, whether in the way of shortening a sentence, or laying by an amount of money to get when he goes out, or to be given to his family while he is there. I think it would be the greatest incentive possible to encourage industry and good conduct; but my observation leads me to the conclusion that it produces an amount of hypocrisy and sneaking in long-date prisons, and perhaps an amount of slighting of work. In short-date prisons however, I am sure, if fairly tried, it would have the most excellent results. I have written to the Warden, and an Act has been passed during the late session, which enables us to do it, and I propose to recommend to the Government, as soon as the Canada Car Company puts us in a position by funds, to do it. We have had nothing yet. In not a single prison does the Government do it, that I know of, but it is the contractor, unless the Government employs the work itself. In any place where the contractors have the prison labour, it is the contractor, being the large benefiter by it, who gives the inducement.

By Mr. Hardy

Q. Keeping in view the modern idea that prisons should be self-sustaining, and that many of them are self-sustaining, how has this one been under 50 cents a day? Keeping that in view, how much would you require to realize to make this self-sustaining? A. About $50,000.

Q. That would be how much per diem? A. There are a certain number of men always required for domestic work. At least 40 are required in this prison for domestic service, and for works that are not productive, works about the building, repairs and that sort of thing: so that really in the prison there would be only about 290 available to make money. if the prison was always full. But say there were the 260 fully paid at 50c. a day, that would be $130 a day. There are about 310 working days in the year, which would make about $39,000 or $40,000. We could not expect to get more than that at 50c. a head.

Q. So that, if the money were paid and all the men were kept employed, that would not pay? A. No, that is for the ordinary maintenance, without reference to capital account at all.

Q. It would not be self-sustaining then? A. It would not pay for the maintenance.

Q. When you speak of prisons on the other side, you do not speak of interest on the capital account? A. No. In no prison is that considered—only the annual maintenance.

Q. 50c. would be short of self-sustaining? A. Yes, unless we employed them in other works. We are making shoes now for several public institutions.

Q. How many does your prison hold? A. 336, but we have 350 in now. There has been a great pressure.

Q. Even at present prices, the prison has not been self-sustaining, and would not be? A. Not at the rates of the Canada Car Company for the first two and a half years' operations. At the 60c. it might pay. Then again, of course, there will be a considerable charge in a short time for renewals of plant and fixtures which, made a charge upon maintenance, will increase the maintenance account somewhat. That being new, we have not had to pay much yet.

Q. Did you write to the various authorities of a number of the prisons in the United States to see what was being paid there, and did you get returns? A. Yes. On the 4th of May, when the Commission was spoken of, I addressed letters to thirty or forty prisons in the United States. I received replies from 16

Mr. GORDON objected to the replies being put in, as the circumstances were entirely different on the other side. He did not see how it could be evidence.

After some discussion,

The CHAIRMAN said the statement might be put in for the information of the Commissioners, though not on the same footing as the sworn evidence. He thought it would have been better if the circular had been submitted to the Commissioners, and prepared with their concurrence, and the concurrence of all parties, and made fuller.

Mr. LANGMUIR then put in Replies to the Circular issued by him.

(Special Exhibit " A A.")

Mr. LANGMUIR also put in a summary of the said replies.

(Special Exhibit " B B.")

Examination continued—

BY Mr. HARDY.

Q. In your visit to Illinois, did you find the price of outside labour in any of these places? A. I did not.

Q. Did you visit any contract prisons last week? A. No, I visited only with a view to short date prisons; I have visited all these contract prisons—long date prisons—before— Auburn, Michigan, and those places.

Q. From your observation of prisons elsewhere, their management and the class of work performed, and of the Central Prison, what, in your judgment, is the value of the prices fixed by this agreement—are they too high? A. My opinion is, that, having regard to the shops and plant and fixtures and privileges given to the Company, and the rates they have agreed to pay for them, extending over 7½ years, it is a fair contract on both sides—that it is a fair rate for the labour; and I think that the operations of a few years, when they are thoroughly organized, will show that; but they have laboured under very great disadvantages, one way and another.

Q. Have they been thoroughly organized? A. They have not. They have been in a state of disarrangement except within the last four or five months.

Q. Judging from business men floating a new business, have they been thoroughly equipped and organized to test the paying capacity of their work? A. No. The car operations were all done at a loss, owing to the commercial depression, and to bad management, may state, on the part of the original manager, who bought a great deal more in the way of machinery and plant than there was any necessity for.

Q. Do you think stopping two hours a day for want of material is an ordinary business way? A. It would never pay in a prison. All the prisons I have visited that are in paying operation, are as closely and well managed as a well-managed firm. Not an hour is lost. Every man, as soon as he has done with one piece of work, goes to another. It is no use idling at all. It is very customary here to find men idling about. We have tried to make rules against it.

Q. It depends largely upon the man in charge, the foreman? A. Entirely so. The employment of prison labour is a speciality that no one man can pick up in a month or a year. That, once acquired, can be successfully carried on, but some men can never acquire it.

Q. And it takes the best men some time to acquire it? A. It does, but, where it has been acquired and put in operation, the prison operations have almost invariably been successful.

By Mr. Gordon.

Q. I think you have made several reports to the Government with regard to this Central Prison? A. Nearly every year for four or five years; every report that has been made to the Government.

Q. When this Central Prison was first thought of, were you not of opinion that the labour could be better managed and worked, and more got out of it if the Government took charge of it than by contractors? A. I have held that opinion as a theory always.

Q. Are you still of the same opinion? A. I cannot say I am still of the same opinion. As a prison specialist, I believed it then, and I believe it now to be the proper system, but it is difficult to manage, inasmuch as a Government has to go before Parliament to get a manufacturing appropriation. You have to show your assets and liabilities, the cost of material—everything has to be ventilated before Parliament; you can have no privacy in your affairs; you are called before the Public Accounts Committee; and therefore the theory may be difficult to work.

Q. More especially, if you have the prisoners in the hands of the Government themselves, they are more easy to manage than in those of contractors? A. I do not think there is any difference now whatever. I do not think that, in the Central Prison, we could take any more than we have given you.

Q. Do you think, if the labour was in your own hands, you could make more than the Car Company can make of it? A. I cannot say that.

Q. That the Government could make more of it than the Car Company? A. I cannot say that.

Q. Did you not make a report in 1871 or 1872 to that effect? A. I cannot say that. My first idea was that the Prison labour should be managed by the Government for various reasons. I gave the reasons there and the methods that obtained in all countries.

Q. I see in your report for 1871-2, page 90, the following words; "There are several points in connection with this important transaction which call for explanation; and, first of all, the adoption of the contract system at all. In my report of last year, I enumerated the various methods of utilizing prison labour, and expressed a decided preference for the system of exclusive Government control over that of the *ordinary* contract system?" A. That is the case; I expressed that opinion.

Q. Then you say—"I am still of the conviction that, theoretically, the former is the best method of utilizing prison labour that can be adopted, and that the latter, as it has ordinarily been carried on heretofore, has been attended with many serious disadvantages?" A. Yes.

Q. Then the ground on which you put that is that you can keep the prisoners better in hand yourselves? A. No, there are many disadvantages attending the contract system, the chief of which is this, that you can never satisfy contractors. If there is any money to be made, they are always there.

Q. You mean the contractors cannot get all they ask for? A. I will say what I mean—if there is any money to be made.

Q. Put it in another way. The contractors are always asking for more than you can give them? A. Exactly; yes.

Q. Do you think all the advantage of this contract was on the side of the Car Company? A. It depends altogether on what view you take of it. If the Government had utilized the labour of the prisoners in some cheaper kind of employment, where you would not require to spend so much for works and shops, the Government would not have required to go to such an outlay, but, having decided that the car business was a good one to employ prison labour at, I think that a great many advantages were given to the Canada Car Company never given to any contractors that I know of in any other prison in the world.

Q. But you had good reason for deciding that the car industry was a good one to employ prisoners at? A. Yes, I have given it fully in one of my reports.

Q. So you thought it was a good thing for the Government to make the contract with the Car Company? A. I stated that, as such a variety of trades and occupations were furnished through this industry, it would serve as an excellent means of employing these prisoners, not only profitably, but with a view to their reformation by being benefited by obtaining a knowledge of some industry, that, when they went out of the prison, they could throw off their lazy habits and go to work.

Q. And you thought there was such a variety of employment? A. I advanced that as an argument.

Q. You had determined, before you made the contract with the Car Company, to put up the buildings you have done at the Central Prison? A. Not at all; the shops were all held back.

Q. You had determined to build the prison there? A. Yes.

Q. And certain shops for certain industries? A. That was left in abeyance. We never decided that. I was pressing on both the Governments the necessity of deciding what was to be done with the prisoners, in order to decide on the style of the shops.

Q. When the Car Company offered to enter into a contract arrangement with you, you were so glad that you gave the contract without tender? A. My reasons were all stated in the report.

Q. That was the case though? A. No, I was not so glad. I considered it the very industry that prison labour should be employed at.

Q. The position of the Car Company's works was so close? A. There is no use in giving a portion of the report. I had excellent reasons for recommending it.

Q. The contract was given to the Car Company without tender? A. Yes for reasons stated. One of the reasons was the suitability of the trade. Other reasons are stated there.

Q. At that time the contract had been given for the building of the Prison, but you were not able to complete the shops because you were waiting to know what industry would be adopted? A. Quite so.

Q. And that was one reason for giving it to the Car Company? A. I have mentioned that reasons are given.

Q. In your report, page 89, you say: "In the early part of the year I c lled the attention of the Honourable the Commissioner of Public Works, to the necessity of deciding upon the industrial labour of trades that should be established in the Prison. The necessity for an immediate decision upon this point arose out of circumstances to which I shall more fully refer hereafter; but chiefly from the fact that the extent of workshop space; its structural and internal arrangement; the amount of steam power required, and the furnishing of such workshops, with the machinery and appliances requisite to carry on the industrial work, proposed to be established, could only be decided upon when the nature and class of industrial labour were determined?" A. Yes.

Q. Then on page 90, you say: "The simple fact is that the work of planning and constructing the workshops, and of furnishing them with the requisite machinery could not have been entered upon before the real nature and extent of the Prison industries had been decided upon. While this question was pending and pressing for a speedy settlement, an opportunity arose of leasing the labour of the prisoners, for that special kind of industry which has all along seemed the most desirable. The Canada Car Company, whose premises adjoin those of the Central Prison, had recently been organized, and after lengthened negotiations to which I shall refer hereafter, they signified their willingness to lease the labour of the Prison on the terms and for the purposes specified in the contract. Inasmuch as the Government thoroughly approved of the character of the work, and as, according to the arrangement under consideration, the Company were to furnish and place in the workshops all the necessary machinery, thus settling the pressing difficulty before referred to, and effecting a considerable saving in capital outlay, with the approval of the Government"—you gave the contract without tender? A. That is right.

Q. What do you mean by "considerable saving in capital outlay?" A. The meaning is, that if the Government had gone in themselves, they would have had to buy all the machinery themselves.

Q. That was another advantage in going in with the Car Company? A. That is as compared with the Goverment carrying it on itself; compare the two systems and that was the advantage of one over the other.

Q. Then the advantages were—one that they were going to employ the labour in a remunerative industry, and of moral benefit to the prisoners, teaching them a trade and not interfering with outside industries? A. I do not think I said that; I never cared a button about that, as a prison specialist.

Q. You speak of that? A. It might be an advantage politically, but I think prisoners should be employed in anything that may pay.

Q. Did you know that Mr. Eddy and Mr. Nelson have presented a petition? A. I did not care about that ; I never considered it.

Q. You have mentioned it? A. I may have mentioned it as a reason why it might be expedient to do it.

Q. You this morning rather gave the impression that all the advantages were on the side of the Car Company. I wanted to know whether there were not some advantages on the side of the Government? A. Speaking about the advantages, when this matter was pending, when the negotiations were going on, I had several interviews with the origina directors of the Canada Car Company ; I refused to express my opinion one way or the other any more than I had founded on my own observation, but recommended them strongly to go to prisons in the States and see for themselves. I mentioned certain prisons where they might go, and others where I had not gone myself, as likely to afford them the information they desired, to arrive at a proper conclusion. A committee of directors did go, saw the operation of prison labour in its various departments, and came back, and were just as full of going into the matter as I was. The advantages were not unduly set forth on one side. They were fairly set forth on both sides at the time. They knew the disadvantages and the advantages at the time.

Q. They were anxious to make the contract with you ? On page 91, you sum up the result of what you stated before : " As a means to its settlement, it occurred to me (as I suggested in a report submitted at the time) that an arrangement might be entered into with the Company for the lease of the prisoners' labour, on terms equally advantageous to them and to the Government ?" A. Quite so.

Q. You were building the Central Prison at that time under contract—Mr. Elliott had a contract, had he not ? A. I think so. It was taken out of his hands about that.

Q. The arrangements with the Company were, that they were to enter into operations on the 1st of January, 1874 ? A. Not with me. They were to have possession of the shops to organize and prepare for prison labour.

Q. In your report you state that, in the contract entered into, "the Government leased to the said Company, for the term of seven and a half years, from the 1st January, 1874, the labour of all the prisoners." Can you tell us as a matter of fact, when the Company got from the Government the proper complement of prisoners ? A. It was tendered several times, but never taken.

Q. In January, 1874, were you in a position to offer to the Company the amount mentioned in the contract, or were you delayed by the buildings ? A. There was no delay on the part of the Government ? All this matter was settled and is embodied in the new agreement—all the differences between the Government and the Company.

Q. Do you remember, as a matter of fact, how much the Company were delayed at the commencement of the operations ? A. They were not delayed by the Government.

Q. Were the prisoners furnished by you up to the number mentioned in the contract ? A. The whole matter is explained in my official report—Eighth Annual Report, 1874-5,

p. 60. A charge was made "for non-completion of workshops at the time stipulated." I replied to that as follows : "This question resolves itself into two heads—1st, When was the time stipulated for ; 2nd, When were the workshops in occupation by the Company. The solicitor of the Company argues that the loss of use of the workshops put the Company to damages, but it was never contemplated that the Company should have the use of the workshops for other purposes than 'organizing,' 'fitting up,' and otherwise preparing for the reception of prison labour. This is evidenced by their letters, the interim contract, and the contract itself, which all show that the giving possession of the workshops before the 1st January, 1874, was a concession not contemplated in the interim contract with the Company, dated 9th August, 1872, and that the concession was made in order that they might 'organize,' and 'fit up,' and for these purposes only and not that they should use the workshops."

Q. I am not referring to the period previous to the 1st January, 1874, but to the period subsequent to that ? A. The contract stated that you were to have such prisoners—no specified number at all, because there are two distinct provisions in the contract : "The said Inspector agrees with the said Company to hire and let to the said Company the labour of as many prisoners as may be received into the Central Prison aforesaid, between the first day of January, 1874, and the first day of July, 1874, except such as may be required for the domestic work of the prison, and to hire and let to the said Company, from the first day of July, 1874, until the thirtieth day of June, 1881,"—then commenced the real contract.

Q. Were complaints made to you or to the prison authorities that the Company could not get prisoners between January and June, 1874 ? A. And this is the reply to it :—The interim contract states only that they were to have the shops for organising and fitting up, preparatory to getting the full number of prisoners in June. Then, as to when the workshops were in operation, "it was never contemplated that the workshops of the prison would be ready to be handed over to the Company for manufacturing purposes by the 1st July, 1873." They claimed they should be.

Q. The Company contended that the shops should be ready for them on the 1st of January, 1874 ? A. No ; in July, 1873.

Q. They contended the Government should be ready to furnish prisoners to them in January, 1874 ? A. They were not ready in January, 1874.

Q. The contract says January, 1874 ? A. As many as were put in the prison.

Q. In January, 1874, the prison was not ready to receive prisoners ? A. The prison was ready, but the shops were not ready. You had not your machinery in October, 1874.

Q. You had no prisoners in January ? A. We were not, because we were not under contract to do it. You used the workshops from October, 1873, and you were utilizing them for manufacturing purposes with your own men.

Q. You did not give us the prisoners in January, 1874 ? A. Because we were not bound to do it.

Q. You said a good deal about the particular advantages the Company derived from the railway connection ? A. I say there is a very great advantage in that.

Q. As a matter of fact, the Company could have received the same advantages if they had carried on this industry on their own premises ? A. They could not.

Q. Why ? A. They had not the Grand Trunk or Northern connection.

Q. Are not their premises as accessible as these ? A. Only to the Western.

Q. Are they not on Strachan Avenue ? A. Yes.

Q. Cannot they switch into them ? A. No, I think not. They switch in direct from our way.

Q. You gave a good deal of evidence as to the value of the shops put up there. I think you put the value at $100,000 ? A. Yes, and the land and the railways.

Q. There have been lately two shops put up, have there not ?—a paint shop and a planing shop ? A. No ; they have been lately reconstructed.

Q. What do you mean by reconstructed ? A. They were what you may call sheds formerly, but they were reconstructed, and they have been lined and fitted, and made into regular shops, and heated.

Q. They are frame shops ? A. Wooden shops.

Q. And occupied by the Company for painting and planing business ? A. Yes.

Q. The Company have charged the Government with these, have they not? A. The Government has paid for it.
Q. For both? A. No; for the erecting and paint shop.
Q. What did they pay for that? A. I really forget. They paid the bill of the Company exactly. I think it was $4,000 or $5,000. That was for putting that in order. I am only speaking from memory.
Q. What is the size of the shops? A. I gave them all.
Q. 190 feet by 68 feet? A. That is the two shops.
Q. And these two large shops were put up at the cost of about $9,000? A. I don't say so —what two shops? I say they were put up originally by the Government as sheds, but they could not be utilized for shops until they were fixed up inside and heated.
Q. I understood you to say re-constructing one of these cost $4,000 or $5,000? A. Yes, I think so. They cost a good deal more for the frame.
Q. Suppose you had had to build the shops *de novo*, what would they have cost? A. I suppose, heated and lighted and all, $8.000 or $9,000, the painting and erecting shop, or more than that.
Q. Can you tell us what was the cost of the north shop, the wood shop, two stories? A. I cannot tell that. It was mixed up with the general account of the company.
Q. I want to get a comparison of the different shops? A. It was mixed up with days' labour of the company, which was afterwards settled by the $16,000.
Q. Have you not charged the prison with so much for each shop, or have you charged a lump sum? A. It was only made up by measurements.
Q. You could not give us a sufficiently accurate idea? A. I could not. There were very expensive foundations.
Q. Do you think it would cost twice as much as the painting shop? A. I cannot express an opinion. The company spent a lot of money in it.
Q. Were all these shops put up by tenders? Were they included in Elliott's contract? A. In some instances they were included in the contract, that is, structures—but they were entirely changed from the original specifications to Elliott. With perhaps the solitary exception of the outside dimensions, the character of the structure was entirely changed, for reasons set forth in my report.
Q. Was the original contract let by tender? A. The original contract for three buildings, attached to the prison, that is, two shops, and what was then called a storehouse, was let.
Q. Was that the old foundry? A. It is now the foundry. The storehouse was afterwards changed into a foundry.
Q. That was let by tender? A. Yes; that is, the buildings intended to be erected originally, but the character of the structures was changed.
Q. Did the same contractor alter them? A. No; it was done by day's work mostly; it was taken out of the hands of the contractor at that time.
Q. These prices are arrived at in that way? A. Some of them were arrived at by measurement; for instance, the foundry was measured, I think, speaking from memory, to cost very close upon $20,000, without reference to the fixtures at all.
Q. By whom? A. By Mr. Sheard.
Q. Alderman Sheard? A. Yes. I will swear it was over $16,000.
Q. After it was erected? A. Yes.
Q. That was his estimate? A. If I recollect right that was his estimate; I will swear it was over $16,000 and under $20,000. That was originally intended for an inexpensive storehouse.
Q. Why did you get him to measure it? A. To settle some dispute between Mr. Elliott and the Government.
Q. And these prices were what the Government were satisfied were the right prices, or were they what the contractor charged in the first instance? A. I think the contractor asked more than that, and I think that Sheard awarded less. You have been speaking of the price of the workshops; I do not give $100,000 as the exact sum, because so much was done on day's work that it was impossible to tell exactly the cost of the shops.
Q. How do you arrive at that figure? A. You take the whole Central Prison premises, which cost about $450,000, and take the area, or volume of brick-work altogether, I take it for granted the shop would take fully that proportion of the whole value.

Q. That is the way you arrive at it ? A. No; and also that the foundry was valued by a competent man, Mr. Sheard, at between $16,000 and $20,000, and the south shop was valued by the same man, I think, at over $20,000. There were a great many changes made in that, at the requisition of the Company. Mr. Baines was always making changes in that and also in the north shop—great changes there. The railways and switches and things alone cost, I think, over $12,000.

Q. I see you stated that the saving to the Company from being able to use these workshops and the lighting and heating, and taxes, and insurance, and water, and other few things amounted to about $16,600 a year ? A. I did not say the saving to the Company, I was taking it as a money investment.

Q. You put it as a saving to the Company ? A. You may, if you wish, put it in that light.

Q. And you say that would reduce the price they are paying for the labour to about 29cts. per man for the first two and a half years ? A. I do, if you allow what the Government paid in money for these things, and take the interest of six per cent. on the buildings and ten per cent. on the machinery.

Q. In arriving at the value of this labour, did you take that into consideration ; at the time the contract was made, in arriving at what you should charge for prison labour ? A. I cannot say it was taken into consideration, because the amount of money spent by the Government for these things was very much greater than had been contemplated.

Q. How much did you put down for these things as a saving to the Company ? Did you take it into consideration at all ? A. I did, and argued that, and mentioned it in my reports. I never put it less, before speaking of machinery, than 10c. a day for 260 men ; but when we came to spend so much—

Q. That is $26 a day ? A. That was only for shop space.
Q. How many working days ? A. 310.
Q. That would be about $8,060, I make it ? A. That is without reference to the machinery at all.

Q. What did you put the machinery as worth ? A. The first appropriation for fixtures, which I thought about right, was only $25,000. Instead of that, it ran up to $66,000.

Q. This is when you were making the contracts ? A. Yes, but I got misstatements from Mr. Baines.

Q. What rental did you put as that the Company should pay for the use of the $25,000 worth ? A. Always ten per cent. That would be $2,500 for the use of the plant.

Q. That would be $10,500 a year which you considered the Company were getting ? A. When the contract was made, I considered the Company was getting, from the use of buildings and the railways, and the other privileges in the way of exemption from taxation, &c., without machinery, between $8,000 and $10,000. Then, when the machinery footed up so much larger, it increased the benefits.

Q. Then, roughly, that would be about 14c. a man a day ? A. I have simply reduced six per cent. on the real estate outlay, and the water and heat and light, upon the same basis as large manufacturing concerns pay in this city, and the machinery and plant I have taken at ten per cent.

Q. Thus arriving at the price the Company should pay for this prison labour and for these privileges, and I understood you to state you would consider that to be $10,500 ? A. I understood 10c. in addition to the rental on the machinery, and that was originally only $2,500—the original estimate.

Q. That is $10,500 ? A. It may be ; I would rather answer questions.
Q. That would be about 14c. off ? A. It would be what it would figure out.
Q. Did you put the labour alone as worth 36c. ? A. No; I did not figure in that way at all.

Q. How did you figure ? A. Mr. Baines' reports will show the concurrence as far as it went. It showed that we would not be asked to give more than would reduce the labour of the prisoners 10c. ?

Q. You put the labour at 40c. ? A. Yes, I did.
Q. I understand that you put the value of the labour at 40c., and the other matters at 10c. ? A. Yes, but the Government spent a greater sum, and that went in the way of privileges to the Company.

Q. At that time you thought the labour worth 40c. ? A. Alone.

Q. It is a fact that $45,000 worth of machinery and material and labour necessary to work the machinery has been taken out and is now utterly useless? A. Belonging to the Company.

Q. That you made your calculations on ? A. I know it has not.

Q. How about the steam hammer ? A. We have nothing to do with the steam hammer.

Q. That is the Company's ? A. That is altogether apart from it.

Q. It is worse than I thought ? A. Mr. Baines spent more money than was necessary. He had four trip hammers alone. What I said was that out of the $66,000 spent by the Government in plant and machinery and fixtures, I think about $45,000 worth is in active use. It may be a little less or a little more.

Q. At the time you came to the conclusion that this labour was worth 40c., did you know that at Kingston, for the long-term labour, they were only paying that price ? A. I never looked at that. I have always looked on that institution as a miserably managed institution—it could not be worse. I based my calculations on short date, well-managed institutions in the States, after inquiring thoroughly.

Q. Did you make any calculation of the price of labour there and the market ? A. Yes, all that.

Q. You evidently thought you made a good contract with the Company ? A. Always, a fair contract.

Q. Favourable ? A. Well, favourable.

Q. "This contract, although in a manner occasioned by the misunderstanding above described, was yet in itself quite as favourable as the Government under any circumstances could have expected to make. The kind of industry provided by it was, as has been shown, by far the most desirable that could be provided ; and the rate of remuneration was far in advance of that received for the convict labour at the Dominion Penitentiary, Kingston, notwithstanding the much shorter terms of sentence of the inmates of the Central Prison." (Report 1872, page 91.) A. Had I known how much more was to be expended for the Company, I would not have used the term "favourable," perhaps, at all, but we spent so much more than I ever anticipated in plant and machinery.

Q. You considered there was some difficulty in making a good arrangement for employing this labour ? A. A thing of that kind in its organization will always be attended with difficulty.

Q. You speak of it as a difficult problem ? A. Yes.

Q. "Now that the most important, and at the same time most difficult problem in connection with the Central Prison scheme has been so satisfactorily solved by the provision of appropriate and remunerative employment for every prisoner sentenced to it, the next most important question that presents itself for settlement is what class of prisoners shall be sentenced to the Prison." (Id. p. 92.) So you thought it a difficult problem ? A. It is, certainly. There was a great deal of feeling against it in the country ; there was a great deal of difficulty in getting Governments to take it up; I had difficulty to get it before the country or the House or the Government.

Q. And difficulty to get contractors ? A. We never could speak of that—it never was submitted.

Q. You made the contract ? A. Yes. Owing to other circumstances, owing to adjoining properties and so on, and it being an industry that was very highly thought of, we took it at once without competition. Whether we would have got more or less, I cannot say.

Q. In your report in 1877 you say 637 had passed through the Prison. Of that number, I see 500 were for 10 months and under ? A. Yes.

Q. 279 under 6 months? A. Yes, that is about it.

Q. Do you consider the class of prisoners in this prison equal to the class in the Penitentiaries ? A. Physically they are.

Q. As equal to do a day's work ? A. I do. Physically, they are just as good, and I think there is the same number, perhaps a greater number, of mechanics, because we have a greater number to select from.

Q. What do you mean by this : "No sooner is the dilapidated physical condition of these habitual offenders rehabilitated by the healthful regimen of a prison, and the enforced suspension of dissolute habits, than they are set free only to return in a short time for a repetition of the same kind of treatment?" A. The argument is in favour of longer sentences. I was speaking of recurrent offenders—not ordinary offenders—men out of one gaol into another. I said it was a great mistake to send these people down for short dates; that they ought to be sent down for longer periods for the prison to have effect upon them.

Q. But it seems to be the general class in your prison. In another part you say: " When it is considered that a very large proportion of these prisoners are habitual offenders of the petty order, who have for many years been oscillating between one gaol and another in the Province, and not a few of whom have been committed to the Central Prison two or three times already." You found there were a large number continually oscillating between one gaol and another? A. Yes.

Q. As a matter of fact, is this the case, that the condition of the prisoner is scarcely repaired before he leaves the prison? A. There may be a proportion.

Q. What proportion? A. I think that report ought to go in.

Q. It will go in. You say a considerable number of these prisoners had not time to repair their condition before leaving the prison? A. I do not say that at all.

Q. You go on to say: " It is not fair to the Province which, at a great cost, has established an industrial prison, that just as soon as this class of prisoners are restored to such a bodily condition as to perform hard labour in the prison, their sentences expire and they are discharged"? A. Yes, there are a certain amount of re-commitments which, unless sentenced for a longer period, would receive little benefit ; but, the oftener they were re-committed to the prison, the more benefit they were to the Company.

Q. Does the clause in which you state that these prisoners are scarcely restored to a fair bodily condition before they leave the prison, refer to the re-commitments, or to the other classes as well ? A. To the re-commitments—to the recurrent cases.

Q. To a limited number? A. To a large proportion, it says.

Q. Is that inaccurate? A. No.

Q. You refer here to a large proportion of the prisoners—do you mean to apply that simply to the re-commitments ? A. Not only that, but to those who have been sentenced several times ; not only the re-commitments to the Central Prison, but also to the gaols.

BY MR. HARDY.

Q. You are speaking of a particular class? A. A class of special cases.

BY MR. GORDON.

Q. You say " when it is considered that a very large proportion of these prisoners "—does that refer to re-commitments or to others as well ? A. The proportion, whatever it is, has a relation to the class of prisoners spoken of.

Q. What class ? A. Those oscillating between one prison and another. A specialist must deal generally with a report, not with figures that a solicitor may take up and try to analyse and dissect. My argument was, that the practice of sentencing prisoners, who were oscillating between one gaol and another, for short periods, was a bad practice, and that it would be better if the Courts would sentence them for much longer periods. I went on to say it took a considerable time to get these men into a condition for work. If they were in the Central Prison before, they would be more valuable. They would have been under discipline before, and would not require to have the same course of discipline again. But, if they were sent to the common gaol, especially for offences against morality, their constitution would have to be built up again.

Q. I don't want to get you in a hole, but only to ascertain what you mean ? A. The Commission will understand exactly what it means. If I read the report to the Commission, I am perfectly satisfied to rest it there.

Q. Can you give us any idea what is the proportion of these people that you refer to ? A. We have been singularly free from hospital cases, except on one occasion, when typhoid fever broke out. Men have generally been able to go into the workshops in a very short time after coming in. Occasionally some old men have come in, and I have sent them back to the gaols again, as soon as the cases were reported to me, and, if it was otherwise reported, they had been in the hospital, or confined in the cells. The regulation is that the prison surgeon must examine the prisoners every day, and the Company has a perfect right to reject that prisoner, or ask for an opinion from the gaol surgeon again, but they must abide by the decision of the gaol surgeon.

Q. How many of these 637 prisoners were registered as intemperate ? A. 441.

Q. Do you think you had any reference to that when you wrote these words as to the physical condition ? A. No. All these statistics taken piecemeal may mean a great deal or very little.

Q. But you give the result of this in your report? A. Yes, but you may use the words that a man is intemperate, but it may not refer in the slightest degree to his work. As a general thing, the man brought into the gaol for intemperance, in a week at the outside, was brought into such a condition as to be able to do a general day's work. The Warden can speak better of that.

Q. How many of these 637 were in for larceny ? A. 258.

Q. How many for vagrancy, drunkenness, loitering and disorderly conduct ? A. 180.

Q. How many of these prisoners were labourers ? A. 316.

Q. Do you think from your experience that the life of an habitual offender is one calculated to enable him to take to industrial work ! A. Not unless he is placed under proper discipline.

Q. At once ? A. He must, as soon as he comes to the prison, be placed under proper discipline to make his work available.

Q. Will the result of that discipline be that he will take hold of the work, and work as well as an ordinary man ? A. Not as well as an outside man.

Q. Or do half as much as an outside man ? A. It is all nonsense talking about proportions—a half, a quarter, three quarters, and so on ; after being in the Central Prison for about a week, the men are in a physical condition to be able to do a full day's work.

Q. They have several things to learn ? A. They have to learn discipline.

Q. You think they can learn implicit submission in a week ? A. Easily.

Q. You gave me some statistics this morning with regard to the average term of the sentences of these prisoners; I think you put it at 7 months, 12·24 days ? A. Yes.

Q. How much would that period be shortened, if you deduct the amount of time these men are under punishment, in the barber's shop and baths, and the amount of time lost from sickness ? A. I never entered into that calculation, but it would be a very trifling percentage.

Q. Would it be easy to make such a calculation ? A. We keep an account of it ; there is a dispute with the Company now ; they contend that, when a man is being barberised, they should not pay for him ; they have signed the last pay-list under protest for that reason ; they refused to sign altogether.

Q. In calculating the percentage, did you include the original sentences of the prisoners transferred from the common gaols? A. All the original sentences.

Q. In some cases, they come only for the balance of their term ? A. Only a very few days elapse.

Q. But not for the whole sentence ? A. Only a few days elapse before they are transferred.

Q. It varies, I suppose ? A. It varies ; but I instruct sheriffs to telegraph whenever a certain class of prisoners are in ; the reason for this is to make up the route of the bailiff, so that it may be made less expensive ; as soon as I have advices along the route—say of the Grand Trunk West or of the Great Western—of enough prisoners, the bailiff is despatched at once, and rarely a week elapses.

Q. He waits for enough to bring in ? A. Often he goes off at once ; very rarely a week elapses.

Q. Have you ever made a calculation on that basis ? A. I never did that.

Q. Do they keep that in the prison ? A. I do not think they do.

Q. Can you give us any idea of what reduction it would make in the average ? A. I do not think in 1,700 prisoners it would reduce it a fractional part.

By Mr. Hardy.

Q. It would not amount to the coming late to work and things of that kind in free labour ? A. It is very small. We remove very promptly—so promptly that we get telegrams so as not to have any delays as to transfers. It is a capital way of transfer that we have. It is done for expedition.

By Mr. Gordon.

Q. This estimate is on the terms of the prisoners in the prison at the present time? A. No; that is the term for the whole period since the prison was opened up to the date named, the 1st May, of all the prisoners committed to the prison.

Q. You stated that, out of these 1,751 prisoners, about 573 or 20 per cent. were mechanics? A. A little less than one third.

Q. Mention what you consider mechanics in that list? I went through it and made a different total. A. I put an architect as a mechanic, because I thought him a valuable man for the Company. I did not put barbers; they are not mechanics. Bakers, I don't know; basketmakers, I did; blacksmiths, brushmakers, bricklayers and plasterers, I did; butcher, I did not; brakesman, I think I did not; the following I did—bellowsmaker, brickmaker, broom-maker, boatbuilder, bookbinder, carpenters, chairmakers, coopers, currier, cabinetmaker (cigar makers, I did not, I think), carriage maker, dyer, engineer, engraver, firemen (because often they are very ingenious men), harnessmakers, hatter (he is valuable to a brush trade at once), jeweller, , locksmiths, lockfitter, moulders, machinists, miners, masons, millwrights, painter, plumber, patternmaker, plasterer, ropemaker, shoemaker, spinner, ship-carpenter, stone-mason, steamfitter, saddler, sailmaker, shuttle-maker, stuffmender, stonecutter, tinsmiths, upholsterer, varnisher, weavers, waiters, watchmakers, waggonmakers, woodjoiners, wheelwright, wool-carder, wool-sorter. "No trade" I took a proportion of.

Q. That is the way you made up 573 skilled mechanics? A. Yes, I call them mechanics, and I have every reason to believe they are mechanics. All I know is that, when a man has said he was a shoemaker, we have found him to be a shoemaker, and a tailor the same. I do not know of any exceptions at all. In the same way with carpenters, using carpenter labour, we would find it out. We have heard a good deal of discussion about their not being as designated, but, as far as my experience goes, I have not found prisoners misstating their former occupations. There may be some poor tradesmen.

Q. Among the prisoners that have been in the prison since the commencement of the works, can you tell us how many before they entered the prison were broom-makers, or how many had worked at any of the industries carried on there? A. Which?

Q. Broom-makers, for instance? A. One

Q. Pail-makers? A. There is no such thing as a pail-making trade. It is part of a trade—a turner and all that.

Q. Brush-makers? A. Twelve.

Q. These are all? A. Ninety-three carpenters.

Q. Blacksmiths? A. Forty-three.

Q. But with regard to pail-makers? A. There is no such trade. It is the turners or machine makers. A cooper would be the next thing to it.

Q. You have coopers, but no pail-makers? A. They may be pail-makers, as a matter of act. In the Reformatory at Penetanguishene, we are coopers, and we make pails.

Q I understand you visited the Cleveland and Detroit Prisons, and found the former nearly self-sustaining? A. Nearly. The Warden this year expects a profit.

Q Detroit Prison also? A. Yes.

Q. Are these carried on by contractors? A. No; by the prison authorities—Detroit, Cleveland, and Chicago. Albany is contract.

Q. You are going to have the Superintendent here? A. Yes, from Cleveland.

Q. Can you tell me what you put the cost of each prisoner for food down at in your last report? A. I think 12c.

Q. 11·3c.? A. Well, that perhaps

Q. What did you put the whole cost of each prisoner down at? A. 44·1c. per day.

Q. That includes the 11c. for food? A. Yes.

Q That is on a basis of 267 prisoners, is it not? A. Yes.

Q. When the prison is full, the total capacity is 342? A. 336.

Q. Had you not 342 in the prison in 1876? A. We may have had 342 at a time. We have 350 to-day. We double them up. 336 is the capacity of the prison.

Q. Is this 44c. based on 267 or on 336 ? A. The statement explains itself: "From this statement, it will be seen that the entire maintenance expenditures for the year amounted to $43,117, and as the daily average number of prisoners in custody was 267·67, the cost for each prisoner for food, clothing, salaries of officials, etc., was $44\frac{1}{10}$ cents per day.

Q. That is on 336 ? A. On 267—the cost on the average.

Q. Would you require more guards if you had 342 prisoners ? A. A great deal more. We have now five or six more. We have increased the appropriation from $43,000 to $47,840—nearly $5,000 more. That is for a full prison—for 336, or perhaps a little less than that. We put in 350 just to do special work.

Q. How much is that a day per prisoner ? A. $44\frac{1}{10}$c.

Q. If you received $44\frac{1}{10}$c. from each prisoner, you would be self-sustaining ? A. We would not this year. I have not struck the average of this year in the estimate. Last year we would have been.

Q. Therefore, if you received the 50c. a day for each man, you would be more than self-sustaining—for each man in the prison ? A. Yes.

Q. Then you would be in a better position than those prisons in the States you have referred to ? A. No, not at all.

Q. I understood you to say that the Cleveland Prison was a little less than self-sustaining ? A. Yes, for the labour, but not for the outlay of the Government. In Cleveland they do not furnish anything like the machinery.

Q. If you put in the whole of the prisoners, what would be more than self-sustaining ? A. You cannot put in the whole of the prisoners. You cannot make them all productive.

Q. Are not these prisoners as valuable on domestic work as on this contract work ? A. Of course they are not. We do not take the best of them for that purpose.

Q. Not for mending shoes and clothes ? A. I think we are making more out of shoes than your contract.

Q. Can you not make 50c. ? A. Not unless we employ them industrially; not on domestic labour, because it will not admit of it.

Q. I thought this was just the kind of work that would pay ? A. Take those who are left, those employed for cleaners, perhaps just out of the hospital, may be slightly sick or maimed in some way or other, they are not as valuable prisoners.

Q. Then the reason is that they are not fitted for the work from physical infirmity or other causes ? A. I do not say that. But, as a matter of fact, we do not in prisons count labour used for domestic purposes to be worth anything at all.

Q. I cannot see how you can expect a contractor to use prison labour for 50c. a day, when you find the rest worth nothing ? A. It may be worth more or less. Take the baker ; I consider him worth $1 a day more to us, and then the shoemakers are worth more.

Q. Is it that you have not the work for them to do ? A. No. Take eight men in one corridor and eight in another—in one they may not be all employed, but they must be there. Is your clerk worth as much as you are ?

Q. They are all the same class of men ? A. No; they are not. Men who are industrially employed are not the same as the others.

Q. If you have the work for all these men to do ? A. If it is the right kind of work. For instance, we are now building stables and additional sheds—storerooms. These men are just as good for that as if we brought men from the outside.

Q. You have not the work for them to do. If you had they would be worth it ? A. I did not say so.

Q. Suppose you had to employ men outside to do the work, what would it cost you ? A. If we did that it would likely cost more than 50c. a day.

Q. And yet you cannot make them worth 50c. a day ? A. There is no value placed upon that kind of prison labour—no money. In order to satisfy Mr. Gordon I will read from my report :—" Labouring work—constructing sewers, drains, and improving the prison grounds, 50c. a day ; farm and garden work, 50c. a day ; tracklaying, macadamizing, and road construction, 50c. a day ; sundry works, 50c. a day. Mechanical work—carpenter work, 50c. a day ; shoemaking, 40c. a day ; tailoring, 35c. a day ; painting, blacksmithing, and tinsmith's work, 50c. a day ; brush and mat making, 50c. a day ; bricklayers, stone masons, &c. &c., 50c a day " That is merely an estimate, but I will not swear that this is the value of it. I say, if we take a contract to make a number of shoes for a public institution, we find them worth more than 50c., or to make a building. we find the stone masons and bricklayers worth more. We get almost as much work from them as from outside men.

Q. If you have a man you can employ some days on things you can sell, and other days in cleaning up your place instead of another man, whom you would hire, it is just as productive as in the former case? A. No; it is not. There is certain routine work you cannot place a value upon in prison labour.

Q. You referred to Mr. Gartshore as having offered $1,000 for the foundry? A. So Mr. McBean told me.

Q. You refused? A. I made a report to the Government, setting forth that it was worth more rental, and that Mr. Gartshore wanted to employ too few prisoners to make it worth while.

Q. If he had employed more prisoners and given a better price would you consent? A. If the Company would consent I was willing to consent to it.

Q. Was the objection he had to employing any fixed number of prisoners? A. I was not made aware of it.

Q. You stated that your opinion was that the length of time made no difference in the capacity of the prisoners as long as they were put on a proper kind of work? A. Yes; I say it depends entirely upon the character of the work.

Q. Would you give us your opinion as to the class of work, from your experience in the United States Prisons, that these short term prisoners can do? A. In Albany they are put on boots and shoes, and become very proficient in a very short time, so proficient that they pay enough for the prison to become self-sustaining; in the House of Correction, in Detroit, they make chairs and boots and shoes—that is more than self-sustaining; in Cleveland they make brushes and paper boxes—there the Warden will speak for himself; then in Chicago they are put upon making brick and, I think, brooms and knitting and things of that kind. The suitability of these industries to prison labour is proved by the fact that the prisons are about self-sustaining.

Q. Is there any machinery? A. Yes; in the chairmaking quite as much as yours, I think.

Q. In the boot and shoe? A. There is not.

Q. In the brushes? A. There is a good deal of machinery.

Q. As much as we have? A. Much simpler; cheaper, I think.

Q. In the paper boxes? A. Some very simple machinery.

Q. In the brick-making? A. There is some machinery.

Q. And the broom? A. The same as your own.

Q. Do you know of any prison where they make pails and tubs? A. I believe they do at Joliet.

Q. That is long term—but in short term prisons? A. I do not know, but I should say the chairmaking and furniture-making in Detroit was fully as intricate as your industry and perhaps more difficult to manage, because one man would require to have a knowledge of a machine—almost of each machine.

Q. Did you come in contact with the Directors at Cleveland? A. I did not.

Q. Just the Superintendent? A. Yes.

Q. The Directors state that the kind of goods which are manufactured, and which seem to be best adapted to unskilled labour are limited to brushes and paper boxes? A. That is their opinion.

Q. Is that your opinion? A. It is not; I think your industry is as good or better, because it gives greater variety than brushes and paper boxes.

Q. They are also of opinion that the Government work is preferable to, if not more profitable, than that done by contractors? A. All theoretically hold that opinion, but the difficulty is to put it in practice.

RICHARD S. WILLIAMS, called on behalf of the Car Company, sworn.

BY MR. GORDON.

Q. You have been accustomed to employ large quantities of free labour? A. Yes.

Q. You have done that for some years, and have had considerable experience? A. Yes.

Q. How many years? A. About twenty years.

Q. You have been carrying on business in the City of Toronto? A. Yes.
Q. You know the value of labour in this neighbourhood? A. I should think so.
Q. During the course of your employment have you ever had apprentices in your establishment? A. Yes.
Q. What was generally the arrangement you made with these apprentices? What term did you take them for? A. Generally about five years.
Q. And what wages did you pay them? A. Generally $1.50 a week for the first year, $2, $3.50, $4, and $5.
Q. Why did you have a sliding scale like that? A. They would be more valuable each year.
Q. Did you find that they repaid their wages the first year, as a rule? A. The first year we used to consider them not worth anything.
Q. The second year? A. They would begin to get useful.
Q. Would they be worth what you paid them? A. Yes, as a rule,—$2 or $2.50, according to the ages of the boys.
Q. From what ages? A. Fourteen, fifteen, and sixteen sometimes.
Q. What industry did you employ them in? A. The manufacture of reed organs.
Q. A good deal of cabinet and wood work? A. Yes, nearly all cabinet and wood-work.
Q. Had you machinery in work? A. Lathes, band-saws, planers, and so on.
Q. Similar to the machinery used at the prison? A. Not quite similar,—more jointers and band-saws, but not so many lathes.
Q. It took nearly two years before these boys began to earn what you paid them? A. Yes.
Q. Do you see any reason why the prisoners should pick up their business quicker than these apprentices would? A. I do not see any reason why they should.
Q. Do you see any reason why they should not so quickly? A. They would not pick it up quicker—being older, they do not learn, as a rule, so quickly.
Q. Would there be any other reasons which would make a difference between them and boys? A. Yes. Of course boys want to learn their trade, and get in favour with their employers. We used to give them bonuses and gratuities and so on, to encourage them.
Q. And do you think that would have an effect on making them work, which would be wanting on the prisoners? A. Yes, certainly.
Q. Do you think the physical condition of the two would be about the same? A. I could not say as to that. As a rule the boys would be more intelligent and apt than the prisoners.
Q. You know the classes of men the prisoners are made up of. Would their physical condition be such that they could take hold of a job at once, when they go into the prison? A. I should think not. Of course we used to select the boys very carefully.
Q. We have a statement here of the Inspector of Prisons, Mr. Langmuir, who, I suppose, is as good an authority as we can find, as to the men going into the prisons, and he says: "Apart from the mistaken leniency of short sentences in such cases, both from a moral and social standpoint, it is not fair to the Province, which, at a great cost, has established an industrial prison, that just as soon as this class of prisoners are restored to such a bodily condition as to perform hard labour in the prison, their sentences expire, and they are discharged." That is Mr. Langmuir's opinion—that it takes the time of their sentences to get them into condition to do their labour—do you think that would make a material difference in the quality of the labour? A. I should think so. If a man is accustomed to get on the spree, the first day after he comes back he would be worth nothing—we would want to get rid of him.
Q. Do you have that often happen in your work—a man going on the spree? A. Yes, some men.
Q. What would be the effect on the work? A. Very bad.
Q. Could you, in your mind, compare the value of this prison labour to free labour? A. I could not make the value of the labour at the prison at all, seeing the short time they are there. I cannot see how they would be of much service. Take a man working at a machine—a free man—he understands the machine thoroughly—a knot comes in the way of a tool which would make the work defective. He is able to stop the machine, take out the tool, and set the machine. I cannot see how possibly a prisoner could do it.

By Mr. Hardy.

Q. If there were a foreman for that, over the whole shop? A. You would have to call him off.

By Mr. Gordon.

Q. Take one foreman for 57 men and 8 machines? A. I should have one for 3 or 4 machines, because a hard knot will often come in the way of a tool and spoil the work.

Q. Do you think that one foreman would be sufficiently taken up if he had the charge of four machines? A. I think pretty nearly taken up.

Q. Would you be willing to enter into a contract to take 250 of these men, when you put 200 of them on skilled work and pay 50 cents a day? A. I would not take them on our work at any price.

Q. And work of a similar nature, with delicate machines, lathes and saws, and so on? A. I think, with the rate of wages now—I am not experienced at all in making pails and tubs, but in a fine class of work like ours—I would rather pay men.

Q. This is an industry in which there is a good deal of competition, and prices have been cut down very low, and it is necessary to have the work turned out very efficiently to get sales at all? A. My experience with machinery is, that we would have a machinist at $3, and another at $1.50; the one at $3 would pay us the best, because the machine does so much of the work that his pay is only an item; if anything went wrong with the machine, we would suffer more; it takes three or four hours to repair a band-saw, besides the cost of material.

Q. Are you of opinion that the better the machinery is, the more skilful the labour ought to be? A. Yes, I think so.

Q. And the contrary is not true, that the better the machinery the less skilful need the labour be? A. Certainly not.

By Mr. Hardy.

Q. Poor men, or men not skilled in their trade would be of no service at all in your business? A. Not at all unless to clean up shavings and rubbish.

Q. You have very little use for many labourers who are not skilled men? A. No.

Q. The manufacture of organs is considered a very fine branch of the business? A. It is a very fine business.

Q. Amongst the finest known of wood-making? A. Certainly.

Q. An ordinary green hand would be of little service in that at all? A. Very little.

Q. How long does it take an ordinary labouring man to learn that class of business completely? A. Three or four years to be skilled.

Q. Then there would be really no parallel between the class of work you do, and the making of tubs and pails which they can learn in 24 hours? A. I think there would be, because the machinery is somewhat similar.

Q. Take a lathe we are told, if one man has skill at a lathe, the others may be ordinary labourers, without special knowledge. There would be no parallel between your work and that? A. I should think you would want one skilled man to work it.

Q. As for the other five, there would be no parallel, and that one man's skill can be learned in three or four months, they say? A. I do not know that. An ignorant man, starting to learn to sharpen tools, and look after a machine, could not learn it.

Q. Then they have a foreman besides this one man? A. One man would be little service to those men. Suppose a belt or pulley gets out of order. I never saw machinery so fine that it did not get out of order.

Q. I ask you whether you consider there is a fair analogy between the class of work you do and the work up there? A. I should say there is some analogy.

Q. Very remote? A. Yes, remote.

Q. Your men will get on a spree? A. Yes.

Q. Frequently? A. Some men very frequently; we discharge them.

Q. When they stop drinking and come in short up, how long before they go on with the business? A. About two days.

Q. If men have to go through trial and sentence and be shut up, and are from a week to three or four months before they get down here, they would not be under the operation of drink when they come ? A. No.

Q. So you obviate that danger ? A. Yes. Still, there would be the effects of the old habits.

BY MR. GORDON.

Q. Did you notice the space that the Company had to work in ? A. Yes, I saw it was very extended.

Q. Did you think there was sufficient room there? A. I thought so.

Q. In the shops ? A. They looked rather crowded, but there seemed to be room enough outside. The shops I should say were a little crowded.

Q. The pail shop ? A. A little too much crowded there, I should think.

Q. The broom shop ? A. I should think there was room enough there

The Commission adjourned.

THURSDAY, July 26th.

The Commission met at ten o'clock.

CHARLES BOECKH, called on behalf of the Government, sworn :—

BY MR. LANGMUIR.

Q. You are a brush manufacturer in the City of Toronto ? A. Yes.
Q. How long have you been carrying on that industry ? A. In Toronto, about twenty-two years.
Q. How many men do you generally employ ? A. We have altogether, perhaps, twenty now.
Q. Have you employed more than that ? A. We used to.
Q. How high have you gone ? A. Nearly double that number.
Q. How do you pay ; by piece or by the day ? A. Some by piece and some by day.
Q. What class of men do you pay by the day ? A. Those doing the combing work, what we cannot easily do by piece. Good men, the best men, are mostly paid by the day.
Q. And the inferior men ? A. Mostly by the piece, except a few boys, that we pay by the week, doing jobbing.
Q. Do you find paying by piece work gets you better value for your money ? A. We know what we pay them.
Q. Do you find the work slighted at all ? A. Some we must do by piece. The drawing of scrubbing brushes, shoe brushes, et cætera, and some paint brushes is done by piece, but the finishing by machinery, combing the brushes and laying out, is done by time. We could not do that by piece.
Q. When you employ your green hands, I suppose at first the work is more or less slighted ? A. It is not so good.
Q. That is a natural consequence of learning ? A. At first they make poor work.
Q. But that is contingent on every kind of industry ? A. Yes, it might be for a day or two, the second or fourth day.
Q. You take in lads ? A. Yes.
Q. What age ? A. About 15 years.
Q. If a lad of ordinary intelligence goes into your wareroom, how long does it take him to earn $3 a week ? A. I am able to put a boy in four weeks by piece work to earn $3 a week.
Q. Does it often go above that in a month? A. It depends upon how he can do it ? Some have pay quicker, some less. We never expect them in a month to be over $3.
Q. Would they on an average earn that—ordinary intelligent lads ? A. Yes, they could do it.
Q. Then how much will these men whom you pay by the piece earn a week at the highest, when learning their trade ? A. I have one now who makes $11 a week.
Q. How long has he been there ? A. Several years.
Q. I am speaking of men less than a year ? A. I have known $5 a week.
Q. How much will the journeymen doing the finer class of work earn ? A. We have some from $14 and $12 a week.
Q. They do that by the day ? A. Most by the day.
Q. That is fine work ? A. Paint brushes, and that class of work.
Q. Do they do a large amount of work—work very steadily ? A. Yes.
Q. What hours ? A. Ten hours a day.
Q. You cannot tell, I suppose, what number of brushes you turn out ? A. No, we know what they can do. I pick out my best men. If they cannot do it, I do not keep them.
Q. But you say, I understand, that in a month a lad of 15 becomes so proficient in his work that he will generally earn $3 to $4 a week. A. Yes, I can make him do that easily.
Q. Have you any apprentices ? A. We have only one now.
Q. What do you pay him ? A. One year we paid him, I think, $2 50, then $3, and then $3 50. After this, he gets regular wages.
Q. Is he in his second year now ? A. He is.

Q. How many men have you working now? A. About 15 to 18, I should say.
Q. How many dozen brushes do you turn out in a week? A. I could not say.
Q. Where are your premises? A. On York Street.
Q. What do you pay for these premises, if it is a fair question? A. Thirteen hundred dollars a year rental.
Q. Do you pay taxes? A. Yes.
Q. What are your taxes? A. $335.
Q. Do you use gas? A. Yes.
Q. What do you pay for gas a year? A. $50 to $60.
Q. Is the water put in by the Commissioners? A. Yes.
Q. What do you pay for it? A. I have to pay now $16, but we do not run our machines, and we used less, and they put in a metre, but still wanted us to pay the whole.
Q. That is, $64 a year? A. Yes.
Q. You use machinery then? A. Yes.
Q. What horse power? A. We used to have 12-horse power, but I have put a smaller one in. Now it is 4-horse power.
Q. Why? A. Because the class of goods do not work any more since we have opposition.
Q. Do you sell brushes to the Canada Car Company? A. We sell what they use themselves.
Q. To their agents? A. Yes.
Q. To McMurray and Fuller? A. Yes.
Q. What kind of brushes? A. Paint brushes.
Q. Do you know the kind of brushes they are making? A. The drawn work—scrubbing and shoe brushes.
Q. The coarser kinds? A. Yes.
Q. That is more adapted to prison labour? A. I am afraid they intend to go further. I have a young man I teach the special work—paint brushes—and the foreman there has asked him to go and teach that kind of work there.
Q. You know they have been making only the coarser class lately? A. As far as I know.
Q. That is more fitted to prison labour? A. Well, yes, and machinery.

By Mr. Gordon.

Q. You have about twenty men in your employ? A. Eighteen or twenty; I cannot say exactly.
Q. How long have you had these men. A. Some have been for years with me, and some are new.
Q. How many have been with you for any length of time? A. I might have four or five who have been with me ten or twelve years.
Q. And how many new men have you? A. Some came in the meantime. I have lately had one or two, but discharged some and got some fresh ones.
Q. You do not get on very well with new men? A. We have to teach them.
Q. You prefer having old hands? A. If I have a good old hand, I do not like to let him go.
Q. You would rather pay a good old man high wages than a green one small wages? A. It depends on the class of goods.
Q. That is, in all work? A. It is always the case.
Q. Better to pay a good price for a good man than a small price for a poor man? A. Well, we pay according to what they can do. If I pay $1 it is only because he is worth it. If he improves I pay him more.
Q. You state you have one apprentice? A. Yes.
Q. Have you had more than one apprentice? A. No, never before.
Q. How is that? A. It is not usual with me. This boy's father wanted me to do so.
Q. You do not care for apprentices? A. No.
Q. You would rather get a man who understood the business? A. I can teach him if he is willing.

Q. Can you give us an idea of the value of the work the men would turn out. You said some men were paid $14 a week? A. Yes.

Q. Can you give us an idea of the value of the work such a man would turn out? A. I could not say. If he works in a common class of goods, he might only turn out $50, but in another class of work a great deal more, perhaps $500.

Q. What I mean is—how much would his labour improve the work he is doing—improve the material? A. I do not know how to answer that question.

Q. What would his work be worth to you? A. Just what I pay him.

Q. It would be worth more than that. You would not pay $14 simply to get $14 back? A. I make the calculation that it costs me so much material and labour, and charge my price accordingly.

Q. What return would his labour at $14 bring to you? A. It depends what price I can get. Our prices are very low now, the competition being so keen.

Q. How? A. I must make my profits, not on his labour, but on material and everything.

Q. I want to know what his labour is worth to you—is it worth $30? A. On all our goods, on the whole thing, we make about ten per cent.

Q. On material and labour? A. Yes.

Q. How much would be the profit on the labour, and how much on the material? Would it be five per cent. on each? A. I did not think—I never calculated that way. It may be; I do not know.

Q. As a rule, when you get a new man into your employment, is he physically fitted to take hold of the work at once? A. Well, some are.

Q. If you discovered that a man was intemperate or dissipated, would you keep him on? A. No man would keep him on if he could help it.

Q. Would you? A. Perhaps not, unless I wanted him badly.

Q. Would he be dear at any price? A. If he would not work. I have had some intemperate men who would work well. I have none now, but, if a man was a good working man, I would keep him on and try to set him straight if I could.

Q. You pay $335 taxes? A. Yes; that is on income and building.

Q. How much of that for building? A. I have not the particulars here now. They tax me on $4,000 or $5,000 income—personal property.

Q. What is the building rated at? A. I could not say, exactly.

Q. Could you produce your assessment paper? A. Yes.

By Mr. Langmuir.

Q. What does it cost to heat your premises? A. We have about eight stoves. It costs me for the heating about ten or twelve tons of coals.

Q. Mr. Gordon asked you about apprentices. When you speak of apprentices, this young man is apprenticed to you? A. Yes.

Q. But you have green hands now and then? A. Oh, yes.

Q. That is what you mean by the men who earn $3 to $4 a week, after a month in the business? A. Certainly, they can earn it.

Q. He asked you what a man who earned $14 a week would turn out. That depends altogether on the class of the work? A. Certainly.

By Mr. Gordon.

Q. I suppose the value would be about the same whether it was on coarse work or fine work? A. It depends upon what we get for the work.

Q. But taking it altogether, the value is about the same? A. If I have an article in which there is no competition, that I can get a dear, reasonable price for, this man makes me more than on an article in which there is competition.

Q. But you do not mean to say that, in very fine work, a man can turn out the same number of fine brushes as he can coarse scrubbing brushes? A. Not the number.

By Mr. Langmuir.

Q. I suppose very green men can turn out the roughest class of scrubbing brushes in a very short time? A. Oh, yes.

Q. If you were running prison labour, you would select the class of brushes most suitable for the prisoners to make? A. What sells the best.

Q. And is most suited to make? A. Yes.

Q. If you found they could not within the two years or six months make a certain class of brush, you would leave it away? A. Yes, and take coarser kinds.

By Mr. Gordon.

Q. Have you ever had brushes returned on your hands for bad work? A. I would not say no; it has been done sometimes.

Q. But it is not a frequent occurrence? A. No.

Q. What would be the effect on your trade if it were constantly happening? A. It would hurt the trade if I made any bad work.

Q. Have you had unskilful men? A. It did not happen through unskilful men, but bad material.

Q. But, if you had such unskilful men, and the product was frequently returned on your hands, would it not badly affect your trade? A. Certainly; but common work always turns out so far good. It is only a certain class of paint brushes.

Q. It should always? A. We never had any returned goods in that class at all.

Q. If the common work was turned out bad, would you suppose the labour had been very unskilful? A. That should be remedied in two or three days.

By Mr. Langmuir.

Q. Would you not rather attribute it to the fault of the overseer not checking it? A. Yes.

Q. How many of these joiners can an overseer look over? A. I might give a man a hundred to look over.

By Mr. Gordon.

Q. But if the men were all thieves and drunkards, how many? A. One overseer could count the brushes and weigh the hair.

Q. Do you think one overseer could look after so many of these men as of your men? A. Yes; because it is all clear work. It is clean work.

Q. But if your shop was full of thieves, and that class of men, would you have one overseer or several? A. Yes, if only this class of goods to make, but, if I had paint brushes and very expensive bristles, I would say no.

By Mr. Noxon.

Q. You speak of the prices being very low owing to competition? A. Yes.

Q. Have the prices been lower since the Canada Car Company commenced? A. I am buying from them what I used to make, cheaper than I can make them.

Daniel Kirkpatrick, called on behalf of the Government, sworn—

By Mr. Langmuir

Q. You are guard in the tub and pail shop at the Central Prison? A. I am

Q. How long have you been in the shop? A. Since March 6th, 1876.

Q. Were you in the Central Prison employ before that? A. Yes.

Q. In what capacity? A. Guard.

Q. What place? A. The tower guard.

Q. How long have you been on the Central Prison staff? A. Two years next September.

Q. How many prisoners are at work in the tub and pail shop? A. To-day there are 69 in that room altogether.
Q. How long have that 69 been on? A. 54 was the average last month.
Q. Has it increased much lately, or has 54 been the average for the last four or five months? A. It has been increasing.
Q. What was the average for the month of May, do you think? A. I think it was less than that.
Q. Now it reaches 69? A. Yes, to-day.
Q. How many lathes are in that shop? A. Six.
Q. How many men to a lathe? A. Six.
Q. That would be 36 at the lathes? A. Yes.
Q. What are the rest doing generally? A. Some are gluing bottoms.
Q: How many about? A. Three.
Q. What is the next? A. One man turning handles; five employed to-day making hoops.
Q. Is that generally about the number making hoops? A. Yes, about the number.
Q. What else? A. Four on the two bottom lathes.
Q. That is in addition to the six lathes? A. Yes, these are a different kind of lathes.
Q. That is where they manufacture the bottoms? A. Yes.
Q. What else? A. Four putting on hoops.
Q. On the pails? A. Yes. Two on the planer. Two barrowmen.
Q. What is that? A. A cleaning up the shop.
Q. What next? A. One tool grinder. Four in the machine shop.
Q. What is that machine shop—iron work on the tools? A. Yes, regular machinists, turning-lathes, and so forth, two firemen.
Q. That is below? A. Yes, firing the boilers. One clerk in the Canada Car Company's office.
Q. Have you charge of him? A. Yes, he is under my charge. Then there is one runner that is carrying water, and so on.
Q. Does this runner not carry water to the Company's men? A. Yes, to the men employed for the Car Company.
Q. Are the runners employed for the benefit of the Company sometimes? A. They are not considered as such. They are for the accommodation of the guards.
Q. What else? A. A man employed in carrying tubs and pails to the paint shop.
Q. You supervise all these men? A. Yes.
Q. You are responsible for them? A. Yes.
Q. Do you keep an account of how these men conduct themselves in the shop? A. Yes, I have kept it since May 1st.
Q. Open it to the month of May. How many men was the average in that month? A. About 54, I think.
Q. How were these men employed? Were they constantly employed, and all the time kept at work by the Company? A. No, sir.
Q. Were they frequently idle? A. Frequently, for want of material.
Q. How frequently? A. On the 2nd, they were delayed for two hours for staves. Four lathes on the 4th, idle all day for staves. No. 1 lathe, on the 4th, idle two hours for staves. Then they have break-downs. The machinery gets out of repair.
Q. Explain that. That is, their machinery? A. Yes, that sometimes stops the whole lathe until the part is repaired which is out of order. Getting driver repaired, that is what they drive the hoop on the pail with.
Q. That stops one lathe? A. Yes.
Q. That keeps six men idle? A. Yes.
Q. Did one lathe break down? A. Yes, on the fourth. They did nothing in the forenoon.
Q. What caused it? A. An accident.
Q. Was it attributable to the lack of care on the part of the prisoners? Do you know what was the cause of the accident? A. They just got out of order. I would not consider it was through the negligence or neglect of the prisoners.

Q. In that particular instance, have you any record of the cause of the breakdown? Was it simply because the machine got out of order? A. Yes.
Q. Were there any other lathes idle that day? A. Yes, No. 1 was idle two hours for staves. On the 5th, No. 1 idle an hour and a half for staves; No. 4—turner on the outside sick—that is the man who turns the wheel on the outside.
Q. The prisoner was sick? A. Yes.
Q. Explain about that; could no other man take his place? A. Yes, I consider if they would train the men properly on the lathe, when one takes sick, the other could take his place.
Q. Did they do that? A. It seems in this instance they were training a green hand. On that day 180 pails.
Q. It did not stop it altogether? A. No.
Q. But it was delayed by the sickness of this turner? A. Yes.
Q. Do you think, under a proper system, another man could have been trained and should have been, to take his place? A. Yes, I believe that.
Q. If they had organized a proper system, it might have been obviated? A. Yes.
Q. On the sixth? A. No. 1 lathe idle two hours for pail staves; No. 4, ditto. On the 8th, two green hands on No. 2 lathe.
Q. That detained No. 2 lathe? A. Yes.
Q. Was that the only cause of detention? A. That is all on that day.
Q. What position did these green hands occupy on the lathe? A. I do not remember.
Q. In your opinion could that detention have been obviated or not? A. I would not say that, on this lathe. This is what we call the churn lathe. It is not a regular pail lathe.
Q. More difficult work? A. Yes.
Q. What was the nature of the detention? A. I forget. I did not mark it here.
Q. Was there any other detention in the shop on that day? A. None. On the 9th, No. 3, a tub lathe, five hours idle, waiting for staves; then they changed the lathe.
Q. What do you mean? A. Suppose we are working No. 1 tubs, the headers are a larger set than for No. 2. They take them off and set the chuch and slide to plane the tubs on the inside. This takes a considerable time—sometimes half a day, sometimes a day.
Q. Did they stop in the middle of the day and go on with some other kind of work? A. Yes. They were five hours waiting for staves and then changed lathe.
Q. How long did that detain them? A. It appears to be all the afternoon idle. They had forty tubs done in the morning when they got idle for staves.
Q. How did that lathe work next day? A. On the 10th, we finished 150 pails in the forenoon, and 130 in the afternoon.

By Mr. Gordon.

Q. Did you not say this was changed, and yet it made pails next day? A. Yes. I have 40 tubs for them on the 9th.
Q. Changed from tubs to pails? A. Yes.

By Mr. Langmuir.

Q. The detention was owing to the change in the lathe? A. Yes, and being idle for staves.
Q. How long did it take to make the change? A. It must have taken all the afternoon, and perhaps part of the next forenoon.
Q. Is it necessary to take so long as that to change the machinery to make another style of pail, or from pails to tubs, or back again? A. It takes longer to change from tubs to pails or back, than from No. 1 to No. 2, or No. 2 to No. 3 pail. They have to take the shafts out and what they call the chuch.
Q. In affecting this change, are the prisoners employed in doing it? A. Yes, with the assistance of the foreman.
Q. How many prisoners are employed in that? A. All of them.
Q. All of them kept busy? A. Not all the time. On the 10th, two bottom hoopers idle all day for want of hoop iron.
Q. Four engaged hooping; two idle? A. Yes.

Q. On the 11th? A. There were three men idle all day for hoops—no iron to make them with; five men idle in the afternoon for want of hoop iron.
Q. What were they engaged at? A. They must have been——
Q. On the general work? A. Yes; three men idle all day, and five in the afternoon.

BY MR. GORDON.

Q. Five in addition to the three in the morning? A. The three all day and five other men in the afternoon.

BY MR. LANGMUIR.

Q. Any of the lathes idle that day? A. No. On the 12th three pail lathes idle nearly all the afternoon for want of staves; on the 14th idle two and a half hours for want of staves.

BY MR. GORDON.

Q. Who were idle? A. It must have been all the lathes.

BY MR LANGMUIR.

Q. All the lathes idle for want of staves? A. It is marked here that. They changed from pine to cedar; it is more difficult to work; it is marked, "Very bad cedar to work;" it is that old dozy stuff lying round the yard, full of holes and rotting at the sides. On the 12th, they changed the tub lathe from pails to tubs again.
Q. What detention was there from that cause? A. They must have lost considerable time; there were only four tubs in the forenoon and thirty-six in the afternoon.
Q. So they must have been most of the day effecting these changes? A. Yes.

BY MR. GORDON.

Q. Is this all the lathes? A. No, No. 3 lathe; two pail lathes idle for want of staves part of the afternoon on the same day.

BY. MR. LANGMUIR.

Q. How long? A. I forget now; lathe wanted fixing; no person to do it; foreman sick. I wish to remark that on the 15th there was no foreman to look after the shop, except that Mr. Brandon would call in once in a while; the only person there was myself.
Q. If you got out of material who was there to direct? A. As I say, Mr. Brandon came in several times.
Q. Was that afternoon or forenoon? A. The whole day.
Q. How often did Mr. Brandon come in? A. I cannot say.
Q. Twice? A. More than twice,—four or five times.

BY MR. GORDON.

Q. Mr. Brandon has a number of other shops to supervise? A. We understand him to be the general manager.

BY MR. LANGMUIR.

Q. On the 16th? A. No. 1 lathe was two hours working culls, that is staves thrown away from the lathe; they are culled out and they try to work them over again.
Q. Then the product is not so great? A. No.
Q. What was produced? A. That lathe did 140 in the forenoon, and 120 in the afternoon.
Q. Would not that produce poorer work? A. I should think so. The pails cannot be so good. No. 3 lathe was idle four hours getting matcher fixed. No. 1 idle 1½ hour for

staves on the 17th, and No. 4 idle 1½ hour for staves, also on the 17th. On the 18th, No. 4 delayed 1½ hour getting lathe repaired.

Q. What was wrong with the lathe ? A. If I remember right, it is this lathe I have heard the prisoners say was not turned off properly in the first place.

Q. There is some defect ? A. Yes, in the saws. The shaft does not run true, and causes too much vibration, and in the chuch the tool catches in the pail, causes it to jump, and in some instances bursts the pail.

Q. Were you informed by some of the prisoners that this was the cause of this break ? A. Yes. Also, on the 18th, 9 men idle all day for want of hoop iron.

Q. Explain that, as there are only 4 hoopers ? A. Perhaps there were the hoopmakers and the men putting on hoops. On the 19th, No. 2 lathe out of repair two hours ; also No. 4, fixing spindle, 1¼ hour ; also 9 men idle all day for want of hoop iron. No. 4 is the lathe that is considered not to be in proper order. On the 21st, hoopmakers and hoopers idle all day—8 men.

Q. Why idle ? A. For want of hoop iron. On that same day, all hands one hour fixing main belt.

Q. How did that belt break ? A. It might get loose.

Q. Ordinary wear and tear ? A. Yes. On the 22nd, 10 men idle all day for want of hoop iron. On the 23rd, 10 men idle all day for want of hoop iron. On the 25th, No. 1 idle 3 hours getting driver fixed. No. 3 changed lathe on that day.

Q. What detention ? A. It does not say. No. 4, fixing matcher, one hour.

Q. How many men kept idle ? A. All hands on the lathe. Complains of having bad staves.

Q. Who ? A. On this No. 4 lathe.

Q. The prisoners ? A. Yes.

Q. And difficult to work ? A. Yes.

Q. Could not turn out the same quantity of work ? A. When they get bad staves, they cannot turn out as much work as with good ones. In the new saw-mill, it appears that the parties attending to it did not set the gauge properly, but sent in one end thinner than the other.

BY MR. GORDON.

Q. How do you know that ? A. I have seen these come into the shop. I was also speaking to the foreman about it. On that partiuclar occasion I believe the Deputy Warden was there, and saw the staves.

BY MR. LANGMUIR.

Q. The next ? A. Bad pail staves to work—not sawed right. Also, on the 28th, very bad staves to work--not cut right. On the 31st, there was one man short on No. 1 lathe, 3 hours.

Q. A prisoner short ? A. Yes.

Q. Why was that ? A. He may have stopped in his cell sick, waiting to see the doctor, and then the doctor ordered him to work, or some other cause. I do not know.

Q. If he was ordered to work, would he not go to work ? A. Certainly.

Q. Was the lathe stopped ? A. Oh, no ; the others went on, with one man short on a lathe. I believe they allow 50 pails less for that man's absence.

Q. The other five went on ? A. Yes.

Q. Was there any reason that another man could not take that man's place ? A. If they had the men properly trained, they could do that quite well.

Q. How was it in June ?—Did these detentions go on, or did they improve a little ?—Was the organization improving after that ? A. I should say it was about the same.

Q. How was it in April,—worse or better ? A. In April I should say it was the worst I have ever seen it.

Q. In February ? A. Doing pretty well.

Q. In March ? A. And in March.

Q. Any more detentions, proportionately, than you have given us in May. A. No, sir ; during the fall and winter months the men did 300 pails a day, on the 8-hour system. Mr. Brandon, one day, said they should work 10 hours steady, and do more work from 7 to 6 o'clock. The prisoners, instead of doing more, did less. I brought it to the notice of the Warden. He spoke to Mr. Brandon, and I believe he told the Warden to let it run a few days, and he would make it all right. I spoke to Mr. Brandon about it. He said, not to bother; he would make it all right by-and-by. On the last day of April he came in and told the men on No. 1 lathe he required 375 pails; on No. 2, I think, 340 or 350; on the other lathe, 340, and any amount over that he would give a cent a pail. The result was, they started on the 1st May, and in the forenoon No. 1 did 300, and in the afternoon 200; No. 2, 250 in the forenoon, and 150 in the afternoon; No. 3 had cedar to work, therefore they could not do as much, and No. 4 the same. After these three or four large days' work, they ran out of material.

Q. When they taxed up to 375, 350, and 340, they not only did the task, but a great deal more? A. Yes.

Q. If they had had the material, and had been supplied promptly, would they have continued? A. I have no doubt they would if they got the money.

Q. When that was being done, did you observe the work slighted or as well done as before? A. I heard no complaint of the work.

Q. Did you see any defects in the work? A. It appeared to me the same as the ordinary class of work.

Q. No defects? A. No.

Q. Although the volume of work was largely increased? A. Yes.

Q. Have they continued to do all that they were asked to do by Mr. Brandon? A. Not at that particular time. I brought the money matter under the notice of the Warden, and the prisoners were given to understand that no person had any authority to offer them any money or bribe, and so they dwindled down, and three or four weeks ago the foreman came to me again, and told me Mr. Brandon would be satisfied now with 325 pails from those pail lathes. This was in the forenoon about 10 o'clock. The Warden came round about 11, and I told him, and he fell the men in, and told them what Mr. Brandon required of them and they should do it, and they have done it every day since when they had material.

Q. Have they, in the face of being stopped frequently for want of staves, executed 325, or have they reduced the quantity when stopped for staves? A. They allow so many pails an hour for the reduction.

Q. In your opinion, what has been the average for detention for these causes on the part of the company—want of material and so on of their own fault—taking one day with another for a month, has there been a third of idle time owing to the want of material and organization on the part of the Company? A. I could not say as to the exact amount, but ever since I went to the shop there has been a considerable amount of lost time owing to the want of material or some other causes.

Q. Has it appeared to you that, under a good state of organization, they have been managing things properly? A. It seemed to me, immediately where I am connected, the whole business could be managed a great deal better than it is, under a better system.

Q. When idleness takes place in one place, they cannot move to another? A. Supposing there are 12 men idle in my shop, they will take them to the drying kiln, and engage with 5 men there, and pile staves into the shop, but there seem to be no more staves piled there than when the others do it.

Q. It does not improve? A. The prisoners take it for granted, if there is a break down, it is a rest for them.

Q. If kept at their own work, do they accomplish everything required of them? A. At the present time they do.

Q. As far as you observe, how many of the men on lathes require to be skilled workmen, on each lathe, and how many will fall into their work in the course of one, two, three or four days? A. In starting a new lathe with green hands, it would only want one man and a week's time to get them thoroughly organised.

Q. So that these men would work well together and produce the complement of pails? A. Yes; we started a new lathe last Friday with new men altogether.

Q. Was it a new lathe built in the prison? A. In the Canada Car Company's works; they were all green men put there but one; he was transferred from another lathe.

Q. Give us the product? A. They had executed 530 up to yesterday evening.

Q. How many days? A. Four days.

Q. What did they produce the first day? A. I could not tell. The pails were not turned out on the inside until they were finished ready for the bottoms.

Q. Were they kept fully employed? A. In a new lathe the new belting will stretch; therefore they have to be delicate, perhaps in cutting a couple of inches out of the belting and stitching it over again. The machinery will not work right. That was the case here.

Q. How long will it take them to work up to 325? A. I should say by the beginning of next week. Yesterday they did 200.

Q. Are they improving all the time? A. Yes.

Q. Do you think, if the Canada Car Company's man pays proper attention to looking after them, and instructing them, they will reach the maximum amount of work in ten days at the outside? A. I should think they would.

Q. Do you say that in ten days one skilled man who has been on a lathe before and five green men will be able to produce about the task—300 to 350 pails? A. I should think they would.

Q. So that, in the pail department, on the lathes, with one skilled man, five can become reasonably efficient in ten days? A. Yes.

Q. In the glueing depaatment, does that require long to learn? A. A man will learn that in one day.

Q. Turning the handles—how long to learn that? A. It will take a few hours.

Q. I am asking you of your own observation; what you have seen yourself? A. Yes. I heard and saw one prisoner put on the glueing; he was considered one of the worst men in the prison, had been in other shops, and could not get on with the foreman; he was sent to the shop I am in, and I asked the foreman how this man got along; at night he said he had done the best day's glueing he had had since he had been in the prison.

Q. Did he complain of the gluers before that? A. Not once, except in regard to one.

Q. In regard to making hoops, how long does it take to learn? A. I should say about half a day.

Q. What is the process? A. Punching holes. A man has to know the length required for that pail or tub.

Q. So the instructor says, "I want you to do so and so," and stays there half-an-hour? A. Then he can make a hoop in half-an-hour.

Q. He goes on quicker and quicker? A. Yes.

Q. It becomes a matter of experience? A. Yes.

Q. In ten days will a man turn out as many hoops as in three months, if properly taught and desirous to learn? A. I should think so.

Q. Could you do it? A. I could.

Q. As to bottom lathes—is that difficult to learn? A. That is more difficult.

Q. How long does it take to learn what is needed of it? A. There is a man putting in the bottoms in the pails. He attends to the man who is cutting them. When they get ahead a few, he will turn round and take hold of the lathe and he will learn. One man learns it from the other in leisure time.

Q. That might be done in idle time? A. Yes.

Q. How long would it take a reasonably intelligent man to learn that trade? A. I should say a day or so would bring a man round to understand it.

Q. It ought to be learnt in a week anyway? A. Oh, yes.

Q. No doubt about that? A. No doubt if a man tried his hand for a week he will go through all right.

Q. Is hooping a difficult process? A. No.

Q. How long would it take to learn it? A. Not long, but a man may get quicker.

Q. Driving a hoop on is it not? A. Yes.

Q. If properly instructed, will a man learn in a week? A. Yes.

Q. Some men less? A. Yes.

Q. It is a question of expertness? A. Yes; just for a man to know enough that the hoop should be the proper size for the pail and then drive it on. The pails and hoops are not all the same size.

Q. If a man be properly instructed he will do a good day's work in a week? A. Yes.

Q. On the planer—that is more difficult? A. There is not any difficulty about that.

Q. Easily done by a green hand ? A. Yes; it takes only a few days to learn to set the gauge.
Q. The cleaner ? A. Any man can do that.
Q. Then the tool grinder—what is that ? A. That is a man who understands grinding the tools on the emery.
Q. Is that always done by a prisoner ? A. Yes.
Q. Is a skilled man required ? A. No; they pick it up round the shop. I believe the man there at present has worked in a pail factory before—I think for Mr. Eddy, in Ottawa.
Q. He does it well ? A. Oh, yes; he is a good hand.
Q. Machine shop—what is that ? A. That is machine work on the lathes.
Q. That requires a skilled man ? A. That requires a practical mechanic; making new work for the lathes. They have built three new lathes there.
Q. By the prison labour ? A. Yes.
Q. All in the shops ? A. Yes, under the instruction of the Canada Car Company's man.
Q. Pail lathes? A. Yes.
Q. And have you observed how the prison machinists do their work? A. There are never any complaints about them.
Q. Do they seem to understand what they are about as machinists ? A. Yes.
Q. Go to work as a machinist would? A. Yes; when I get a prisoner from the Deputy-Warden for the machine shop, I hand him over to the foreman in charge, and soon after I ask the foreman whether he is a good hand or not.
Q. What is the result of your enquiry in reference to the department that we are on ? A. Except in two instances, where they were not, I always found them machinists.
Q. In these two instances, were they not good machinists, or not machinists at all ? A. Not machinists; there are two of the four who are there now who are not machinists, but they are good hands in a machine shop; the others are two good practical machinists.
Q. The firemen ? A. That is firing the Company's boilers.
Q. Carrying pails away ? A. Any ordinary strong man can do that, I suppose; the more pails he carries the better they like it.
Q. You say then that of the sixty-nine men six are required for the six lathes, and on everything else five, taking the machinists and all, making eleven out of sixty-nine who would require to have some experience—is that so ? A. What I mean by that is that if you put on green hands——
Q. They all come in from one day to ten ? A. Yes.
Q. And become reasonably proficient in their work ? A. Yes.
Q. From your observation of these men, have they done their work reasonably well and faithfully when watched and instructed ? A. In very few instances have they ever refused to do what they were told.
Q. What have been the instances generally ? A. Perhaps the prisoner would not like the job.
Q. And murmured ? A. Yes.
Q. To whom would he complain ? A. To the foreman.
Q. As far as you know, and from your observation as guard, have they done as much as they have been asked to do, provided the material was found ? A. Yes.
Q. Since they have attempted to task, have they kept up to it ? A. Yes, until Mr. Brandon interfered with them.
Q. Is it frequent for men to be taken away by the doctor ? A. Yes, the doctor's book is sent out. That is an every day occurrence of one man or the other.
Q. He complains of being sick ? A. Yes.
Q. Is he detained or sent back ? A. Nearly always sent back.
Q. How long are they kept away ? A. Perhaps five or ten minutes, or perhaps more.
Q. That is in going to see the doctor ? A. Yes.
Q. As to the health of these men, are they broken down, useless fellows, or good, active, able-bodied men ? A. All good able-bodied young fellows.
Q. Mostly young ? A. All young—not strapping built fellows, but about the proper size for that work—light and active.

Q. All active? A. All appear to be active.
Q. Are they generally reasonably intelligent? A. They seem to be intelligent.
Q. Are they as intelligent as in any other shop outside? A. As the ordinary class of men.
Q. Pick up quickly? A. Yes.
Q. And altogether seem as good as outside people physically, and in capacity for learning? A. Just about the same. I do not believe out of the sixty-nine, there is a man maimed in the shop, either in the legs or arms.

BY MR. GORDON.

Q. Is it your opinion that prisoners in the Central Prison are equally good workmen with men outside who have never been in the prison? A. Certainly I do.
Q. You think a prisoner who is a constant occupant of the Central Prison is as good a workman as a free man outside, who is not degraded by crime? A. I do. That is my opinion.

BY MR. LANGMUIR.

Q. Under the discipline of the prison? A. Yes.

BY MR. GORDON.

Q. When were you first asked to keep this list? A. I do not believe I was ever asked.
Q. Was it your own notion? A. Yes.
Q. How long have you been keeping this list? A. I started about the 1st May.
Q. Have you kept it up to date? A. Up to yesterday.
Q. Can you give us in detail what the lathes have done from the 1st June up to date? A. Yes. On the 1st June, No. 4 delayed seven hours fixing spindle; No. 5—this is a new lathe—green hands on that lathe. On the 2nd, No. 3, changing lathe, broke down.
Q. What was the matter with it? A. I do not remember.
Q. Something wrong with the machinery? A. Yes. Green hands again on No. 5. On the 4th, No. 1 idle two hours getting driver fixed; No. 4 had a green hand; and No. 5 green hands. On the 5th, a green hand on No. 4; No. 5, green hands. On the 7th, No. 1 idle four hours, fixing shaft. On the 8th, No. 1, one man short six hours.
Q. How was that? A. I forget now.
Q. Was he not furnished by the prison? A. You see there would be a man taken off a lathe, and the Company would not accept a man in his place, unless he was discharged, or had gone to hospital. If he was ordered to his cell for punishment, or some other reason, they would prefer waiting to taking a green man.
Q. The consequence was, the whole lathe was standing still? A. No. They allow 50 pails for that man. They go on. On the 8th also, one green hand setting up on No. 2. On No. 3, changing lathe.
Q. Do they make the same allowance for a green hand when he comes on—50 pails a lathe? A. I do not understand so.
Q. As I understand you, 325 pails a day is the stint? A. Yes.
Q. When a green hand comes, do they make any allowance? A. No, I do not think they do. The lathe is still required to turn out the same.
Q. Do you know that? A. Suppose a man was turning off; he leaves; then perhaps a man who is setting up, understands turning off; they put him on turning off, and the man who is jointing goes setting up.
Q. They shove them up? A. Yes.
Q. That is the way they get them to learn from the lowest grade to the highest? A. Yes. They put a green hand on the lowest grade.
Q. What difference does it make to the lathe, getting a green man? A. None at all, if the other men are properly trained.
Q. Will the green man do as well the first day as in two weeks? A. On putting off he will, but not on matching or setting up. No. 3 on the same day changing lathe.
Q. What was that for? A. Changing on to cedar house buckets.

Q. Why does this change take place? A. The Company gets an order for a different kind of work, and it is to supply the demand.
Q. That is really a proper business operation to change their work? A. Certainly.
Q. And I understood you to say the prisoners were employed in the change? A. Yes, some on the lathe; others are not; as many as they require; the rest stand by. On the 9th, No. 2, changing lathe. On the 11th, No. 4, three men idle all day for want of hoop iron. On the 12th, No. 4, green hand setting up.
Q. Why do you take a note of the green hand on the lathe? A. That is in case they do not do the amount of work required of them.
Q. In consequence of the green man being there? A. I take a note of it.
Q. In some instances, they do not do the whole work in consequence of that? A. Sometimes they cannot, because they do not place them properly; I have seen them put the green man in the most critical part of the work.
Q. Why was it done? A. I do not know.

BY MR. HARDY.

Q. It is a mystery? A. It is a mystery; perhaps it depends on the ideas of the parties responsible at the particular time.

BY THE CHAIRMAN.

Q. Do you know what was the out-turn of each of these lathes on these particular days? A. Yes.

BY MR. GORDON.

Q. Go back to the 1st June, when they were all green hands on No. 5? A. There was no stint at that particular time; the stint commenced about the 16th June.
Q. On the 1st June, what did No. 1 lathe turn out? A. 240.
Q. No. 2? A. 7 union churns and 40 butter-pails; No. 3, 70 tubs in the forenoon, and 60 in the afternoon; No. 4, 80 in the forenoon and 30 in the afternoon; No. 5, 70 in the forenoon and 50 in the afternoon.
Q. That is the one the green hands were on? A. Yes.
Q. On the 2nd, No. 3? A. Changing lathe, and broke down.
Q. How many were turned out by No. 3? A. Fifty in the forenoon and thirty in the afternoon.
Q. How many of No. 2? Eighty altogether.
Q. No. 5 on the 2nd? A. Eighty in the forenoon and fifty in the afternoon.
Q. On the 4th, how many did No. 1 turn out? A. 100 in the forenoon and 120 in the afternoon.
Q. No. 4, one green hand? A. 100 in the forenoon, 130 in the afternoon.
Q. No. 5? A. Seventy and one hundred.
Q. On the 5th, No. 4? A. Ninety in the forenoon and 140 in the afternoon.
Q. No. 5? A. Eighty and ninety.
Q. On the 7th, No. 1? A. Forty in the forenoon, 110 in the afternoon; idle four hours.
Q. On the 8th, No. 1? A. 210.
Q. I thought it was six hours waiting? A. One man short six hours.
Q. No. 2? A. Butter pails, 40, changing lathe, green hand, setting up.

BY MR. LANGMUIR.

Q. Is that the best thing to put green hands on? A. No it is not.

BY MR. GORDON.

Q. No. 2, that day? A. Forty butter pails.
Q. No. 3? A. Forty-five in the morning, twenty in the afternoon, changing lathe.

Q. On the 9th, No. 2, changing lathe, how many ? A. None marked. They were changing from butter pails to cedar churns.

Q. That is for our own benefit, so I will not ask you as to that in future. No. 4, on the 12th, green hand on the lathe ? A. Eighty in the forenoon and seventy in the afternoon.

Q. 13th, what note against that day ? A. Cedar churns, No. 2, 15 in the forenoon, 4 in the afternoon, changing lathe ; No. 3, 90 cedar horse buckets, and 15 No. 2 tubs in the afternoon.

Q. Any delay ? A. There must have been a delay in changing lathe. No. 4, 3 men idle all day—that must have been the hoopers.

Q. On the 14th ? A. No. 1 idle nearly all the afternoon for want of hoops ; 16 pails only ; No. 2, fixing lathe, 32 cedar churns, and none in the afternoon ; No. 4, idle two hours for want of hoops, 110 in the forenoon and 116 in the afternoon ; No. 5, idle all the afternoon for want of hoops, they turned off 106 in the forenoon. On the same day three men idle all day for want of hoops. On the 15th, No. 1, idle all day for want of hoop iron ; No. 2, in the forenoon changing lathe, 20 in the afternoon ; No. 4 idle all day for want of hoops ; No. 5, idle all day for want of hoops ; 3 men idle all day for want of hoops.

Q. When you say these lathes are idle all day, that does not necessitate the prisoners being idle all day ? A. In some cases it does. They take them round the yard picking up chips and so on.

Q. As a rule, are they not put on other work ? A. I never saw them put on work profitable for the Company.

Q. That is not a question for you ? A. They are put round the yard picking up chips, and in the foundry.

Q. Do you mean to say they go round and pick up chips ? A. Yes, they do ; little chips not as large as your hand.

Q. In the foundry what do they do ? A. Move stuff from one part to the other.

Q. On the 16th ? A. No. 4, 2 hours idle for want of hoop iron. On the 17th, No. 2, 18 cedar churns in the forenoon, and in the afternoon changing lathe. On the 21st, delayed one hour on account of fire in the wash-house.

Q. How many did they turn out on that day on the different lathes ? A. This is ashwood pails—different from the pine. No. 1, 50 in the forenoon, 40 in the afternoon ; No. 2, 25 in the forenoon, 17 butter tubs in the afternoon ; No. 3, 50 and 40 No. 1 tubs ; No. 4, 170 and 120 ; No. 5, ashwood pails 60 and 76. On the 22nd, No. 1, idle 1½ hour, breakdown, ashwood pails 91 in the forenoon, and pine 20 in the afternoon ; No. 3, changing lathe, 45 in the morning, 34 in the afternoon ; No. 4, 120 in the forenoon, nothing in the afternoon. On the 23rd, No. 3, changing lathe ; No. 4, idle all day getting spindle fixed. On the 25th, No. 2, changing lathe ; in the afternoon 24 churns. On the 26th, No. 2, 6 churns, break down 8 hours ; No. 3, 20 No. 1 tubs in the forenoon, 70 in the afternoon, changing lathe. On the 28th, No. 2, changing lathe, 15 churns ; 6 men idle one hour for hoop iron. On the 29th, No. 2, 10 churns in the forenoon, changing lathe ; No. 3, 40 tubs in the forenoon and 70 in the afternoon, changing lathe. On the 30th, No. 3, 30 tubs in the forenoon, 40 in the afternoon, changing lathe.

Q. During that month they were not idle once for want of staves ? A. I believe they had staves enough that month.

Q. The only cause for idleness under the Company's control seems to be want of hoop iron ? A. Yes.

BY MR. LANGMUIR.

Q. And the constant changes ? A. Yes, and the break-downs.

BY MR. GORDON.

Q. Can you account for the majority of these break-downs ? A. I should suppose it was in the ordinary course of running machinery.

Q. Do you think that if there were more supervision, more free labour and superintendence, or if you had skilled men working on the machines, the break-downs would be less frequent? A. I don't know; I would say that if they had more free men there supervising, it would be much better than it is.

Q. Do you think there are not sufficient free men to the number of prisoners? A. I do not.

Q. How many free men do you think there should be to the number of prisoners? A. I think there should be at least four free men in that shop.

By Mr. Brockway.

Q. How many prisoners? A. Taking the men who work in the machine shop, and so on, that would be 62.

By Mr. Gordon.

Q. You think instead of one the Company should have about four? A. Yes; I see they have another man there this morning; I will just explain that to you. Supposing that at this end of the shop a lathe breaks down, and there is only one foreman, he is employed an hour or two in getting that lathe fixed; the other men, forty, fifty, or sixty, are working at the other end without any one looking after them, except the guard walking up and down.

Q. Can you give us any idea as to the amount of time, or the number of times, the men are taken away from these shops for punishment, or to attend the doctor or the barber, or to fill any prison regulations? How often does it happen? A. There may be one or two men going to the doctor a day, some days there are none; it is very seldom that any men leave that shop for punishment during working hours.

Q. Are these supposed to be the best men you have in the prison in that shop? A. No, they are ordinary prisoners.

Q. Are not they the picked men of the prisoners? A. They have been picked by Mr. Brandon and the foreman; they went to the outside gang and fetched men in there; I have fetched men in.

Q. How often does it happen that a man is taken away from that shop to be punished, or to attend the barber or others, except the doctor? A. Once a week they are shaved.

Q. Every man in the shop? A. Yes.

Q. How long does that take? A. About from five to seven minutes.

Q. How long will it take before the man gets back to his work? What loss of time? A. I should say five to seven minutes.

Q. You mean the man is shaved and gets back again in seven minutes? A. Yes.

By Mr. Brockway.

Q. Where do they shave? A. Just outside the door; or, in cold weather, in the shop.

By Mr Gordon.

Q. You have relays of men,—they wait and stand round for the barber? A. No.

Q. You do not return a man to the shop and take another? There is always one waiting when the other gets out of the barber's chair,—if they have a chair? A. Yes.

Q. So they are waiting? A. Yes.

Q. There are two out always? A. I will explain how that happens. There are always some men at the lathes who get out of work.

Q. Is not that the case that two or three men are out waiting for the barber? A. Not in all cases.

Q. As a rule? A. No; sometimes the prisoner may not have anything to do, and he walks out there when notified to go and be shaved.

Q. How often does it happen that a man is taken for punishment? A. I think there has been only one man in all last month.

Q. What was the extent? A. He went in about 9 o'clock and did not return till the next morning.

Q. What was the punishment? A. I do not know; I did not enquire.

Q. What is his name? A. Hugh Riley.

Q. Was he in the cells or what ?   A. I do not know. He was in the cells.
Q. What was he punished for ?   A. Fighting in the shop.
Q. You have that occurrence sometimes ?   A. Oh, yes.
Q. Very frequently ?   A. No.
Q. Did they fight with the foreman or among themselves?   A. With another prisoner.
Q. Was the other prisoner punished too ?   A. He was gone in for a few minutes and returned to the shop.
Q. The man punished was found to be the culprit ?   A. Yes.
Q. Is the work often stopped for men fighting ?   A. No, that is the first fight we have had for six months.
Q. And this man was returned to the Company next day ?   A. Yes.
Q. What did they do in the meantime ?   A. They had other men.
Q. Did the prison authorities furnish another man ?   A. Yes, they brought another man into the shop.
Q. What was he doing ?   A. He was setting up No. 3 tub lathe.
Q. Did the Company accept the man ?   A. Yes, they put him in a different place. They put another setter-up who was idle at the time in his place.
Q. When was it ?   A. One day last week.
Q. Have you an account of it in your book?   A. No, I did not note that in my book.
Q. Was not the lathe delayed in consequence ?   A. I think not. They put another setter-up there, just as competent as he was.
Q. Was it not delayed by his being taken away ?   A. No.
Q. But they had to put another on ?   A. It was an old hand.
Q. They were fighting—did not that delay the lathe ?   A. No ; that was not more than two minutes. That did not delay the lathe.
Q. Not even for two minutes ?   A. I do not suppose it did.
Q. The other men did not stop to look on ?   A. Perhaps they did.
Q. Did you see it ?   A. Yes.
Q. Did all the men in the shop stop ?   A. They did not.
Q. Did the men stop on this lathe ?   A. They were stopped at this time doing something —fixing some part of the lathe, and these two men got arguing about it, and the result was, they resorted to blows, got one down, and I happened to catch them coming round the pile. I sent them in.
Q. Did not that cause delay ?   A. Not long.
Q. How long ?   A. About 3 or 4 minutes. I told the foreman, and he got the other man and put him on at once. That particular day, the men did as much work as was required by the Canada Car Company—the number fixed by the manager, Mr. Brandon.
Q. Give the date ?   A. I cannot fix the date.
Q. This man came back next day ?   A. Next morning.
Q. What was his capability for work after being punished ?   A. He had to go through the same as the day previous.
Q. Was he as capable as the day previous ?   A. Yes ; he might have felt a little rougher, but he had to do it.
Q. Do you think punishment has no effect on prisoners the next day ?   A. They may feel a little rougher, according to the punishment they receive.
Q. No effect on their work ?   They have to do it all the same.
Q. Do they do it as well ?   A. I think so.
Q. A man in the dark cell for three days?   A. I have not seen any man in the dark cell for three days.
Q. A man chained up for 24 hours—will he do his work as well the next day ?   A. I do not know when I had a man under me chained up for 24 hours, so I cannot say.
Q. Would he do his work as well ?   A. He would not feel as comfortable under it.
Q. Will he do his work ?   A. Certainly, if compelled.
Q. It makes no difference to the quantity of work ?   A. No, I do not think it does.
Q. You said prisoners were as good as free men ?   A. I said under prison discipline they were.
Q. Is there any duty cast upon you when the prisoners are idle ?   A. Yes, I am to ascertain the cause, and if I find that they are idle for want of material, I am to place them

in the centre of the shop until they are required to go to work by the foreman. If I find they are lounging or loitering around the shop, I am to report them.

Q. On each of these occasions you have referred to, where they have been idle from want of material, did you place them in the centre of the shop? A. I did, until the shop was so crowded I could not do it any more.

Q. How crowded? A. Full right through with material, caused by this delay.

Q. There is not sufficient space in the shops? A. There is if there were a proper system.

Q. What system? A. Taking the material away to the other shops as required.

Q. Is there sufficient space in the other shops? A. Certainly.

Q. Were these men employed to take away? A. No, there were no bottoms in through the want of hoop-iron.

Q. Then they could not have been taken away, no matter how good the system? A. For the want of hoop-iron.

Q. But when there was a delay for the want of staves, did you make the men stand in the middle of the shop? A. Except those who were taken out to the yard by the foreman. Not on all occasions. When I considered it in compliance with the Warden's orders, I did so.

Q. Are not your orders peremptory? A. Yes, but if a man has a tool in his hands——

Q. You did not obey your instructions? A. Oh, yes, I always do. If a man wants to clean his lathe——

Q. He is not idle then? A. But perhaps he was pronounced by the foreman as having nothing to do.

Q. With regard to this glue man you spoke of as wonderfully good, has he continued to be such a good man, or was it only on the first day that, like a new broom, he swept clean? A. He has continued up to the present day. He is not glueing now. He is on one of the lathes.

Q. Does he turn out to be as good a man on the lathe as on the glue? A. Yes.

Q. It must be pretty difficult to find out sometimes what these prisoners are best fitted for. There must be a good deal of changing round the shops to find out? A. I never saw much trouble in placing them.

Q. Have not men asked to be changed two or three times to get work suitable? A. Yes, I have known men to ask to be changed to get what they call a fancy job.

Q. And they have worked better when they have been changed? A. Yes; they seemed to be better satisfied.

Q. How many guards have you in the prison? A. About 18, I think, working guards.

Q. Do you think that is sufficient for the number of men? A. From what I hear of the amount in other prisons, I suppose it is.

Q. What is your own opinion on that point? A. My opinion is that, if there were more guards, it would be better.

Q. Do you think that you can give a proper supervision to these 69 men in this shop, or do you think it would be better if you had an assistant to superintend these men, keep them at their work and so on? A. I could do it now as it is, if the material of the shop were placed so as to do it, but it is impossible for four guards in the present state of the shop to supervise the men.

Q. The shops are not sufficiently large for the industries carried on? A. Yes, sir; I have 69 men there, and sometimes I will stand in particular parts of the shop and cannot see more than three or four at a time.

Q. And the inclination of these men is not to do too much work if they can help it? A. They have a task now to do, and that they must do.

Q. You never heard of their doing more than their task without some inducement? A. I have known it.

Q. On many occasions? A. Several occasions; not many.

Q. How many since the task was set? A. I do not suppose that they have done any, but I have known instances where they did more than the foreman asked of them.

Q. You would be surprised if they took to doing more than their task? A. Some men, I would not.

Q. Would you be surprised if any particular lathe turned out for a week more than their task ? A. I would not be surprised.

Q. Would you ask to find out if the Company were giving an inducement ? A. I would be led to believe there was something wrong.

Q. With regard to these machinists—there are 4, are there not ?—A. I said two, and two good hands.

Q. I mean four prisoners working at it ? A. Yes; two of them are machinists.

Q. How many free men are there in that department ? A. One ; they had three or four others there, and discharged them about the 1st of this month.

Q. Up to that time how many ? A. One discharged prisoner, and two other free men.

Q. You had four free men to four prisoners in that department ? A. Yes, but for a very short time.

Q. Can you tell from your general recollection about how many are the number of recommitments—how often do you see old friends come in again ? A. Frequently.

Q. As many as one-third ? A. I could not say that.

Q. Two out of a dozen ? A. Yes, I should say so ; a man we have in the shop to-day, a cooper by trade, is a recommitment—he worked four months in the shop before.

Q. How often do these men change ; you have got 64 prisoners—about what is the change per week—men going out and others coming in ; do you have a change every day ? A. No ; some weeks there is no change at all.

Q. Does it average two a week ? A. No, not so much.

Q. Would it be one a week ? A. I should say it would average about one a week.

Q. Would you have about 52 new men a year ? A. There are quite a number of men who were there when I went there.

Q. You have the long term men ? A. No, the average. The long terms are in the broom and brush shops.

[Witness to prepare a statement of the result of the work in May.]

By Mr. Langmuir.

Q. There is a want of system, you think, in the lumbering up of the shop ? A. I do.

Q. Many pails standing in the middle of the shop without bottoms ? A. Yes.

Q. If the bottoms were made and the hoops on, and everything complete, they would be removed ? A. Yes.

Q. Under a proper system that would be done ? A. Yes.

Q. Do you know that a whole flat is vacant in the south machine shop ? A. The top floor is all vacant.

Q. It could be all used for piling material ? A. Yes.

Q. Is the foundry vacant ? A. Yes.

Q. There is no want of shop-room ? A. None.

By Mr. Gordon.

Q. As a matter of fact, you move these things out twice a day ? A. There are pails there that have been there for three months.

Q. How many ? A. There are the tobacco tubs, they were manufactured there before Mr. Warren left. They have been in the shop over a month.

Q. How many ? A. Twenty or thirty.

Q. That is all ? A. They take up a considerable space.

By Mr. Langmuir.

Q. As for the machinery and the men working, is there ample room, if all the stuff was removed as it is manufactured ? A. Yes ; and more than that, there are staves enough in and around the shop to last the lathes for two or three weeks, and they keep bringing in piles.

Q. Which cumbers up the shop ? A. Yes.

Q. But there is plenty of space for manufacturing purposes ? A. Yes.

Q. But want of system in removing the stuff ? A. Yes.

Q. In the report given for the month of June, there is not such a lack of staves?
A. No.

Q. The saw-mill was not in operation in May? A. Not in operation.

Q. But now that is remedied? A. Yes; Mr. Brandon said it was owing to not having the number of stave saws.

Q. I see you have a list here of the dates of men. Do you know the average? How many two years men—how many over twelve months? A. There are twenty-seven men of twelve months and over.

Q. How many two years men? A. Four I think.

Q. You have long date men there comparatively? A. Yes.

By Mr. Gordon.

Q. Do you know how many pails on an average are turned out each day? A. When they are working on pine, they average since the Warden spoke to them 927 pails on three lathes.

Q. On the whole five, tubs and everything, it would probably be 1,200? A. They are supposed to turn out 100 No. 1 tubs.

Q. How many would these machines turn out in a day, as a rule? A. 36 churns or butter tubs, 100 No. 1 tubs—about 1,200.

Q. Towards the end of the day then the shop must get pretty crowded? They are all piled in the shop at the end of the day, I suppose? A. They are taken away from the lathes after dinner.

Q. Are they moved twice a day? A. One man is kept carrying all day long.

Q. One man is employed moving these out during the whole day? A. Yes.

Q. How many does he move? A. He moves as many as are hooped.

Q. How many? A. He could move 1,200.

Q. Then they are moved out as fast as they are made? A. No, they are not. I say he could move them. He moves them as fast as they are ready. He has to wait for these men who are idle for want of hoop iron.

Q. As fast as they are completed, he moves them? A. Yes, and when there is an overplus they put on extra men.

Q. Have you any experience in a manufacture of this kind before you went into the prison? A. Not in a pail factory, but I have in others.

Q. Do you know anything of the difficulties in organizing a thing of this kind? A. No I do not profess to, except what I have picked up in the prison.

Q. It is a large thing to put in order all of a sudden? A. It seems to be.

Q. Do you think the officers of the Company are working as well as can be expected? A. I think the foreman in my shop has done more than can be expected.

Q. As to Mr. Brandon? A. That I do not know. I would not swear that he takes a great interest in it.

Q. But the other foremen; do you think they do as much as can be expected? A. I hear considerable complaints about other foremen.

Q. Do you think Mr. McBean does as much as can be expected? A. He just passes through there, and that is all I know about him.

Q. Is he not often there, considering the Company cannot pay him? A. I do not know anything about that.

By Mr. Hardy.

Q. Mr. McBean talks a good deal? A. Yes. If you would allow me to remark, I think if the thing was managed a little better, it would pay a little better.

By Mr. Gordon.

Q. Did you ever find a business managed as well as it could be? A. I think it could be managed a great deal better with very little difficulty.

By the Chairman.

Q. Are you a mechanic ? A. No. I never served my time to any particular branch of business.

Q. Had you no knowledge of mechanical work or machinery before going in there ? A. I worked a little on it on the other side.

Q. What kind of work ? A. I worked in an axe factory. I have seen a good deal of work carried on.

Q. What is the exact process of making a hoop for these pails ? A. In the first place, they roll the iron through little rolls, then cut it to the length required.

Q. How do they ascertain the length ? A. They measure the size of the pail, and then they have little spikes stuck on the bench, and they set these accordingly. First, they punch a hole in the end of the hoop, place the hoop on this peg, and put it in the machine and cut it. Then it is given to another man, and he puts a rivet in and strikes it with a hammer.

Q. Are two men employed in it? A. There are six employed.

Q. In making one hoop ? A. No. One man cuts them on the knife and throws them out to the other men, and they rivet them.

Q. When these men have a task, after they have made the specified number, supposing the hour has not expired, what do they do then ? A. They clean up around the lathe, and put in the time until the whistle blows.

Q. They do not go on making any more ? A. No; no more than is required.

Q. You said these men were all young. How do you get the information as to their ages and periods of sentence—is it supplied to you ? A. When I get a man in the shop I generally ask him the length of his sentence.

Q. It is from his statement? A. Yes ; they are generally correct.

By Mr. Noxon.

Q. You have spoken of frequent breakages of machinery, do not the Company keep duplicate parts to replace, instead of waiting, as one part gives way ? A. No, they have not done it. I think they are now.

JACOB P. WAGNER, called on behalf of the Government, sworn——

By Mr. Hardy.

Q. What business are you in ? A. Manufacturer of sashes, doors, blinds, &c.

Q. How long have you been engaged in the business ? A. About sixteen years in that line. I am a builder as well.

Q. How many men have you employed now. A. At present, 54.

Q. Do you rent your premises, or have you built them ? A. Built them all.

Q. What would the rental come to at 6 per cent., say—are they brick or frame ? A. Partly brick and partly frame. I calculate 7 per cent—$1,300 per annum.

Q. For 54 men ? A. Yes ; I can put double that.

Q. Do you think 7 per cent. is a fair charge for rental of shop property ? A. I think so, the way money is going now.

Q. What would you consider a fair rental per annum for steam engines, boiler, shafting, belting, and that sort of machinery ? A. We generally calculate $100 the horse power.

Q. Could you fix a percentage ? A. I could not do that without going into some calculation.

Q. Would it be more than 7 per cent. for the use of that machinery ? If you rented it how much would you want ? A. I should want at least 25 per cent.

Q. Covering wear and tear ? A. Yes.

Q. You think 10 per cent. would not be enough, including the wear ? A. No. Take a machine. You calculate it will wear out in ten years.

Q. It is a boiler and engine ? A. It is the same thing.

Q. Do you calculate the life of a boiler at about ten years ? A. Yes.

Q. An engine longer? A. It is according to how it is used. An engine may go 20 or 25 years if you keep it well and take care of it.
Q. Do you use machinery pure in the manufacture of doors, sashes, blinds, &c.? A. Pure.
Q. How many machines have you running—take the blind department? A. In the blind department I have seven machines.
Q. How are they worked? How many men? A. At present I have only four men working in that department. They do nothing but prepare the material. It is carried away into another part of the shop and put together.
Q. What part of these are skilled men? A. Only one man. The rest are boys from 12 to 18 years old.
Q. What do you pay them? A. From $3 50 to $5 00 and $6 00 per week.
Q. What do you pay the skilled man? A. $1 75 a day.
Q. Is there a pretty close analogy as to the amount of skill required in the manufacture of this sort of thing, and in the manufacture of pails and tubs? A. It is pretty much the same.
Q. You do not require more than the one skilled man? A. One skilled man.
Q. To how many? A. To attend to 10, 15, or 20.
Q. And the lowest you pay is $3 50 a week to the boys? A. Yes.
Q. And you furnish the whole of the motive power, machinery and buildings, and so on? A. Everything.
Q. Have you seen the pail work in operation? A. I have not.
Q. Are you familiar with it at all elsewhere? A. No.
Q. Do you know what taxes you pay on your shop? A. $450.
Q. What insurance? A. $840.
Q. Have you water connected with it? A. $200 for water.
Q. Gas? A. I do not burn it, I do not work by candlelight.
Q. Assuming that the class of work—pails, wheelbarrows, washboards, and so on, is practically similar to the class of work which you carry on? A. From my knowledge, I believe it is pretty much the same, it is all done by machinery, and that is so perfected that it is only to stick it in and take it out.
Q. Assuming that it was similar, what would be your opinion that the men at the Central Prison would be worth a day, getting them free of taxes, insurance, water rate, rental, heating, machinery, boilers, and running gear—I do not mean the hand tools or the lathes—the machinery for the motive power, the engine, the boiler, the shafting, the belting? A. We charge $4 for a man and machine. Then the machine and everything is supplied. Deducting his wages gives the profit.
Q. Well, if the contractor gets house-room, what would be a fair rate of wages for these men, as competing fairly with outside labour? A. I should say 75 cts. to $1. They are mostly all young strapping fellows up there.
Q. You find everything and pay even boys at least $3.50 a week? A. Yes.

BY MR. GORDON.

Q. These taxes—is that on real estate? A. That includes everything that is on the premises.
Q. How much of that is for the real estate; how much for the land and buildings, and so on? A. I do not recollect exactly.
Q. Have you your assessment paper here? A. I have not.
Q. Would you have any objection to send it down here? A. No; I can do that.
Q. You employ machinery in your establishment? A. I do.
Q. As a rule do you put your green men on the machines, or skilled men? A. I generally keep one skilled man to set the machines up, and anyone can put the stuff there.
Q. Do you take the common labourers to work the machines or skilled men? A. I take boys. I train boys.
Q. Would you be inclined to take ordinary labourers off the street—men working for the corporation—and put them on your delicate machinery? A. Yes.
Q. And give them the sole control of those machines? A. By a little showing they can run as well as the skilled man.

Q. Can as well control it ? A. No. I would get the man to set the machine up, and they would put in the stuff.
Q. Supposing you had to pay $2.50 a-day to a good man, and could get a poor man at $1, which would you prefer ? A. The poor man.
Q. You would prefer for choice having a poor man of that description at that rate ? A. As far as the profit is concerned, of course, if I could get a good man for the same price as a poor man, I would take him.
Q. Would it be more profitable to have that class of man at $1 a-day, than a skilled man at a higher rate ? A. Certainly.
Q. Do you consider it safe to leave that class of man in charge of a machine ? A. Not entirely.
Q. How far would it be safe ? A. Just so long safe until the machine gets dull and wants sharpening up.
Q. How often ? A. Perhaps every hour.
Q. Would it with that class of man ? A. Some saws every two or three hours.
Q. Would you require to have a skilled man working near the machine worked by these men ? A. To look after them.
Q. How many skilled men to say 10 of that class of men ? A. I have different departments, and I keep one skilled man in each department.
Q. How many men in each department ? A. Some of them five, some six, some three, some four.
Q. And the rest are boys ? A. Yes.
Q. Are these boys apprentices ? A. Yes.
Q. What term are they with you ? A. Three to four years, according to their age.
Q. You pay them on a sliding scale—something less the first year than the last ? A. Yes.
Q. Why ? A. Because they are always considered worth more the second year than the first.
Q. Have you ever taken in apprentices for less than three years ? A. No.
Q. Why do you fix it at that ? A. Because, we take it, it takes them that to learn to set the work for themselves.
Q. Do you make much out of these apprentices at the end of the three years ? A. I suppose so, or we would not take them.
Q. It is a good operation to have them ? A. Yes.
Q. Would you rather have apprentices at that sliding scale than men at $1.75 a day? A. Certainly ; a boy will earn just as much as a man getting $10 to $12 a week.
Q. But how soon would he do that ? A. I suppose, working a year he could do as much work on the machine as a man getting $10 a week.
Q Would you think it a good operation to take a contract for 250 boys or men for a fixed rate over a period of five years, taking into consideration the fact that the price of labour and all the other circumstances which, as a business man, you would look into before you made the contract, may be altered ? A. It depends altogether on how low a rate I would get them at.
Q. Do you think it would be a good operation at any rate ? A. That depends altogether on circumstances.
Q. In your business? A. I would not take such a quantity. There is not the work to do it.
Q. Would you bind yourself to take 100 men ? A. I would not.
Q. Fifty ? A. I would not.

BY MR. HARDY.

Q. Not in your special business ? A. No.

BY MR. GORDON.

Q. As a business man you would not think it an operation to pay to take any fixed number of men—you prefer to hire and discharge men as you want them ? A. Decidedly, I would not be bound.
Q. Where is your establishment ? A. On Adelaide Street.

Q. Do you know what land is worth a foot there ?   A. Some was sold next to me at $120 a foot.
Q. Pretty nearly the centre of the city is it not ?   A. Yes.
Q. Did you put these buildings up yourself ?   A. Yes.
Q. Then you calculate this $1,300 is 7 per cent. on the cost ?   A. Yes, I take the land as worth $80 a foot.
Q. When did you put these builoings up ?   A. Some about 16 years ago and some later.

BY THE CHAIRMAN.

Q. In reference to the yearly value of machinery, if you were renting a steam engine with the lying shafts necessary for driving the machinery, and were furnished the first belting connecting the steam engine with the lying shafts, without furnishing the power or the men who are driving it, what do you consider the yearly value of that would be?   A. I should say from 15 to 25 per cent.
Q. Fifteen per cent. ?   A. At the least.
Q. You consider the period that boilers will last averages about ten years ?   A. That is my experience.
Q. An engine will last ?   A. Twenty or twenty-five years if taken care of.
Q. This shafting and the bearings and pulleys, how long will they last ?   A. I think they would average about ten years. They would break down occasionally and wear out.

BY MR. GORDON.

Q. Have you had any experience in the value of prison labour ?   A. No.
Q. Therefore from your personal knowledge you cannot state what the value is ?   A. I have been up there and seen them work. I judge from that more than anything else.

BY MR. BROCKWAY.

Q. In your business, do the boys remain with you a good many years ?   A. I have some 10 and 12 years and longer.
Q. It is usual for them to continue on at one place or another ?   A. Yes. If they turn out good we generally keep them on.

The Commission adjourned.

The Commission reassembled at 3 o'clock.

Captain WILLIAM STRATTON PRINCE, called on behalf of the Government, sworn—

BY MR. LANGMUIR.

Q. You are Warden of the Central Prison ?   A. I am.
Q. How long have you occupied that position ?   A. I was sworn in on the 12th November, 1873, and assumed my duties on the 1st January, 1874.
Q. And have continuously occupied it ?   A. Yes.
Q. You see every prisoner who comes into that prison, unless you are absent on leave ?   A. Yes.
Q. Will you state to the Commission what is the physical condition of the prisoners that are tendered to the Canada Car Company ?   A. Very good indeed. They are generally an active, able bodied set of young men. When I say young men, I mean men under 40— varying from 20 to 40.
Q. Are not cripples or physically dilapidated men tendered to the Company ?   A. None. There have been some occasions on which they have been tendered. There was a man tendered to the Company who was sentenced to 18 months' imprisonment. He was minus a leg. He was a capital worker for the brush shop, and of course the deprivation of a leg did not

operate against the work of his hands ; but the Company objected, and I took him and put him on domestic work.

Q. When the Company objects to a man, what do you do? A. He is never given over to the Company. I must have a medical inspection, though, before I receive the Company's objection.

Q. According to the contract ? A. Yes.

Q. That is a provision of the contract ? A. Yes.

BY MR. GORDON.

Q. The Company may object to a man, but you may not consider it sufficient ? A. Yes, I must have a medical report.

Q. Unless your surgeon ratifies what the Company says ? A. Then the Company are obliged to take him.

BY MR. LANGMUIR.

Q. In other words, the opinion of the surgeon is final. A. Yes.

Q. That is the provision of the contract ? A. Yes.

Q. Is every man examined by the surgeon on coming into the Prison ? A. Yes, on his arrival, and reported upon.

Q. And if they are found to be in bad condition, physically disabled, what is done with them ? A. Then they are put to domestic work, and I report it officially to the Department of the Inspector of Prisons.

Q. And if they are fit subjects for the hospital ? A. They are sent to the hospital.

Q. But, in any case, is a man unwell, sick, or in a bad state of health tendered to the Company. A. No.

Q. In your report, you state that a large proportion of the men are intemperate. That is taken from statistics, is it ? A. From statistics, and from the transfer returns which are kept in the register.

Q. What is the proportion in your report of last year ? A. With regard to intemperate people, of course, they are placed in the transfer returns as intemperate.

Q. But not found to be intemperate of your own knowledge ? A. No. I should like to state that, from my experience in police duties, a great number of these people come out from England—discharged soldiers a great many of them—get drunk, are arrested and sent to gaol for six months under the Vagrant Act; but, from their actual appearance, they are not intemperate actually, but are carried away by meeting friends, and perhaps those of them who are sent to the prison are as capable of work as I am—strong able-bodied men.

Q. In other words, though a man is put down as an intemperate man in statistical returns, very frequently, it does not interfere with his work ? A. Never or rarely.

Q. Is he tendered to the Company if it does ? A. No.

Q. Classing him as intemperate does not interfere with him as a good worker ? A. No.

Q. Are any men brought into the prison in an intemperate condition ? A. There have been some, but we never tender them until they are perfectly well ; they are reported upon as unfit for work by the surgeon, for the time being.

Q. What is the *modus operandi* in tendering prisoners ? A. On their arrival at the prison their description is taken down, and a list made out for the information of the Company ; that list contains their names, occupations, and the unexpired portion of their imprisonment.

Q. To whom is that sent ? A. To the Canada Car Company's office; then Mr. Brandon selects from that list what prisoners he chooses.

Q. Are they immediately placed at his disposal ? A. Yes.

Q If he rejects a man, do you force him to take him ? A. Yes ; unless the medical man reports him unfit for labour.

Q. But they have not the full number ? A. No ; they had 216 ; it was reduced to 213 ; my duty is to keep them up to their complement, but they have refused for the last two months to take the prisoners.

Q. How many are there now ? A. 215 now.

BY THE CHAIRMAN.

Q. Employed by them? A. Yes, by the Company.

BY MR. LANGMUIR.

Q. When they have taken 215 under their contract, they are compelled to keep that number, not to go down any lower? A. No. They went down to 214 and 213. For some weeks they were at 216.
Q. They are under contract to take 260? A. Yes, since January 1st.
Q. They are short forty-five of their contract to-day? A. Yes.
Q. Was a statement of the occupations of the prisoners before commitment—prisoners within certain dates—made out under your supervision? A. Yes.
Q. What is the period? A. From September 18th, 1876, to June 18th, 1877.
Q. That is correct? A. Yes.
Q. As a general thing, do you find prisoners report themselves incorrectly as to previous occupation? A. No. Sometimes they report as a carpenter, when they have only been working a year or two—have been working in wood. I have had some misrepresentations.
Q. Many? A. Very few. Very exceptional.
Q. When you have employed prisoners in the industries of the prison, do you find they report themselves as tailors, without being tailors? A. No. It has occasionally taken place, but very seldom.
Q. How many shoemakers have reported, who have turned out not to be shoemakers? A. I do not think I have had a single instance.

BY MR. GORDON.

Q. Do you mean, about the carpenters, that they like the occupation, and so report themselves? A. They have been employed as carpenters, but do not come up to the standard I should expect.
Q. Do they report themselves carpenters in preference to any other trade? A. No.

BY MR. LANGMUIR.

Q. You mean men who had only a slight knowledge of it? A. Yes, only a year or a year and a half at it.
Q. Have you another statement as to ages? A. Yes.
Q. Is that also taken from the register? A. Yes.
Q. That is correct? A. Yes.
Statement put in.

(Exhibit " N.")

Q. You have a statement of the terms of sentences of prisoners now employed? A Yes, up to the 18th June.
Q. Read the statement below? A. "The following long sentenced prisoners, now employed at domestic work, were first accepted by the Company, and then were rejected."
Q. How many. A. Nine.
Q. Over what periods? A. Four of two years, two of one year 11 months, and three of 12 months.
Q. Do you know why they were rejected? A. I do not know why. As far as I knew, or my judgment carried me, these men were perfectly fit for the service, except John Baxter, who was reported physically unfit for labour.
Q. But do you know the reasons why the nine men were rejected? A. Patrick McCabe is minus a finger, but perfectly capable of work, a strong, able bodied, active man.

BY MR. GORDON.

Q. What is Baxter? A. Reported physically unfit by the surgeon. I do not know why.

By Mr. Langmuir.

Q. Do you know the reasons in every case ? A. No. This John Breen was a man Mr. Brandon said was addicted to quarrelling with the men.
Q. These were all long-date men. A. Yes.
Q. And you took them back ? A. Yes. John Breen has been in the shoemaker's shop ever since, and does his work as well as anyone else.
Q. Did you force the Company to take any of these long date men ? A. No.
Q. Had the surgeon passed them ? A. Except one or two. McCabe, John Fair and McKeown he had passed. Thomas Brooks was a man who is now employed in the shoemaker's shop. He is as capable of work as any one in the prison.
Q. Why did the Company reject Brooks ? A. They said he had something the matter with his leg, and so he had when he entered, but the doctor pronounced him fit for work, and I tendered him and they refused him.
Q. Were most of these men pronounced fit for labour by the surgeon ? A. Yes.
Q. But you did not force the Company to take them ? A. No ; I told Mr. Brandon I regretted it, and it would be an advantage to the Company to have these two young men.
Q. What do you find as a general thing with these prisoners in their disposition ; are they given to malicious destruction of property, or damaging machinery wilfully ? A. I do not think there have been more than three cases of the kind brought under my notice—damaging machinery, that is just taking a spring out, there was one case of that ; another case was sawing bone work with the Company's saw. Of course this was put a stop to at once, and the man well punished.

By Mr. Gordon.

Q. Did that improve the saw ? A. I do not know whether it damaged the saw or not, but the foreman said it would, if continued.

By Mr. Langmuir.

Q. The man was punished? A. Very severely punished, in irons.
Q. Only three cases have come to your notice ? A. Yes.
Q. They would, if serious ? Yes, immediately.

By Mr. Gordon.

Q. What was the third case ? A. Something connected with a churn—altering or injuring the paint-work or something like that ; I read out the orders to the prisoners that any of them would be punished with corporal punishment for injuring machinery.

By Mr. Langmuir.

Q. Have any of the Company's officers reported damage to property except these ? A. None except these ; they have reported sometimes missing files ; I have examined the prisoners' cells ; sometimes they will take a file for working bone-work or something of that kind ; it is found afterwards, and immediately restored to the Company.
Q. In your official capacity, have you had occasion to enquire of the Company's officers of the manner in which these prisoners performed their work, both in the manufacture of cars and in the new industry ? A. It was my practice when Mr. Baines was at the head, to go round among the different foremen, and enquire if they were satisfied with the work of the prisoners ; the general answer was that they were perfectly satisfied, and in some instances that free men could not work better.
Q. Many of these are not there now ? Q. Yes, they have left.
Q. Were there any very marked instances at any time ? Was there a test of manufacturing cars by free men against prison labour? A. One day, I happened to make a match between free labour men and prisoners, and in 30 wheels the free labour men had 7 failures, and the prisoners only three.
Q. That is the quality of the work ? A. Yes ; that was two years ago.

By Mr. Gordon.

Q. Was the casting all done by prisoners? A. Yes, in this case; free labour men came in, and they wanted to test them.

By Mr. Langmuir.

Q. How long has the present industry been in force? A. Since the last Spring twelve months.
Q. Have you made similar enquiries in regard to that? A. I have.
Q. What has been the result? A. I have found universal satisfaction. I spoke to the foreman of the brush shop, and he said he had excellent men, and no free labour men could do better; he told me that on two occasions; the foreman of the machine shop said the same thing.
Q. Have you been very anxious to find out the actual capacity of these men to perform a day's labour? A. For months past Mr. Brandon and others have complained to me they thought they ought to get more labour out of the prisoners; I have said, "I should be happy to meet your views if you will arrive at some decision as to what a prisoner can do, which I cannot." This went on for weeks and weeks; at last I wrote to them a letter, which I should like to produce for the information of the Commission; I said, "You had better write to me officially about it." and I got a letter from Mr. Brandon about it, to which I replied.
Q. You received a letter from one of the officers, calling your attention to the fact that not sufficient work was got from the prisoners? A. Yes, in the box factory.
Q. What is the date of your reply? A. March 14th; it might have been a complaint verbally by the foreman.
Q. What was the tenor of it? A. That the prisoners did not turn out a sufficient number of boxes in their daily labour.
Reply put in.

[Exhibit "O."]

Q. Did you have any information from the officers as to what constituted a day's labour? A. Not for some time—probably a month.
Q. Before they took notice of your letter? A. Yes, they took verbal notice of it by acknowledging it and saying they were making up some statistics.
Q. Have you those statistics? A. Afterwards I had a letter, signed by Mr. Bailey, complaining of the want of a proper number of guards in the prison, and also of the pails not being turned out in the number they ought to be, I am not certain about the other, whether it was a letter or not.
Letter of May 8th, put in.

[Exhibit "P."]

Witness, continuing.—I did not reply to that because it was signed by Mr. Bailey, Mr. McBean, the Managing Director, was absent, and it was necessary for me to ascertain whether he had authorised such a letter being written, and to find what the outside labour was.

By Mr. Gordon.

Q. Mr. Bailey is secretary of the Company, is he not? A. I was not aware of it then. I handed the letter to Mr. McBean when he returned, and he said I was to take no notice of it whatever: "Don't take any notice of it; it will be all right by and by."

By Mr. Langmuir.

Q. Did you take any notice of it? A. No.
Q. Did you make enquiry as to whether their statement was correct as to the product of outside labour? A. I understood that with outside labour they could throw 90 a day.
Q. Did you give a stint to the prisoners then? A. Yes; then I consulted the foreman of the broom shop and he said he would be satisfied with 60. Then I informed the

prisoners they had to turn out 60 or 65 a day, which they immediately did and they have stuck to it since.

Q. In regard to the pails, Mr. McBean said take no notice of it at present? A. He said "It will all come right ; take no notice of it." There was no disrespect to Mr. Bailey in not taking notice of it. Mr. McBean is the Managing Director, from whom I always receive my orders.

Q. Were you ever informed Mr. Bailey was Secretary-Treasurer of the Company? A. No.

Q. Were you aware, when you received this letter, that Mr. Bailey was the Secretary-Treasurer? A. No, only by signature. He puts himself Secretary when he writes to me.

Q. How long has he been so? A. I do not know. I have never been officially informed anything about him.

Q. With whom have you officially come in contact? A. Mr. Brandon and Mr. McBean.

Q. And you have come in contact with them always? A. Always.

Q. Why did you wish to consult Mr. McBean? A. Because he was absent.

Q. Had you previously spoken with him about it? A. He had spoken about it : "They are not doing enough ; I do not wish you to take any action about it, but I will speak to the Government about it ; I know prisoners cannot do as much as free men."

Q. Did you ever receive from Mr. Brandon as an officer of the Company, other than this letter, what was considered a good day's work on the lathes with pails? A. Mr. Brandon came to me one day, after this I think. He said he had got 500 pails turned out one day by a certain number of prisoners on a lathe. I said : "How did you manage this?" He said : "I gave them one cent a pail above 375." I said I would not tolerate that ; it was contrary to prison rules and subversive of discipline and would not do. He said it would be advantageous to the Company. I said I would not allow it without the sanction of the Government.

Q. Had he paid them? A. He had not paid them, but he promised to pay them. I told the foreman to report anything of the kind again. Then they complained that the number fell off in a day. I then enquired how many a day they should do. He said 325 or 335 a day. I sent for the prisoners and told them I expected them to accomplish that work during the day, and if they did not I would punish them severely until they did. They set to work, and turned out the amount required per day, and I said : "I will not allow anything of this to be done in a rush ; you shall work all day long ; no idleness ; but you must accomplish the 325."

Q. Did they do so to your satisfaction? A. They did so.

Q. Had you any complaints from Mr. Brandon or anyone else after that? A. None.

Q. What is your opinion of this industry as compared with the car building industry? A. I should think it far more adapted to the industry of a prison.

Q. I am talking about the labour, not about its paying? A. We can supervise it far better. It is more under control.

Q. Do you think it is a kind of industry that is well suited to prison labour? A. Yes, and one which prisoners take an interest in.

Q. It is only a question of good management and organization, then, provided you can sell the goods, to make it successful? A. I should think so ; that is my opinion after observation.

Q. What is your opinion as to whether the organization and management of the Canada Car Company is a good one? A. It requires improvement decidedly. I do not see why a shop like the north machine shop should be filled everywhere with unfinished pails, tubs and churns. I am not a mechanic, but I think when you turn out a pail or other article, it should be moved out of the workshop into a reception shop, a storage. Now, it is impossible to supervise the men properly. The whole place is stacked up to the ceiling.

Q. Have you complained about that? A. Months and months.

BY MR. GORDON.

Q. To whom? A. To Mr. Brandon and Mr. McBean, twenty times, I suppose. The other day I said, "Mr. McBean, if you do not move these things, I will move them by force ; I will not have them here at all ; you must tell Mr. Brandon to take them away."

Q. What reply did Mr. McBeau make? A. He said he would go and see, and he came back to say it was impossible to take steps at present.
Q. Why? A. Because, he said, they were not finished.

BY MR. LANGMUIR.

Q. Were you led to understand why they were not finished? A. No, he did not say. The foreman said, "Material is wanted; they are unfinished, and you cannot remove them till they are finished."
Q. That is a great drawback to the discipline and supervision of the shop? A. It is impossible to supervise the men properly because they are hidden in little batches.
Q. Are they not compelled under contract to keep the shops clear? A. Yes, and remove the manufactured goods, There is the large foundry only about a third occupied.
Q. Any other places for storage? A. There is the upper part of the south machine shop, and the foundry, an enormous establishment.
Q. In going through the shops do you find the men always busy at work, occupied, properly engaged? A. No, I frequently find different lathes idle. It has been so for months and months.
Q. What are the answers when you enquire? A. I ask the guard why the men are not properly occupied at work. He says "It is not my fault, but the want of material." I speak to the foreman and he says "I have no work for them."
Q. Does he ever tell you that it is because he cannot get proper prisoners? A. No.
Q. Did he ever, on any one occasion, tell you it was because the prisoners were not of a proper kind? A. Not a single instance of the kind has taken place since I have been in the prison.
Q. Have we increased the number of guards this year? A. Yes, one. That is in the shoemaker's shop.
Q. Is it true that one guard has charge of 70 prisoners, some of them 500 or 600 yards apart, as Mr. Bailey says? A. Yes. For instance, take the forge guard, McCormack had charge of the forge, there were 30 or 40 men in the forge, but the yard party is taken out into the yard and works under an officer of the Canada Car Company. If every small working party is to have a guard, we would want 30 or 40 guards. The outside working party is outside the shop.
Q. For a special purpose? A. Every day the same—unloading cars and lumbering and working at the drying kiln. Guard McCormack has charge of that gang attached to his inside gang.
Q. What is the number? A. 65.
Q. In the shops proper, is there, in your opinion, any lack of sufficient guards on the part of the Government? A. Not at all.
Q. But there might be with gangs outside occasionally? A. Yes. This gang is divided into two parts. When that letter was written, there was a guard dismissed, and afterwards I put on another, in the south machine shop.
Q. You have heard what Mr. Bailey said about a lack of discipline—holding conversation—is that allowed? A. Oh, no. They are immediately punished if they are caught. Of course, covering a large space of ground like the Central Prison, prisoners may be seen in conversation by the members of the Canada Car Company, where the foreman being in another part of the ground would not be at the moment. But, as far as we can, we prevent conversation among them.
Q. In the north shop, while it is lumbered up with material, it would be impossible to prevent them? A. Entirely.
Q. Would not that be a fault of the Company? A. Entirely, because of not keeping the shop clear.

The further examination of Captain Prince was deferred.

FREDERICK HILL, called on behalf of the Government, sworn—

BY MR. LANGMUIR.

Q. You are a guard in the Central Prison? A. Yes.

Q. When were you appointed guard? A. For the Canada Car Company, Jan. 20th, 1875.
Q. How do you mean? A. The Canada Car Company then had to supply two guards.
Q. You were employed by the Canada Car Company then, first? A. Yes, sworn in on approbation.
Q. And permanently sworn in, when? A. In March, 1875.

By Mr. Gordon.

Q. Do you mean the Car Company paid you? A. The Warden swore me in, but I never received pay from the Canada Car Company.
Q. You did not get that pay? A. I had to wait three months.

By Mr. Langmuir.

Q. What was your position first, when you were appointed? A. On the wall, and on night duty.
Q. How long did you continue there? A. Four or five months, and then put on the front grounds.
Q. In charge of prisoners? A. Yes.
Q. What are you doing now? A. In charge of the paint shop.
Q. How many prisoners? A. There are two shops included in the one.
Q. Alongside of each other? A. Yes. There are 37 men in the two shops.
Q. What is the other shop? A. Paint and carpenter shop. There is only a wooden partition between the two.
Q. Is that the average number of men you have had lately? A. 32 was the number on the 30th April, when I went in. Now there are 37.
Q. How are the 37 men employed? A. It would be almost next to impossible to say how, from day to day, because they would be at different kinds of work.
Q. But painting and graining? A. Yes. There would be two men to grain, and there would be two varnishing, two striping, four puttying, two men painting the pails, three men baling, putting the handles on the tubs and pails, and one man packing the pails into dozens ready for shipping, and one shipper. He ships the articles for the Company. That is about 17. That is the paint shop.
Q. What is the other shop you supervise—the carpenter's shop? A. I could not tell the articles they are working at.
Q. Tell me what they are at? A. A man named Cook would be sawing the legs of the churns off to a proper length with a Tennent saw. The next man would be assisting to fit the iron castings to the union churns.
Q. Where are the castings made? A. I think they are made down town and brought up to the north machine shop, all ready to fit. The next is Waddington, making churns. The turning is all done in the north machine shop. The next man, Sindbad, is at the same. Then Smith is making knife boxes.
Q. Do you mean boxes for domestic purposes? A. Yes, the same as you see on tables, separating the knives and the forks. Wade is fitting hose reels for Gordon hose.
Q. Where are they made? A. Made there.
Q. Does he make them altogether? A. No, the material is prepared by machinery in the north machine shop. He puts them all together, and Murray also does this. There are six making boxes.
Q. What kind? A. Dry goods and packing boxes. Then there is a man fitting up. He is making various changes, and so on, for the Company—fitting up forms for lathes. There was a pattern maker, but he went out last Thursday.
Q. Any men cleaning or doing labouring work? A. There is one boy, who carries the glue pots and so on to prevent a more skilled man going. Then there are men making tobacco boxes at the north end of the shop—tobacco caddies. There are three at that.
Q. Will you explain the nature of this graining? Is anything done by machinery? A. No. Of course, it is machinery, but it is not complicated. It is a crank—just simple turning.
Q. Anything mechanical about it? A. No.

Q. How long would it take a green hand to learn it? A. A reasonable man could learn to grain a pail, if the foreman would stop and instruct him, in one day. Of course, in a week, he would be far more able to do it, because there is a certain pressure of the foot required to make a proper impression on the pail.

Q. But with care and application a man may become a good grainer in a week? A. Yes.

Q. What kind of work is done by them? A. Very good; I have heard Mr. McBean express——

Mr. GORDON objected.

Q. As to varnishing—anything intricate about that? A. No, it is very simple; they just dip it in and turn the pail round; it is put on a spindle, and they turn a handle like grinding an organ.

Q. What is the nature of striping; is that done by hand? A. It is put on a spindle similar to painting and varnishing, and they hold the brush against while turning it round.

Q. It requires a little practice? A. At the outside 3 or 4 days; but any man going into a paint shop sees how not to daub the outside of the pail.

Q. As to puttying? A. Any man who has any head at all could do that.

Q. What do you call painting? A. Painting the outside of the pail; after the pail has been puttied, it has to have one coat of white paint; that is done similarly to the varnishing process; it is put on a regular spindle for it.

Q. Putting the handles on—is that very difficult? A. A man could thoroughly understand how to do that in a day or in half an hour you might say.

Q. A packer—is there any great trick about that? A. No.

Q. The shipper—the same thing? A. Yes.

Q. Have you a great many painters come into the prison—men whose former occupation was painting? A. I have asked the former occupation of any man who has come into my gang; one man in the paint shop was formerly a pail painter, and worked in the paint shop at Cleveland.

Q. Have you many? A. Only two. I had three, but one has gone out.

Q. Is it important for a man to be a painter? A. We have a carriage painter as well, I did not speak of him.

Q. Then, as far as these seventeen men are concerned, as far as your opinion goes, can men who are bodily fit learn all that is required to be learned in a week, so that they are worth as much as any man outside would be in a week? A. Yes, thoroughly.

Q. What is sawing with a Tennent saw? A. Just putting the leg in, and there is a mark and it is sawn off?

Q. Is that difficult to learn? A. No.

Q. Fitting castings—must a man be a machinist to do that? A. No. There is a little crank that goes on the outside of the churn. The hole may not be quite large enough for it to go in, and he takes a round file for it.

Q. That is not very difficult? A. No. The foreman is there to give any instruction.

Q. Making packing boxes—is that a difficult operation? A. No. All there is to do is to put the two edges together.

Q. They can all be attained very quickly, with a few rare exceptions? A. Yes. The most experience would be required in the construction of the churns, and we have men at this who were professional carpenters outside.

Q. They become handy at once? A. Yes We have Waddington, who has eighteen months, at the churns. He was a carpenter outside.

Q. Have you a carpenter at the boxes? A. We have one man, John Williams, who came in this morning.

Q. The pattern maker? A. He was a thoroughly experienced man.

Q. A very capital man was he? A. He did the best, I fancy, of any who were in the prison; they were always calling his powers into work.

Q. Did the Company consider him an excellent pattern maker? A. Yes.

Q. Are these men kept always fully employed? A. No.

Q. Is that the fault of the Government or the fault of the Company? A. Since I have been in the shop, since 30th April—and orders were issued then—it was the first shop I was in; I was doing Government work previous to this——there was a lack of material to exact the proper work, and I made complaint to the Warden.

Q. What material? A. Varnish from the 18th June to the 30th June.

By Mr. Gordon.

Q. How do you know there was a lack of varnish? A. By conversation with the foreman.

Q. Were men kept from work in consequence of a lack of varnish? A. The men were at work, but not in regard to painting, as they would have been otherwise.

By Mr. Langmuir.

Q. Did the foreman tell you there was a lack of varnish? A. Yes.

Q. Were the prisoners delayed for any other reason? A. There were eight men idle one hour and a half, because there was no material coming over from the north machine shop, and they stood on the floor with their arms folded.

By Mr. Gordon.

Q. Give us the date of that? A. 28th May.

By Mr. Langmuir.

Q. Why? A. There was nothing for them to do—no tubs or pails coming over. We sent over to the north machine shop, and there was nothing coming over, so I made them stand up and fold their arms; that was the only time I have ever had occasion to fall any men in. I had gone to Mr. Brandon and the foreman to ask if there was anything for them to do—they had been puttying up—and to say that, if there was nothing, they would have to stand on the floor; and I was told by the foreman that he had been told to give them something to do, but on no account to have them standing on the floor.

Q. Did he give the men anything to do? A. Piling up pails and taking them out into the foundry and that.

Q. Did they take away any unfinished, unvarnished or unpainted? A. They took some unvarnished into the packing shop.

Q. Did they bring them back again? A. They would have been, but they shifted the stuff out and varnished them there.

By Mr. Gordon.

Q. You came in in April last? A. Yes.
Q. Whose place was it you took? A. Guard Mansell's.
Q. Where did he go? A. I think he was sick the first day that he went.
Q. Is he dismissed? A. Not that I know of.
Q. He is given some other place? A. Yes.
Q. Do you know why you were substituted for him? A. I do not know.
Q. You did not hear that Guard Mansell had been ordered to leave on account of the complaint of the Company—that he did not attend to his duty? A. I may have heard so.
Q. Do you know that, when he was in charge there, one of the prisoners allowed the varnish in a barrel to run dry? A. I do not know anything about it.
Q. And that, in consequence of that, he was ordered to leave? A. I do not know anything about it.
Q. Now, with regard to this graining business that you say is so easy to learn, have you seen, since you have been in the shop, any unskilful work in the graining of these pails? A. I have seen at times that Mr. Brandon has complained about the graining being a little too dark or too light, and the foreman has consequently altered the colour to suit.
Q. How often? A. It might have been once or twice, or more.
Q. Any complaint as to being put on badly? A. Not to my knowledge.

Q. Was any complaint made as to the mould being injured by the prisoners? A. There was.

Q. What happened to the mould? A. I did not examine it. Mr. Brandon made a report to me, and I sent in the written report to the Warden; the date was the 15th May. Mr. Brandon reported that prisoner George Hill had been sent to clean a mould, and that he had, to a certain extent, spoiled it. I wrote a note to the Warden, and the man was taken inside, and the Warden and Mr. Brandon had some conversation about it.

Q. Do you know that that would cost the Company $50? A. I do not.

Q. What was done to the man when he was taken in? A. I cannot say the nature of the punishment.

Q. Was he punished? A. He was.

Q. Did he come back at once? A. He came back on the 16th.

Q. When did this happen—on the morning of the 15th? A. I could not say. I rather think it was in the forenoon, between 10 and 11 o'clock. He came back on the 16th.

Q. Morning or afternoon? A. He resumed work at 10 o'clock on the 16th.

Q. In the meantime, was his place supplied? A. By a man named George Moscow.

Q. What did he do? A. Took up painting—what the foreman set him to.

Q. Had he been in the shop before? A. Not while I was in charge of it.

Q. This new prisoner was put on the work that the other man had been doing? A. No, they do not put them on the same individual work.

Q. Did they put anyone on the same work? A. Yes, some older man, and gave this man puttying, or something else.

Q. When this man came back on the 16th, how did he work? A. Just the same as usual.

Q. Have you required to give particular attention to this man since? A. No, I have never been called to this man in particular.

Q. Are not your instructions to give particular attention to this man? A. Not particularly, more than others in the shop.

Q. Since he spoiled the mould in this way? A. No.

Q. In regard to the box work, you say it is pretty easy work? A. I mean to say it does not require a large knowledge of carpentering to do it. The timber is sawn the exact length, and all needed is to put the pieces together.

Q. Do you know that 500 of these boxes have been returned to the Company's hands in consequence of unskilful work? A. No, I do not.

Q. Do you know that there are a large number of boxes lying at the foundry at this time? A. No, I do not; I rather think not.

Q. As to the idle men, I understood you to say there was only one occasion when you put the men in the centre of the room because they had nothing to do? A. Yes.

Q. On other occasions they were put at something? A. Yes.

Q. Either carrying tubs into the foundry—the manufactured material—or sorting the shop, or something—always occupied, more or less? A. Yes, except on the one occasion with 8 men.

Q. Have you had complaint made to you of things being stolen from these shops, putty-knives and things of that class, for instance? A. The foreman in the carpenter's shop, some six weeks or two months ago complained about losing a putty-knife of his own, which he had brought for the convenience of the men putting the churns together, and asked me to look out for it. I did so, but was never successful in finding it.

Q. Anything else—material or tools? A. Not that I recollect.

Q. Were other complaints made of brushes and other things being destroyed? A. There were complaints, but before I went into the shop. A pot of green paint was brought back which had been found in the snow. It was supposed to have been stolen before I went there.

Q. Since you have been there, have there been any complaints of brushes or material destroyed by the prisoners? A. Not to my knowledge. I have never heard of it.

Q. Have you been accustomed to prison labour before you came to the prison? A. I was sailing for 14 years before I went to the prison—sailor and marine diver.

Q. You have altogether 37 men under you. Have you a change in those men once a week? A. I can tell you every change made since I have been in the shop. On the 5th

May, Maclear. He was an extra man at painting pails; he had been once before in the prison and had been working in the pail shop in Cleveland. He came back then, and Mr. Brandon wished him placed instead of one other man. On the 7th a man was sent in sick, and we did not get another in his place because it was half-past five.

Q. Did he come back on the 8th? A. Yes.
Q. Was he fit for work? A. Yes. On the 11th, William Denton, discharged and George Swan in his place. On the 15th, George Hill sent in under punishment and George Moscow in the lieu of him. On the 16th, a man sent into his cell sick and John Donahue came in his place.
Q. At what o'clock? A. I have not the hour.
Q. What was he doing? A. He was baling pails.
Q. Did the other man know anything about baling pails? A. I do not know that he did.
Q. Was he put in the first man's place? A. Yes.
Q. Have you an account of what was done that day, in baling pails? A. No. On the 17th, Snooks, who had been sent in sick on the 7th, came back. I make a mistake; Moscow came in his place; he came back, and Moscow was returned to the yard gang.
Q. He was a better man, then? A. Yes, he was a carriage painter. On the 19th, at one o'clock, one additional man was tendered to the Company, who professed to be a painter. On the 26th, prisoner John Sweeney was sent to the dark cell.
Q. What for? A. For skylarking.
Q. When? A. During his work.
Q. What was he doing? A. He was a painter by profession. This man had been reported by the Prison Surgeon unfit for labour, but Mr. Brandon would have him, knowing he was a painter. I said, "Sweeney is reported unfit for prison labour, and the Warden is going to send him back to the Lunatic Asylum." I said: "He will joke, and make the other men laugh."
Q. He was punished for skylarking, though fit for the Lunatic Asylum. A. Yes. My view and the Surgeon's are not the same.
Q. Sometimes you and the Surgeon differ as to the capability of a man to do a day's work? A. Yes. I am not proficient enough to understand that.
Q. Have you had occasion to differ with the Surgeon since you have been there? A. It is not a part of my duty to do so.
Q. Have you had a different opinion? A. No. J. Streakle came in place of Sweeney.
Q. Did he come back again? A. He was kept in his cell then as rather troublesome. Then we sent him out to the Company. He was sent painting cars, and we never charged him. On the 29th, the foreman of the carpenter's shop complained of John Baxter, a man with heart disease. He was making boxes, and was in for a long term—2 years—and they substituted Waddington, who has 18 months, in his place.
Q. This was the man the Surgeon had passed as a man fit for duty? A. No, I think, in the Warden's evidence, he remarked that the Surgeon had reported him unfit for prison labour. He was not to do any hard work.
Q. How was he handed to the Company? A. I do not know. Sweeney was discharged from the prison and John Clancy substituted. On the 31st, H. Johnson, new man, painter. George Swan, discharged on the 20th; William Anderson in lieu of Swan.
Q. Johnson was again under punishment on 18th July? A. Yes.
Q. What for? A. Giving some insolence to the foreman, talking something to him as of his knowledge of painting.
Q. That was at 9:30 in the morning? A. Yes.
Q. How long was he away? A. I cannot say.
Q. J. Ray on the 26th is reported sick? A. Yes. That is to-day, another man, professional carpenter, came in his place.

[Statement in detail to be prepared by the witness.]

BY THE CHAIRMAN.

Q. When these men go out from these various causes and another man is substituted, where is he brought from? A. From the yard gang.

Q. He is taken from among those who are already engaged for the work of the Company? A. No. At present all the surplus men that the Company do not require are at digging drains and making other sheds round the hospital and that kind of work. In the event of a man being sent in sick or for punishment, a notice goes to a sergeant of the prison, and he takes one of the Government men and puts him in lieu of this man.

EDWARD GURNEY, junior, called on behalf of the Government, sworn :—

BY MR. LANGMUIR.

Q You are a member of the firm of E. & C. Gurney & Co., founders? A. Yes.
Q. Where? A. In Toronto and Hamilton.
Q. Where is your manufactory in Toronto? A. On King Street West, west of Brock Street.
Q. How many men are you employing at the present time? A. Between 100 and 200.
Q. According to the volume of work you are doing? A. Yes.
Q. Are you in the habit of having apprentices? A. Yes.
Q. What ages do you take them at? A. From 18 to 23.
Q. What do you pay your apprentices? A. According to the time they have been with us. We commence at from $2.50 to $3 per week.
Q. Not below $2.50? A. No.
Q. How long do you retain them generally as apprentices? A. About 3 years.
Q. And up to what sum per week do they reach? A. Well, we pay them $2.50 or $3 during the first year and if, during the year, they show a greater amount of ability than usual, they are placed on a floor to work by the piece, and sometimes they will make more wages in that way. We demand from them, as a consideration for shop room and all that, that they shall make equal to $9 a week before we give them anything for themselves.
Q. You consider immediately on entering your manufactory they are worth to you from $2.50 to $3 per week? A. Oh, no; they are not worth that. We cannot get apprentices in this country at all, and we must give them enough to pay their board. They are really worth nothing at first.
Q. How long does it take them to be worth something? A. Well, a boy would begin to be useful in about 6 months, I should think.
Q. That is as moulders? A. Yes.
Q. Have you any departments of your trade where skilled work is not required? A. Labouring work, yes.
Q. Much of that? A. Not a very great deal, I should think we must employ between 20 and 25 labourers.
Q. What do you pay them? A. $6 to $8 a week.
Q. They have had no knowledge of foundry business up to the time they enter your place? A. No.
Q. What is the size of your premises in Toronto? A. The premises cover two acres.
Q. Including the court on the inside—the quadrangle? A. Yes.
Q. And how many stories high? A. Four stories.
Q. Do you know the superficial area of your buildings? A. About 100,000 square feet.
Q. What are your taxes on the property? A. I think about $2,200 a year.
Q. Does that include your income? A. That is income as well; the taxes on the property would be about $900, taking my own valuation for it.
Q. What do you value your property at? A. $60,000; that is what the buildings cost.
Q. What did the land cost? A. $9,100.
Q. That is $70,000 then. Do you take water from the Commissioners? A. Yes.
Q. What is your water rate per annum? A. During the last four years it has been at the rate of $280 a year; they put a meter on, and it was at the rate of $1,000 a year for a quarter, and $6 a quarter for the rest of the year.

BY MR. GORDON.

Q. Which rate are you going to take? A. I think about $70 a quarter would be about right.

By Mr. Langmuir.

Q. Do you heat your shops? A. Yes.
Q. What does it cost? A. I should think about 75 tons of coal.
Q. I suppose compact shops are much more easily heated than those which are straggling about? A. I should suppose so.
Q. Do you light? A. No.
Q. You have shafting, and boilers, and engines in your shop? A. Yes.
Q. What do you consider the annual value, the percentage value, of boilers, engines, running gear, shafting, main belting, and pulleys and things of that kind? In a general way, what would be the rental of it per annum? A. There is a great shrinkage on that kind of material—a great deal of wear and tear; it would depend on who was to keep that up; if you were renting shafting to me and you agreed to keep it up, you would want more.
Q. The Company have to keep it up for fair wear and tear, but when it is worn out it has to be renewed? A. It would be worth 10 per cent.
Q. Railways do not enter your premises? A. No.
Q. Would you consider it of considerable value to your operations if you had a switch going into your premises? A. No.
Q. It would depend altogether upon the character of the industry? A. Yes; in light goods such as ours, I would not consider a switch going in there of any value at all; it would not be material.

By Mr. Gordon.

Q. Your goods are stoves, and so on? A. Yes.
Q. Ours are pails and brushes—I suppose you would consider these light goods—lighter than stoves? A. Yes.
Q. Would you consider a railway running in would be of much advantage in that case? A. No.

By Mr. Langmuir.

Q. How about large carloads of raw material, lumber, and so on? A. I should think so.

By Mr. Gordon.

Q. Have you not raw material? A. Yes.

By Mr. Langmuir.

Q. Would not that be of advantage to you in that? A. Yes, in that respect; but we do not take that as of much importance; suppose we have 1,800 tons of pig iron coming in a year, we can get that laid down at 25 cents a ton—$450. That would be the real value to us.

By Mr. Gordon.

Q. Would it make much difference whether the road ran right in, or you had to cart it? A. I say $450 a year.
Q. Is that what it costs to cart from the railway depot? A. Yes, that is what would be saved.
Q. That is carting from the railway depot? A. Yes.
Q. Do you not make your contracts to deliver? A. Yes, mostly always. Somebody has to pay for that, I suppose.
Q. How do you know that that would be the cost? A. Because, in purchasing, I have to find out all these things to find out what people can deliver for.
Q. Have you ever acquired the knowledge of the difference between delivering to you at the station and at your factory. A. Yes.
Q. And you say the difference is $450? A. Assuming 1,800 tons as the basis, yes.
Q. You stated seventy-five tons of coal would heat the shops—suppose they were heated by refuse steam? A. One reason why I did not build down on the front was that I would

rather be up in the centre of the town and have the advantage of that, than be in the front for all I could gain by it.

Q. Do you think the advantage of being in the centre of the town would more than compensate you for that? A. Yes, that was my purpose.

Q. If you heated with refuse steam instead of coal, what would be the cost—very large or small? A. It would be less, but you cannot send even exhaust steam through pipes without costing something. It would not be more than a-half.

Q. Would it be less? A. Rather. It would not be that.

Q. As an employer of labour, would you rather pay a good price for a good man, or a smaller price for a poor man? A. A poor man we never keep at all.

Q. Do you find it would be too expensive and impolitic to employ poor men at low rates? A. Yes.

Q. You would rather pay a good price for a good man? A. Yes.

Q. With regard to these apprentices, I understood you to say they would not be of much use to you for six months? A. No.

Q. Would they pay their way at the end of six months? A. Yes, they would begin to turn the corner then. In the early time they turn out a good deal of work, but so much is spoiled, it costs so much to mould the iron for them and it is sent back as scrap.

Q. Do you think at the end of six months an apprentice would earn $3.50 a week? A. Yes.

Q. These apprentices are bound to you for three years? A. Yes.

Q. And they have the inducement of getting on the floor and working by the piece at the end of the year? A. Yes.

Q. Have you had any experience with prison labour? A. No.

Q. Would you care to? A. I do not know anything about it. I feel sometimes as if I would like to thrash some of my men.

By Mr. Brockway.

Q. What kind of work is yours—castings? A. Stove castings.

By Mr. Noxon.

Q. Moulding is the most difficult part of your work, is it not? A. Stove mounting is about the finer part of the work now.

Q. You employ a class of men as drillers, and so on, a class of mechanical work of that kind that no class of mechanical skill would form it? A. Labouring men would begin to be useful in a month.

Q. In the lower grades of your work an ordinary man would be quite useful in a month A. Yes.

By Mr. Gordon.

Q. Is casting a delicate kind of work? A. Very.

Q. If a man does not understand it, he is likely to make a mistake? Yes.

The Commission then adjourned.

FRIDAY, July 27th.

The Commission met at 10 o'clock.

JOHN W. LANGMUIR, recalled, and examination continued :—

BY MR. HARDY.

Q. Did you receive a telegram from the Warden of the Cleveland Workhouse, stating that he cannot come ? A. Yes. I had arranged to have him here, but I have just received a telegram from him saying he had not received my letter, although I addressed it properly. Probably there was some interruption in the mail. In his telegram he says he cannot come under two weeks.

BY MR. GORDON.

Q. I think you said in your previous evidence that you were theoretically of opinion that short term labour could be more profitably employed if in Government hands, than if let out to contractors ? A. I have always held the theory, and it is not singular to me, but it is generally held by prison officials that the Government authorities, or the authorities having control of the prison, are the best ones to manage and direct prison labour, whether in a long or short date prison.

Q. More especially in a short date ? A. I do not know that I have ever expressed that opinion.

Q. Does it not apply more to short date than long ? A. I do not know that it does.

Q. What is your opinion on the point ? A. I think it is equally applicable to both long and short.

Q. When this Central Prison was first projected, the intention was that the Government would work this labour themselves, was it not ? A. It was my intention—not the Government's. My intention was to introduce the most advanced mode of utilizing prison labour, and all specialists held, and do hold that theory, that the control of the discipline and the labour, the character of the industry can be better directed and managed in the hands of the controlling authorities of the prison. I wished to carry that out, but I fully recognised the very great difficulties in the way, and knew I would have to meet them when I brought down my scheme to the Government of the day.

Q. How was it then that you came to give the contract to the Car Company, and not to work the labour yourself? A. For various reasons, having regard to this fact, that, for a manufacturing appropriation to carry on the prison industry, it would require to come every year before Parliament. The fullest kind of information would require to be given to Parliament, by way of report, and before committees.

Q. Is that appropriation in regard to material ? A. Manufacturing on Government account.

Q. Material ? A. Material, certainly. In talking with members of Parliament, and I think members of the Government as well, I found it was going to be attended with a great deal of difficulty, and in fact I saw it was going to endanger the scheme to a certain extent. I therefore modified my views about that, and in order to make it a certain thing —the establishment of an industrial prison in this Province—I thought it was better to make a sure thing of it, by leaving it to a contractor, if we could get him. The whole thing is then given in my reports. Then we received letters from the Canada Car Company, or rather, then, the Steel Iron Works, making application for additional lands, and the whole transaction sprung out of that.

Q. Did you feel there would be any difficulty, if the Government took it, in organizing the industries ? A. If left in my care, I should have taken good care to have the very best men in charge.

Q. Did you feel there would be difficulty in organizing, and is that one reason ? A. I frankly confess I saw there would be some difficulty. I could not see my way that the Government could pay the salaries, sometimes, that such men might ask to manage that industry. That was one.

Q. And also that it was probable it might not be a success for the first year or two? A. As all schemes of that kind, I certainly thought it would have to pass through an experimental stage to a reasonable degree.

Q. Had you in your own mind fixed any time that it would take before the organization was perfect? A. I thought it would be in the second year.

Q. You did not take into consideration, then, the change in the labour market and the markets generally? A. I certainly had not calculated the chances so closely as that.

Q. Such a crisis as we have lately met with you did not take into consideration? A. I frankly confess I did not foresee the stagnation in railway supplies and goods of that kind.

Q. Had you in your own mind fixed upon any amount necessary to get from the Government to put in suitable machinery, if the Government had carried it on themselves? A. I had not fixed it. I had not got so far as that. As my reports will show, I was urging upon the Government the necessity of deciding the character of the industries, in order that we might be able to decide upon the shop room and the arrangement of the shops; and, while these recommendations were going on to the Government, this presented itself in regard to the Canada Car Company.

Q. But did you consider that a considerable appropriation would be necessary? A. Most assuredly it would be necessary, and that was another reason why I fell into leasing the labour by contract, because I knew there might be a difficulty in getting an additional appropriation from Government for the machinery.

Q. And the Car Company having agreed to provide that themselves, it relieved you to a certain extent? A. It did.

Q. Are there any other prisons or reformatories in the Province under our control the labour of which you let to contractors? A. Yes.

Q. What are they? A. The labour of little lads at the Reformatory, Penetanguishene.

Q. What industries are there? A. Only cigar manufactures.

Q. How many boys do they take? A. Eighty.

Q. Are they bound to take them? A. Yes.

Q. Have they the option of more? A. Up to 100, but if they take that number they must continue it.

Q. How long is the contract for? A. Five years.

Q. When was it made? A. On the 28th October, 1872.

Q. Have they the option of an extension? A. It is renewable by mutual agreement.

Q. What are the terms of the contract? A. For the first year, 15 cents; for the second year, 20 cents; for the third year, 25 cents; for the fourth year, 35 cents; for the fifth year, 40 cents, and a bonus to be given to each boy in addition for the second year, three cents; the third year, four cents; the fourth year, five cents; and for the fifth year, six cents, by the contractors.

Q. What age boys do they take? A. Under 12, I think.

Q. For what terms are these boys in there? A. From six months to five years.

Q. What is the average? A. I cannot tell you. I should say about two years. I am quite sure it cannot go over that.

Q. The boys have to do a certain amount—there is a certain stint, is there not? A. No; the bonus is for industrial habits and good conduct.

BY THE CHAIRMAN.

Q. Is that to be given under all conditions absolutely? A. Under all conditions, unless they have forfeited it by bad conduct.

BY MR. GORDON.

Q. Has the contractor the choice of the boys? A. He has not. He is to get a certain number over twelve and a certain number under, and he must take a certain number under.

Q. Cannot he choose the number over and under? A. No; as a matter of fact we do allow him to have a good deal to say in the matter.
Q. There is nothing to prevent him from having it? A. No.
Q. Nothing in the contract? A. No. We have a considerable amount of unemployed labour.

BY MR. HARDY.

Q. How many? A. He must have 80 or up to 100.

BY MR. GORDON.

Q. Have you any complaints as to the work of these boys from the contractor? A. Now and again.
Q. What is the nature of the complaints? A. That they do not do as well as they should, which, of course, is very natural, being boys.
Q. Any other kind? A. Occasionally of stealing cigars.
Q. Any others? A. A few times, of not making the most of material, and possibly on one or two occasions of cutting straps or something. The complaints of the grosser kind have been very few indeed. I have gone up frequently and tried to settle the matter, but I found the complaints were very much magnified.
Q. The complaints were so frequent that you thought it advisable to go up and make enquiry? A. Not at all. On one occasion I went up and made a special enquiry, and found the complaints were so very much magnified that I think it was shown to the contractors.
Q. Have there been any complaints with regard to delays in furnishing the boys, taking them away for punishment or anything of that kind? A. No. The complaint on the other side was that we did not furnish enough.
Q. No complaints for loss of time by the contractor? A. None.
Q. Have you had any claim on the ground that the labour was not such as it should be? A. I have.
Q. What is the claim? A. They claim the pay should not go above twenty-five cents, owing to the stagnation in trade; German goods were putting their goods out of the market.
Q. When was this complaint made? A. A year ago.
Q. Was this the first complaint? A. I think so.
Q. Have you had a claim for damages on account of loss of time or the boys not doing work? A. None.
Q. Do you furnish the contractor with anything in addition to the labour? A. Shop room, heated.
Q. No machinery? A. None.
Q. Water? A. By the pailful.
Q. Do you charge him by the pailful? A. No; it is for the boys to drink—not in the hydraulic business.
Q. Light? A. They do not work at night. They only work eight hours per day. That is the arrangement.
Q. Eight hours per day? A. I think it is only six. There are three sessions of school, and the contract is subordinate to the school.
Q. Is that deducted from the contractor? A. If we do not give him the right time it is deducted. School is the only thing.
Q. Do you barberize the boys? A. Their beards are not growing yet.
Q. When you take them away for any of these things, is that deducted? A. No.
Q. Are there any other prisons where you let the labour? A. None.
Q. You had one of the reports from Cleveland? A. Yes.
Mr. GORDON put in the report of the Cleveland Directors.

[Exhibit R.]

By Mr. Hardy.

Q. They take in both boys and women? A. Young men, not boys; but there are women.

Q. What work are the women at? A. Paper boxes.

Q. It has been very nearly self sustaining? A. Yes, last year; and the Warden showed me it would be quite self-sustaining this year.

A. How old are the boys? A. There are very few boys,—very much the same as our own in regard to that; about the same number as we have, as far as the youths are concerned.

By the Chairman.

Q. In this statement of the periods of sentence of the prisoners, I see there are prisoners of two and a half years up to five years. They are not sentenced directly to the prison? A. There are some transferred from the Reformatory; two years is the longest for prisoners sentenced direct. Boys reported to be incorrigible have been removed from the Reformatory to the Central Prison, but now we only remove them to the Penitentiary.

Q. Then in fact there will be no prisoners over two years that the contractors can avail themselves of? A. No.

Q. As a matter of fact and experience, do you think that men of this class who are found in this prison, are not physically and mentally impaired in some respects by the kind of life they lead generally before they go there? A. Undoubtedly they are; a portion of them are impaired; but we have a very large selection, and we compel the surgeons of the gaols to report that they are fit, and do not remove them from the gaols until they are reported fit. They remain in the gaol until they are reported fit, physically and mentally, to do a day's work, and then they undergo another medical examination when they come to the prison, so really there are two examinations by medical men before they are tendered to the contractors.

Q. But don't you suppose that this kind of life has a permanent effect upon them? A. Naturally it must. They must be impaired to a certain extent, but I do not hold the opinion that some do, that the proportion is so very great. We find that many of those prisoners who are included in statistics as being intemperate, are, as a general thing, rather above the average—intelligent, sharp, and that many of them are exceedingly physical and active. Many of them must certainly impair their constitutions by their vicious habits.

Q. Can you tell us what is the cost of keeping prisoners? A. From 11 to 12½ cents per day for food. It is from 42 to 46 cents per day all told—including food, clothing, the salaries' and wages' list, everything,—varying with the requirements of the prison, from time to time. In that we allow an amount for current repairs.

Q. Do you know the cost of keeping prisoners in any places in the United States—in Detroit, for instance? A. I have had occasion to inquire as to that, but I cannot furnish you with the exact figures. I think that it is about the same in Detroit as with ourselves, but in many penitentiaries it is a great deal more, for instance in the Cleveland workhouse.

Q. Do you know if, in these prisons, which you have referred to as being self-supporting, the business is carried on on account of the prison? A. It is in Cleveland, Detroit and Chicago.

Q. In making up their accounts do they make allowance for the capital invested in the machinery? A. I believe they do. I know they do in Detroit; they keep an account of each shop; they take an inventory of the previous year, and then they take an inventory at the close of the year, and charge the amount to the balance. That would indicate that they make an allowance for the value of the plant and machinery. In the Central Prison, we keep the maintenance account entirely separate from everything. I see that in Cleveland, the cost per day is 34¼ cents, which is rather lower than ours. I see also that there are a greater number of boys there than in ours.

By Mr. Brockway.

Q. Are there any prisoners sent directly to the Central Prison here? A. There are.

Q. What proportion are transferred from other prisons? A. I may mention that had the Canada Car Company's Works not stopped in 1875, the prison would have been almost exclusively occupied by prisoners sent direct. The judges were getting into the habit of sending prisoners for short terms, but that was stopped, and they were afterwards sent to the penitentiary.

Q. What was the number removed of those sent to the common gaols? A. About 75 per cent. out of the whole number in the common gaols.

CAPTAIN PRINCE, recalled, and examination continued :—

By Mr. LANGMUIR.

Q. You have got with you the Labour Distribution Book, which shows where the prisoners are? A. Yes.

Q. How were they distributed yesterday? A. North machine shop, 93 men ; south machine shop and works, 19 ; in the yard, 38 employed in loading cars, handling staves, &c. ; steam fitters in the south machine shop, 1 ; blacksmiths' shop, 6 ; broom shop and carpenters' shop, 40 ; paint shop, 17 ; brush shop, 7. There were altogether 221 employed yesterday.

Q. Is that about the proportion generally in the yard? A. Yes, it has been so for months.

Q. The work is all of a labouring character? A. Yes, unloading wood, unloading cars, and putting these staves into proper order.

Q. How many shop guards have you? A. North machine shop, 2 ; forge shop, 1 ; broom shop, 1 ; constructing and paint shop, 1 ; yard gang, 1 ; which includes the south machine shop.

Q. You have other guards in charge of other works? A. Yes, the outside gang has one guard in charge.

Q. There are certain instructions to guards for the performance of their duty? A. Yes, laid down in the rules and regulations. I have also issued orders since they were prepared.

Q. You are aware that free labour is allowed to be introduced to a certain extent by the Company. Do you know the proportion? A. I do not. There is one foreman with every gang.

Q. The contract shows that 43 should be employed. Have the Company ever asked you to allow free labour to go in, and you have prohibited it? A. I have prohibited it in this way, I discharged a prisoner——

Q. Have you refused any free men—any artizans? A. Oh, no.

Q. You would have admitted the 43 if they wished? A. Oh, yes.

Q. There were those men on the lathes—could they have put one man to every lathe if they wished? A. Certainly if they wished to do so.

By Mr. GORDON.

Q. I think you stated yesterday that the work turned out by these men was as good as the work outside—as free labour turned out? A. No, I don't think so. I am not a judge of work at all.

Q. You are the Warden, and you go around and examine the work sometimes? A. I think the work is very neatly done ; I have taken up pails, and they seemed to be very well made.

Q. Do you know of any case of any work being badly done? A. I think there was one time a churn was badly made, and a tub badly painted, or something of that kind.

Q. But you have generally found them to be very well turned out? A. Oh, yes.

Q. Do you remember writing a letter to the Company, dated the 22nd March—you do not state the year—in reference to some work the Company did for you—some buckets, or something of that kind? A. Yes. I sent them this letter :—

(Take in letter marked " Exhibit S.")

Q. That is your experience with regard to the only class of pails or tubs that were manufactured for you? A. Yes, for me.

Q. And yet you came to the conclusion that the work turned out by the prisoners for outside parties is properly made? A. Yes, but this was different work, for they had machinery for it, and the very long time they were in turning out these buckets and pails was just through the want of machinery.

Q. Do you think their work is equally good in the broom department, and brush department? A. I think it is very good indeed.

Q. Have you had any personal experience as to that? A. Not to my knowledge.

Q. Have you occasion to go around and examine the work? A. Yes, I visit the shops three or four times a day. I think the broom work is perfectly admirable.

Q. Do you remember writing a letter of the 7th March, with regard to some brushes turned out for you? A. Yes, I wrote the following letter:—

(Take in letter marked "Exhibit T.")

Q. How can you in the face of that letter, state that the work turned out is good? A. I am speaking of the work done lately. These were made about the beginning of this year. I was so informed by the Superintendent.

Q. Have you had any other experience with regard to the commodities turned out by this Company? A. I do not remember it.

Q. With regard to the prisoners that have been tendered to the Company by the prison authorities, I understood you to say yesterday, that you had not known of a case where a prisoner had been passed by the surgeon, and afterwards found incapable of work? A. I said this—that a prisoner passed by the surgeon would not.

Q. Can you say there was no such case? A. There have been a few cases. A man named Brooks, I remember, was sent to work at the brush shop. He was afterwards found to have an injured leg, and he was sent to the hospital. The doctor made an operation on him, which was successful, and he got well immediately afterwards; was sent back to the brush shop, and the Company would not accept him. He was consequently sent to our shop, and is as well able to work as anybody.

Q. Was that the only case? A. There was another man we tendered, and the doctor said he was perfectly capable of doing any work at which he might sit down. He was sent by mistake.

Q. Do you remember a case where a prisoner was passed by the surgeon. The man said he was unfit for work, and yet was sent into the pail or broom shop. The guards saw he was unfit for work, and after keeping him there for three or four days, he was sent back, and had to go to the hospital. Do you remember that case? A. Yes, I do.

Q. What was the name of that prisoner? A. I do not know the name. There were not more than three or four such cases.

Q. Can you tell us how much time was wasted in that way? A. Their places were supplied by other men. There have been several cases where men are sent to the hospital and their places are supplied by other men. It must be an event which occurs weekly or fortnightly. I think this man's name was Fizzell; he was in the broom shop. He seemed rather delicate after he had been passed by the surgeon, and he was taken from the broom shop and sent to the hospital. The surgeon afterwards said he was quite capable of work, and he was sent back, but the Company refused to take him.

Q. Have you had any complaints as to the guards not doing their duty? A. Two or three times, and the complaints have been immediately acted upon.

Q. Do you remember having received a letter from the Company, dated the 24th April, 1877, with reference to a guard stationed in the paint shop? A. Yes, I received a letter on that subject.

(Letter put in, "Exhibit U.")

I made inquiries about it, and the Sergeant Deputy Warden and Sergeant Dean denied it. I substituted a guard in his place.

Q. Well, you came to the conclusion that the Company was right? A. No, I thought they exaggerated it. He was constantly in the habit of talking, which guards are forbidden to do.

Q. You came to the conclusion that the guard was sufficiently wrong to remove him, and you did it ? A. Yes, I did.

Q. Have you had any other complaint ? A. Yes, I had a complaint with regard to one guard, instead of watching his prisoners, being in the habit of dozing. Mr. Brandon and the foreman of the prisoners gave testimony on oath, and I dismissed the guard.

Q. Have you had any complaint from the Company with regard to insufficient prison inspection ? A. Yes, there was a letter written on the 8th of May.

Q. Is that the only complaint you have had with regard to an insufficiency of guards ? A. The only written complaint, I think.

Q. Do you remember receiving a letter from the Company on the 26th May, 1877, to the same effect ? A. No, I have not got it here.

Mr. GORDON read a letter.

WITNESS.—I think I did receive that letter.

Q. Will you find it and bring it down ? A. I will try.

Q. Now, I will come to the complaints with regard to delays in consequence of men being taken away to the barber shops, and so forth. Have you had any complaints of that kind ? A. In the guards' time books they have deducted so many days for shaving. I have put a memorandum on every weekly book, "This reduction not recognised by me." Why I do so is, because I follow the practice adopted in the United States.

Mr. HARDY.—You will see that the agreement allows two hours each week.

Mr. GORDON.—But they get that on Saturday afternoon, do they not ? A. Yes.

Q. And this time is wholly outside of those two hours ? A. Each prisoner is shaved once a week. There is one man in the room at a time, and after him another is taken in.

Q. Does the guard bring one man to the barber shop, and then take another, or are there any waiting around ? A. The former is my instruction.

Q. But you do not know whether this is done or not ? A. No, I do not know.

Q. That is your letter to the Company, dated March 19th ? A. Yes, that is my letter.

(Exhibit " V.")

Q. Have you received complaints as to putting on men that the Company did not desire ? A. Yes.

Q. Did you receive a letter, dated 15th March, 1877, as to that ? A. I do not remember.

Mr. GORDON read a letter.

WITNESS.—I think I did receive that ; I do not exactly remember it, but I will look and see.

Q. Have you had complaint from the Company for taking men away from their work without any notice from the Company ? A. I do not think so. They spoke one day about taking men away for punishment. I have been verbally spoken to. It was some long time ago, when the prison was first opened.

Q. Do you remember receiving a letter of the 5th March, 1877, on that point ? A. No.

Mr. GORDON read a letter.

WITNESS—I remember receiving that letter.

Q. That prisoner was never returned to the Company ? A. No.

Q. Why not ? A. Because he was not offered to be tendered.

Q. Then the Prison authorities have the first choice in that way ? A. Yes, and we are entitled to men for the domestic work of the Prison.

Q. Do you know why it was that the Company wished to have this man, Irish ? A. Because I believe he was a useful man for clerk ; but I had just discharged my clerk and I wanted him. I substituted a man just as good.

Q. I think the understanding with the Company is, that no prisoners are to be tendered to them under two months' sentence ? A. Yes.

Q. Every day that prisoners come in you furnish the Company with lists of them, and the terms of sentence ? A. Yes.

Q. Look at that list sent on the 17th of July? A. I can say that was a mistake made by the clerk who sent it to the Company.

Q. Look at this sent on the 19th July. Was that a mistake? A. That was a mistake also, as regards these two months' men.

Q. You stated yesterday, in reply to a question by Mr. Langmuir, that the stint of 325 pails per day was fixed by Mr. Brandon? A. I was informed by Mr. Brandon that it was all they required, and by the foreman of the shop.

Q. Notwithstanding that you received a letter from the Secretary of the Company, to the effect that it was unauthorized? A. No, I wanted to see Mr. McBean first. I spoke to him, and asked him if he had seen this letter, and whether it was approved by the directors and himself. He laughed, and said, "Oh, never mind that," or something of that kind, "it will all come right."

Q. Did he say that Mr. Bailey had no authority to write that letter? A. No, he did not say so.

Q. And you had previously recognised Mr. Bailey as secretary of the Company? A. Yes.

Q. That was in reply to your letter of the 14th March? A. Yes.

Q. The reason you wrote that letter was because you did not think that these unskilled men could turn out as much work as skilled labourers? Did you form any idea of what unskilled labourers could do? A. I thought that 600 pails a day was too much even for a skilled man.

Q. Did you make any enquiries as to the work done in other factories? A. I made enquiries about brooms, at Nelson's shop, and I understood that a good man could turn out between 90 and 100 brooms per day.

Q. Did you find the class of brooms from him? A. No; I asked about first-class brooms.

Q. You knew there were different classes of brooms made at the prison? A. Yes, but I merely asked for first-class brooms.

Q. Did you go anywhere else? A. No, I did not.

Q. Did you make enquiries with regard to pails? A. No.

Q. How did you come to your conclusion then? A. I judged that 600 pails a day was too much, according to my own judgment; afterwards I went to Mr. Brandon, and asked him what amount of pails should be turned out, and he said 325 per day.

Q. Now I want you to be careful about this—325 pails per day? A. I think it was that.

Q. Was this in conversation? A. This was in conversation in the presence of the guards. I am not sure whether it was 325 or 335.

Q. It was on Mr. Brandon's statements, without making enquiries anywhere else, that you made your calculation? A. Yes, but I said, "If you think they can accomplish more, I will try and make them work more."

Q. With regard to the boxes? A. I did not make any enquiries about the boxes at all. I think they reduced the box gang shortly after.

Q. Do you know if there have been great complaints with regard to boxes? A. No.

Q. Do you know that a large quantity of these boxes have been returned, and are now stored at the Central Prison? A. No, I did not know.

[Mr. Gordon here put in Exhibits "W," "X," and "Y."]

Q. With regard to the destruction of property in the prison, we heard something from one of the guards about one of the prisoners turning the tap of a varnish barrel, and letting the varnish run off? A. Yes, I remember that.

Q. Do you remember causing the punishment of a prisoner for destroying a mould in the same shop? A. Yes.

Q. Did that occur only once? A. Yes, only once. I remember I went with Mr. Brandon and examined the mould.

Q. And the result was, you punished the prisoner? A. Yes, I punished the prisoner.

Q. Are you in the habit of searching prisoners for stolen property? A. Yes, I am. I do it suddenly, leaving it till Saturday.

Q. What are the results of these searches? A. I often find knives, tobacco, pipes, and so on. The fact is, that the prisoners are so mixed up with the free labour men, that it is difficult to keep them apart.

Q. I am referring to things stolen? A. Yes, but it is principally the case that free men bring things in to them.

Q. Did you ever find any material on prisoners? A. I think one day some flax was found on one of the prisoners.

Q. Anything else? A. No; I don't think anything else.

V. Do you remember receiving a letter of the 16th January, 1877, on this subject? A. No.

Mr. GORDON read a letter.

WITNESS.—I acknowledge that letter; I will try and find it.

Q. Now, Captain Prince, I want your opinion generally, with regard to the number of prisoners there that the Company are bound to take. Does it appear to you that the Company have too many prisoners—that they are unable to find work for them? A. I think, as they are situated at present, they are not able to employ them, perhaps for the want of material.

Q. Would you say that they can employ them now—from your observations? A. I do not think so, because they have not got the material.

Q. Do you think there is sufficient work for them, and room and accommodation and demand? A. I cannot form an opinion.

Q. Do you think the Company are doing all they can to employ this labour? A. I do not think they can employ it all.

Q. Were you accustomed formerly to the employment of large bodies of men? A. Yes. In building trenches.

Q. But in manufactures? A. Oh, no.

Q. You have been employed in military service and the police? A. Yes.

Q. Your police were, as a rule, picked men? A. Yes.

Q. And you have had no experience with regard to this class of men before you went into the prison? A. No.

Q. We heard a good deal about getting hoop iron? A. I don't know anything about that.

Q. Do you know that it is customary in large establishments of this kind to allot a certain time every month to cleaning machinery and putting it in order? A. I have been informed so.

Q. Do you know that in some cases as many as three or four days a month are occupied in that way? A. No, I am not aware of it.

Q. And that when these delays take place, men whom the Company have employed are engaged in cleaning machinery? A. The guards told me so, I think.

Q. Can you say how many times the guards asked the prisoners to stand up when they had nothing to do? A. Up to January or February I found that a great many of the men were idle, and the Company were complaining that the men were not performing enough work, and I asked a guard about it and he made them stand up in the middle of the room.

Q. Can you tell me how often these were idle and were asked to stand up in the middle of the room? A. I cannot tell you.

Q. Could you furnish a statement of that kind? A. I understood a guard furnished that yesterday.

Q. You made a statement yesterday with regard to the returns given in to you when the prisoners entered the prison—as to their previous employment, and as to their being temperate or intemperate. I understand you keep a register? A. Yes.

Q. Does that register show the employment of the prisoner and his previous occupation, and whether he is addicted to drink or not? A. Yes.

Q. You think it is absolutely necessary to classify the prisoners in that way? A. Yes, they are registered according to the previous return.

Q. Then I suppose you try to keep that register accurate? A. Certainly.

Q. And therefore we may take it that register is correct? A. Yes. You must remember that when a man is entered as intemperate, that implies that he is found drunk on the street. These returns are taken from other returns furnished by the sheriffs.

Q. Do you think that a man who has been addicted to drink all his life, although he may be sober three or four days, is able to perform as much work as a man who does not drink at all? A. Certainly not: what I mean is if a man is sentenced under the Vagrant Act he is put down as intemperate, and if he is sentenced for being drunk he is put down as intemperate.

Q. I see you had 180 vagrants last year? A. If a man was as sober as a Judge he might be put down as intemperate.

Q. Do you find that a man who is found lying drunk on the street is as sober as a Judge? A. No, certainly not.

BY MR. LANGMUIR.

Q. You have returned 441 as intemperate, but out of that there are only 180 for vagrancy and drunkenness, and there may be only 100 of them who are really drunken? A. Yes, that's it.

Q. Now, is Irish's case an isolated one? A. This very rarely happens—I think it is the first of the kind that has happened.

Q. If a prisoner is forced upon them it is only now and again? A. Yes.

Q. As a matter of fact, if the Canada Car Company were prevented in any way it was because the men were without staves; could you have classed the prisoners so as to have a certain number of pails made in a day, while they were without hoop-iron, while they were without staves—could you have turned out, one day after another, a given number of pails? A. No, I could not.

Q. As to taking away files, pipes, &c., is not that usual with prisoners? In visiting prisons in the States have you found the same thing? A. Yes, of course.

BY MR. GORDON.

Q. Do you know that the Company had to pay $400 to the Canada Southern Railway for bad wheels furnished to them? A. I don't know; I spoke to one or two of the foremen, and they said the men were doing very well, and free men really could not do better.

Mr. LANGMUIR.—But you knew the free men did make bad wheels.

JOHN WHITE, called on behalf of the Government, sworn and examined:—

BY MR. LANGMUIR.

Q. What position do you hold in the Central Prison? A. Master shoemaker, or instructor in the shoe-shop.

Q. When were you appointed? A. On the 21st February I began my labours there.

Q. Did you commence manufacturing shoes at once? A. Not at once. We had to remove our shop to another part of the building.

Q. Had you already the implements on hand, or had they to be bought? A. They had to be bought.

Q. How many prisoners have you employed? A. From nine men up to eighteen.

Q. In buying the leather, have you been present when it was bought? A. Yes, sir.

Q. Has it been bought at the lowest market rate? A. At the lowest market rates.

Q. Do you know the prices of boots and shoes? A. Yes, sir.

Q. Taking the average price of leather, and all the raw material, and charging the boots and shoes at the lowest wholesale rate, what are these men worth? A. Taking into account what they have manufactured, they are worth 54 cents per day.

Q. Have you any machinery? A. No machinery.

Q. What do you think these men would be worth with machinery? A. Supposing I was running an outside factory with all the appliances necessary, they would be worth from 75 cents to $1 per day.

BY MR. HARDY.

Q. Have you any particularly skilled men among them? A. No, sir; during the whole time we have had 1,844 men at this labour altogether, and there were 228 skilled men out of the 1,844.

Mr. HARDY.—That would be in the proportion of nine unskilled men to one skilled man.

BY MR. GORDON.

Q. Were those delays you have referred to in moving the shop, the only delays you had? A. It took some little time to organize the place into some proper shape.

Q. How long did that take? A. About a fortnight.

Q. Have you made allowance for the prisoners being taken away for punishment? A. No, they are not taken away frequently.

Q. How many times? A. Three or four times, I think.

Q. Have they been kept a whole day? A. Yes, sir.

Q. Substituted another man? A. No, sir.

Q. Why didn't you get another man substituted? A. Because we have no machinery, and no machinery stands idle.

Q. Do you think it is better to have no one substituted? A. I think it is.

Q. Have you had any experience with outside labour? A. Oh yes.

Q. What? A. I have had four years' experience in this city, and all my life before that in the Old Country. I have been in John Turner's in this city.

Q. Did they take green men at John Turner's? A. Yes, but not much. They would take on men who are comparatively green.

Q. They work by piece-work usually? A. Yes, piece-work.

Q. What do they get for piece-work, usually—for manufacturing? A. It depends altogether on the kind.

Q. The kind you are making at the prison? A. They get from $3.50 to $5 per dozen for putting bottoms on, and they get so much more for fitting up. Putting everything together, I think they would want about 45 cents per pair for making brogans.

Q. How many of these boots do they turn out in a day? A. Some make three, some four. They would probably make about three pairs a day where our men make two.

Q. How long would it take these men to get into the work? A. Not very long. We divide it up, and in one week I could teach a man to do pretty well on one thing. In two months there are men who can turn out work just as good as anything in a factory in the city.

Q. You are able to give them a good deal of your time? A. Yes.

Q. You do nothing else? A. I do the cutting.

Q. In most prisons they do this kind of work? A. Yes, I believe they do it in Kingston Penitentiary.

THOMAS SHORT, called on behalf of the Government, sworn and examined:—

BY MR. LANGMUIR.

Q. You are bursar of the Central Prison? A. Yes, sir.

Q. And have been so since the opening? A. Since the opening.

Q. In that position you have charge of all the financial affairs of the prison? A. Yes, sir.

Q. Have you made a statement as to what the expenses are likely to be this year? A. I have.

Q. Say that all the prison labour that could be utilized in the shoe shop and tailor shop, and every place was credited at fifty cents per day, and you only deducted the domestic work, what would the expenses be this year? A. Taking 330 prisoners for the whole year, and the cost for food, clothing, and everything at 43 cents per day, in a year of 365 days, it amounts to $51,793.50.

Q. That number is greater than we had up to this year in the prison? A. Yes, we never had so large an average as that.

Q. What number would be available at fifty cents per day? A. Taking off the number that we use for domestic purposes, there would be 264 prisoners for 313 days, at fifty cents per day—$43,316; which would be reduced by holidays and short time to $38,148, leaving a deficiency of $13,545.50.

[The witness here put in Exhibit " Z."]

Q. Then this $13,500 would be the full deficit for this year? A. Yes.

Q. I instructed you to find out what quantity of water is used by the Company? A. I did so.

Q. Whom did you find it from? A. The engineer.

Q. And what did it come to? A. I have not got the figures.

Q. Do you think it was $900? A. If that is my return to you, it is right.

Q. Was the return you made to me based upon actual examination? A. It was based upon the actual quantity used.

Q. With regard to gas? A. We have not used gas to any extent; but if they asked for it, we would give them gas, and it was estimated that one jet would consume about three feet an hour.

Q. About the fuel? A. The fuel was used by actual consumption, as returned by the engineer.

Q. Did you charge any of the engineers' or stokers' wages? A. We did not enter anything of that kind, only the fuel.

BY MR. GORDON.

Q. What is the capacity of the prison? A. The full capacity is 336. There are four cells set aside for punishment cells—332 would be the number.

Q. Why do you make your estimate on the number of 330? A. That was the probable estimate of the current year.

Q. But if the prison were full, it would be 332? A. Yes.

Q. "Available labour, 264"—are not all the 332 prisoners available? A. No, there are so many for domestic work.

Q. Is not that available work? A. No.

Q. Don't you make money by saving it in that way? A. My estimate is only with regard to productive work.

Mr. GORDON.—Taking 332 men, and supposing them to work 300 days at 50 cents per day, that would amount to $49,800; then taking 332 men for 365 days, at a cost of 43 cents per day, it would amount to $52,107.40. That would show a deficit against the prison of about $2,300.

Mr. LANGMUIR.—The expenses must increase, because we are running from capital, and not from maintenance.

Mr. GORDON.—In Mr. Langmuir's last Annual Report, page 87, he says the cost was 43 cents per man per day. Supposing the number of prisoners increased to 332, what additional cost would there be to the prison?

The WITNESS.—There would be an extra guard, clothing, and food——

Mr. GORDON.—Food is 7 cents per day; bedding, clothing, and shoes would be $5\frac{3}{10}$ cents per day.

Mr. LANGMUIR.—Would there not be an increase in groceries, in laundry appliances, in stationery, in the library a larger number of books, etc.? Having started the prison with capital account in the way of clothing, bedding, etc., will not the charge for maintenance be more in the future?

The WITNESS.—Yes, certainly.

BY MR. GORDON.

Q. How much do you consider every prisoner increases the expenditure of the prison? A. I have not made any calculation.

Q. Would 20 cents a day cover the cost? A. I do not know without figuring,—it would only be a guess.

Q. As the number increases will not the expense decrease per prisoner? A. Yes, I suppose so.

This concluded the evidence on behalf of the Government.

Mr. GORDON put in the Reports of the Inspector of Asylums and Prisons for 1873, 1874, and 1876, which were marked respectively as "Exhibit 2 A," "Exhibit 2 B," and "Exhibit 2 C."

The Commission took recess.

The Commission re-assembled at 3 o'clock.

Mr. GORDON proposed to call witnesses in rebuttal.

ALEXANDER MANNING, called, sworn, and examined—

BY MR. GORDON.

Q. The only question I wish to ask you, Mr. Manning, is what do you think would be the cost of putting up such buildings as would enable the Canada Car Company to carry on the industries which they now carry on at the Central Prison. You have had a good deal of experience in the employment of labour, I believe? A. Yes, a good deal.

Mr. HARDY objected to the question proposed to be asked, on the ground that the original agreement provided what kind of buildings should be put up, and that the new agreement embodied that portion of the original agreement.

Mr. GORDON—I will ask you if you have been up to the Central Prison, and have seen the nature of the industries carried on there? A. Yes.

Q. The number of the prisoners taken by the Company is 260. Do you think the buildings we have there at the present time are suitable for carrying on these industries? A. Yes, there is one very large building there that is very suitable for the purpose.

Q. Do you think the Company could have carried on their industries in the buildings there at the present time? A. Yes, they could carry on the larger portion of their business in the one shop.

Q. How many other shops are there? A. Two other shops.

Q. Do you think that with these two other shops we could carry on the whole of the industries? A. I think you could.

Q. Can you give us any idea of what you think these buildings would cost? A. I made no calculation, for I was only there a few minutes; I suppose about $20,000.

Q. Supposing that the Company had had to erect buildings in the Central Prison suitable to this industry, what do you think it would cost? A. That would cover a great deal of ground, because you would have to take machinery into account.

Q. I am only talking about buildings? A. They could put up wooden buildings for $25,000.

Q. Do you think wooden buildings would be as suitable as brick for carrying on this work? A. They would not be as safe in case of fire, and for heating, but for other purposes they would be just as good.

Q. Can you see any advantage for the Company to carry on this work in buildings erected by the Government? A. No, I think it is a disadvantage, because they are not buildings erected for the class of work they are doing. The shops are separate, and this causes more handling, and more expense.

BY MR. HARDY.

Q. Do I understand that you refer to buildings outside the prison walls? A. Yes.

Q. That are now erected? A. Yes, where they built their cars.

Q. Wooden buildings? A. Yes. They are finishing some cars there now. There is one building about 150 feet long and 75 feet wide.

Q. When was that started? A. That was there when they first started the Car Company.

Q. The reason they don't use it is simply because they have failed in their car business? A. That is the reason they don't use it.

Q. Wouldn't they require heavier buildings for the iron work of the cars? A. No, because they use the ground floor.

Q. The blacksmiths' work, for instance—they require a heavier building for that?
A. Oh no, a wooden building would do as well.

Q. You think it is advisable to put up a wooden building for that purpose? A. Not permanently, of course; but if you wished to be economical, I think it would do.

Q. By the agreement, they may resume their car works at any time? A. But they don't need them now.

Q. We cannot tell how good the car trade will become in the future? A. I think there are too many car works in the country now.

Q. Do you think there are too many buildings at the prison for the Company? A. No, but they are too far apart; if they were close together they could run the cars from one to the other. With an addition of $20,000 to remove them and fix them up, the whole might be worth $40,000.

Q. When were you over them? A. I was over them two years ago, and I was over them to-day.

Q. When did you sit down to make your calculation as to the value of these buildings? A. I did not sit down at all.

Q. You just did it by guess, then? A. Yes, just by guess.

Q. What do you think the land there worth? A. I think it worth about $2,000 an acre.

Q. You did not examine to see whether these buildings cost too much in construction? A. I do not think they have cost too much. They are plain buildings.

Q. Can you make a calculation to find what a brick building costs per superficial foot—say 10,000 square feet? A. I cannot exactly tell. Brick buildings cost about seven cents per cubic foot.

Q. Will it cost more to build a second floor on one building, or to put up two buildings with a ground-floor? A. It will cost more for two buildings, because one roof would do for two floors.

Q. Do you know Gurney's foundry? A. Yes.

Q. Do you know what that cost? A. I do not know; I have no particular knowledge of Mr. Gurney's place.

Q. But you have knowledge of the buildings up at the prison? A. I simply make the calculation for those outside.

Q. The testimony Mr. Langmuir has given is that they cost more than $100,000, including the switches. Have you ever put an estimate upon the rental value of steam fixtures, boilers, engines, belting, &c.—what percentage on the value should you get? Supposing the machinery cost $10,000, and you were going to rent it to a man, how much percentage should you get? A. I would expect to get fifteen per cent.

BY MR. GORDON.

Q. I did not understand your statement about $40,000? A. With the present buildings to utilize them, and if you were to have this machinery, and make it all suitable, it would cost you $20,000 additional.

Q. What do you consider the buildings to be now worth? A. I think they are worth $20,000.

Q. Do you know anything about the car works at Port Hope or London? A. I have seen the buildings, but I cannot say what they are worth.

BY MR. HARDY.

Q. You have no stock in this Company? A. No, I never had, and did not want any.

BY MR. GORDON.

Q. Was it because you thought they could not make enough on the prison labour?
A. I thought they could not succeed.

Q. Then you do not believe in prison labour against free labour? A. If you could keep them after teaching them, I think they might be of use; but otherwise I do not think they would be profitable.

is a provident thing for a Company to take a fixed number of
e? A. If they understood their business; but if they knew
t, I think it would certainly be a failure.
yourself—supposing your contract limited you to one freeman to
That is their own look out; I have considered this thing a good
the Company could get good men to manage their work, they
ir at 33 cents on the dollar; that is, if they got a free man at one
hird to a prisoner would be about right.
hat price per man? A. If I were to have them only for three
t, because you could not teach them in that time.

BY THE CHAIRMAN.

y price as to what you think the Company should pay for 260
ional option to have all that are in the place, with the buildings,
cessary for the first connection, the Company being obliged to take
ed from two months up to two years? A. I would say it was a
enter into, if the prisoners had on an average ten months' impri-
according to its present value and what it is likely to be for some
a very bad contract for the parties; labour can be had for 90c. per
I think it will be very much less before it will get better; looking
ough there are great advantages at the prison, I would prefer my-
ys, and put them on apprenticeship for five years, than take prison
an could get 250 lads at a very low price now—people would be
you are sure of their services for five years, and they are a different
r from prisoners; and where you have to train a man, where the
ten months, of course it would give very little chance of making
u trained him.

BY MR. HARDY.

bour do you employ? A. I have employed all kinds.
nt years? A. I have both built houses, and I have been railway

aying on the Welland Canal for instance? A. We are paying
lollar and a quarter.
ying to your skilled men—stone-masons and so on? A. We are
em.
ny men in Toronto? A. Not many; I have been getting three
for $1.25 per day.
ighbour with contracts at the canal? A. There is Mr. Jackson

aying? A. They are paying nine shillings.
ak of 90 cents here, then? A. Mr. Laidlaw can get as many
cents per day, and stone-masons can be got for $2.25 per day,
t the canal, simply because there is a union there.
ere you paying? A. Labourers, $1.25; stone-masons, $3 a day.
y now for stone-masons? A. We pay the same.

BY MR. GORDON.

ou have yet answered the Chairman's question, as to what you
of this labour? A. I say that labour of that description I would
could get boys to teach them the business; but in the position
quarter of a dollar per day would be enough.

BY MR. HARDY.

Q. But you have not considered the interest on the machinery and the plant, and the rent of the buildings there; so the fact is they ought to get the labour for nothing? A. No; but I think it is a very bad bargain.

Q. In the Cleveland Prison they have about 250 prisoners on short terms, and they are paying 40 cents per day for them? A. There are more people there to supply than here; and when you want skilled labour there you can get it better than here.

BY MR. BROCKWAY.

Q. Have you ever employed prison labour at all? A. I have not.

JOHN HARPER, called on behalf of the Company, sworn and examined—

BY MR. GORDON.

Q. You are an architect of considerable experience in the city of Toronto, I believe? A. I am a builder, architect, and valuator.

Q. I think you have been architect for many of the Government buildings here? A. I was clerk of works for the new post-office, appointed by the Government.

Q. Have you been up to the Central Prison, and seen the class of industries carried on there? A. I saw the different kinds of work there.

Q. Did you see the character of the Company's buildings, and the adjacent premises? A. I did.

Q. I want to ask you what, in your opinion, it would cost to put up buildings suitable to carry on the industries that are now carried on there, for 260 men,—not saying anything of machinery or anything but the buildings? A. That would depend on the nature of the buildings.

Q. Buildings that would be suitable for the work? A. I made a little calculation that suitable buildings would cost $35,000.

Q. Did you examine the three old buildings there? A. Yes; there is one building about 350 feet long, by about 75 feet wide.

Q. What do you think it would cost to put up that building, for instance? A. It is now an old building; I counted the whole of the buildings as worth about $18,000; I think that building would be worth about $7,500.

Q. Then there is one to the south? A. Yes, longer but not so wide.

Q. What is the value of that building? A. It was a sort of a guess, a bird's-eye view that I got of the whole thing; I valued one at $7,500; one at $4,500; and the rest at $3,000 more, besides allowing $1,000 for odds and ends.

Q. Do you think there is enough accommodation for the Company to carry on their business in those buildings, which you value at $18,000? A. Yes, I think so.

C. T. BRANDON, called on behalf of the Company, sworn, and examined :—

BY MR. GORDON.

Q. We have heard a good deal about the prisoners being idle. From your position as superintendent of the work, can you tell us of any occasions when the prisoners have been idle, from want of material or anything else? A. There has been no time when the prisoners were idle only for an hour or two when the foreman had to look around, or was engaged at anything else. Sometimes when they have been short of material, they had to be left standing at the lathe for an hour or two.

Q. Were they idle at those times? A. Yes, idle, with the exception of dressing up their tools, or something of that kind—they were not turning out any work.

Q. In an establishment of this kind, is it possible to go on for a week without having any stoppages of this kind? A. Oh, that is done in every shop.

Q. Do you think it is possible to keep them constantly at work? A. No, I think not.

Q. Would it be advisable to do so? A. It is not a loss of time, for the men are put at dressing up the machinery or piling up staves.

Q. Is it not customary in every establishment of this kind to give the men an hour or so a week, for the purpose of cleaning up their machinery? A. It is usual on Saturday afternoon to give them about an hour and a half to clean up the machinery.

Q. What is the average number of days that they work the year round? A. The average would be 23 or 24 days a month.

Q. Do you think, with the stoppages we have heard so much about, the time would be much less than that? A. In the two years we have run that place, there has been no stoppage for more than half an hour at a time for any breakdown of the machinery, and that does not extend to more than half a dozen instances in the whole two years.

Q. There were some questions put yesterday about bad work that was turned out. Do you know anything about some boxes? A. Yes, there are some there.

Q. How many? A. About 1,000 or 1,200 that have been returned as badly made.

Q. What is wrong with them? A. Nails not being driven properly, and the boxes not being fit for packing up.

Q. Can you estimate what the loss would be to the Company? A. The loss would be about eight cents a box.

Q. With regard to pails—can you recollect any case where the Company have suffered loss in consequence of bad work on pails? A. A very few instances. They have pails that are damaged, and not properly made.

Q. Have you had pails returned to you? A. No, not for improper make.

Q. Well, brooms? A. We have had them returned—as many as 50 or 75 dozen at a time on two or three occasions.

Q. Could you form any idea as to the round number? A. No, I could not.

Q. These brooms the Company sell for about $1.50 per dozen? A. Yes, $1.50 to $2.00.

Q. We heard yesterday about the conduct of the prisoners in the shop. There was one case of two prisoners fighting in the shop, and the evidence of the guard was that that was a solitary case, and those prisoners were removed. A. That is not a solitary case; last year it was almost a daily occurrence. The names of the parties who were fighting are Guinness, McCabe and others, and the result was black eyes.

Q. What would be the effect of that on the rest of the men in the shop? A. They would stop to look on.

Q. Do you think that would have anything to do with the number of pails and other things turned out? A. Of course. That wouldn't do in a free shop.

Q. Captain Prince said the estimate fixed on was 325 pails per day. Have you any recollection about that? A. I went round one time with the Captain and the guard, and the amount was 375 per day—the prisoners' own proposition—provided you paid them for all they made above that.

Q. Do you think the prisoners could do 375 per day? A. I think they should readily do that number.

Q. Can you speak as to the exact number of pails turned out from the 28th of April to the 21st of July? A. I could not say as to the exact number. Mr. Bailey can.

Q. With regard to the building—do you think that it is of any advantage to the Company to have the tracks on the north side? A. From my experience there of two years, with reference to getting in the material and the shipping of goods, I think it has been a damage to the Company to have anything to do with the railroad. The railways only come in on one line, and we have all the shunting to do with men or a team. They frequently run in cars and block up the track from one end to the other, and we have to shunt all the cars through the lumber yard or down the side track to get out one car.

By Mr. Hardy.

Q. Isn't that all a question of management between you and the railway authorities? A. One road will not take their cars out unless the others do, and we have had a great deal of difficulty about shunting cars, especially in winter time, and the track has probably been the cause of more difficulty that all the good we have derived from it.

By Mr. Gordon.

Q. With regard to the buildings in which the industries are carried on—is there any particular advantage in carrying on the industries in these buildings? A. I do not think so. I think it is a disadvantage. The buildings are separate to a great extent, and the shops are too small to carry on any particular branch in one department or one room. If we enlarge our pail business we would have to make two separate businesses of it, putting it into two buildings. The buildings should be built two or three stories high.

Q. Do you think the Company could have utilized those buildings on Strachan Avenue? A. The buildings there are better adapted for the business carried on than the buildings we occupy.

Q. Could you have carried on your pail business in that large north shop? A. We could have carried it on much better, and have had more room. The shop is 350 feet long and 75 feet wide, and we should have room for machinery on both sides, and be able to stack goods in the middle.

Q. Would it be of any advantage with reference to the guards to have the work in one building? A. I think if we had the work in one building, the guards could watch it better.

Q. With regard to the brush factory—do you think you could carry it on better in the Strachan Avenue buildings? A. Yes, I think so. The size of the room is of more importance than the manner in which it is built.

Q. Would there have been any more difficulty in heating these buildings? A. I do not think so.

Q. Is the heating in the shops as it should be? A. No. I have frequently called the attention of the engineer to it, saying that the heating was not as good as it ought to be, and that the men were cold, and he said that the pipes were all heated, and the heat could not be made greater.

Q. What do you think it would cost to put up suitable buildings to carry on this work? A. I think to build them of brick, with the same amount of floorage that we occupy, would cost $50,000.

Q. What in wood? A. I don't know.

Q. Would wood be less? A. I should think it would.

Q. Considerably? A. It would depend to a great extent on how they were built. The principal buildings we are using are built of wood.

Q. You were with the Union Manufacturing Company of Toledo before you came here. A. Yes.

Q. Did they make pails and so forth? A. They were confined exclusively to hardware goods—churns, butter-tubs, &c.

Q. Did they turn out as much work as you do here? A. They turned out twice as much.

Q. Could you tell how their buildings are placed? A. They have two buildings, built at right angles to each other, each is 100 feet by 50 feet, and two storeys high. They have also a wooden building three storeys high, built of wood. The second storey is used for painting and so forth, the lower part is used for shipping and offices.

Q. Could you have carried on the work in the buildings that you carry on here? A. We could not carry on all the work and employ the same number of men; pails and tubs require more room.

Q. Do you know what those buildings cost? A. I could not say anything positive about it.

Q. Could that help you? It seems to be a report of the industries carried on there, could you give us any idea as to the cost of those buildings? A. I have no knowledge of what they did cost.

Q. Do the prisoners ever work after dark? A. No, sir.

Q. Since you have been Superintendent of the works you have never had occasion to use the light? A. We have had occasion to use the light, but it has never been in such a state that we could use it; in the winter time it has been so dark when we worked on short time, that it has been impossible for the men to work in the evening for about a quarter of an hour.

Q. At what time of the year would that be? A. That would be in the fall of the year, and would last for a week or two; sometimes the Warden came to us and asked if it was light enough for the prisoners to work, and we informed him that it was not paying and that we would have to work on shorter time.

Q. There was a letter written by Mr. Bailey on the 16th of February, 1877, on this subject, asking for a change of hours on this account. Do you know anything about it? A. I believe it was in order to obviate the need of gas-light and to get day-light.

Q. Do you know anything of the value of the machinery put in by the Company? A. I have not estimated the value.

Q. Can you tell us anything about the delays on account of hoop iron? A. All the delays I know of are the delays of the shipment of the iron when it was expected, and the iron was of a size that we could not get in the city. The iron is always ordered and means taken to procure it in proper time.

THOMAS BAILEY was re-examined on behalf of the Company:—

BY MR. GORDON.

Q. Did you prepare a list showing the number of pails turned out by the prisoners from the 28th April to the 21st July last? A. I did.

Q. Was the number less than 325 or 375? A. Yes, less than 225.

Q. Look at that, and say if it is a correct statement? A. That is a correct statement, taken from my books; I prepared it.

Q. That shows an average of 224 per day. Supposing 325 was the task, what loss would that be to the Company at the price they were getting during that period? A. $411 about.

Q. Supposing 375 was the task, what would the loss be to the Company during the same time? A. That would increase it about $321, but to that would have to be added the labour on the overplus, and a little allowance to be made for hooping iron.

(The statement was put in and marked "Exhibit 2 D.")

BY MR. HARDY.

Q. That only covers the period from April 28th to July 21st? A. Yes, sir.
Q. You did not show that to the guard? A. No, it was taken from our books.
Q. Did one of the guards test it with you? A. No.
Q. Why didn't you submit it to them? A. We have nothing to do with their own testimony.

HON. GEO. BROWN, called on behalf of the Company, sworn and examined—

BY MR. GORDON.

Q. Mr. Brown, I believe you have taken a great deal of interest in the question of prison labour? A. At one time I did, but not so much of late years.

Q. At one time, I think, you visited the prisons in the United States? A. Yes, I went as a commissioner for the Government to see the prison management in the United States.

Q. And I believe you have some knowledge of prison employment at Kingston? A. Yes.

Q. You have studied the question very thoroughly? A. I did then, very thoroughly. I examined the different systems all over the world, along with the other commissioners.

Q. I would like to get your views, Mr. Brown, on the employment of prison labour. What do you think as to the adaptability of prison labour to the business of manufactures? A. I suppose that the thoroughly accepted view on that point is, that labour should only be used subsidiary to the reformation of the convicts. I apprehend that when you look at the matter as a whole, the only point you bring before you is, that here is one who must be dealt with in order that he may be turned from his evil life, and everything else is entirely subsidiary to that.

Q. Do you look upon a prisoner, then, as a different class of a man from others? A. No, I think he is the same as all of us.

Q. Do you think he is capable of doing as much work as a free man? A. You cannot make a comparison between the labour of a convict and that of a free man.

Q. Do you think it would be advantageous to the convict? A. No. I think it would be decidedly disadvantageous to the convict.

Q. Why so? A. The question would come up as to whether it is desirable to pay them for their labour, and the moment you do that you may give up all idea of their moral reformation.

Q. Do you think you can get any kind of work from them? A. Oh yes. If you gave to the prisoners that are in for some time a business which they would like to know, and by which they thought they would be benefited after they left the prison, I think you would get a good deal of work out of them, especially if they were educated.

Q. Are the generality of them well educated? A. There are—many of them. But my experience was that those in the Penitentiary were below free men, as a class.

Q. Do you think it is necessary, then, to give them some inducement to make them do anything? A. I won't say that, you know they are, many of them, idle there, and some of them like it. There is a kind of *esprit de corps* among them. The work in the gaols, I think, must be more objectionable than that in the Penitentiary, for the prisoners in the Penitentiary are there for long terms while those in the gaols are for short terms.

Q. But don't you think it is possible to teach these men so that you could get as much work out of them as from free men? A. You could get more out of some of them. Of course their whole time is given to it—there is no moping, no talking, or anything of that kind to interfere with them, so that when you get a really good man, he is liable to turn out more work.

Q. What would be the percentage of such prisoners, do you think? A. I think it would not be half.

Q. But, with regard to the other half—do you think you could get any work out of them? A. The best criterion would be what you would get for their labour.

Q. Have you made any investigation about that? A. Yes, very thoroughly; I have given out contracts and have had a good deal to do with the subject.

Q. What is your experience about it? A. There is a difference with regard to the branches that are taught them. My own opinion was that those branches only should be taught the men that would benefit them when they go out; and that was the first consideration, I thought, which should be held in view. I thought a prisoner should be taught something at which he could afterwards work in his own house, and not in a workshop, where other men might find out that he had been in prison, and, if so, there would be little hope of keeping him from crime.

Q. What were the industries carried on at the time of which you speak? A. At first, stove-making, but we changed to shoe-making, which the prisoners could work at in their own houses after they got out. We also used the Asylum system. If you cannot get thorough moral improvement, you can get the habits of the men improved by keeping them still and quiet, and by having a moral instructor go around among them. We found that tobacco and whiskey, and so on, were brought in among the men while they were at the stove-making.

Q. Was there cabinet-making there? A. Not while I was there—after I left. It is very necessary to have good contractors, men of intelligence, and men who have some regard for the purposes of the institution.

Q. At what prices was the labour employed then? A. I think it was about 30 or 35 cents a day.

Q. Did that include anything besides the shop room, engine, boiler, machinery, et cætera? A. I do not think that there was any occupation of that kind while I was there. My impression is that no other branch was carried on except those which were carried on quietly.

Q. Do you know what the wages were that were paid in the States at that time A. I think they were 45 or 50 cents at that time. Of course there are two ways of conducting a Penitentiary—to make it pay, to rectify the failings of the mass of population on your hands.

Q. Do you think there can be any improvement on the way the prisoners are employed in the Central Prison? A. Oh, decidedly. I think I may be allowed to say that I believe there is great harm done in mixing up those on short terms with those who are there for two years. I think that view was first expressed in the report which we presented to the Government. There were the most shocking deeds committed under that system. A girl or boy, perhaps untouched by crime when they went in, would come out of prison greatly injured. And we were all of opinion that those serving long sentences should be removed from the gaols, and that the term of punishment for such as are in the Central Prison should not be less than two years. But they have prisoners here, I believe, for all terms.

Mr. LANGMUIR.—Not less than six months.

Mr. GORDON.—But you have a good many for two months.

Mr. LANGMUIR.—Not many.

WITNESS.—My idea was, that there should be a House of Correction for those of short terms. There was such a House of Correction at Boston, and it was very successful. Of course, the industries for short-term men would be very different from those for the long-term men.

Q. How? A. Because you would have to teach them something.

Q. From your experience, Mr. Brown, at Kingston and elsewhere, do you think that these short-term men, whose sentences average from two to ten months, should be made available to turn out tubs and pails, and such things, with the use of machinery? A. I presume so, but it would not be skilled labour. The class of people sent in for two or three months, are not the class suited very well for mechanical employment.

Q. In 1876, I see by Mr. Langmuir's report, there were 441 classed as intemperate? A. That is just the difficulty with these men. They are usually men of that class, and it would be absurd to place them with long-term men, who would be a good deal superior. We divided our occupations, and took short-term men. One of the arrangements we had with the contractors was that we would have only a certain proportion of three-year men; the great object was to get life men.

Q. I suppose I should scarcely ask you about the value of these short-term men? A. It would depend upon the employment they were put at. It was customary to put them at picking oakum for ships, which was very profitable, and they could do that, and such kind of mere manual labour, very well.

Q. But taking the two years' men and the six months' men, what would be the comparative value of these men? A. There is no comparison between them. Drink would bring in a great many short-term men, wasted in body and wasted in mind.

Q. Have you visited the Central Prison since the new industries have been there? A. No.

BY MR. HARDY.

Q. You speak of two theories, Mr. Brown, one to make a prison pay, and the other to subordinate that to the reformation of the prisoner. Which theory did you adopt? A. We took the view that you should endeavour to combine them both by the selection of industries, and by seeing to the way the inspection is managed. For instance, when we first went in there, the Penitentiary cost the Government $65,000 a year. The first year, we reduced it to $40,000; the second year, we reduced it to $30,000, and my opinion was that, if we continued, we would have eventually made it self-sustaining.

Q. What years were those? A. 1848, 1849, and 1850.

Q. Whom do you refer to when you say "we"? A. The Hon. Adam Ferguson, Mr. Sheriff Thomas, of Hamilton, Mr. Brostom, of Montreal, Mr. Emery and myself. We closed our proceedings in 1849, I believe, and then I took the Superintendency of the Penitentiary without payment. With reference to the gaols, I must express my opinion very strongly, that the point is not to keep the prisoners locked up, it is to try and make such a change in them, that they will not come there again. For instance, I got a circular yesterday, asking me to attend a meeting for the formation of a Prison Discipline Society, whose members would go and see these prisoners, and help them to get employment when they came out. This is being done, I believe, in the United States, and with very good effect. But above all, the idea of the money consideration should be abandoned ; it is a wrong idea; it is a poor economy ; and if there is one thing we ought to keep in view it is the reformation of these prisoners—that is everything. They watch the slightest injustice. They know what every man is in for, and what his term of punishment is. They know all about each other.

BY THE CHAIRMAN.

Q. Do you know anything of the value of outside labour at the time of the prison labour to which you referred ? A. I should think that, at that particular time, there would be very little discrepancy from what it is now, if there was any. There was a panic in the United States in 1847, from which they suffered more than we did. The difficulty we found was to get a really good man as contractor. One who would continue for three or four years, it was worth a good deal to get.

Q. Do you think three years was the shortest term of imprisonment at that time ? A. Yes, I think so.

Q. What is your opinion as to the effects on the physical and mental condition of these men of their mode of life before going into the prison ? Did it affect them to any great extent ? A. Oh, very much. We used to mark that very much. A man would come in bloated and wasted, and the quiet life he pursued, would have an immense effect upon him after a year or so.

Q. Would you be prepared to give us an opinion as to the value of the labour of these men, sentenced from six months to two years ? The Company agree to take 260 prisoners ; they may take more, but they are not obliged to do so. They have the shops and shafts, and the first connection by belting to give them their motive power. What is the value of this labour under these circumstances? A. If you put it the other way—what is the value of the machinery ? I would say it would be very considerable if they had good labour. It is an enormous advantage to a contractor to have machinery.

BY MR. HARDY.

Q. Since you were a member of this commission, there has been a good deal of machinery put in prisons for doing the work ? A. There is not very much difference. There was very fine machinery at the Penitentiary, put in by Mr. Stevenson, of Napanee.

BY THE CHAIRMAN.

Q. Have you given this matter special thought, as to what the value of this labour would be under these circumstances ? A. I have had a good deal of correspondence and reading on the subject. The impression on my mind is that the contract these people made was a very poor one for themselves ; and when the Government was condemned for having made a poor contract, I was obliged to say that I thought they had an advantage over the contractors in the price they got.

BY MR. GORDON.

Q. Then your opinion is that the proportion they could make would not be 50 cents ? A. We were quite willing to take lower rates in order to secure the moral ends.

BY THE CHAIRMAN.

Q. There is one point that has a double bearing—it has a bearing directly on the value of the labour, and also with regard to its effect on the men ; that is, giving to the men themselves something for their labour—holding out some inducement ? A. It is one of those questions that nobody can establish what is the conclusion to be arrived at in the matter. Of course, circumstances alter the cases; but the idea is a wrong one of coaxing the men to be right. You have to avoid everything that elevates them in their own estimation—that is, you may influence them to have self-respect, but not self-confidence. The moral lesson you have to teach them is that they have been guilty of a great offence, and the moment that you begin to buy them and coax them, my opinion is that the end of your hope of reformation has come.

MR. GORDON here put in "Exhibit 2 E."

The Commission adjourned until Thursday, the 23rd August.

The following communication, enclosing an Order in Council, extending the time for the completion of the enquiry, was received by the Chairman:—

TORONTO, 31st July, 1877.

SIR,—I am directed to transmit herewith for your information copy of an Order in Council, approved of by His Honour the Lieutenant-Governor the 28th day of July instant, extending the time for the completion of the inquiry into the value of the labour at the Central Prison supplied by the Government to the "Canada Car Company," from the 1st of August until the 1st day of October next.

I have the honour to be, Sir,
Your obedient servant,
I. R. ECKART,
Assistant Secretary,

Hon. W. P. Howland, C. B.,
&c., &c., &c.,
Toronto.

COPY of an Order in Council approved by His Honour the Lieutenant-Governor, the 28th day of July, A. D. 1877.

Upon the recommendation of the Honourable the Provincial Secretary, the Committee of Council advise that the time fixed for the completion of the inquiry into the value of the labour at the Central Prison, supplied by the Government to the Canada Car Company, and the return of the evidence and the report thereon, be extended from the 1st day of August until the first day of October next.

Certified.
(Signed)   J. LONSDALE CAPREOL,
Assistant Clerk, Executive Council,
30th July, 1877.   Ontario.

On the 23rd August the Commissioners met and proceeded to visit Prisons in the United States, the final meeting in Toronto being deferred till September 13th.

THURSDAY, September 13th, 1877.

The Commissioners re-assembled.

The CHAIRMAN read and submitted the replies received to the circular issued by the Commissioners to the Prison authorities of the United States. The circular and replies are appended:—

TORONTO, 3rd August, 1877.

SIR,—A Commission having been appointed by the Government of Ontario, composed of Messrs. Z. R. Brockway, Superintendent of the State Reformatory, New York, Mr. James Noxon, of Ingersoll, and myself, to inquire as to the value of the Prison Labour furnished by the Government to Contractors at the Central Prison, Toronto, I am requested to inform you that the Commission will be greatly obliged if you will kindly answer, at your earliest convenience, the interrogatories attached hereto.

I have the honour to be,
Sir,
Your obedient servant,
W. P. HOWLAND,
Chairman of Commission.

Albany Penitentiary, Albany, N. Y.

1. What are the dates of your existing contracts ? June, 1874.
2. Have any contracts recently expired ? No.
3. Have new tenders been asked, and what was the highest tender received ? No.
4. Have you any available labour remaining unemployed for want of contractors to hire it ? No.
5. Are your contractors bound to pay for a certain number of prisoners, whether they are required or not ? Contract calls for 650, and we consider the contractors bound to take that number and keep them *constantly employed.*
6. For what periods are the prisoners sentenced ; giving the *minimum* and *maximum* ? Three months to life.
7. What do you consider the present contract value per day of your prison labour ? Forty cents per day for all sentenced for *less* than one year, and sixty cents per day for all sentenced for one year or over.
8. What is the value of the same when employed on account of the State ? None so employed, excepting a few of the poorest class of short-term men and women, at seating chairs. Will not average *above* thirty cents per day.
9. If you have long-term labour and short-term labour in your prison, what do you consider to be the relative value of the two ? See answer to No. 7. The value, however, of our prison labour depends upon the discipline maintained.

L. D. PILSBURY,
Superintendent Albany Penitentiary.

Auburn State Prison, Auburn, N. Y.

1. What are the dates of your existing contracts ? 1875, 6, 7.
2. Have any contracts recently expired ? No.
3. Have new tenders been asked, and what was the highest tender received ? We do not advertise our contracts, and therefore make our own terms as to price of men.
4. Have you any available labour remaining unemployed for want of contractors to hire it ? Yes.
5. Are your contractors bound to pay for a certain number of prisoners, whether they are required or not ? They must pay for all contracted for.
6. For what periods are the prisoners sentenced ; giving the *minumum* and *maximum* ? From one year to life.
7. What do you consider the present contract value per day of your prison labour ? We charge 50 cents on new contracts, and think that a fair rate in present condition of business.
8. What is the value of the same when employed on account of the State ? Cannot estimate with accuracy, say from 35 to 50 cents. The best men 90 cents on contracts. State carries on no business.
9. If you have long-term labour and short-term labour in your prison, what do you consider to be the relative value of the two ? Sentences of 2 years being about as short as we have here, we have no means of estimating. Our contractors choose from 2 to 10 years in preference to life or 20 years. Should say that 5 years would be as desirable as longer sentences.

Chicago House of Correction, Illinois.

1. What are the dates of your existing contracts ? Have only one contract to furnish prison labour. Contract dated June 13, 1877 ; to furnish fifty able-bodied prisoners—none of less than sixty days' sentence—with allowance without charge, of ten days' apprenticeship ; price each per day, thirty cents ; ten hours labour.
2. Have any contracts recently expired ? None.

3. Have new tenders been asked, and what was the highest tender received? Have repeatedly, but not recently, asked for tenders, but none received since 1873.

4. Have you any available labour remaining unemployed for want of contractors to hire it? None such as contractors would employ.

5. Are your contractors bound to pay for a certain number of prisoners whether they are required or not? Yes.

6. For what periods are the prisoners sentenced; giving the *minimum* and *maximum*? City prisoners from a single day to six months; county and state prisoners from thirty days upward; have several under one year sentences.

7. What do you consider the present contract value per day of your prison labour? Thirty cents for able-bodied prisoners having terms from sixty days to one year; city prisoners would be valueless to a contractor, but may be employed on institution account.

8. What is the value of the same when employed on account of the State? Such male labour is utilized at value not less than thirty cents per day, when used.

9. If you have long-term labour and short-term labour in your prison, what do you consider to be the relative value of the two? We have not what is called "long-term labour"—a year prisoner with us is so called, but should be considered in a contractor's eyes, as simply "apprentice labour."

Respectfully,
CHAS. E. FELTON.
Superintendent.

House of Correction,
Chicago, August 9, 1877.

Detroit House of Correction.

1. What are the dates of your existing contracts? The labour is employed directly by the city, without the intervention of contracts, the Superintendent being the General Manager.

4. Have you any available labour remaining unemployed for want of contractors to hire it? All labour fully employed.

6. For what periods are the prisoners sentenced; giving the *minimum* and *maximum*? The large majority of sentences are under three months, with a sprinkling ranging from that time to life, there being, however, only five in all under life sentence—three females and two males.

8. What is the value of the same when employed on account of the State? Have not estimated the value per day.

Iowa State Prison, Fort Madison.

1. What are the dates of your existing contracts? January 1st, 1875.

2. Have any contracts recently expired? One expired on January 1st, 1875.

3. Have new tenders been asked, and what was the highest tender received? We have let three new contracts at 43 cents and 48 cents per day per man.

4. Have you any available labour remaining unemployed for want of contractors to hire it? None.

5. Are your contractors bound to pay for a certain number of prisoners, whether they are required or not? They are bound to pay for the number contracted for, if we can furnish the men.

6. For what periods are the prisoners sentenced; giving the *minimum* and *maximum*? Minimum, one day; maximum, life.

7. What do you consider the present contract value per day of your prison labour? From 43 cents to 60 cents.

8. What is the value of the same when employed on account of the State? Have no estimates.

9. If you have long-term labour and short-term labour in your prison, what do you consider to be the relative value of the two? The long-term labour is considered by contractors to be far the most valuable.

Yours respectfully,
H. CLAY STUART,
Clerk.

Maryland Penitentiary.

BALTIMORE, August 10th, 1877.

DEAR SIR,—In answer to first interrogatory would state: The date of contract for female labour is September 15th, 1872, which contract was renewed a few days ago. The date of the marble contract, June 3rd, 1874; the shoe contract, December 1st, 1875; foundry contract, August 4th, 1875. A contract for the manufacture of round baskets and splint boxes begins to-morrow, August 11th.

2. As stated above, the contract for female labour has just been renewed, the old contract being about to expire.

3. No new tenders have been received other than the contract mentioned for the manufacture of baskets and boxes.

4. We have no available labour unemployed for want of contractors to hire it.

5. Our contractors engage to take a specified number of men, the number to be increased as the exigencies of their business may demand. A man once employed must be retained until the end of the contract, if not released from the prison, or is not pronounced by the physician to be permanently unfit for service.

6. The sentences of our prisoners range from twelve months up to twenty-one years, and several have been sentenced for life.

7. Fifty cents per day is as much as we can get for prison labour in this section of our country, and we regard it a fair price, especially as our labour is measurably inferior to that of some of the other States; they receiving a higher percentage of skilled hands. A large proportion of our convicts are negroes.

8. We have no labour at present employed on account of the State. This was done several years ago, but was abandoned because it could not be made profitable. We did recently employ a number of men on State account caning chair-bottoms and backs, by the piece, but our utmost efforts only enable us to realize an average of about twenty-five cents per day for each man.

9. Unquestionably long-term men are more preferable, because long experience enables them to attain a degree of proficiency that makes their services of value to the contractor; while, on the other hand, men who are sent for short terms, by the time they become of value their terms are ended.

Very respectfully,
THOMAS S. WILKINSON,
Warden.

W. P. Howland, Esq.

Massachusetts State Prison, Charleston.

1. What are the dates of your existing contracts? Made in '75 and '76, to "as long as the Prison remains at its present site." We shall move into our new Prison next spring.

2. Have any contracts recently expired? None.

3. Have new tenders been asked, and what was the highest tender received? No.

4. Have you any available labour remaining unemployed for want of contractors to hire it? None.

5. Are your contractors bound to pay for a certain number of prisoners, whether they are required or not? Yes.

6. For what periods are the prisoners sentenced: giving the *minimum* and *maximum*? From three years to life.

7. What do you consider the present contract value per day of your prison labour? Fifty-two cents.

8. What is the value of the same when employed on account of the State? Always contract.

9. If you have long-term labour and short-term labour in your prison, what do you consider to be the relative value of the two? No division of terms of sentences.

Michigan State Prison.

JACKSON, August 16, 1877.

SIR,—Enclosed please find hurried answers to the interrogatories of your Commission, received under cover of yours of August 3, 1877.

I regret the lack of time to give better attention to the subjects suggested by the interrogatories, and especially by the last one. The mode, adaptability and value of prison labour are subjects to which the best thought of prison men should be turned, and upon which their ripest judgments should be exercised; and I hope the work of your Commission will, by turning attention in that direction, be productive of good in that direction.

Very respectfully,
W. HUMPHREY,
Warden.

W. P. Howland,
Chairman of Commission,
Toronto, Ontario.

1. What are the dates of your existing contracts? The following tabular statement gives dates of contracts existing October 1, 1876, the prices paid, and other data relating thereto:—

CONTRACTORS.	When Contract took Effect.	Length of Contract.		Expiration of Contract.	No. of Convicts required to fill contract.		Per Diem Contract Price for Labour.		Total per Diem Earnings by Contracts.		What Manufactured.
		Yrs.	Mos.		1875	1876	1875	1876	1875	1876	
Austin, Tomlinson & Webster M'f'g Co.	Oct. 1, 1873	10	..	Sept. 30, 1883	50	50	$1 00	$1 00	$50 00	$50 00	Wagons.
Chas. Hollingsworth	June 1, 1871	5	..	{ Annul'd Dec. '75 }	75	....	50	......	37 50	......	Cigars.
Chas. Hollingsworth	Sept. 1, 1873	5	..	{ Annul'd Dec. '75 }	50	....	65	......	32 50	......	Cigars.
Withington, Cooley & Co.	May 1, 1873	5	2	June 30, 1878	100	100	65	65	65 00	} 101 25	Farming Tools.
Withington, Cooley & Co.	Oct. 1, 1873	4	9	June 30, 1878	50	50	72½	72½	36 25		Farming Tools.
Henry Gilbert & Son	Oct. 1, 1872	5	..	Sept. 30, 1877	100	100	55	55	55 00	55 00	Furniture.
Filkins & Crane	April 1, 1874	10	..	M'ch 31, 1884	40	50	60	65	24 00	32 50	Barrels.
Pingree & Smith	Jan. 19, 1875	5	..	Jan. 18, 1880	50	50	45	55	22 50	27 50	Shoes.
Sutter Brothers	Oct. 18, 1875	5	..	Oct. 17, 1880	....	50	......	53	......	27 50	Cigars.
Totals					515	450	$5 12½	$4 67½	$322 75	$293 75	

Average per diem contract *price*, in cents, was, Sept. 30, 1875.... .64.06
Average per diem contract *price*, in cents, was, Sept. 30, 1876.... .66.78
Average per diem earnings, per convict, in cts., was, Sept. 30, 1875 .62.67
Average per diem earnings, per convict, in cts., was, Sept. 30, 1876 .65.27
Average per diem earnings, per contract, was, Sept. 30, 1875 .... $40 34
Average per diem earnings, per contract, was, Sept. 30, 1876 .... $41 96

2. Have any contracts recently expired? None. The contract with Filkins & Crane was cancelled in the spring, and the contract with Gilbert will expire by limitation September 30th next.

3. Have new tenders been asked, and what was the highest tender received? New tenders have been asked, and the highest tender received is 45 cents per day per convict.

4. Have you any available labour remaining unemployed for want of contractors to hire it? But little—not enough to fill contracts now let until the contract of Gilbert & Son expires.

5. Are your contractors bound to pay for a certain number of prisoners, whether they are required or not? They are for the number given in the above Table, but in addition to these they employ others, that can be thrown off at their option.

6. For what periods are the prisoners sentenced; giving the *minimum* and *maximum*? The following gives the lengths of terms and the number of commitments for each term during the year closing September 30, 1876. It may be presumed to be a fair average of the lengths of terms of a course of years:—

	Aggregate.		Aggregate.
Average of terms..................	3 2-12	5 years	33
		4 years 9 months	1
		4 years 6 months	1
Totals..............................	364	4 years	23
		3 years 6 months	4
		3 years	63
Life, solitary, at hard labour	3	2 years 6 months	14
20 years	1	2 years 3 months	1
18 years	1	2 years	74
15 years	6	1 year 9 months...................	1
12 years	1	1 year 8 months	1
		1 year 6 months	23
10 years	10	1 year 3 months...................	5
8 years	3	1 year	59
7 years six months...................	1	10 months	5
7 years	15	9 months	5
6 years	4	6 months	6

7. What do you consider the present contract value per day of your prison labour? The *contract* value of *our* prison labour *now* is the value of the labour of selected convicts whose terms of service average about five years. The average price of our contract labour, as appears in the tabular statement included in the answer to the first interrogation, is sixty-five cents *per diem*. The average *per diem* that we will receive after the Gilbert & Son's contract expires, and the contracts just made take effect, will be *fifty four* cents and six mills; and I consider our contract prison labour worth fully that price.

8. What is the value of the same when employed on account of the State? We have no established industries, and hence no basis for a definite answer to this interrogatory.

9. If you have long-term labour and short-term labour in your prison, what do you consider to be the relative value of the two? We have both longer and shorter term labour here, but our shortest term convicts do not go on contracts. As to the comparative value of the two, the same considerations would enter into the consideration as in the case of free labour. If the short-term convict be a skilled workman, his labour will be worth more than the long time unskilled convict. Skill is the essence of value in labour. If the short-term convict is unskilled, his labour is of little value as compared with the long-term convict in so far as skilled work is required. Prison *contract* work is manufacturing of a class into which the use of machinery largely enters, and the skilled labourer is but a completing part of the machinery. It takes a long-time convict no longer to acquire the necessary skill than a short-time one. Suppose the time required be six months, and the terms two years and ten years, the skilled to the unskilled labour performed would be for the shorter term as three to one; while in the case of the longer term it would be as nineteen to one,—or the shorter term would put in one-fourth of his time as an unskilled labourer, while the longer term would put in only one-twentieth of his time as an unskilled labourer.

This, when skilled labour is required. But in every manufacturing establishment there is a considerable portion of work for which only a common labourer is required. For this class of work the short-term convict is as valuable as that of the long term one.

The question of "relative value" as applied to the labour of long or short-term convicts, is not a simple one, and its solution can be reached only by a careful consideration of all the conditions under which the labour is performed, and upon the comparative qualification of the different labourers for the work they will be required to perform, as also upon the extent to which the organization of the manufacturing business will admit of such a division of labour, as that the various grades of convicts can readily adapt themselves to their work.

For a business which admits of *such a division* of labour, both classes of convicts would be of equal value as labourers, and the farther from such a division of labour it is necessary to keep, the greater the difference in the value of the two classes of convicts.

New Hampshire State Prison, Concord.

1. What are the dates of your existing contracts ? Oct. 1, 1876, to Oct. 1, 1881.
2. Have any contracts recently expired ? No.
3. Have new tenders been asked, and what was the highest tender received ? None been asked.
4. Have you any available labour remaining unemployed for want of contractors to hire it ? No.
5. Are your contractors bound to pay for a certain number of prisoners, whether they are required or not ? Yes.
6. For what periods are the prisoners sentenced ; giving the *minimum* and *maximum*? One year to life.
9. If you have long-term labour and short-term labour in your prison, what do you consider to be the relative value of the two ? Our labour is all of one class.

New Jersey State Prison.

TRENTON, August 18th, 1877.

SIR,—Enclosed with this you will find answers to the several interrogatories in your circular letter of August 3rd. I will send by same mail my two last reports from which you may possibly gather some additional information.

Very respectfully,
W R. MURPHY,
Supervisor.

W. P. Howland, Esq.

1. What are the dates of your existing contracts ? First—June, 1876 ; second—November, 1876 ; third—December, 1876.
2. Have any contracts recently expired ? One—November, 1876.
3. Have new tenders been asked, and what was the highest tender received ? One offer for 100 convicts at 70c. per diem.
4. Have you any available labour remaining unemployed for want of contractors to hire it ? All our available labour is employed.
5. Are your contractors bound to pay for a certain number of prisoners, whether they are required or not ? All our contracts specify the number to be employed, and must be paid for unless prevented from work by us.
6. For what periods are the prisoners sentenced ; giving the *minimum* and *maximum* ? Minimum—6 months ; maximum—40 years ; and for life for murder in the second degree.
7. What do you consider the present contract value per day of your prison labour ? Average about $2.50.

8. What is the value of the same when employed on account of the State? None employed on State account except for labour incident to the Prison.

9. If you have long-term labour and short-term labour in your prison, what do you consider to be the relative value of the two? Contractors generally prefer to hire convicts, possessing equal capacity, whose sentences run from two to five years.

Ohio State Penitentiary, Columbus.

1. What are the dates of your existing contracts? April 1, 1873; May 6, 1874; July 1st, 1873; August 6, 1874; April 12, 1873; November 1, 1873; November 4, 1873; January 3, 1876; April 6, 1875; May 6, 1874; July 31, 1873; April 12, 1873; May 6, 1874; April 1, 1873; March, 1876.

2. Have any contracts recently expired? Seventeen have expired since October 31st, 1876.

3. Have new tenders been asked, and what was the highest tender received? Yes. 50c.

4. Have you any available labour remaining unemployed for want of any contractors to hire it? Plenty.

5. Are your contractors bound to pay for a certain number of prisoners, whether they are required or not? If they contract for a certain number they are compelled to pay for the same.

6. For what periods are the prisoners sentenced; giving the *minimum* and *maximum*? One year and life.

7. What do you consider the present contract value per day of your prison labour? Fifty cents.

8. What is the value of the same when employed on account of the State? I do not know.

9. If you have long-term labour and short-term labour in your prison what do you consider to be the relative value of the two? We have no such division.

You will see that we could employ our labour at fifty cents, which is all that I think it worth now, but the law here forbids letting for less than seventy cents.

Hoping this will be satisfactory,
Yours with great respect,
JOHN H. GROVE,
Warden.

Rhode Island State Prison, Providence.

1. What are the dates of your existing contracts? June 5th, 1877, contract for fifty men at shoemaking at forty cents per day.

2. Have any contracts recently expired? No, sir.

3. Have new tenders been asked, and what was the highest tender received? Forty cents per day.

4. Have you any available labour remaining unemployed for want of contractors to hire it? We have many jail prisoners employed on State account, also a few State prisoners.

5. Are your contractors bound to pay for a certain number of prisoners, whether they are required or not? Yes, sir.

6. For what periods are the prisoners sentenced; giving the *minimum* and *maximum*? From one year to a life sentence.

7. What do you consider the present contract value per day of your prison labour? Forty cents per day.

8. What is the value of the same when employed on account of the State? Much depends upon the management and success in disposing of goods made by State. I think favourably of the contract system.

9. If you have long-term labour and short-term labour in your prison, what do you consider to be the relative value of the two? We realize forty cents per day for short-term jail prisoners on unskilled labour, but to work at skilled labour jail prisoners cannot be considered worth but little.

Very respectfully,
NELSON VIALL,
Warden R. I. State Prison.

State Prison, Sing Sing, N. Y.

1. What are the dates of your existing contracts? January 1st, 1873; December 1st, 1876; March 29th, 1877; April 18th, 1877.
2. Have any contracts recently expired? No.
3. Have new tenders been asked, and what was the highest tender received? No.
4. Have you any available labour remaining unemployed for want of contractors to hire it? No.
5. Are your contractors bound to pay for a certain number of prisoners, whether they are required or not? Yes.
6. For what periods are the prisoners sentenced; giving *minimum* and *maximum?* Minimum, one year; *maximum*, life.
7. What do you consider the present contract value per day of your prison labour? Fifty cents.
8. What is the value of the same when employed on account of the State? Fifty cents.
9. If you have long-term labour and short-term labour in your prison, what do you consider to be the relative value of the two? I am not prepared to answer this question; for the reason, that my experience in the management of convict labour has been very limited.

B. S. W. CLARK,
Agent and Warden.

Prison, August 11, 1877.

The two following, previously received and marked Exhibits "J" and "K," were also submitted:—

HALIFAX PENITENTIARY,
11th July, 1877.

To the Hon. Wm. Pierce Howland,
Chairman of Commission on Prison Labour, in Central Prison, Toronto.

At the request of the C. C. & M. Company, and with the permission of Jas. G. Moylan, Esq., Inspector of Penitentiaries in the Dominion of Canada, I beg to make the following statement as to convict labour in this penitentiary:

1. The total number of male prisoners is 77.
2. The minimum term of sentence for convicts is 2 years. Common prisoners are now confined to offenders from the army and navy who are to be dismissed from the service, and whose sentences range from 42 to 672 days.
3. There are at present 10 men employed in the manufacture of brooms; and a like number at work in the shoe department. The rest of the prisoners are employed in improving the prison grounds, and in other occupations of a domestic character.
4. The earnings of the Broom department have fallen off very much of late, as will be seen by the following statement, taken from our book, for the months of April, May and June:—

	Cost of material.	Value of labour.
April	$313 64	$363 25
May	213 56	244 00
June	97 43	114 65
	$624 63	$721 90

Those ten men whose labour is represented by the above figures, could nearly quadruple the amount, if the trade were as brisk as it was two years ago ; but the market has been so flooded by outside competition, that even after reducing our prices to an almost nominal rate, we are able to make very few sales indeed.

In the Shoe department our work is principally supplied from a single manufacturing house in town, and consists of "*bottoming*" boots, and for which we received 20 cents a pair. This gives an average of about 30 cents per day—some of the workmen can make 2 pairs daily ; others not so many, according to their skill and disposition.

In my opinion, taking the prisoners one man with another, I do not think that a contractor could afford to take the whole and pay more than 35 cents per man, per day.

The disadvantages of prison labour as against free labour are : 1st. They do not turn out the same *quantity*. 2nd. They do not turn out the same *quality*, when compared with free hands.

A prisoner, although he may be a good workman, sometimes gets into a bad humour, and the only way in which he can get satisfaction for some wrong which he conceives has been done to him, is making bad work and doing as little of it as he possibly can.

The men employed in this department are generally those of comparatively long sentences, say from 3 years and upwards, as it requires considerable time for them to acquire the necessary dexterity and skill to perform suitable and paying work.

In the Broom department it is different ; there the prisoners acquire the necessary amount of skill in from 3 to 6 months, according to their aptness and the branch of the trade in which they are engaged.

In my last Annual Report, I have shown that the average value of prison labour for that year was from 30 to 40 cents per day, for each man.

Hoping the foregoing will be of some service to you,

I have the honour to be, Sir,

Your obedient servant,

JOHN FLINN,

Warden.

ST. JOHN PENITENTIARY,
July 12th, 1877.

To the Hon. Wm. Pierce Howland,
Chairman of the Commission as to Central Prison Labour, Toronto.

With the permission of the Inspector of Penitentiaries, I beg, for the information of the above Commission, to make the following statement as to prison labour in this Penitentiary.

The total daily average number of male prisoners for the past six months, is 138. The terms of sentence will be found in the Report of the Minister of Justice, page 170. There are at present employed in the manufacture of pails, twelve men. They turn out about 15 dozen ordinary size (3 hoops), per day. There are about fifteen men employed at the manufacture of brooms ; they make about 17 dozen per day. I append hereto a list of the present prices for these articles.

Probably with six or seven additional men, and another turning-lathe, double this quantity of pails could be turned out.

At the prices above referred to, which are the utmost that can at present be obtained, the profit over and above the cost of material is very small, and does not represent more than 20 cents per man per day for pail making, and 50 cents per man per day for broom making, —that is of men actually employed at it.

Having a large surplus of prisoners over what I can profitably employ upon the above articles, I am enabled to employ thereon the best men, or those having the longest time to serve.

I find that there is a great difference in the capacity for work, or rather in the turn-out of free labour and prison labour. The men have little or no heart for this work, and they will, as a rule, not do more than they can help doing.

I found from experience that for the prisoners I employed upon pails, that 15 dozen per day was a fair average day's work, and I accordingly fixed that as a "stint," and expect that quantity from them. The same with regard to brooms.

About half of the prisoners are sentenced to terms under two years, as will be seen from my report above referred to. For the reason given I have not been obliged to employ these, except for domestic and other purposes about the prison yard and farm.

In my judgment it would be almost impossible to employ these prisoners profitably upon pail or broom making, as their term would expire soon after they acquired skill in their work. This remark would probably apply with greater force to some industries than others, depending of course upon the amount of skill required for the particular industry. The very limited market we have in the Maritime Provinces for almost every article in large quantities, is a serious drawback on making prison labour profitable.

I should consider it very fortunate if all our spare labour was let to contractors for 35 cents per day per man.

I have the honour to be, Sir,
Your obedient servant,
CHAS. KETCHUM, *Warden.*

PRICE LIST.

Brooms, No. 1 .... $3 00 per dozen.
" 2 Ex. Velvet .... 2 75 "
" 2 Ex. .... 2 50 "
" 2 .... 2 05 "
" 3 Ex. Velvet... 2 00 "
" 3 Ex. .... 1 75 "
" 3 .... 1 45 "
Pails .... 1 60 "
Half-pails .... 1 45 "
Quarter-pails .... 1 00 "
Wash-boards .... 2 10 "
Wash-tubs Nests (6) .... 2 60 "
" (3) .... 1 75 "
Clothes-pins .... 90 box of 5 gross.

Exhibits "2 F," "2 G," and "2 H" were put in.
The Balance Sheet of the Canada Car Company was submitted.

(Exhibit "2 I.")

THOMAS BAILEY, recalled.—I declare that the Balance Sheet now produced and marked as Exhibit No. 103 ("2 I") is a correct statement of the affairs of the Company, as exhibited by their books.

Mr. Gordon (Morrison, Wells & Gordon), representing the Car Company, and Mr. Hardy, representing the Government, each entered very fully into a review of the evidence; after which the Commissioners adjourned to consider their report.

The following is the

COMMISSIONERS' REPORT.

To *His Honour the Honourable Donald Alexander Macdonald, Lieutenant-Governor of the Province of Ontario.*

SIR,—The undersigned, your Commissioners to examine into and report upon the value of the labour of prisoners in the Central Prison, having regard to the value of the works, machinery, and plant provided by the Government of Ontario in connection therewith, to be furnished the Canada Car and Manufacturing Company (limited) under certain agreements between the Government of Ontario, represented by the Inspector of Prisons and the Commissioner of Public Works of the Province, and the said Company, beg leave to report, submitting at the same time a record of the proceedings of the Commission, a full copy of the testimony taken, and the several exhibits mentioned therein and attached thereto.

The Commissioners, to properly inform themselves, upon their first meeting (20th of June), immediately after organizing, visited the Central Prison, where they observed for themselves the nature of the industries carried on by the Company, the organization of the labour, and the efficiency of the business administration ; also the machinery, plant, &c., supplied by the Government, and the thoroughness of the discipline maintained by the prison authorities. Afterwards, and at a later date, Commissioners Howland and Noxon personally visited three of the prisons in the United States corresponding nearest in the class of prisoners confined, and in the character of the employment supplied to the Central Prison here, viz., the House of Correction at Detroit, Michigan, the Workhouse or House of Correction at Cleveland, Ohio, and the Erie County Penitentiary at Buffalo, New York. At each of these establishments every opportunity was afforded the Commissioners to obtain such information as they desired, and they beg leave to here acknowledge their obligations to the several superintendents in charge for the kind courtesies received. Also a circular letter (copy of which and the replies thereto is hereto appended), was addressed to all, or nearly all, of the American and Canadian prisons, bringing in return replies of considerable value from seventeen of them, including, however, one of those the Commissioners had previously visited. In the taking of evidence, the parties to the inquiry have been allowed full scope to bring forward such testimony as they chose to present, and neither of them has been remiss in that regard, as is evidenced by the fact that the Commission has occupied eight days in receiving it, as well as by the extent of the record containing it, submitted herewith.

The Commissioners have sought to exclude from the considerations governing their conclusions topics of great general importance, such as the question of public policy in regard to the employment of prisoners at mechanical pursuits or otherwise; whether prisoners so employed should be contracted out at a given rate *per diem*, as is customary, and as is the case at the Central Prison, or be employed directly for the Government, and without the intervention of contractors ; whether under a different system of sentences, or with possible additional inducements to industry and good conduct generally, to be supplied, through rewards, and improved methods of discipline, their labour might or might not be made more valuable. Nor do they attempt to determine whether the current rate for prisoners' labour in all the prisons is less or more than the real value as compared with the rates paid for similar work when performed by free labour and under ordinary circumstances, but rather assume that the price generally paid by contractors is the better standard of value for the purposes of this inquiry. And the simple statement of the Company here that they have made no profit, or have suffered loss by their contract at the Central Prison, is not deemed of itself sufficient to determine the fair value of the prisoners' labour.

There is now, and has been always, a wide difference for mechanical or manufacturing purposes in the estimate placed by contractors upon the labour of prisoners and that of free labour ; it is to be explained in that the prisoners cannot be relied on for experienced work except after considerable time consumed in instructing them, and then only for the period of their imprisonment, which is short, as compared with the period of time citizens usually work at a given occupation. Under present prison administration, the labour of prisoners is measurably a forced labour, the prisoners not being actuated actively by the ordinary incitements and ambition belonging to citizens and freemen at their work. Contractors employing prisoners must continue the business and pay for their labour, whether the market for their commodities is favourable or not. There is also always some embarrassment to the manufacturer employing prison labour to be anticipated from the necessarily divided control of the prisoners' operations. Of course, there are certain advantages to be had in the employment of prisoners, and much might be said on that side also ; but the considerations cited have great weight with employers, and have the effect to depreciate the current value of prisoners' labour very much below that of citizens employed in similar pursuits, so that it can be disposed of at only about one-third of the price paid for free labour.

The value to contractors of prison labour is affected, as is the value of all labour, by the general conditions of trade throughout the country at any given time, and the Commissioners are not unmindful of the present depression, but take into account also that the contract of the Company extends over a number of years, during which it is not unreasonable to expect some improvement in that regard. So too, the productiveness of prisoners' labour is affected by the degree of adaptability of the work to be done, to the class and capacity of the prisoners employed; by the tact and ability with which the contractor organizes the employees, arranges the factory, directs the labour, and generally conducts the business; by the wisdom and thoroughness of the management of the prison and prisoners by the prison authorities; by the degree of harmony and co-operation between the contractor, his agents, and the government of the prison; and by the character of the shops and value of machinery, plant, &c., supplied with the prisoners. But mainly, and very apparently, it is affected by the class of prisoners confined, and the duration of their terms of sentence.

There are generally two classes of prisons:—The one designed for custody of criminals sentenced to imprisonment for one year and more, even to sentences for life. These prisons have many prisoners under sentence for three, four, five, and from that to ten years. The other prisons are variously styled, namely, Workhouse, House of Correction, and Penitentiary. Their prison population consists mainly of misdemeanants under sentences of from ten days to a few weeks or months, and large numbers committed in default of payment of fines, and in default of sureties for good behaviour (liable, of course, to be released at any time), and also a small proportion sentenced for one year or more. The Detroit House of Correction is a notable illustration of this class of prisons. The Central Prison here, more properly belonging to the latter class, should not really be classed with either, because, as the Commissioners are informed, there is, on the one hand, a *maximum* limit, so that two years is the longest term of sentence, and on the other, through the regulations under which prisoners are transferred to this prison from the gaols of the Province, the worthless class included among the short-term prisoners in this class of prisons in the United States, are in a great measure excluded.

The Commissioners are of opinion that, so far as the first above-mentioned particulars affecting the value of prison labour are concerned, there is no essential difference between these conditions at the Central Prison and at other prisons on this side of the Atlantic, and that the sentence and system of selecting the prisoners here, and the machinery, plant, &c., so liberally furnished by the Government, makes their labour of about the same value as the average value of prison labour in all the seventeen prisons from which replies to their inquiries have been received, including, as it does, prisons of both the classes named, and also the Canadian prisons at St. John and Halifax (no reply having been received from Kingston). It is ascertained, from a calculation made from the returns from these prisons, that the average contract price per *diem*, on contracts entered into during 1876 and 1877, stating it exactly, is ($44\frac{23}{100}$c.) forty-four cents and twenty-three hundredths. Or, if the price of prison labour in the two classes of prisons be considered separately, it is seen that in the long date prisons it averages $45\frac{1}{4}$ cents, and in the short date prisons 39 cents; or, including the Erie County Penitentiary, where the sentences average extremely short, and the contract price is, therefore, extremely small, the average is 35 cents, but it must be remembered that in these prisons only workshops with their bare walls are furnished by the Government with these prisoners.

In the course of the examination, it has been estimated by the most competent experts (as has already been stated) that the fair value of prison labour of the class we are specially considering is—taking one year with another—one third of the current rate for wages of citizens similarly employed outside. Now, if it is adjudged that the wages for unskilled labour outside is one dollar per *diem*, and for skilled labour one dollar and a half, and that 21 per cent., or thereabout, of the prison labour at the Central Prison may be classed as skilled labour; then, upon the basis of one-third value, and the employment of the number contracted for, namely, two hundred and sixty, we have 37 cents as the average value of the whole, to which an addition should be made for the unusual amount of machinery, plant, &c., supplied with the prisoners.

Finally, after having given due consideration to the voluminous testimony submitted, the Commissioners have concluded that, were they called upon to name one sum per *diem*, as their opinion of the fair value of the labour at the Central Prison, having regard to the machinery, plant, &c., supplied by the Government, that sum would be forty-two (42) cents, but believing it more equitable to all concerned, and less likely to suggest further differences in future, they have unanimously agreed to report that a fair price to be paid for the labour aforesaid is—For all prisoners whose term of imprisonment shall expire in less than one year, *forty cents per diem* (40c.) ; and for all prisoners whose term of sentence shall exceed one year, *fifty cents per diem* (50c.). These rates per day to cover, of course, the use of all machinery, plant, &c., as agreed to be supplied by the Government.

All of which is respectfully submitted.

W. P. HOWLAND,
Z. R. BROCKWAY, } *Commissioners.*
JAMES NOXON,

Toronto, Sept. 15th, 1877.

APPENDIX.

(EXHIBIT " A.")

Agreement between the Government and the Canada Car Company, of date March 17th, 1873. (*See* page 3.)

(EXHIBIT " B.")

Agreement between the Government and the Canada Car Company, of date January 27th, 1876. (*See* page 6.)

(EXHIBIT " C.")

Report of the Michigan State Prison for 1876.

(EXHIBIT " D.")

Weekly Return of work done for the Company.

(EXHIBIT " E.")

Orders for the Regulation of Shop Gangs.

1. The Guards in charge of shop gangs shall not allow any Prisoner to sit down whilst at work. No lounging or loitering shall be permitted.

2. Should a Prisoner be observed by a Guard standing idle, and the Guard having ascertained from the foreman that he, the Prisoner, has nothing at the time to do, the Guard shall order the Prisoner away from his place of work to the centre of the shop where he shall *remain in view of the Guard with his arms folded* until the Guard is notified by the foreman that he should resume work. Should there be more than one Prisoner, the Guard shall place them four feet apart.

3. In event of a Prisoner being found in a shop who does not belong to that shop gang, the Guard in charge shall at once require of the Prisoner to state under whose directions he was sent there, and if the Prisoner's reply is not to the satisfaction of the officer, the Guard shall deliver the Prisoner over to the Deputy-Warden who will commit him to the Dark Cell, pending the decision of the Warden.

4. Should a Prisoner report himself sick in the morning, and unable to work, and upon medical inspection *is sent to work by the Surgeon*, that Prisoner shall be rationed upon bread and water for that day and the following day, and be deprived of his tobacco till further orders.

285

5. Guards in charge of shop gangs and working parties are on no account to allow mor than one Prisoner at a time to repair to the buckets; and the Prisoner *shall report himself* t his *Guard immediately on his return.* The bucket is to be placed in close proximity to the shop or spot where the gang is at work, and the Guards are to be particular that Prisoner are not away from their work for a longer period than is absolutely necessary, as Prisoner are apt to idle and absent themselves from their work upon the plea of answering the call nature.

W. S. PRINCE,
Warden.

(EXHIBIT " F.")

Fifth Annual Report of the Directors of Penitentiaries of the Dominion of Canada fo the year 1872.

(EXHIBIT " G.")

Statement showing periods of sentence and previous occupations of Prisoners in the Central Prison.

PERIOD OF SENTENCE.	Number of prisoners committed in 1874.	Number of prisoners committed in 1875.	Number of prisoners committed in 1876.	Number of prisoners committed in 1877.	Total number committed up to 1st May, 1877.
One month	....	....	18	....	18
Two months	69	13	77	13	172
Three do	54	38	85	34	211
Four do	50	56	93	21	220
Five do	5	18	6	11	40
Six do	97	205	187	140	629
Seven do	....	2	1	1	4
Eight do	6	8	4	....	18
Nine do	4	7	21	3	35
Ten do	1	4	6	1	12
Eleven do	1	....	2	....	3
Twelve do	38	45	94	53	230
Thirteen do	....	....	1	....	1
Fourteen do	....	....	....	2	2
Fifteen do	2	1	7	1	11
Eighteen do	10	12	17	15	54
Nineteen do	1	....	....	....	1
Twenty do	2	....	....	....	2
Twenty-one do	....	....	1	....	1
Twenty-two do	1	....	1	....	2
Twenty-three do	4	3	8	6	21
Two years	10	14	8	15	47
Two and a half do	1	....	....	....	1
Three do	3	....	....	1	4
Three and a half do	1	....	....	....	1
Four do	5	....	....	....	5
Four and a half do	1	....	....	....	1
Five do	4	....	....	1	5
	370	426	637	318	1,751

Occupation of Prisoners prior to Commitment.	1874.	1875.	1876.	1877.	Total.
Architect			1		1
Barbers	6	6	6	5	23
Bakers	3	6	5	2	16
Basket-maker			1		1
Blacksmiths	11	13	11	8	43
Brushmaker	10		1	1	12
Bricklayer and Plasterers		8	4	4	16
Butchers	3	5	15	6	29
Brakesmen			2	2	4
Boiler-makers			8	3	11
Brick-makers			2		2
Broom-maker			1		1
Boat-builder			1		1
Book-binders			3	1	4
Book-keepers				2	2
Bar-tenders				2	2
Carpenters	18	29	28	18	93
Clerks	5	7	16	7	35
Cooks	3	2	5	1	11
Chair-makers		1	2		3
Chemist			1		1
Coopers	2	2	6	5	15
Currier			1		1
Cabinet-makers	3	2	4		9
Cigar-makers	3	5	6	1	15
Confectioner	1				1
Carriage-makers				3	3
Cab-drivers				2	2
Dyer			1		1
Dispensers	2	1			3
Dentist		1			1
Engineers	3	6	1	2	12
Engraver				1	1
Farmers	21	10	15	14	60
Firemen		3	3	3	9
Fur-dresser	1				1
Fisherman		1			1
Grooms	2	1	1	2	6
Gardeners		2	1	1	4
Grain-dealer				1	1
Harness-makers			3	4	7
Hatter			1		1
Hostler				1	1
Jockey			1		1
Jewellers		1		1	2
Locksmiths			2		2
Labourers	133	188	316	123	760
Lock-fitter				1	1
Musician			1		1
Moulders	6	8	12	9	35
Machinists	5	5	9	6	25
Miners			3		3
Merchants			3		3
Miller			1		1
Masons	4	1			5
Millwright				1	1
No Trade	53	23	3		79
Printers	1	4	5	1	11
Peddlers		1	6	3	10
Painters	18	11	26	12	67
Plumbers			7	1	8
Proof-reader			1		1
Pattern-maker			1		1
Photographer			1		1
Polisher				1	1
Plasterer		1			1
Ropemaker				1	1
Sailors	16	26	23	14	79
Shoemakers	11	19	18	16	64
Spinner			1		1
Ship-Carpenter			1		1
Salesman			1		1
Stone-masons		3	7	3	13

Occupation of Prisoners prior to Commitment.	1874.	1875.	1876.	1877.	Total.
Steam-fitter			1		1
Saddlers	1	3			4
Saw-maker		1			1
Suttle-maker		1			1
Stove mounter		1			1
Soldiers	2				2
Stone-cutters	3				3
Tailors	11	11	10	9	41
Teachers	1	1	1		3
Tobacconist			1		1
Tinsmiths		1	5	4	10
Traveller			1		1
Telegraph operators		2		2	4
Teamsters	5				5
Tavern keeper				1	1
Upholsterers		1	1		2
Varnishers			3		3
Weavers	1	2	2	1	6
Waiters			2	3	5
Watchmakers	1		3		4
Waggon-maker			1		1
Wood-turners			1	1	2
White-washer	1				1
Wool-carder				1	1
Wool-sorter				1	1
	370	426	637	318	1,751

(Exhibit " H.")

Returns of work done in Carpenter and Trades Department, work done on Permanent Improvements, and Statement showing cash returns for articles and labour, Carpenter Department, Kingston Penitentiary. Pages 38, 39 and 40 of the Report of the Minister of Justice as to Penitentiaries in Canada, for the year 1876.

(Exhibit "I.")

Report of the Minister of Justice as to Penitentiaries in Canada, for the year 1876.

(Exhibit " J.")

Statement of Warden of St. John, N.B., Penitentiary (see page 279).

(Exhibit " K.")

Statement of Warden of Halifax Penitentiary (see page 278).

(Exhibit "L.")

STATEMENT of Machinery, Fittings and Fixtures placed in the buildings for the exclusive use of the Canada Car Company.

		$ cts.	$ cts.
Dickey, Neill & Co	Steam engines, boilers, shafting, &c	20,052 41	
Neil Currie	Cupolas, &c................................	9,177 88	
Canada Car Company	Sundries	7,000 00	
Sundries	Connected with machinery	1,404 65	
Repairs of Machinery	Engine-house, Lake Shore	1,946 28	
Dickey, Neill & Co	Account steam-engines, boilers, shafting, &c..	2,750 12	
Neil Currie	Tanks	1,000 00	
Canada Car & Manufacturing Co.	Sundries........	3,941 33	
John Fensom	Spiders, countershafts, pulleys, &c..........	85 78	
Neil Currie	Scaffolding to cupolas	100 00	
George Harding	Sundries	886 00	
			48,344 45
Sundries.................	Wages—cost of overseeing labour...........	1,125 30	
Do		600 00	
Do		679 61	
			2,404 91
Canada Car Company	Paid under agreement	15,576 07	
			15,576 07
			66,325 43

(Exhibit "M.")

CENTRAL PRISON.

YARD AREA.

	Feet.	Feet.
Lumber Yard	453 by 264½	119,818
Prison "	599½ " 496	297,352
Total		417,170

SPACE OCCUPIED FOR PRISON PURPOSES.

Quadrangle in centre and road space opposite	209 by 140	29,260	
Water closets	51 " 20	1,020	
Bucket space	40 " 38	1,520	
Laundry, bake-house, store-house & weigh scale	80 " 40	3,200	
Coal shed	103 " 25	2,575	
Root house	50 " 24	2,100	
Proposed stable	40 " 38	1,520	
			41,195

Leaving for Car Company shops, &c 375,975

DIMENSIONS OF SHOPS OCCUPIED BY CANADA CAR COMPANY.

North Wood Shop. *Inside Measurements.*

Lower floor........	196 by 46.4	9,081	
Less prison boiler and coal bin		351	8,730
Upper floor...............			7,208
			15,938

South Iron Shop.
                Lower floor............................ 196 by 46.4   9,081
                Less prison boiler house, coal bin and
                        engineer's room   526   8,555
                Upper floor............................ 156 by 46.4   7,208
                                                                            ——— 15,763
Foundry Building and Connections.
                Lower floor, main building............157.6 by 77.6   12,206
                Workshop in upper flat of .... 157 " 50   7,850
Connections.
                Brick coal-house....................... 17.6 " 16   280
                Cupola   "   15   " 19   285
                Wooden shed .... 34 " 26   884
                2nd brick cupola house 15   " 19   285
                Brick core oven 10   " 14   140
                                                                            ——— 9,724
Forge building, fitted as shops.
                Ground floor centre ....109.8 by 49.6   5,429
                        "   west wing .... 52 " 24   1,248
                        "   east wing .... 64 " 24.6 1,578
                Second "   ....107 " 49   5,243
                Third "   ....107 " 16   1,712
                                                                            ——— 15,201
Erecting and Paint Shop.
                Ground floor ....190 by 68   12,920
                Less angle S. W. corner..................   165   12,755
                Upper floor in part ....190 by 13.9   2,612
                                                                            ——— 15,367
Broom Shop.
                Ground floor   ....186.6 by 31.6   3,733
Brush Shop.
                One floor .... 70 by 18.6   1,295
*Large drying kiln......   .... 70 " 17.6   1,225
*Small   "   .... 33 " 11   363
*Two sheds to drying kiln, each............. 20 " 10   400
                                                                            ———
                        Total inside floor, space of feet........................... 91,224

(EXHIBIT "N.")

FOUR HUNDRED AND FIFTY-FOUR PRISONERS RECEIVED IN THE CENTRAL PRISON
    FROM 18TH SEPTEMBER, 1876, TO 18TH JUNE, 1877.

OCCUPATIONS.

Tanners	22	Brush-makers	1
Labourers	190	Fullers....................................	1
Butchers	10	Waiters	6
Sailors	16	Barbers...................................	6
Harness makers	4	Engineers	4
Coopers	5	Grooms	2
Shoe-makers	20	Peddlers.................................	4
Carpenters	24	Carriage-makers	4
Painters	16	Clerks	9
Moulders	11	Wool-carders	1

Stone-masons	4	Printers	2
Tinsmiths	6	Bar-tenders	2
Polishers	1	Lock-fitters	2
Bakers	4	Plasterers	3
Blacksmiths	11	Brakemen	3
Tailors	11	Weavers	1
Turners	1	Cooks	3
Millwrights	2	Tavern-keepers	2
Hostlers	2	Gardeners	2
Telegraph operators	2	Wool-sorters	1
Engravers	1	Grain-dealers	1
Cigar-makers	1	Plumbers	2
Book-binders	2	Bricklayers	4
Boiler-makers	3	Machinists	11
Cab-drivers	2		
Firemen	6		454

AGES.

Under 18 years	12
From 18 to 20 years	70
" 20 to 30 "	200
" 30 to 40 "	100
" 40 to 50 "	40
" 50 to 60 "	27
" 60 to 70 "	5
Total	454

Warden's Office, Central Prison, June 18th, 1877.

(EXHIBIT "O.")

MARCH 14th, 1877.

SIR,—The foreman having the supervision of the prisoners employed in the construction of boxes has complained to me that the prisoners employed at that work fail to accomplish their proper amount of daily labour.

Now, it is my duty to see that all prisoners who are not incapacitated from labour, by medical direction, perform an ordinary day's labour. And if a prisoner does not do so he shall be punished until he does. But, in order that I should not make a mistake in enforcing *more* than an ordinary day's labour, I shall be glad if you will ascertain and inform me what amount of labour per day is expected to be performed by these prisoners, and what, in the judgment of experienced and skilled foremen, they are able to accomplish in a day's work, so that I can come to some conclusion whether they really perform an ordinary day's labour or not.

Unskilled men cannot, of course, turn out the same number of boxes in a day as a skilled workman could, but what I desire to guard against is, that the prisoners are not forced to accomplish a larger amount of labour than they are capable of, and that the statutory application of the term "ordinary day's labour" may be properly interpreted to guide me in the infliction of punishment.

Your obedient servant,
(Signed) W. S. PRINCE,
Warden, C. P.

To the Managing Director,
    Canada Car Company.

(EXHIBIT "P.")

CANADA CAR & MANUFACTURING Co., (LIMITED.)
TORONTO, May 8th, 1877.

DEAR SIR,—I beg to call your attention to the fact that there is only one guard appointed to control some seventy odd prisoners, stationed in three different shops, and they situated some five or six hundred yards from each other, thus rendering their being looked after properly, a physical impossibility.

Also to the utter disregard of what is understood to be a prison rule, viz. : prisoners sitting down during a temporary stoppage of work and holding conversation with each other, or grouping together in less than six feet from each other.

For the past two months we have kept returns of work done in the different departments, and are now able to report what is an ordinary day's labour outside, what the prisoners can easily do, and what they have actually done.

	Outside Labour.	Prisoners can do.	Are doing.	Should do each day.
No. 1 lathe	600 Pails per day	500 per day	165 Pails	400 Pails.
2 " (Churn)	500 " "	400 "	120 "	375 "
		125 }		110 No. 1 tubs.
3 " (Tub)	125 Tubs "	150 } "	75 Tubs	135 " 2 "
		175 }		160 " 3 "
4 "	600 Pails "	500 "	165 Pails	400 pails.

This allows for all drawbacks such as new men, &c.

In the Brush Department there are six men drawing, and the number of holes drawn by outside labour is 8,000 holes ; they are only doing at the rate of 3,200 holes per day, and should do at least 6,000.

In the Broom Department, the winders on the hand machines, of whom there are six, have only been doing 25 and some 30 brooms per day ; they are capable and have done 60 of the best and 75 of the common, while the sewers, who have been turning off only 25 to 30, are capable of sewing 75 of the best and 100 of the common brooms.

The prisoners engaged baling the pails acknowledge themselves they can each do 1,200 per day, whereas on Saturday they only did between 600 or about a quarter of a day's work.

The results, as shown by the weekly returns, are very discouraging to the Board of Directors, and will, if continued, prove disastrous to the Company ; we have orders for more goods than we can produce, and only require your co-operation to very materially increase our present out-put.

I am, yours truly,
THOMAS BAILEY,
Sec-Treas.

The Warden,
Central Prison, City.

(EXHIBIT "Q.")

Terms of sentences of prisoners now employed by the Canada Car Company, Central Prison :—

```
5 years ................................................................. 1
3   " ................................................................. 1
2   " .................................................................26
1 year and 11 months.................................................. 4
18 months.............................................................18
12 months.............................................................71
9 months.............................................................. 4
6 months.............................................................77
3 months.............................................................10
2 months............................................................. 3
```

Total... 215

The following long-sentenced prisoners now employed at domestic work, were first accepted by the Company and then were rejected :—

Thomas Brooks........................... 2 years.
Charles Stephens.......................... 2 years.
Moses Fizzell............................. 2 years.
John Baxter.............................. 2 years, physically unfit for prison labour.
Patrick McCabe .... 1 year and 11 months.
John Fair................................ 1 year and 11 months.
Joseph Colton........................... 12 months.
Richard McOwen........................ 12 months.
John Breen.............................. 12 months.

(EXHIBIT " R.")

Sixth Annual Report of the Directors and Superintendent of the Cleveland Workhouse.

(EXHIBIT " S.")

CENTRAL PRISON, ONTARIO
TORONTO, March 22nd,

I return 8 of the night buckets as useless, owing to leakage.

(Signed)   W. S. PRINCE,
Warden.

To the Superintendent Car Co., Central Prison.

(EXHIBIT " T.")

CENTRAL PRISON OF ONTARIO, TORONTO.

I send you some brooms of yours which I should think are indifferently made. The nly work that they have been put to is to sweep a plain floor.

W. S. PRINCE,
Warden.

To the Superintendent, Canada Car Company.

(EXHIBIT " U.")

CANADA CAR AND MANUFACTURING COMPANY (Limited.)
TORONTO, April 24th, 1877.

DEAR SIR,—I have to inform you that the guard stationed in the paint shop has for some time past been utterly incapable of controlling the prisoners employed there, either by preserving that discipline necessary to a proper discharge of the work placed in their hands, or by preventing a very large waste of tools and material.

He is continually talking and joking with the prisoners, and is so *familiar* as to occasionally have three or four around him—this Mr. Brandon and the foremen of the shop can testify to.

This morning some of the prisoners turned the tap of a barrel of varnish and wasted all its contents on the floor ; this is a very serious matter to us, and I hope you will take such steps with regard to the whole matter as will protect the interests of the Company.

I am, yours truly,
THOS. BAILEY,
Secretary-Treasurer.

The Warden, Central Prison, City.

(EXHIBIT " V.")

CENTRAL PRISON OF ONTARIO,
TORONTO, March 19th.

I cannot consent to any time being deducted for shaving purposes. It has never been the practice in this prison, neither in the prisons in the States.

W. S. PRINCE,
Warden.

To the Managing Director,
Canada Car Company.

(EXHIBIT " W.")

WARDEN'S OFFICE, CENTRAL PRISON OF ONTARIO,
TORONTO, March 14th, 1877.

To the Managing Director, Canada Car Company.

SIR,—The foreman having the supervision of the prisoners employed on the construction of boxes has complained to me that the prisoners employed at that work fail to accomplish their proper amount of daily labour.

Now it is my duty to see that all prisoners, who are not incapacitated from labour by medical direction, perform *an ordinary day's labour*, and if a prisoner does not do so, he shall be *punished until he does.* But in order that I should not make a mistake in enjoining more *than an ordinary day's labour,* I shall be glad if you will ascertain and inform me what amount of labour per day is expected to be performed by these prisoners, and what, in the judgment of *experienced* and *skilled* foremen, they are able to accomplish in a day's work ; so that I can come to some conclusion whether they really perform an *ordinary day's labour* or not. Unskilled men cannot, of course, turn out the same number of boxes a day as a skilled workman could, but what I desire to guard against is, that the prisoners are not forced to accomplish a larger amount of labour than they are capable of, and that the statutory application of the term—*ordinary day's labour*—may be properly interpreted, to guide me in the infliction of punishment.

Your obedient servant,
W. S. PRINCE,
Warden, C. P.

(EXHIBIT " X.")

PRISONERS RECEIVED, JULY 19TH, 1877.

James Welsh,	Labourer	6 months.
Edward Howard,	Shoemaker	6 "
John Hannings,	Plumber	3 "
James McIver,	Labourer	3 "
John Williams,	Gardener	40 days.

William Murray,	Joiner	2	months.
Francis Walker,	Grocer	2	"
Samuel Degear,	Carpenter	2	"
James Griffin,	Labourer	1	"
Richard Morrison,	Labourer	40	days.
Joseph Strau,	Labourer	2	months.
John Riddell,	Butcher	3	"
James McMahon,	Labourer	12	"
James Moore,	Labourer	3	"
Charles Womsley,	Tailor	2	"
Robert Brown,	Mason	2	"

Central Prison, July 19th, 1877.

(EXHIBIT " Y.")

PRISONERS RECEIVED, JULY 17TH, 1877.

George Murphy,	Baker	3	months.
William Furlong,	Shoemaker	30	days.
John Daley,	Blacksmith	2	months.
Edward Hall,	Cabinet maker	2	"

Central Prison, July 18th, 1877.

(EXHIBIT " Z.")

Estimate of the cost of maintenance of the prison for one year, and the revenue derivable from available labour on the basis of an average of 330 prisoners for each day.

330 prisoners for 365 days, or 120,450 days, at 43 cents $51,793 50

Available Labour.

264 prisoners for 313 days, or 82,632 days, at 50 cents $41,316 00
Liable to be reduced by
holidays 5
16 weeks of short time $19\frac{1}{3} = \frac{1}{5}$ of 96 days

$24\frac{1}{5}$ days or 6,336 ds. at 50 cents $3,168 00——38,148 00

Or about 26 per cent. deficiency $13,545 50

(EXHIBIT " 2 A.")

Sixth Annual Report of the Inspector of Asylums, Prisons, &c., for the Province of Ontario, 1872-3.

(EXHIBIT " 2 B.")

Seventh Annual Report of the Inspector of Asylums, Prisons, &c., for the Province of Ontario, 1874.

295

(EXHIBIT " 2 C.")

Ninth Annual Report of the Inspector of Asylums, Prisons, &c., for the Province of Ontario, 1876.

(EXHIBIT " 2 D.")

PRODUCT of Lathes when less than 321 per day from April 28th to July 21st, 1877.

				Pails.	Pails.	Pails.	REMARKS.
April 28	No. 1 Lathe,			190	No. 2, 310		No. 1 broke down.
" 30	" 2	"		220			
May 1	" 4	"		250			Green hands
" 2	" 4	"		305			Green hands.
" 4	" 1	"		140	No. 2, 120	No. 4, 80	
" 5	" 1	"		208		" 4, 180	
" 7	" 1	"		190		" 4, 160	
" 8	" 1	"		290		" 4, 250	
" 10	" 1	"		250		" 4, 230	
" 11	" 1	"		280		" 4, 230	
" 13	" 1	"		180		" 4, 160	
" 14	" 1	"		150		" 4, 120	....No. 4 broke down.
" 15	" 1	"		220		" 4, 180	
" 18	" 1	"		260		" 4, 260	
" 19	" 1	"		175		" 4, 180	
" 21	" 1	"		250		" 4, 180	
" 22	" 1	"		320		" 4, 260	
" 23	" 1	"		300		" 4, 300	
" 25						" 4, 210	
" 26	" 1	"		240			
" 28	" 1	"		280			
" 29	" 1	"		260			
" 30	" 1	"		230			
" 31						" 4, 200	......Green hands.
June 1	" 1	"		240			Green hands.
" 2	" 1	"		180			No. 1 broke down.
" 4	" 1	"		220		No. 4, 240	......Green hands.
" 5	" 1	"		240		" 4, 230	......Green hands.
" 6	" 1	"		260		" 4, 280	......Green hands.
" 9	" 1	"		180	No. 5, 180	" 4, 240	
" 11	" 1	"		250	" 5, 220	" 4, 300	
" 13	" 1	"		250	" 5, 240	" 4, 170	......Green hands.
" 14	" 1	"		152	" 5, 106	" 4, 226	
" 28	" 1	"		180	" 5, 240		
" 30	" 1	"		260	" 5, 260	" 4, 260	
July 5	" 1	"		315	" 5, 300	" 4, 280	
" 6					" 5, 225	" 4, 225	
" 7	" 1	"		180	" 5, 180	" 4, 160	
" 11	" 1	"		260	" 5, 230	" 4, 290	
" 12					" 5, 275		
" 14	" 1	"		260	" 5, 264	" 4, 260	
" 16	" 1	"		175	" 5, 230	" 4, 300	
" 17	" 1	"		225	" 5, 283	" 4, 288	
" 18	" 1	"		225	" 5, 225	" 4, 225	
" 19	" 1	"		225	" 5, 225	" 4, 225	
" 20	" 1	"		225	" 5, 225	" 4, 225	
" 21	" 1	"		180	" 5, 180	" 4, 180	
				2,710	3,342	2,910	

(Exhibit "2 E.")

Return of Work executed daily by Prisoners in the North Machine Shop, Central Prison, for the month, May, 1877.

Date		Lathe		Quantity		Remarks
May 1	No.	1	Lathe,	500	Pails	Six men employed on each lathe.
" 1	"	2	"	400	"	On April 30th Mr. Brandon told the
" 1	"	3	"	380	"	prisoners he would give them a cent
" 1	"	4	"	250	"	for every pail they would make over 375, that being the number he required of them for a day's work.
" 2	"	1	"	360	"	Delayed two hours for staves.
" 2	"	2	"	370	"	Do do
" 2	"	3	"	360	"	Do do
" 2	"	4	"	300	"	Do do
						On the 3rd idle all day for staves.
" 4	"	1	"	260	"	Idle two hours for staves.
" 4	"	2	"	200	"	Do do
" 4	"	3	"	5 Tubs		Do do
" 4	"	4	"	150 Pails		do and getting driver fixed.
" 5	"	1	"	208	"	Idle one hour and a half for staves.
" 5	"	2	"	90	"	Do do
" 5	"	3	"	60 Tubs		Do do
" 5	"	4	"	180 Pails		Do do
" 7	"	1	"	190	"	Two hours idle for staves.
" 7	"	2	"	130	"	Do do
" 7	"	3	"	80 Tubs		
" 7	"	4	"	160 Pails		Do do
" 8	"	1	"	290	"	
" 8	"	2	"	190	"	Two green hands on this lathe.
" 8	"	3	"	90 Tubs		Green setter up.
" 8	"	4	"	250 Pails		Five hours idle waiting for staves, then changed Lathe.
" 9	"	1	"	330	"	
" 9	"	2	"	230	"	
" 9	"	3	"	40 Tubs		
" 9	"	4	"	280 Pails		
" 10	"	1	"	250	"	
" 10	"	2	"			Changed from pails to churns.
" 10	"	3	"	280 Pails		Two bottom hoopers idle all day for want of hoop iron.
" 10	"	4	"	240	"	
" 11	"	1	"	280	"	Three men idle all day for want of hoops; five men idle afternoon for want of hoop iron.
" 11	"	2	"	9 Union Churns		
" 11	"	3	"	280 Pails		
" 11	"	4	"	280	"	
" 12	"	1	"	180	"	Three pail lathes idle near all afternoon for want of staves.
" 12	"	2	"	12 Union Churns		
" 12	"	3	"	150 Pails		
" 12	"	4	"	160	"	
" 14	"	1	"	160	"	Three pail lathes idle for two hours and a half for want of staves.
" 14	"	2	"	16 Union Churns		
" 14	"	3	"	160 Pails		Very bad cedar to work.
" 14	"	4	"	120	"	
" 15	"	1	"	170	"	
" 15	"	2	"	14 Union Churns		

					REMARKS.
May 15.....	...No. 3	Lathe,	40 Tubs and Pails......	Changed from pails to tubs.
" 15.......	" 4	"	160 Pails...............	Two pail lathes idle for want of staves. Lathes wanted fixing. No person to do it, foreman being sick.
" 16........	" 1	"	260 "	Two hours working culls.
" 16	" 2	"	19 Union Churns	
" 16........	" 3	"	60 Tubs......	Four hours idle getting matcher fixed.
" 16........	" 4	"	230 Pails......	
" 17........	" 1	"	280 Pails.....	Idle one hour and a half for staves.
" 17........	" 2	"	20 Union Churns	
" 17........	" 3	"	80 Tubs...............	
" 17.........	" 4	"	230 Pails.........	Idle one hour and a half for staves.
" 18........	" 1	"	260 "	
" 18.........	" 2	"	16 Union Churns	
" 18.........	" 3	"	110 Tubs.............	Nine men idle all day for want of hoop iron.
" 18	" 4	"	260 Pails........ ,.........	Idle one hour and a half getting lathe repaired. New hand setting up.
" 19........	" 1	"	180 "	
" 19........	" 2	"	11 Churns...............	Out of repair two hours.
" 19.......	" 3	"	80 Tubs........	Nine men idle all day for want of hoop iron.
" 19........	" 4	"	180 Pails................	Fixing spindle one hour and a half.
" 21.........	" 1	"	250 "	
" 21........	" 2	"	17 Churns	Eight men idle all day for want of hoop iron.
" 21	" 3	"	110 Tubs	
" 21......	" 4	"	240 Pails	
" 22........	" 1	"	320 "	Ten men idle all day for want of hoop iron.
" 22........	" 2	"	11 Union Churns	
" 22	" 3	"	110 Tubs......	
" 22	" 4	"	260 Pails	
" 23.........	" 1	"	300 "	
" 23.........	" 2	"	19 Churns	Ten men idle all day for want of hoop iron.
" 23........	" 3	"	90 Tubs.....	
" 23.........	" 4	"	260 Pails	
" 25.........	" 1	"	150 "	Idle three hours getting driver fixed.
" 25...... ..	" 2	"	11 Churns...............	Changed lathe.
" 25	" 3	"	70 Tubs	Fixing matcher one hour.
" 25........	" 4	"	150 Pails	Complains of having bad staves.
" 26	" 1	"	240 "	
" 26........	" 2	"	18 Union Churns	Bad pail staves to work, not cut right.
" 26......	" 3	"	110 Tubs ......,.........	
" 26........	" 4	"	200 Pails...............	
" 28........	" 1	"	280 " .... ·	Very bad staves to work, not cut right.
" 28..	" 2	"	21 Churns	
" 28........	" 3	"	150 Tubs	
" 28......	" 4	"	260 Pails........	
" 29.........	" 1	"	260 "	
" 29	" 2	"	23 Churns...............	
" 29	" 3	"	140 Tubs...............	
" 29.........	" 4	"	70 Pails..	Fixing new lathe forenoon.
" 30	" 1	"	250 "	
" 30	" 2	"	30 Churns	
" 30........	" 3	"	140 Tubs........	

May 30........No. 4 Lathe, 160 Pails..................Fixing spindle.
" 31...... " 1 " 230 " ....One man short on this lathe.
" 31....... " 2 " 32 Union Churns......
" 31......... " 3 " 120 No. 3 Tubs ....One man short three hours.
" 31........ " 4 " 200 Pails ....
" 31......... " 5 " 60 " .... New lathe, training green hands.

(EXHIBIT "2 F.")

List and number of prisoners who have been tendered to and employed by the Canada Car Company from the opening of the Prison, May 29th, 1874, to the 1st June, 1877:

Terms of Sentences.	Number.
5 years...	1
3 years...	6
2 years...	27
23 months..	12
18 months..	32
15 months..	7
14 months..	2
12 months..	142
11 months..	3
10 months..	7
9 months...	14
8 months...	7
7 months...	2
6 months...	228
5 months...	9
4 months...	62
3 months...	79
2 months...	35
Total...	675

W. S. PRINCE,
Warden.

Central Prison, August, 1877.

(EXHIBIT "2 G.")

BURSAR'S OFFICE, CENTRAL PRISON OF ONTARIO,
TORONTO, July 28th, 1877.

SIR,—Agreeable to the instructions of the Commission on my examination yesterday, I have the honour to transmit herewith--to be attached to my evidence as an Exhibit—a statement showing the number of prisoners in custody, and the actual expenditure on maintenance account for the half year ending on the 30th of June last.

Agreeable to the contention of the Company's Solicitor, I have placed to credit of the account all the available labour of the prisoners at fifty cents per day, including that portion employed for the domestic service of the prison, and have charged to the account the labour actually employed for that purpose.

I have the honour to be, sir,
Your obedient servant,
THOMAS SHORT,
Bursar.

Hon. W. B. Howland,
Chairman, &c., &c.

CENTRAL PRISON OF ONTARIO.

STATEMENT of Expenditure on Maintenance Account of the Prison for the half year ending 30th June, 1877.

Prisoners in custody 59,972 days. An average for 181 days of 330¼ prisoners per day. Placing the whole of the available prison labour to the credit of the account, the expenditure will be as follows :—

For cash expenditure for the six months, or an average of 45⅓ cents per day....................................	$27,128 26	
For 300 tons of Coal used during that period, not included in the above expenditure, at $4.........................	1,200 00	
For 8,797 days' labour of prisoners actually employed in the domestic service of the Prison, at 50cts.............	4,398 50	
		$32,726 76

CR.

By labour account, 155 working days of 330¼ men per day..................		51,189	
Less—			
In Hospital.........................	884		
3 Holidays..................................	990¾		
41 days of 8 hours......................	2,708		
12 " 9 "	396	4,978¾	
		46,210¼ at 50cts.	$23,105 13
		Balance not provided......	$9,621 63

Being a deficiency equal to $19,243 26 per annum.

Correctly compiled from Prison Accounts.

THOMAS SHORT,
Bursar, Central Prison.

(EXHIBIT " 2 H.")

KINGSTON PENITENTIARY, 11th August, 1877.

SIR,—I am instructed by Mr. Moylan, Inspector of Dominion Penitentiaries, to " send you certified copies of Advertisements for Tenders for Prison labour, and the answers thereto." The following is the advertisement which was published in Toronto, Montreal, Boston, Albany and New York, but I received no response to it from any quarter.

I am, Sir,
Your obedient servant,
JOHN CREIGHTON,
Warden.

(Copy.)

"CONVICT LABOUR.—Sealed Tenders marked ' Tender for Convict Labour,' will be received by the undersigned till Tuesday, 23rd November next, at noon, from parties willing to contract for one, two, or three years, for the labour of 150 or 200 convicts, to be employed at shoemaking at the Kingston Penitentiary. About fifty of the convicts are more or less skilled in the business.

"The hours of labour in the summer will be about 9½ hours, and in the winter about 8 hours per day.

"A large, airy, well-lighted workshop—200 feet long by 40 feet wide—will be set apart for the use of the contractor.

"The contractor to furnish skilled instructors, all material, tools, furniture, &c., required. The Penitentiary will heat the shop and supply such supervision as may be necessary to maintain discipline, and if pegging machines are used steam power will be supplied for the same.

"Payments for convict labour to be made monthly.

"Any further information may be obtained on application to the undersigned.

"JOHN CREIGHTON,
"Warden.

"Kingston Penitentiary, 28th October, 1875."

EXHIBIT "2 L" (103.)

BALANCE SHEET Canada Car and Manufacturing Company, dating from Sept. 15, 1875; for new industry to July 7th, 1877.

DR.	$ cts.	$ cts.		$ cts.	CR. $ cts.
OLD INDUSTRY.			**OLD INDUSTRY.**		
Capital Stock, paid up	269,390 00		Land, buildings, tracks, sidings, scales, transfer and turntables, machinery, chimneys, hammers, movables, machinery in south shop, also flat cars	117,925 53	
Creditors' Debentures, outstanding	26,728 04		Machinery (old stock), in use by new industry	5,541 13	
Shareholders' Debentures	12,314 46		Iron, pig, wrought and cast scrap	7,220 63	
Government of Ontario Labour Account, 1875	14,040 24		Stoves, including copper coin	4,105 19	
Consolidated Bank, Special Account	87,714 13		Lumber, oak for cars	9,025 52	
Sundry Credit Accounts	2,173 58		Office furniture	400 00	
		412,410 45	Sand	363 00	
NEW INDUSTRY.			Patterns and pattern material	250 00	
Bills Payable, outstanding	24,746 16		Horses, vehicles, and harness	392 05	
Shareholders Debentures	34,060 54		Land in Vespra	400 00	
McMurray & Fuller, mortgage and interest	5,684 36		Canada Southern Railway	90,816 54	
Sundry Credit Accounts	11,468 73		Sundry Debtor Accounts	5,302 33	
Government of Ontario, Labour Account, 1876	9,072 17				241,741 92
do do 1877	15,171 38		**NEW INDUSTRY.**		
		100,202 34	Goods manufactured and in process	7,315 86	
			Lumber	4,757 35	
			Material	11,617 60	
			Machinery	16,401 34	
			Dry kiln	3,653 80	
			Waggons	522 55	
			Forge and Scrap Shed	5,456 85	
			Patents	557 80	
			Sundry Debtor Accounts	7,677 36	
			Government of Ontario	1,339 69	
			Victoria Railway (spread over 4 years, cost value, $11,500)	12,883 75	
					72,183 95
New........ 28,018 39					188,686 92
Old........ 170,668 53					
Balance..$198,686 92		512,612 89	Balance..		512,612 79

(SPECIAL EXHIBIT "AA.")

REPLIES to Enquiries addressed by the Inspector of Asylums and Prisons of Ontario :—

OFFICE OF THE INSPECTOR OF PRISONS AND PUBLIC CHARITIES, ONTARIO,
TORONTO, 4th May, 1877.

DEAR SIR,—As three Commissioners are shortly to be appointed to enquire into the value of the prison labour furnished to the Company, who are under contract to employ the prisoners confined in the Central Prison of Ontario, I should be extremely obliged if you would inform me, at your earliest convenience, (1st) of the nature of the industries carried on in your prison, (2nd) if the labour is let to contractors, the price charged them per man, per diem, and (3rd) if, in addition to workshops, the contractors are supplied with the motive power, plant, machinery, etc.

Yours truly,
J. W. LANGMUIR,
Inspector.

TRENTON, May 7th, 1877.

DEAR SIR,—Your favour of the 4th is before me. In response I would say :

1st. The only mechanical employment followed in this prison is shoemaking.

2nd. The labour of the convicts is hired to contractors ; the present price is 50 cents per day.

3rd. The State owns the engine and steam boilers, but allows the contractors the use of them, they (the contractors) keeping them in repair.

Very truly,
W. R. MURPHY,
J. W. Langmuir, Esq., *Supervisor.*
Inspector, &c.

CLERK'S OFFICE, AUBURN PRISON,
AUBURN, N. Y., May 7th, 1877.

DEAR SIR,—The manufacturing carried on in this prison consists principally of shoes, horse collars, harness, axles, tools, baskets, &c. The labour is let to contractors. Under the old system, the price per man has ranged from 35c. to 42c. per day. Under the new rule the price is 40c. per day for the first year and 50c. for each subsequent year up to 5 years. All contractors furnish their own power except one who has the use of water power owned by the State.

Yours truly,
LEONARD R. WELLER,
Agent and Warden.

J. W. Langmuir, Esq.,
Inspector of Prisons and Public Charities, Ontario.

ILLINOIS STATE PENITENTIARY, WARDEN'S OFFICE,
JOLIET, ILL., May 9th, 1877.

DEAR SIR,—In reply to your esteemed favour of 4th inst., would say that the following convict labour is at present let to contractors in this Institution :—

43 men manufacturing wire fences at...... .... 55 cents per man per day.
150 " cigars, averaging about... ...... 25 " "

45 tailors, averaging about.....................	50	cents per man per day.
397 manufacturing boots and shoes, averaging about ...	42	" "
196 coopers, averaging about	44	" "
91 manufacturing Butt's hinges and small hardware...	48	" "
64 " mantels, table-tops, etc.......	45	" "
70 " harness, collars, etc., averaging......	45	" "
27 knitting socks, etc.	43	" "
16 granite-workers	50	" "

Another contract for 225 stone-cutters, at 50c. per man per day, was annulled a few weeks ago ; the men have not been re-leased yet. We furnish power, etc., without any additional charge, to the Wire Fence Company, to a portion of the shoe department (for sewing machines), and to the tailor department (sewing machines); cooper and Butt departments furnish their own power, as did also the stone department; the Mantel Company and Granite Works are charged at about actual cost for power furnished them by us.

Very respectfully, your obedient servant,

R. W. M'CLAUGHRY, *Warden.*

J. W. Langmuir, Esq.,
Inspector of Prisons and Public Charities, Toronto, Ont.

SING SING PRISON, AGENT AND WARDEN'S OFFICE,
SING SING, May 9th, 1877.

MY DEAR SIR,—Your letter of 4th inst is at hand. In reply I beg to say that at the present time we have employed on contracts, at forty cents per day, 150 convicts manufacturing saddlery hardware ; 125 convicts manufacturing felt hats. These contracts expire with the present year, and we shall not renew them at less than fifty cents per day for each convict. We are running a laundry on our own account, employing 260 convicts. This industry pays us at least sixty cents per day for each convict. We have recently entered into contracts for 300 men to be employed manufacturing boots and shoes; and 500 men to be employed manufacturing stoves; both of these contracts are for five years. The first year we receive forty cents per day, the last four years fifty cents per day for each convict. We confidently expect that both these contracts will be running with their full complement of convicts by July 1st. We do not furnish motive power or machinery, only shop room.

Very truly yours,

B. S. W. CLARK,
Agent and Warden.

J. W. Langmuir, Esq.,
Toronto, Ont.

NEW HAMPSHIRE STATE PRISON, WARDEN'S OFFICE,
CONCORD, N. H., May 9th, 1877.

DEAR SIR,—Yours of the 4th just received, having been mis-sent. In answer to your enquiries, would say,—

1st. Our convicts are *all* engaged in the manufacture of *bedsteads.*

2nd. The men are let to contractors for five years, at $46\frac{1}{2}$ cents per day per man.

3rd. The State furnishes the contractor with shops, engine, boilers, and *main line* of shafting; all minor machinery, belting, etc., he has to furnish. Also the fuel for the boilers and oil, tallow, etc.

Very truly yours,

J. C. PILSBURY, *Warden.*

J. W. Langmuir, Esq.,
Toronto, Canada.

WARDEN'S OFFICE, IOWA PENITENTIARY,
FORT MADISON, IOWA, May 10th, 1877.

DEAR SIR,—The Warden has just handed me your favour of 5th May for answer.
The industries carried on here are agricultural implements, boots and shoes, chairs, and cigars.
The labour is contracted to contractors, who pay for the same 43 and 48 cents per diem.
The contractors are only furnished workshops, they furnishing their own power, machinery, &c.
This, I believe, answers all your interrogatories.

Yours truly,
H. CLAY STUART,
Clerk.

J. W. Langmuir, Esq.,
Toronto, Canada.

MARYLAND PENITENTIARY, BALTIMORE, May 7th, 1877.

DEAR SIR,—Yours of 4th instant duly received. In reply to your first inquiry as to the character of our industries, I would state that we manufacture iron and shoes, and carry on stone-cutting and cane chair seats. Our female convicts are employed in the manufacture of ready-made clothing.

In reply to your second inquiry, whether our labour is let to contractors, I would answer in the affirmative. As regards the price paid per diem, our contractors are loth to have this information imparted to any one, but I will inform you the average price per diem is fifty cents.

Third, with reference to workshops, motive power, &c., the workshops are rented to the contractors, they furnish everything themselves, machinery, instructors—in a word, all things requisite for the conduct of their business. We merely furnish an officer for each department, whose duty it is to enforce order and compel adherence to the discipline.

Yours truly,
THOS. S. WILKINSON,
Warden.

J. W. Langmuir, Esq.,
Inspector, &c.

WISCONSIN STATE PRISON,
WAUPUN, WIS., May 10th, 1877.

DEAR SIR,—In answer to yours of 4th instant, the convicts confined at this prison are not leased; I am therefore unable to state the value of that class of labour.

Respectfully yours,
H. N. SMITH,
Warden.

Inspector of Prisons and Public Charities, Toronto.

RHODE ISLAND STATE PRISON,
PROVIDENCE, May 7th, 1877.

DEAR SIR,—It gives me pleasure to reply to your inquiry of the 6th instant. We let our prisoners as far as possible to contractors, but work a portion on State account. We have a small number on an old contract on wire goods at 80 cents per day. We have recently let 50 men to be employed in the manufacture of boots and shoes, at 40 cents per day, for one year—this is more than we could realize when working them on State account in seating chairs and making furniture. We do not furnish power to contractors, but do furnish suitable workshops.

By this mail I forward you a copy of our last report, hoping it will give further information relative to the Institution.

Very respectfully,
NELSON VIALL,
Warden.

J. W. Langmuir, Esq.,
Inspector of Prisons, &c.

WARDEN'S OFFICE, OHIO PENITENTIARY,
COLUMBUS, May 12, 1877.

SIR,—Yours of a recent date is before me, and contents noted. We have quite a variety of industries in our prison: small or hand agricultural implements, buggy material, carpenter and other tools, stoves, chairs, children's carriages, iron bolts, brushes, coffins, cooperage, car wheels and other castings, stove or hollow ware, wire, and a general line of harness furnishings. Each of the foregoing is carried on by different contractors, except the last two, which are done by one contractor, and all of the labour is let to contractors that is let.

We get from 70 cents to 94 cents for able-bodied men, and 40 cents for minors and old men. We have a *minimum* for full men, which is 70 cents. We can go higher, but no lower. We furnish nothing but the shop, guards and men.

The question of our labour has been much discussed during the last winter, and a strong effort made by the contractors to have the *minimum* removed or reduced; but our General Assembly declined to do anything, except to place prisoners sentenced for one year on the same footing with minors and old and infirm men.

Hoping this will be satisfactory to you,

I am, most respectfully, &c.,
JOHN H. GROVE,
Warden, O. P.

J. W. Langmuir,
Inspector of Prisons,
Toronto, Ontario.

CLINTON PRISON, NEW YORK,
DANNEMORA, June 11th, 1877.

DEAR SIR,—I beg you to pardon delay in replying to your inquiries of May 4th, the letter being mislaid. We are making nails and iron at the prison entirely by convict labour, under the personal supervision of the Agent for the State. The machinery is run wholly by steam power.

Again asking pardon, and trusting this may be satisfactory,

I am, dear sir,
Respectfully yours,
JAMES C. SHAW,
A. and W.

J. W. Langmuir,
Inspector of Prisons, &c.,
Toronto, Ontario.

WARDEN'S OFFICE, STATE PRISON,
NASHVILLE, TENN., May 21, 1877.

SIR,—I received yours of the 18th to-day, and send you Prison Regulations for both officers and guards ; also for convicts.

A sober, watchful guard, on outside labour, armed with double-barrel shot and a pistol (six shooter) can hold from six to eight convicts. The guard should be careful not to allow convicts to approach nearer than fifteen to twenty paces, or near enough to seize his gun or inflict a blow.

It is seldom a convict will run from under a gun, in the hands of sober, vigilant guards. Escape from outside labour, in nearly every instance, is chargeable to negligence of duty on the part of the guard. The eyes of convicts are never idle, always watch the guard, ready to take advantage. This, doubtless, is the experience of all prison officials.

It is important on farms to work the convicts in squads, and never allow them to go beyond the range of a gun.

I should think you could employ convicts in quarrying stone—cutting stone and in breaking stone, to macadamize streets and public roads, as well as on farms.

On farms, three day guards and one night watch will hold from sixteen to twenty-five convicts, but the guards must be sober, watchful men, or escapes will occur.

For the past two years have worked from five to six hundred and fifty convicts on outside. To-day, five hundred on outside and five hundred and twenty-nine in prison here.

Very respectfully yours,
H. F. CUMMINS,
Warden.

J. W. Langmuir, Esq.

WARDEN'S OFFICE, STATE PRISON,
NASHVILLE, Tenn., May 12th, 1877.

SIR,—In reply to your inquiries, the prison, including tools, patterns, motive power and prisoners, numbering over one thousand, are leased out to a company, who pay the State fifty thousand dollars and bear all expenses of clothing, feeding, guarding and medical attention. The State pays the salaries of Superintendent, Warden, Assistant-Warden, Physician and Chaplain. The lessees have the privilege of working the convicts anywhere in the State, in coal-mines, on public works, railroad construction, and on farms, not less than fifty in a gang on the latter.

Within the prison walls the lessees manufacture common furniture, waggons, and run a foundry for the manufacture of stoves and hollow-ware. The value of goods manufactured in the prison is about one hundred and ninety-five thousand dollars for the year 1876. The labour of convicts on the outside works will average forty cents per day nett, or in other words, the hirer on railroads and coal-mines will pay 40 cents and pay all expenses of feeding, guarding, clothing and medical attention. Second-class hands to work on farms pay *nett* about seven dollars per month. The prison has yielded to the lessees, for the past five years, a clear profit of about ninety-thousand dollars per year, after paying their rent to the State. The State allows convicts to be worked an average of ten hours per day, to be regulated by the Warden, winter and summer. The police supervision of the prison and prisoners is entirely under the control of the Superintendent and Warden, who are appointed by the Governor. No convict can be punished only by authority of the two officers named. It is their duty to see the prisoners are properly taken care of and that they perform their labour. It is a congregated system of labour. All work together, eat at the same table, and worship in the same chapel. Convict labour can be made profitable in coal mines and on public works like railroads, but require strict guarding to prevent escapes. In the shops the mechanics can earn one dollar per day average clear of all expenses. They should lease at 50 to 60 cents nett, and 40 cents nett for first-class on outside ; 2nd class 25 to 30 cents nett, on farms of not less than forty to fifty in a gang. Temporary prisons have to be erected at the expense of contractors or hirers at the coal-mines, on railroad construction, or on farms for the safety of convicts at night. The women in prison are used for washing and ironing clothes for officers and convicts at the prison. Shoes and clothing for convicts in the prison at Nashville are manufactured by the convicts. The motive power, tools, machinery of every kind belonging to the State is leased, with shops and outbuildings owned by the State, but all expenses are borne by the lessees. The prison is now advertised to be leased again for six years from the first August next. Bids will be received till first of June, but no bid under fifty thousand dollars will be received.

I herein in a hurried way have given such information as you directed, but not in the order of your questions.

I will add one remark: out of four or five hundred prisoners in this prison under my charge, have not been compelled to flog a dozen a year for neglect of work, and never inflict more than from five to ten stripes with a strap.

I regard convict labour in the South as the only fixed labour, you can place it and hold it. No strikes for higher wages, and they perform as much work as any outside free labourer with proper management; always see that they are clothed and fed well, and not cruelly treated by guards or contractors.

Very respectfully,
Your obedient Servant,
H. F. CUMMINS,
Warden.

J. W. Langmuir, Esq.

VERMONT STATE PRISON,
WINDSOR, May 15th, 1877.

DEAR SIR,—Your letter of May 4th at hand, and contents noted.

We manufacture wholly women's shoes by contractors, they paying 35 cents per day for each man, contractors furnish all plant, all machinery, and motive power.

Yours truly,
H. P. SPENCER,
Superintendent State Prison.

MAINE STATE PRISON,
THOMASTON, Maine, May 12th, 1877.

DEAR SIR,—In reply to your inquiries, under date of 4th instant, I have to say that the industries of this prison consist of the manufacture of carriages, harnesses, and boots and shoes, all on account of the State.

We use no steam power, only hand machinery. In my judgment the labour of convicts should never be sold to contractors, for the reason that the interests of contractors always conflict with the interest of the State. Both systems have been pretty thoroughly tried in this State, and the contract system is very generally condemned by our law makers. I forward with this the last annual reports of the officials of this prison.

Yours truly,
W. W. RICE,
Warden.

J. W. Langmuir, Esq.

MASSACHUSETTS STATE PRISON.
BOSTON, Charleston District, May 7th, 1877.

DEAR SIR,—In reply to yours of the 4th inst., I would call your attention to the following tables of contents :—

Contractors.	Trade.	No. of convicts	Price per day. cents.
Liverus Hull	Spring beds	75	75
Fearing & Swift	Chain making	40	75
Averill & Hunting	Brush-making	30	60
Ira Blanchard	Shoemaking	125	40
Davis, Whitcombe & Co	"	125	40
Rice & Hutchings	"	125	40
J. C. Nichols	Cotton ties	25	60
A. Batchelder	Cabinet work	50	50
E. B. Wilds	Foundry	20	60

The State furnishes shop room, with officers to maintain discipline, free, and motive power at the rate of $100 per horse power per year.

Respectfully yours,
S. E. CHAMBERLAIN,
Warden.

J. W. Langmuir, Esq.

MICHIGAN STATE PRISON.
JACKSON, Michigan, May 7th, 1877.

DEAR SIR,—Except to your 3rd question, you will find answers on page 33 of the report I send you by mail with this.

We do not find power for contractors but only shops, they putting in their own machinery and placing it.

Respectfully,
WM. HUMPHREY,
Warden.

ERIE COUNTY PENITENTIARY.
BUFFALO, May 5th, 1877.

DEAR SIR,—I enclose our contract, for your benefit, which I think will give you the desired information. You can use it, and if you should desire to keep it any length of time, please copy, and return the original. You will please be cautious and preserve it so as you can send it back when through.

I am Sir,
Very respectfully yours,
M. H. PURCELL,
Clerk.

J. W. Langmuir, Esq.

Articles of agreement, made this thirteenth day of January, in the year of Our Lord, one thousand eight hundred and seventy-four, between the County of Erie, acting by J. Nichols, Whitford Harrington, and Henry Atwood, Commissioners appointed by the Board of Supervisors of said County, for the care, custody, and management of the Erie County

Workhouse or Penitentiary, party of the first part, and Pascal P. Pratt, and Josiah Letchworth, doing business under the name, firm, and style of Pratt & Letchworth, of the City of Buffalo, in the said County, party of the second part,—

WITNESSETH :—

The party of the first part in consideration of the covenants and agreements of the party of the second part herein contained, covenants and agrees to hire and let, and does hereby hire and let unto the party of the second part for the term of three years from and after the first day of January, one thousand eight hundred and seventy-five, the work, labour and services, of all the able-bodied men, and all the able bodied women, who shall or may from time to time be confined in said Workhouse or Penitentiary, under sentence of imprisonment, to be employed by the party of the second part in the manufacture of saddlery, carriage, trunk and harness, hardware or other goods ; it being understood and agreed, however, that the Superintendent or Principal Keeper of said Workhouse or Penitentiary may reserve and retain a sufficient number from said able-bodied men and women, to do the usual necessary work, in and about said Workhouse, and in case the aforementioned Commissioners of the said Workhouse or Penitentiary deem it advisable so to do, that the Superintendent may also reserve and retain from said able-bodied men, whose several terms of sentence do not exceed three months' imprisonment, a number not exceeding a daily average of twenty men to work upon any contemplated prison enlargement. Provided, ever, that when any male convict or convicts shall have been placed in the shop of the party of the second part, under the provisions of this contract, the same shall continue in the employ of the party of the second part during the term of their confinement in said Workhouse or Penitentiary, unless they shall be unable to work in consequence of illness or other inability, or shall be useless or unmanageable, in consequence of misconduct, or withdrawn with the consent of the foreman or superintendent of the works of the party of the second part. And the said party of the first part further covenants and agrees to let and furnish, and does hereby let and furnish free of rent the buildings now erected on said workhouse premises, and now occupied by the party of the second part, and keep the same in repair, and also sufficient ground around the same for the storage of wood, lumber, and materials for carrying on their business, and also to allow and permit the said party of the second part, their clerks, agents, and workmen, the general superintendence of the business, and free ingress and egress thereto at all necessary times, and further that the said party of the second part shall have the right to employ a sufficient number of persons of their own selection, other than the said convicts, to instruct said convicts in and about their work. The deportment of persons so employed, while in the said workhouse, to be orderly, and such as shall not interfere with the discipline of said workhouse.

The party of the first part further covenants and agrees to furnish such men as the keeper of said workhouse may select to empty buckets at the workshop, and perform such other duties as the Commissioners may think proper without charge to the party of the second part.

The party of the first part further covenants and agrees to maintain a good and competent keeper in the lower or main shop, also a matron or male keeper in the upper shop or packing room, and also to maintain good order and discipline among said convicts, so that the same shall correspond, as nearly as the circumstances will permit, to that maintained during the past year in said Penitentiary. And in case any of the convicts selected by the party of the second part shall neglect or refuse to work, the time which said convict shall so neglect or refuse to work shall be deducted, so that the party of the second part shall be obliged to pay only for such time as convicts shall actually perform work and labour of able-bodied men and women, as the case may be.

And the party of the second part, in consideration of the covenants and agreements of the party of the first part herein contained, hereby covenant and agree to pay to the party of the first part for the work, labour and services of said convicts for the time which each convict shall actually work, as follows, to wit :—

Male convicts, for each man who shall work twenty days or more, the sum of thirty cents per day. For each man who shall work less than twenty days, the sum of eighteen cents per day.

Female convicts, for each female convict under sentence of one year or more, twenty-five cents per day. For each female convict under sentence of less than one year, twenty cents per day. Such payments to be made at the expiration of each and every three months during the continuance of this contract, it being mutually understood and agreed that the labour of said convicts shall average not less than ten hours a day during the whole of each year.

It is mutually agreed and understood that said party of the second part shall have the right at the expiration or other termination of this contract to remove and take away from said workhouse, shops and warehouses, all machinery, fixtures and improvements heretofore or hereafter made and belonging to them, and to remove all walls, fences, &c., necessary for such purpose. Provided, however, and it is also mutually understood and agreed that the party of the first part may purchase from the party of the second part at any time within ten days from the expiration of the term of this contract, the boiler chimney (or smoke stack) now owned by the said party of the second part at the sum of six hundred dollars.

And it is also further provided, that in case the party of the second part do not contract for the labour in said workhouse or penitentiary at the expiration of the term of this contract, the said party of the second part shall remove their property from the said workhouse buildings and grounds within thirty days from the said expiration of the term of this contract.

It is understood that in case of the death or retirement of any one member of said firm, all the rights, duties and obligations of this contract shall appertain and be confined to the surviving or continuing members of said firm.

In witness whereof, we have hereunto set our hands and seals the day and year above written.

J. NICHOLS, [L.S.]
W. HARRINGTON, [L.S.]
HENRY ATWOOD, [L.S.]

PASCAP PRATT, [L.S.]
JOSIAH LETCHWORTH, [L.S.]

(SPECIAL EXHIBIT, " B. B.")

Summary of Replies contained in Special Exhibit, "A. A."

www.ingramcontent.com/pod-product-compliance
Lightning Source LLC
Chambersburg PA
CBHW031902220426
43663CB00006B/733